SURVEY RESEARCH
Second Edition

Charles H. Backstrom
University of Minnesota

Gerald Hursh-César
International Communication Agency
United States of America

John Wiley & Sons
New York • Chichester • Brisbane • Toronto

Library on Congress Cataloging in Publication Data:

Backstrom, Charles Herbert, 1926–
Survey research.

Includes index.
1. Public opinion polls.   2. Social science research.
I. Hursh-César, Gerald.   II. Title.
HM261.B18   1981   303.3′8   81-1738
ISBN 0-471-02543-7   AACR2

Printed in the United States of America

10 9 8 7 6 5 4 3 2 1

For Mauricette, Gabrielle, and Barbara

PREFACE

A reviewer of the first edition of Survey Research suggested that we could have entitled "this delightful 'cookbook'... *The Joy of Surveying.*"[1] We were pleased that we communicated something of the exhilaration of scientific study of public opinion.

We have apparently convinced many researchers that there is no mystery in conducting surveys, only rigor in the method of doing it; no magic, only hard work. This is our feeling from countless personal conversations, from observations of worn copies of *Survey Research* on office shelves all around the world, and from seeing widespread use of our model format, checklists, and procedures in government, academic, and commercial surveys and in other books about survey research.

The best tribute, however, came from a reviewer who, although he didn't seem too excited about the book's intensely practical focus, concluded:

> But for the neophyte, student or professional, who actually wants to make a survey, the volume should be useful.[2]

Exactly what we had in mind! We really meant to lead a first-timer—someone who wants to do a survey, or someone who is about to hire someone to do it— toward the collection of useful data.

But times have changed. Few persons now have to be convinced to do a survey. Everybody's doing one already. But the proliferation of surveys, and the changed climate in which they must be done, makes the need for an update of this book greater than ever.

Beginning researchers still need a step-by-step account of how to do a survey. Experienced researchers still need criteria for examining their own methods. And survey consumers and clients are in constant need of help in making survey plans and dealing with survey results.

Every decision on what to include in this book was based on whether it was *practical*—helpful to a person actually *doing* or *using* a survey. We believe this can best be done by illustrating all the steps involved in developing a Model Survey, describing the process from start to finish in plain language. Once users understand the whys and wherefores of survey research, they can readily adapt the principles and practices shown in the Model Survey to their own specific needs and circumstances. As before, we have used checklists of things to think about and do to make

[1] David Nasatir, *The American Journal of Sociology*, **70**, 387 (1964).

[2] Warren O. Hagstrom, *American Sociological Review*, **29**, 634 (1964).

sure no vital activity is overlooked. Detailed interviewer instructions are presented in the form of a ready-to-use training manual.

Some major changes from the first edition are necessary. Everywhere, computers have replaced unit-record machines for processing data more quickly than we had expected. Luckily, simple data handling and statistical packages have enabled present-day researchers to produce usable survey results without having to know much about the computer itself or about programming languages. We show how anyone can ask a computer to process data. Beyond this, we now provide assistance in analyzing and interpreting survey data.

The Model Survey is a one-time, in-person, at-the-door, general population opinion poll. But in each chapter we describe features of other modes of interviewing—telephone surveys, mail questionnaires, panel studies, and intercept surveys (election day exit polls).

Lastly, we have incorporated throughout several more years of experience in how to design better studies that use surveys, how to continue to do surveys in the face of changes in the social and political climate, and how to make survey data more useful to decision makers who need information that only surveys can provide.

In sum, we are satisfied that the first edition of this book expanded the cadre of competent survey doers and users. But because of increased demand for surveys, even more people now need instruction in how to do surveys well themselves and how to judge whether surveys are done well by others.

It is to these people that this book is addressed.

Our special thanks go to Wayne Anderson, our editor at Wiley, for his faith that this book would happen. We are grateful to Deborah Herbert and Douglas Gower who polished the prose, and to Cathy Starnella who supervised production. Valuable suggestions were given by John Sonquist, Bob Agranoff, Bill Lyons, Burt Russick, Tom Danbury, Phil Voxland, David Nolle, Leonard Robins, and Bob Coursen, while Cheryl Mattson and Joan Breeser helped in practical ways. We are particularly and gratefully indebted to Stanton H. Burnett.

The authors will attribute any errors any errors to each other.

Charles H. Backstrom
Minneapolis

Gerald Hursh-César
Washington, D.C.

CONTENTS

LIST OF FIGURES

LIST OF TABLES

LIST OF CHECKLISTS

Planning Surveys

This book is a practical guide to survey research. Popularly called "polling," a survey here is the scientific study of people—their personal characteristics and aspects of their knowledge, attitudes, and behavior. Chapter 1 describes how to plan surveys. The rest of the book shows how to carry out all other steps in doing a survey.

Our purpose is to show how to do survey research—how to gather information about a large number of people by interviewing only a few of them. The people interviewed are called *respondents*, because they respond to our questions. Together, respondents form a *sample*—a small-scale replica—of the *population* under study. The population may be any size: a group, a city, the nation. The sample is drawn by certain rules that assure that within an acceptable margin of error it is a miniature of the larger population.

Rather than describing surveys in general terms, in this book we will construct a *Model Survey*. That is, we explain in nontechnical language every phase from start to finish in doing a survey. Our main intent is to help those who actually want to do a survey themselves. They can proceed step-by-step following the Model through the book and end up with a good survey. But seeing in detail how surveys are done can also aid those who instead must hire others to conduct surveys for them. And, for those who may never do a survey or commission one but who read and use survey data, knowing the details of the process can help in judging whether the surveys they read about are competent enough to be trusted.

Our Model Survey is of the "field survey" type, in which people are personally interviewed in their homes. Face-to-face interviewing is the traditional form of survey research, and it is still the type that people seem to trust most. Academic studies that seek basic knowledge about human behavior are most likely to be done through the in-person, at-home survey. Journalistic and marketing surveys, however, today are more likely to contact people by telephone and mail samples than in person.

The same principles of sampling, question writing, and data analysis apply to surveys regardless of the method of interviewing. But in each chapter, after presenting the face-to-face procedures of the Model, we will describe various adjustments required for telephone and mail surveys, as well as for "intercept" surveys, such as the "exit polls" done at polling places on election day by news organizations.

Choosing to describe a Model Survey, instead of using a more general approach to surveys, means explaining certain topics and leaving others out; but working through a model from start to finish is also a practical way of ensuring that the essential topics are covered. The Model Survey must be thought of as a starting point from which adaptations will have to be made for each real-life survey situation; it helps show the need for and consequences of choosing alternative procedures.

The Model is intended to provide enough knowledge to help beginners move to more advanced readings and to enable them to seek guidance from professional survey researchers without fear of asking naive questions.[1]

A survey is a formidable task and shouldn't be undertaken lightly. By breaking down the process into individual, understandable steps, we hope to avoid unnerving the novice researcher and, at the same time, to develop a healthy respect for the complexities of the survey approach to knowledge.

WHAT SURVEY RESEARCH IS

In the grocery store as well as in the voting booth we make choices based on our assumptions of what the world is like and what we can do to change it. *Assumptions* are our personal interpretations of information we have about the world. When this information is based only on hearsay, hunch, limited experience, or casual study, the assumptions on which we act may not be sound. The use of survey research can improve our assumptions by providing timely and accurate information, the validity of which we can check.

Why Do a Survey

We do research on human beings for both theoretical and practical reasons. Besides trying to understand the world, we would like to help solve its problems. Because

---

[1]Further readings are listed at the end of each chapter.

effective policy making requires that we thoroughly understand both the nature of such problems and any proposed solutions, a sound base of information is needed about people's conditions and behavior, their states of awareness, their feelings, attitudes, and beliefs.

This search for more knowledge is not intended to enable would-be leaders to manipulate the citizenry, although they may try. In a democratic society where the desires of people are the test of acceptable public policy, a continuous flow of information about themselves will enable people to make more enlightened judgments about that policy and to better communicate their desires and reactions to the decisionmakers.

Finally, in a world where change is the only certainty, past studies are quickly outdated. Speculation about the present human condition is widespread, but it needs constant testing for reality.

It is for these reasons that we continue to do research. But under what conditions do we use the survey method instead of other forms of information gathering?

Survey research is a set of orderly procedures specifying what information is to be obtained and from whom and how. From among other research approaches, we choose to do a survey when the people from whom we need information are too many and too dispersed to contact all of them. Some nonresearchers may think it's always preferable to ask everyone, to include every area, to process every piece of paper. But with large populations, such efforts are massive, costly, time consuming, and so prone to mistakes that we are almost always better off using only a sample of some kind.

Survey research differs from informal techniques because it tends to be a more systematic and impartial means of getting information. Since, in a survey, only a few people must represent the views of many, it is essential to keep our personal feelings out of the process of selecting the respondents. The survey is thus a formal *procedure*, a way of getting information that is more or less insulated from the personality—the values, beliefs, predispositions—of the researcher. Personal values are, of course, important for deciding which problems should be researched, and by which methods. But once the method is specified, a survey can be carried out reasonably free of the personal biases of the user. This way it can produce information that is more reliable for decision making than our personal judgments and guesses.

Checklist 1 summarizes important characteristics of survey research.

CHECKLIST 1

Characteristics of Survey Research

Survey research is:

1. **SYSTEMATIC:** it follows a specific set of rules, a formal and orderly logic of operations.

2. IMPARTIAL: it selects units of the population without prejudice or preference.
3. REPRESENTATIVE: it includes units that together are representative of the problem under study and the population affected by it.
4. THEORY-BASED: its operations are guided by relevant principles of human behavior and by mathematical laws of probability (chance).
5. QUANTITATIVE: it assigns numerical values to nonnumerical characteristics of human behavior in ways that permit uniform interpretation of these characteristics.
6. SELF-MONITORING: its procedures can be designed in ways that reveal any unplanned and unwanted distortions (biases) that may occur.
7. CONTEMPORARY: it is current, more than historical, fact-finding.
8. REPLICABLE: other people using the same methods in the same ways can get essentially the same results.

The survey differs from other kinds of research in an important way: the survey can *generalize* about many people by studying only a few of them. Social science is concerned with describing human conditions. Because we cannot know all conditions, we generalize about them. The cook tasting the soup from a spoon generalizes about the contents of the pot. Likewise in science, a generalization is a statement that describes all people or circumstances similar to those studied, but not necessarily studied themselves.

In everyday life we generalize when we say things like ''the average voter'' or ''the typical Southerner.'' Because the world is so complex and so much of it is outside our personal experience, we need generalizations to understand it. But our personal experience is so limited that our generalizations are often seriously flawed: ''All politicians are crooked'' or ''All teenagers use drugs.''

Everyday generalizations are stereotypes that vary from person to person depending on who is making them. The generalizations of science cannot, however, vary from scientist to scientist; if they do, they are not generalizations. Science provides methods to produce generalizations that are mostly free of personal biases and that enable us to describe with assurance people and conditions beyond those studied. This is what distinguishes survey research from other types of inquiry. The survey allows us to ''see'' conditions beyond our direct experience. Moreover, its procedures enable us to repeatedly test and affirm or refine these statements of how, under varying conditions, people are similar to or different from others in aspects of their knowledge, attitudes, or behavior.

Kinds of Information from Surveys

Relative to other types of research, the survey can obtain in a short time a lot of information about many people in many places. Checklist 2 shows some of the characteristics of survey information.

CHECKLIST 2

Characteristics of Survey Information

The information from surveys is:

1. ORIGINAL: not already existing in some usable form.
2. PARTIAL: obtained from *some* (a sample), not all, of the people (the population) it describes.
3. MEDIATED: obtained by *interviewers* acting as third parties between the researcher and the people in the sample (respondents).
4. SELF-REPORTED: primarily people's testimony about themselves.
5. STANDARDIZED: obtained by *uniform procedures* for asking and answering questions.
6. TIMELY: *collected quickly*—surveys are in and out of the field in a rather brief time.

Compared to other research approaches, surveys are the best means available for describing certain characteristics of large populations. These are personal characteristics that people provide about themselves—how they feel, what they think, what they know, how they act. Until we find a substitute method of getting the same information *without talking directly to the people themselves* (decoding brain waves?), the survey will remain the best means of describing these characteristics.

At present there is no preferred research alternative to surveys for determining, with a known degree of confidence and a known level of precision, the characteristics of large populations. There are many different kinds of characteristics that surveys discern best; the following provides a few examples:

About individuals:

- *Information:* The percentage of people correctly identifying the campaign slogan of the labor-endorsed candidate for senator.
- *Attitudes:* The feelings of people over 55 years of age about a proposed extension of compulsory retirement age.
- *Behavior:* The proportion of Democrats in the state who watched the presidential candidates debate on television last night.
- *Physical states:* The average height and weight of boys and girls in inner-city and in surburban neighborhoods.
- *Needs and demands:* The numbers of people desiring more insulation in their homes.

About institutions:

- *Agencies:* Reactions among employees of the U.S. Department of Labor to new restrictions on youth job-training programs.

- *Associations:* Reasons given by members of the National Rifle Association for opposing gun-control legislation.
- *Bodies:* The mood of the state legislatures in 14 Southern and Western states regarding passage of the Equal Rights Amendment.
- *Organizations:* Attitudes of management and labor officials about the impact of their new contract on federal wage guidelines.

About communities:

- *Ethnic groups:* Personal experiences with job discrimination among citizens of Mexican-American and Asian descent living in Southern California.
- *Neighborhoods:* Opposition among surburban residents to busing students to schools in South Boston.
- *Cities:* Proportion of registered dog owners in New York City and in San Francisco complying with city ordinances prohibiting pets from littering the streets.
- *States:* The proportion of voters in South Dakota, Texas, and New Jersey favoring passage of spending controls on government.
- *Nations:* The prevailing sentiments of the peoples of Great Britain and United States regarding diplomatic accommodations with the Soviet Union.

The examples above are only suggestive. There are many ways of classifying the kinds of information obtainable from surveys. Moreover, surveys are not limited to conclusions about individuals. As illustrated by our examples, we can sum up our findings from contacts with individuals to draw conclusions about *groups*— associations, cities, nations, and so on. Additionally, surveys can study *things*— objects, events, land areas, whatever. For example, we can do surveys of the crime rates in major U.S. cities, of the amount of public funds collected through state sales taxes, of the number of gasoline stations participating in voluntary rationing programs, of the percentage of public buildings in a downtown district that violate fire codes. The Model Survey in this book, however, is concerned with surveying people to generalize about people.

Limitations of Surveys

Survey research has many limitations. To generalize for large populations, surveys must follow certain strict procedures in defining whom to study and how to select them. Following the rules can be very expensive. For one thing, the sample of people studied must be of large enough size and of sufficiently varied characteristics so that as a group they can be trusted to be a miniature replica of the population. In terms of *size,* the survey must include enough people so that statistics used to describe them are based on numbers that mathematically permit reasonably safe conclusions. In terms of *characteristics,* the people studied must include the same kinds as in the larger population—blacks and whites, Puerto Ricans and Italians, men and women, Catholics and Jews, conservatives and liberals.

The *costs* of achieving a proper number and mixture of people can be enormous. But because surveys deal with hundreds and even thousands of people, they have limitations other than just high costs. With so many people to interview, time is precious. That is, if the survey intends to study many people under comparable conditions, there simply isn't time to go into great detail on each and every respondent. As a result of these limitations, survey data is usually *superficial*. With little time and artificial interviewing circumstances, we are not capable of digging deeply into people's psyches looking for fundamental explanations of their unique behavior.

Time and cost are important concerns, but the fundamental limitations of the survey arise from its intrinsic nature. The essence of the survey is that it is a process of people (researchers) talking to other people (respondents) through still other people (interviewers). The process is entirely *human*. Its principal frailty is the point at which the interviewer asks questions and records answers, the point at which the interviewer intervenes between the intentions of the researcher and the intentions of the respondent.

Surveys are *obtrusive*. Interviews are unnatural intrusions into the individual's everyday life—something extraordinary. As such, people are fully aware of being the subjects of study. They often respond differently from how they might if they were unaware of the researcher's interest in them.

A somewhat related factor is the unreality of the survey exchange. Surveys are *structured* situations. The interviewer and the respondent have well-defined, almost mutually exclusive, conversational roles. One asks the questions; the other answers. This exchange is more like an interrogation than a conversation. Further, the questions (and admissible answers) are determined by the researcher in advance, who thus runs the risk of introducing issues that are irrelevant to respondents or that are outside of their experience and therefore unreal in terms of assessing their opinion.

Also troublesome is that most of the information we get from respondents about their own characteristics is *self-reported,* which is not always undiluted truth. What is more, not everyone is home at the time of the interviewing attempt, and not everyone who is agreed to be interviewed. With these and other types of *nonresponse,* we suffer from not getting information from all of the people we should, thus risking distortions of the representativeness of the sample.

These limitations are not to be interpreted as failures that could be overcome with better survey management. They are instead inherent features of this type of research, which must be kept in mind so that we temper our reliance on the resulting data.

CHOOSING THE RESEARCH APPROACH

Tools are designed for specific tasks. A good carpenter doesn't use a chisel for a screwdriver. Similarly, certain kinds of knowledge are better obtained by surveys than by other means of study. But the reverse is also true. To use surveys appropriately we must be aware of their position in the research spectrum.

Different research approaches produce different kinds of information. Our basis for deciding which approach to use depends on the information needed for the problem at hand. For example, we might do a small, informal study of a single community simply for the purpose of developing some ideas to be formally tested later in a large-scale study of many communities.

Approaches and Methods

In this book we make a distinction between research approaches and research methods. Taking a census of all of the people or doing a survey of only some of them are different *approaches* to a problem. But both a census and a survey can be conducted by any one of different interviewing *methods*—in person, by telephone, by mail.

We distinguish among research approaches by the kinds of information each produces, while we distinguish research methods by the manner in which information is collected. Any method can be used with any approach, but some work together better than others. For example, we could use the telephone interview method to ask senators how they voted, but it would be more accurate to observe the rollcall from the Senate gallery, and more efficient to read the printed rollcall.

The difference between approach and method is important because:

* The purpose for which we do research defines which *approach* must be used. Each approach places certain known limitations on the information obtained. These limitations are *known and planned for* in advance of the study.
* The *methods* of gathering information may place *unknown and unplanned* limitations on the information obtained. These limitations are human failings, called "biases," that distort the quality of research.

Bypassing methods for the moment, let us consider the kinds of information produced by a census, a survey, and a small-group study. A *census* is a study of all people, thus permitting us to describe them without errors due to sampling. A *survey* is a study of some people done in a way that permits us to describe all people, but with some margin of error due to sampling. The *small-group study* is a study of only a few people that is performed in a way that does not permit us to describe the whole population, but because they are few we can afford to study them in depth.

As required by the Constitution for apportioning U.S. representatives among the states, the Bureau of the Census conducts a national census every ten years (with a mid-decade census allowed), in which it attempts to contact every single household in the nation. Censuses of large populations are expensive and time-consuming. Sampling is faster and more economical. Moreover, sampling can be more accurate than large, complete counts because clerical errors are more likely in handling huge masses of census forms and data, and because professional interviewers can be used who will seek out hard-to-find respondents who are missed in the "total" count.

Because of costs, time, and potential for error, the Census Bureau gets most of its information from sample surveys. Its annual *Continuing Population Survey* and other studies are surveys, not censuses. What is more, only about one-fourth of the 10-year census output is true census data; the rest is from sample surveys, which are additional schedules filled out by every fifth household, every twentieth, and so on.

Criteria for Selecting a Research Approach

Deciding which research approach to use depends on knowing the answers to several questions:

- Does the information already exist?
- Why do we need the information?
- What population are we trying to describe?
- What resources do we have?

We answer these questions first, before worrying about how the information can best be obtained, which is a question of method.

Does the Information Already Exist? Surveys are unnecessary to gather much of the information desired by decisionmakers or students. We do surveys to get only data that does not now exist in usable form for the problem at hand. This is called *primary* data—information that must be gathered in original form from the "field." *Secondary* data, in contrast, already exists in usable form.

Checking secondary data sources, such as libraries, public offices, and private association headquarters, is one of the first steps in undertaking any study. If this initial process of "backgrounding," largely library research, is carefully done, a wasteful survey may never be undertaken. For example, if we want to know how many men and women of various races live at different income levels in our city, we would consult published U.S. census data. If we want to know how many registered voters voted in the last election and for which candidates, we would consult voter registration lists and published election abstracts. But we probably could not find a published record that puts these kinds of information together—to show, for example, the percentage of black women in middle-income families who voted for the conservative mayoral candidate. We would have to do a survey to find that out. We would, however, use existing data to help define the population for study. Likewise, we could find out about accident rates from the state's drivers license records, and we could estimate average family debt from credit bureau files. But if we wanted to find out whether people in credit difficulty had more accidents than the norm, we would have to do a survey.

Why Do We Need the Information? If we are dealing with human problems, we need to know what people think and do in relation to those problems. We also need to know why they think and act as they do.

Describing and explaining human behavior are two different types of information. Describing behavior tells *how* without telling *why:* "Public support for new clean air laws has increased from 30 percent to 45 percent in the past month" is a description. Explaining behavior is more difficult: "Two-thirds of the people exposed to the direct mail campaign changed from nonsupport to support for the proposed clean-air law, compared to one-third of those who did not receive the mailings."

To explain behavior means to show the relationships between certain "causes" and certain "effects." If we want to generalize these cause/effect relationships to the larger population with certainty, we have to take surveys of the same people at different points in time. And even with that base, we must take great care to ensure that some unknown influence is not the actual cause of the changes we find from one time to the next.

The purpose for which we do research defines the approach we must use. We can illustrate the point by classifying various research approaches according to two sets of information objectives: (1) whether to generalize *or* not generalize from the persons studied, and (2) whether to describe *or* to explain their behavior. Figure 1.1 shows these alternatives for the two objectives, with study approaches that fulfill each pair of alternatives.

Approaches that Describe Behavior Without Generalization. The *small-group study* is the classic approach of the anthropologist: this is an intensive study of one or a few communities, such as an ethnic group, a neighborhood, or an association. The researcher often lives among the persons studied, unobtrusively observing, questioning, and recording behavior. The purpose usually is to describe the total system of the group's behavior. Although small-group studies are capable of delivering much in-depth information on a few people, they describe only the unique group studied.

The *depth interview* is an exploratory approach. Each topic is probed deeply—following up important leads with further questions—until a well-rounded picture emerges. Obviously, the results of this time-consuming inquiry cannot be applied to a larger group, because we cannot know how representative are the few respondents we have time to talk to.

The *key informant* approach is what a journalist might choose; this is a depth interview of someone in a position to observe or affect what is happening in a situation. Although that person may be very well informed, the findings cannot be reliably generalized even to other close observers, who will have a different perspective.

A survey *pretest,* usually done as a small "dress rehearsal" in advance of a

Figure 1.1. Comparison of major research approaches by goals of information[a]

	No generalization[b]	Generalization
Describes what behavior exists	Small-group study Depth interview Key informant Pretest Any nonprobability study	Census One-time survey Multiple-time survey (independent samples; panel studies)
Explains what causes behavior	Nonexperimental case study Quasiexperimental study Demonstration project Critical incident/ focused interview Human laboratory (class) experiment	Controlled field experiment Simulation Physical laboratory experiment

(THE MODEL SURVEY → One-time survey)

[a] Adapted from Gerald Hursh-César, *The Research Information Workshop: Using Research for Public Policy Decision Making* (Berkeley: Office of the Academic Vice President, University of California, 1977), Chapter II (mimeo).

[b] If broad conclusions are drawn from these studies, they are not generalizations but are *extrapolations*. A generalization describes people and conditions similar to those studied. An extrapolation is used more broadly to describe people and conditions different from those studied.

large-scale study, is a miniature survey performed under the same conditions and among the same population as expected for the main study. The purpose is to get insights into the people and problems under study as a basis for improving the chances of achieving a successful survey. Its numbers of respondents are too few, and probably not sufficiently well distributed, to warrant generalizing to the population at large.

In a *nonprobability sample* people are chosen deliberately for certain characteristics believed to be relevant to the study. But because they are selected intuitively rather than scientifically, they cannot be relied on to represent the whole population fairly.

Approaches that Describe Behavior with Generalization. In a *census,* everyone in the population being studied is contacted for information. We therefore can describe the whole population without any errors due to sampling.

The *one-time survey,* which is able to cover large populations rapidly, provides timely generalizations. This approach takes the findings of small-scale studies and tests their wide-scale application to the whole population. With large samples, the survey can study different subgroups in order to quantify differences and relationships among them, as well as in the whole population.

Most surveys are one-time efforts (the Model Survey is of this type) that describe behavior at a single point in time. Like a photographic snapshot, they record conditions. But since they glimpse only one point in history, the most hazardous use of such surveys is to try to reconstruct prior events and behavior (subject to faulty memory) or to predict future behavior (subject to changing conditions). Even so, we often use these point-in-time surveys as a basis for predicting how people will behave in the future. For example, voting surveys have this objective. So do marketing surveys for new products, or government surveys of people's responses to the teaching of the metric system. And we can have some faith in our predictions if reliable data exists on the relationships of important characteristics of the people studied—we assume until shown otherwise that those relationships will continue. But, like all other survey approaches, the one-time survey is an obtrusive technique, obtaining rather superficial self-reported data in a highly structured situation.

The *multiple-time survey* provides a reliable basis for describing changes in large populations over time. Identical surveys of the same population at two or more points in time permit us to check our predictions, based on the first survey, by looking at the second, and they also allow us to discover the antecedents of findings in the second survey as they existed in the first.

Multiple-time surveys that reinterview the same individuals each time are called *panel studies.* These show net changes in *individuals* from one time to another (people who said they saw the candidate's television commercials between surveys were more likely to change their minds against him). Other multiple-time surveys continue to study the same population but interview new (independent), comparable samples each time. These show gross changes in *classifications* of people from one time to another (Republicans show a larger increase than Democrats in opposing the Equal Rights Amendment). Unlike panel surveys, however, surveys of independent samples cannot track changes in specific individuals for the purpose of relating changes in them to changes in events and circumstances.

Approaches that Explain Behavior Without Generalizations. A *case study,* as defined here, is a special type of small-group study. It differs by its focus on changes over time. Small-group studies focus on the group itself; case studies focus on change in the group. The case-study researcher, usually involved intensively in the study situation, witnesses the entire process of change—before, during, and after. Case studies are usually called ''nonexperimental'' field studies.

As in any small-group study, care must be taken so that the presence of the researcher does not disrupt the normal functioning of the group. The researcher must guard against losing perspective by accepting the group's values as his or her own.

Because of the often small numbers of people involved, it is usually meaningless to quantify the data—what is the point of writing about ''33 percent'' of 12 people? Neither is any attempt made to compare the study group with other groups, whether under similar or different study conditions.

Quasiexperiments differ from full experiments, which require careful before-and-after measures, with adequate controls. Anything less rigorous may explain behavior in one instance but will not have the power to generalize to other people or other conditions beyond those studied. That is why they only *resemble* true experiments, as their name implies.

A *demonstration project* is a special kind of case-study. Working with a pilot demonstration project, the researcher's aim is to try out a specific program to provide evidence that would convince us to expand it to reach a larger audience. It is quasiexperimental, often using highly quantified before-and-after measures, but since it usually involves only one group without controls, the results cannot be generalized.

Focused interviews are like depth interviews, but they focus on the sequence of events surrounding a critical incident, such as the capture of hostages or a nuclear accident. The focused interview explores connections between events, communications, attitudes, and actions in order to explain behavior. Because the respondents usually are people who were involved in a specific event, the power to generalize to other people and other events is weak. The focused interview is also known as a critical incident study. It is often confused with semistructured depth interviewing.

The *human laboratory experiment,* a psychology classroom experiment with human subjects, is designed to explain behavior by noting what happens as some new element is introduced. This is sometimes called ''the science of college sophomores.'' Subjects used are either ''captive'' or whoever voluntarily signs up. Conclusions drawn from such experiments, therefore, cannot be applied to just anyone, anywhere.

Approaches that Explain Behavior with Generalizations. To explain what causes what in the real world is difficult. *Controlled field experiments* attempt to do this. Studying causes and effects requires a special kind of rigorous structure, called *experimental design*. Although our experiments occur in the field, their form is like that of the chemistry experiment in the laboratory; we observe a real-world group (the ''before''), add a new ingredient (the ''treatment''), and observe any changes (the ''after'').

To ensure that any change is due to our treatment and not to other factors, we leave comparable groups untouched (as controls) to see if any changes occur in them at the same time. To ensure that any change is not a fluke or caused by our biases, we assign people at random to treatment and control groups. To ensure that any change is not due to unique study conditions, we are careful that both our groups are representative samples of the larger population. The result of a controlled field experiment is the most highly quantified statement of cause and effect we can get from any method.

Such experiments are typically very costly. Large numbers of respondents are usually required. Great care is exercised in selecting groups for study and in preventing contamination of them by outside influences. Experiments usually extend over lengthy periods of time, in order to let the treatments have "natural" effects. For example, it might take months to measure the cumulative effects on people's attitudes of a major public relations campaign in support of clean-air laws.

The principal limitation of controlled field experiments is that we cannot actually control the real world. The effects of our hypothetical public relations campaign could be wiped out by one bill passed in the state legislature, or unduly magnified by a sudden killer smog. Moreover, we risk sensitizing people to their participation in the experiment through our repeated before-and-after measurements of them. People aware of being studied may act unnaturally. Special experimental designs are thus required to monitor this possible effect.

Simulation is usually a mathematical, computerized model of the real world. By duplicating the "world" with statistical techniques and by varying the values of different parts of the "world," this approach attempts to predict how conditions will change in response to new values. (Another form of simulation is *role playing,* in which the real world is "re-created" by assigning people to roles in a mock confrontation.) Simulations are generalizable to the extent that the data and relationships used in them have been previously verified by separate research.

Physical laboratory experiment: Because conditions in the chemistry or physics laboratory are so carefully controlled, and because there is so much less variability in the physical realm compared to the human realm, we have confidence in our ability to generalize from a laboratory experiment about cause and effect. The same results are very likely to happen every time in any laboratory and, when conditions are the same, in the world outside.

What Population Are We Trying to Describe? Important considerations in picking the study population are: (1) whether the findings are to be unique to the persons studied or to be generalized to a larger population, and (2) whether conclusions are to be drawn for individuals, institutions, or communities.

For example, a sample of police statistics for 20 large cities may be sufficient to generalize for crime rates in metropolitan areas in the nation. A census of all members of the state legislature may be required to predict the vote on a closely

contested bill. An in-depth interview with the governor may be sufficient to conclude about chances of tax legislation being vetoed.

Survey populations are either residential or institutional. *Residential* settings
are the natural settings of the community. We usually think of surveys being
conducted in these natural settings. But much of our scientific knowledge comes
from *institutional* populations, for example, school children, prison inmates, army
officers, factory workers. Any research approach—case study, survey, or field
experiment—can be used in an institutional population.

The major research challenge in an intact group is to minimize the study's
intrusion in the environment, so that the presence of the study itself is not a cause of
behavior. Also, a study of a specific institution is a unique study of a unique
situation. It does not generalize to other institutions or natural communities. In other
words, if we want to conclude about prison inmates nationally, we have to take a
national sample of prisons.

Usually survey researchers want to draw conclusions about people. We can, of
course, sum up our findings to draw conclusions about an institution or community.
As we will see, however, it may require studying as many people in a *single*
community in order to describe that community as it would to describe the entire
nation.

What Resources Do We Have? This is the crunch. We want to do the best study
that can be designed for the problem, but it may be unrealistic given the competition
for resources. Studies run on time, money, staff, supplies, and equipment. Although a case study may require a lengthy period of time in the field to describe
causes and effects in a small group, it needs few staff and minimal supplies and
equipment. A survey, in contrast, requires little time in the field but usually requires
substantial investment in staff, salaries, supplies, and equipment. An experiment
typically requires large investments in all resources.

A realistic appraisal of resources is essential to designing a study. We can
never do the ideal study, and we usually do much less than we originally intended.
If we know in advance the realistic limits of our resources, we can plan a useful
study accordingly, instead of being hit with the disaster of a fund shortage midway
through a survey. If a survey is too costly, a small-group study can be launched
instead that may give important insights into a problem and provide exciting
hypotheses for further studies of other kinds when resources are more plentiful.

Where Surveys Fit Among Other Approaches

The several research approaches that have been described are in fact complemen-
tary. Although each is more suitable than others for certain projects, one or another
may be used at different phases of the same study.

If we are considering embarking on a major research project, we might well do

Figure 1.2. Choosing among research strategies[a]

Approach	Use When You Want To Know:	Advantages	Limitations
Small-group study	A lot about a little: Early research Generate hypotheses	Natural Unobtrusive High validity In-depth	Unique Impressionistic Uncontrolled Low quantification
Survey	A timely generalization: Test hypotheses Subgroup differences	Generality Quantitative Timely Replicable	Superficial Obtrusive Structured Self-reporting
Field experiment	Causes and effects: Changes Time order	Control Powerful conclusions Across time Highest quantification	Costly Time-consuming Vulnerable Sensitizing

[a] Adapted from Gerald Hursh-César, *The Research Information Workshop,* op. cit., 1977, Exhibit 11-3.

a small-group study early in the project's life. The richness and variety of such intensive data can yield great insight into the basic processes of behavior. These insights will generate concepts and hypotheses to be tested later in a larger-scale survey, and they may help improve our survey measures. Any field experiment we undertake is likely to be based on one or more small-group studies or pilot projects, and it will use the survey method as well to provide the before-and-after comparative measurements sought.

Figure 1.2 summarizes several features of small-group studies, surveys, and experiments—the three main models of field research in the study of human populations.

CHOOSING THE RESEARCH METHOD

Knowing the objective of our research automatically defines which approach to take; we do a survey because it is best suited for delivering data on our problem. But the same is not true of choosing the *method* of getting information. Which method to use depends on what we want to know, in how much time, and how we can best get the particular information.

Ways of Getting Information

Information can be obtained in three distinct ways: by direct measurement, by observation, and by interviewing. To an extent we choose among them depending on the access we have to the people studied and the time we have to gather the information, but mostly we choose because one or the other is more suitable for the kind of data we want. In a single study, we may even use the measures sequentially, or in combination.

Direct Measurement. This is straightforward counting or testing. Four examples of direct measurement are: (1) clinical—testing blood pressure; (2) field verification—checking the air-pollutant emissions of heavy-duty trucks; (3) physical measurement—mapping and measuring distances families travel for shopping; and (4) records—compiling attendance data on elementary students in various areas of the city.

We sometimes use direct measurement to supplement and verify subjective data already collected from people in surveys. A form of field verification used by commercial researchers is the "pantry survey," in which the interviewer inspects the kitchen shelves to verify the presence of, say, brands of breakfast cereal. Monitors attached to television sets supplement oral interviewing about viewing habits. Checking official city voting records is a way of verifying respondents' claims that they voted in an election.

Observation. People do not or cannot always tell the truth. We can learn much about people's behavior from watching them. A survey is obtrusive—people are aware of being studied. Thus, observing audience reactions to a campaign speech may be a more valid indicator of the candidate's impression on people than are interviews in their homes the next day. Observation has been a classic tool of anthropologists and sociologists, generating rich insights into behavior.

Observation techniques can be classified according to how the observer participates in the group under study. Three types of observation are:

1. *Participatory*—hanging around with a street-corner gang.
2. *Sociometric*—observing from the gallery the patterns of interaction among members of a legislature during debate.
3. *Nonparticipatory*—listening to people in the supermarket talk about food prices.

Interviewing

Interviewing techniques are the subject of Chapter 5. Briefly, however, the feature that distinguishes interviewing from other methods of gathering data is that interviews rely on people's self-reported testimony about their own characteristics.

Because of the frailty of this aspect of human behavior, we often try to verify interview data with observation and direct measurement.

Mode of Interviewing. There are several ways of classifying interviewing methods, but only one will be considered here—the physical mode of the interview. The physical mode includes information that is gathered in person, by telephone, and through the mail. Figure 1.3 contrasts these three techniques.

Figure 1.3. Choosing among interviewing modes [a]

Interview Mode	When To Use:	Advantages	Disadvantages
Personal	When timely generalization is desired When combined with observation When visual stimuli are used When rare groups are defined by geography	Complicated topics Probing Better rapport Better control of respondent	Interviewer biases Respondent availability Interviewer-respondent perceptions Expensive
Telephone	For immediate results For general issues, general audiences For simultaneous national/regional interviewing To verify survey data	Anonymous Fast, cheap Geographically flexible 90% + homes have phones Free of many perceptual biases Monitors interviewer biases	Disruptive Uncomplicated topics Less control of respondent Underrepresents minorities and low-income groups Imprecise local areas
Mail Questionnaire	For nose-counting sample enumeration For specialized, well-defined populations For low-risk populations For diary keeping To verify personal interviews	Cheapest Capable of census Free of perceptual bias Pictorial, technical content	Low response rate No control of respondent Junk mail irritation Slow returns Requires literate respondents

[a] Adapted from Gerald Hursh-César, *The Research Information Workshop,* op. cit., Exhibit 11-4.

A critical aspect of most personal and telephone interviewing, in contrast to mail, is that the researcher probably does not gather the data. Instead, the data is collected through intermediaries—interviewers—who are not likely to see the objectives of the survey in the same way that the researcher sees them, nor are they likely to conduct the interview in the same manner. It requires great care to safeguard the quality of the data from the personal biases (values, abilities, beliefs, expectations, predispositions) of the interviewers.

Face-to-Face Interviewing. This is the traditional form of survey research. The interviewer gathers information in the physical presence of the respondent. The Model Survey used later in this book employs the face-to-face interview in the home, but personal interviews can also be conducted in offices, in shopping malls, at polling places, in farm fields, etc. We will look at two special types of in-person surveys in later chapters, in addition to the Model; these are (1) the previously mentioned panel study, in which the same people are interviewed more than once to see what changes occur in their behavior; and (2) the intercept survey, in which people are stopped as they leave the polling place on election day and asked about their voting behavior, or stopped in the shopping mall and asked about their purchases.

Personal interviews are the standard by which survey research gained credibility. Many clients do not yet trust telephone studies for information critical to decision making.

In the home, interviewers are able to develop a personal rapport with respondents through eye contact, sharing coffee, and other kinds of visual behavior that can enhance the completion of an interview in difficult situations. Physical presence gives the interviewer greater control over respondent behavior than does telephone interviewing, in which the voice is the interviewer's only means of holding the respondent's attention. For this reason, in-person probing usually can penetrate complicated subjects in greater depth.

Length of interview alone may dictate the use of in-home interviewing. A 20-minute call is a long phone interview, and 30 minutes is considered the practical maximum. Therefore, interviews that contain hundreds of variables, requiring more than an hour to obtain answers, almost surely must be obtained in person.

Personal interviewing is the only means of visually observing people's characteristics in order to acquire or verify certain data. For example, it may be more reliable for the interviewer to visually observe a respondent's race than to ask this by telephone. The same might be true if we wanted to check food products in the pantry, measure the dimensions of the living room, verify the number of television sets, conduct a literacy test, and so on.

Personal contact is necessary if we want to demonstrate a product or some device as part of the questioning. Further, we often present visual stimuli—photographs, pictures, objects, measuring scales—and ask people to respond to them, which can be done only personally. In campaign surveys, for example, people are sometimes shown photographs of various candidates or mocked-up illustrations of billboards; they are then asked to say which ones they have noticed, or which they like most and why.

Frequently we study issues for which there are many alternatives, for which the only fair approach is to let the respondent consider all alternatives together at the same time. For this, we may use response cards (see Chapter 4), which aid understanding and recall of the issues involved. The trend is toward the use of more visual materials in presenting response alternatives in face-to-face surveys.

At-the-home interviewers have certain other advantages in ensuring completion of the sample. Listings of people's telephones or mailing addresses are usually somewhat out of date. Personal interviewing will obviously find who the current family is at a particular residence.

Some elements of the population can be reached only by going to their door. The few people without telephones are most often in the lower-income groups and will therefore be represented in their proper proportion only by a personal survey. Interviewers suitable to ghetto or barrio neighborhoods are more likely to get cooperation of suspicious people in those neighborhoods.

In-person interviews are most efficient when we are trying to reach rare subgroups in the population who can be identified by their location in time or place. For example, personal interviewing will be more productive when the survey is of delegates at the Republican National Convention; the same can be said for trying to find Spanish-speaking residents in a specific neighborhood.

For surveys in precisely defined geographic areas, such as congressional districts in large cities or catchment areas for a neighborhood social service center, telephone exchanges usually will not coincide with the district boundaries. Personal interviews will be required to ensure getting only the intended respondents.

Other site-related reasons include situations where interviews must be conducted at the workplace, where records must be consulted (such as at schools), where simultaneous interviews with husband and wife are desired, where all residents of a household are to be interviewed, where a respondent must be verified by sight, and where proof of interviewing is essential.

Finally, U.S. government contracts for survey research typically specify personal interviewing—it's the form most trusted.

On the negative side, high cost is the main limitation of personal interviewing. Travel takes interviewers' time while they are on the payroll, and transportation costs continue to escalate. If the study design requires tracking down specific, hard-to-locate respondents, such as young, single, mobile professionals or segments of the transient populations of the inner city, costs are especially likely to mount.

Guarded-access apartments require special strategies (see Chapter 5), and the personal security of interviewers requires special precautions in high-crime areas.

Perhaps the most negative aspect of personal interviewing is, however, the researcher's lack of control over interviewers' behavior in the field. We cannot constantly check their activities or fidelity to learn how carefully they follow instructions or how their personal feelings may be intruding on data collection.

Despite its traditional merit, personal at-home interviewing is no longer the dominant survey mode. Many more people are contacted each year in commercial surveys by telephone or by mail than in person.

Interviewing by Telephone. Although personal interview surveys provide timely generalizations, only telephone surveys can deliver almost instant generalizations, because the completed questionnaires are available at survey headquarters as soon as the interview is completed. The telephone is the preferred interview mode of newspapers, television, and radio stations that are competing for public attention by adding survey responses to their coverage of fast-breaking news events. In particular, the television networks have led the movement toward telephone surveys to improve their political coverage on election night.

Telephoning is most appropriate for surveys of general issues and general populations or for any population that can be located faithfully by a directory, such as a list of company officials, association members, agency staff, school principals, or university students. Going to each of these people's scattered residences would entail unreasonable travel time. Government agencies use telephone surveys to collect institutional data by calling, say, hospital staff.

Telephone surveys have virtually unlimited geographic reach. It is far easier and cheaper to conduct national surveys by phone than to maintain a national field staff or to assemble one for a single survey. Moreover, local, regional, and national interviewing can be conducted simultaneously, and the results can be analyzed and made available at the same time, without even a day's delay. Individual personal interviews may be scattered over a large area, and the interviewer may be able to complete only one per day, phoners let their fingers do the walking. When the survey design calls for interviewing specific members of the family who may be away (for example, on a business trip, at college, or in the armed forces), they can be reached by phone. There also are no physical risks to phone interviewers.

Since more than nine-tenths of all U.S. homes now have telephones, samples of general populations can be pretty thorough in their coverage; although weighting techniques may have to be used to balance the sample for certain kinds of people less likely to have phones (see Chapter 2).

Completion rates of telephone surveys are usually no worse and often better than completion of in-person samples. City apartment buildings, some comprising hundreds or even thousands of residents, are today often locked and guarded; the telephone can reach these people. The problem of telephone directories excluding unlisted numbers has been overcome; computerized methods now select sample numbers randomly from telephone exchanges known to be working.

The attitude once held that telephone data is of lower quality is no longer supportable. Studies show that for the most part the quality of data gathered by telephone and personal interviewing is comparable.[2] In terms of interviewer-respondent rapport, the telephone survey is free of many biases caused by the reaction of a respondent to an interviewer's appearance, dress, or manner. The interviewer's voice, and the mental image conveyed by it, is the principal source of bias. The anonymity that people feel in telephone interviews may help them to feel in control of the interview when responding to sensitive questions.

People will respond to questioning over the telephone for nearly the same period of time that they will be patient for an in-person interview, although interviewers at the door are in a better position to ingratiate themselves or to press harder to complete a very long questionnaire. Generally, however, people who refuse to complete an interview do so at the point of introduction; only a small percentage break off the interview after having agreed to participate.

Using questions broken down into simple parts, it is feasible to handle fairly complex topics over the telephone. Other than noise disturbances on telephone lines, there appears to be little difference in people's ability to understand well-worded questions when asked face-to-face or by telephone. A good question must be understandable regardless of the mode of interviewing.

Lastly, telephoning done from a central research office has a major virtue: we have greater control over interviewers' behavior—both in work schedule and in manner in interviewing—because of our ability to monitor them continuously.

On the negative side, telephone calls are disruptive in the home and easier to reject. Of course, because many low-income families do not have telephones or share a phone with other families, there is danger of failing to represent these persons in sufficient number or accurate proportion in the sample.

Interviewing by Mail. Mail surveys fall under the more general category of *self-administered* surveys: respondents themselves read and answer the questions. Our concern here is only with questionnaires by mail. The chief use of mail questionnaires is to conduct very large surveys of general populations when there is little risk of making a bad decision based on the data.

Mail is efficient for counting simple characteristics of large populations (families with pets), for studying populations that are well defined by address (magazine subscribers), or for reaching interest group members with high concern for the subject (teachers' associations). Mail is most efficient for collecting extensive written information, such as daily diaries of television viewing over a period of time, and for getting people's reactions to visual content like colors or photographs, such as in the testing of advertisements.

[2]Robert M. Groves and Robert L. Kahn, *Surveys by Telephone: A National Comparison with Personal Interviews* (New York: Academic, 1979).

A major advantage of mail surveys is that they are the most inexpensive kind of survey in terms of absolute costs (though postage is substantial). For the same amount of money, a mail survey can make contact with many more would-be respondents than can telephone or in-person surveys. They are also free both of the biases of interviewers and of any threat that interviewers may represent to people.

A major disadvantage of mail surveys is that response rates are notoriously low, and such surveys are often biased toward people with great interest in the issue who are more likely to respond.

Since mail surveying is relatively inexpensive, however, a much larger sample can be drawn to ensure enough usable responses for analysis (although this may merely accentuate the bias toward willing respondents). Money or other incentives can be used in mailed surveys to encourage higher response rates. Short question-naires have the highest return, but the same proportion will respond to a very long questionnaire (12 pages) as to a moderately long one (8 pages).[3]

An additional, invisible weakness of mail questionnaires is our inability to control who actually responds, and how they respond. For all these reasons the quality of the data will likely be somewhat lower for mail surveys than for the other modes.

Mailings are often used in connection with other kinds of surveys, whether to check information already provided by personal or telephone surveys, to alert in-tended respondents of an upcoming survey, or to verify that a personal interview actually took place.

Self-administered questions also are often used in personal interviews, so the mediation of interviewers can be eliminated. In voting studies, for example, inter-viewers may carry a ballot box. They give a ''secret ballot'' to the respondents and ask them to check off the candidate(s) they favor in the forthcoming election. The respondents put the ballot in the box without the interviewer seeing the choices marked. In other surveys, respondents might be given a set of questions about their attitudes on sensitive topics, such as personal health practices, or they might be asked about technical subjects that require reading for comprehension.

THE SURVEY PROCESS

The steps in doing a survey are laid out according to a *research design*. The research design is more than a flowchart of activities. It combines the theory and practice by which the project is undertaken.

Checklist 3 shows the steps in doing a survey. The first five steps concern

---

[3]Thomas Danbury, *Large-Scale Mail Surveys of the General Population: Some Methodological Observations,* a paper presented to the Advertising Research Foundation, October 19, 1976, New York (mimeo).

survey planning, and these are discussed in this chapter. Steps 6, 7, and 8 each rate a separate consideration, and they are examined in Chapters 2, 3, and 4, respectively. Steps 9 through 12 are covered in Chapter 5, and Steps 13 through 20 in Chapter 6.

CHECKLIST 3

Steps in Survey Research

1. DEFINING: deciding exactly the problem to be studied.
2. BACKGROUNDING: checking existing information on the problem.
3. HYPOTHESIZING: specifying the relationships to be studied.
4. DESIGNING: establishing study principles and procedures.
5. ORGANIZING: marshaling staff, funds, and materials.
6. SAMPLING: choosing the people to be interviewed.
7. DRAFTING: framing the questions for use in the field.
8. CONSTRUCTING: shaping the format of the questionnaire.
9. PRETESTING: discovering whether study methods elicit the desired data.
10. TRAINING: teaching interviewers good data-gathering techniques.
11. BRIEFING: showing interviewers how to use the questionnaire.
12. INTERVIEWING: securing data from respondents.
13. CODING: assigning numerical values to responses.
14. CLEANING: assuring that all data is usable.
15. PROGRAMMING: instructing the computer how data is to be manipulated.
16. COMPILING: organizing data into tables.
17. ANALYZING: relating responses on two or more variables.
18. TESTING: applying measures of statistical significance.
19. REPORTING: presenting the findings and conclusions to the client.
20. USING: applying the findings to the problem at hand.

Defining the Problem To Be Studied

Suppose we are concerned with a proposal to create a drug-abuse program for Model City teenagers. (Model City is a hypothetical locale we will use in this book. Although the name "Model City" has been used for the federal government's Great Society programs of the 1960s, our usage of the term dates back even earlier, to this book's first edition. And since it so aptly describes the idea of a fictional city in which to conduct a Model Survey, we will continue to use the name.) Assume that the drug-abuse program proposal is to be submitted to the voters by referendum in a special election next month. We want to know whether the referendum is likely to pass. Our motivation might be strictly scholarly: we would like to know more about the processes of direct democracy or political communication. Or, it might be activist: we would like to influence the outcome by helping to ensure the referendum's passage or defeat, and we need a better understanding of public opinion in order to effectively intervene. The questions to be explored in the Model Survey are: (1) Who is likely to vote in this referendum? (2) What are their present understandings and opinions about the issue? (3) What characteristics do they have that are related to these attitudes? (4) What kinds of appeals are likely to motivate them to take one side or the other? And (5) through what communication channels can they most efficiently be reached?

Variables. To define this problem for research means to specify the important items for study and to determine what are the relationships among them that we must know in order to conclude correctly about the referendum vote. The survey will try to learn about respondents' physical characteristics, behaviors, knowledge, and attitudes. These characteristics are the *variables* for this study.

As to the term "variable," research is the study of human conditions that are diverse and changeable. In the population as a whole, these human conditions exhibit differences in quantity, size, frequency, direction, or in some aspect of quality—that is, they have different numerical measures called *values*. These differences are the variability in the population. For an individual respondent a particular condition may have different values at different times, that is, it can be changeable. A person's age is a variable. In a panel study a respondent's age will be different between survey and resurvey. But in a one-time survey, each respondent's age is recorded as a set figure; yet *age* will still be considered a variable because respondents all together will report many different ages.

A single respondent's gender is not ordinarily thought of as changeable, but the population will show variability between two values: *male* and *female*. Likewise, in our one-time study on the drug-abuse program, each respondent will show only one attitude—some degree of support or opposition—but respondents will differ from each other in their *level* of support. This is the survey variable in the population that we want to detect, and therefore we designate "Level of Support for the Drug-Abuse Program" as a variable.

Relation Among Variables. We distinguish variables by their relationships. The three of interest to us are dependent, independent, and intervening variables.

Dependent Variables. The major variables under study are dependent variables, those we wish to predict. In this survey, the likelihood of voting for passage of the referendum might be the major dependent variable. We think of dependent variables as being "caused" or "forced" by other variables (called independent variables) or as coming later in a time series. For example, how people vote on the drug-abuse referendum is thought to be related to—dependent on—the level of information they have about it. In summary, a dependent variable is the objective of our research. It is the condition we are trying to measure and to understand well enough to possibly effect a change in it.

Independent Variables. The variables that we start from—that is, accept for this study without wondering what made them what they are—are independent variables. They are the variables that we predict *from*. We think of them as "causing" or "forcing" the dependent variables, or as coming earlier in time. Typical independent variables identified in surveys are people's age, gender, education, occupation, income, and other personal characteristics. In the present example, a relationship might be found showing that parents with teenage children are more likely than parents without teenagers to vote for the drug-abuse program. Family composition would thus be an independent variable.

Intervening Variables. Voting in favor of the referendum may depend on conditions that come between the independent and dependent variables. Such intervening variables, difficult to classify in advance of the study, are conceptually somewhere between the two major variables. For example, a person's education may predict the level of his or her information about the referendum, and the level of information may in turn be related to support for the drug-abuse program. Thus, information level is an intervening variable between the respondent's education and the dependent variable of support for the program.

Defining clearly what the important variables are for this study, and determining which are independent, dependent, and intervening, is the first step in planning a survey. Some may wonder why we are setting out to identify the important pieces of information in the study before we have done the study itself. The answer is that unless we figure out what topics are likely ones to inquire about, we may end up with very little relevant data. We can't go to respondents and ask just one question, "Tell me all about yourself," and go back to the office to sort through the massive junk heap of information we would then have in hopes of finding something pertaining to our study problem. Instead we must acquire a carefully guided collection of information from every respondent, if we are to stand any chance of drawing conclusions that will be helpful.

The identification of possible variables is a study in itself. Their relationships are often circular and obscure. The more we can learn about the subject matter of the problem, the more likely we will be to end up with a useful inventory of study variables.

Many of the study's ultimate variables will not be identified by specific questions in the survey. Instead, these will be constructed later out of items that are asked. As an example, we may want to study the attitudes of high media users. We would not ask someone if they were a "high user" (what would they have to compare themselves to?), but instead we will ask specific questions about how much TV they watch, about whether they read a daily newspaper or a weekly news magazine. In the data analysis stage, we will then combine the separate answers to these specific questions to come up with a new variable, in this case: "media use" (see Chapter 6). Likewise, we will do the same to develop such concepts as "socioeconomic status" and "split-ticket voter." The point is that these concepts must be thought through at the problem-definition stage of a survey, so that we are sure the necessary ingredient items are included for later use.

Background Research

Having defined the problem, we immerse ourselves in background research. Being familiar with the problem means more than a scattered reading of a few texts or articles. Backgrounding is the careful study of available written material—texts, newspaper stories, magazine articles, reports, government documents, other research studies, scholarly monographs, institutional records. It includes audio-visual materials such as maps, photographs, tape recordings, satellite photos, movies, and TV kinescopes. It embraces data storage repositories—archives, computer files, microfiched census reports, and congressional documents. Backgrounding also includes consulting academic experts, other researchers, government officials, and community activists in the subject area.

Vast amounts of information exist now on virtually every problem we might research. An earlier survey on drug-abuse programs may even have been done already somewhere else. The Census Bureau, as is well known, has volumes of detailed aggregate data on every larger community in the land. Less well known is the Census Bureau's public use sample. This is individual respondent data, although everything that could possibly identify an individual has been removed. All information from each household can be analyzed like any other survey. Three basic sample sizes are available: 1 in 100 (every one-hundredth home is in the sample—a 1 percent sample of the total census), 1 in 1000, and 1 in 10,000.[4]

The census, however, is concerned with people's personal and economic demographic characteristics, not specific behavior or opinion. For surveys having such data we turn first to various academic and journalistic survey research organizations. Academic survey organizations publish monographs on separate parts of their results. Journalistic surveys usually publish a series of one-topic reports from a single survey over several weeks or months. But if we fail to find the information we need in such reported studies, that does not mean useful data does not exist. Every study uncovers more data than can be published. We can turn to various archives of social, economic and political data. Individual respondent data, together with codebooks showing how to use it, can usually be obtained by outside researchers. Prominent among these are the Survey Research Center, Institute for

[4]U.S. Bureau of Census, Public Use Samples of Basic Records for 1970 Census: Description and Technical Documentation (Washington, D.C.: Government Printing Office, 1972). These samples are available only for governmental areas of 250,000 or larger population.

Social Research, University of Michigan, and the Roper Center, University of Connecticut. The Gallup organization's monthly publication *The Gallup Opinion Index* tabulates questions from its surveys in the United States and abroad. *Public Opinion Quarterly* reports many current poll results, as does *Public Opinion* in its centerfolds, "Opinion Roundup."

Of the thousands of surveys done each year, unfortunately few have been systematically collected or indexed. For data from these surveys we have to rely on local archives such as state and county historical societies, although not many are yet alert to the lode of survey data being mined in their localities. We also can go directly to the organizations that have sponsored polls—interest groups, government agencies, political campaign managers, newspapers. After their current use of such polls is past, many sponsors would be willing to share their data with researchers, but few have the time to organize it for ready access.

One other kind of backgrounding source is the professional survey researcher. Regardless of his or her field of interest, the professional can identify practical weaknesses in questioning, field work, and budgeting.

On topics for which very little is known, we often do an early-stage pilot survey, which has the strictly exploratory objective of sharpening concepts for further research. But usually this objective can be better met with another technique, such as small-group observation or depth interviewing of a few people closely identified with the problem at hand.

The purpose of backgrounding in general is to cast up all possible, and relevant, variables and then to narrow the range of study objectives, identify measures and methods of achieving them, and detail the expected relationships among those variables.

Specifying Hypotheses

A hypothesis is a research expectation: what we believe we might find in the data. A hypothesis states that a certain relationship will be found between two or more variables. For example: "Married women are more likely to vote for the drug-treatment referendum than other women or any men." The statement may not turn out to be supported by the data, we hasten to add, but the expected relationship needs to be written out to show how we are defining the problem to be studied.

Inventory of Variables. Ultimately, a complete inventory should exist of all variables to be included in the study. The list will reveal whether any are missing, incomplete, or repetitive. One such list, continuing the referendum example, is shown in Figure 1.4. Note that the variables are classified according to whether they are independent, intervening, or dependent variables.

Figure 1.4 is only the barest illustration, because actually there would be a great many more variables besides those listed. Since the relationships can become

Figure 1.4. Inventory of study variables

Independent Variables (Those we predict from)	Intervening variables (Those we predict from and to)	Dependent Variables (Those we predict to)

Personal
  Age
  Gender
  Ethnic group
  Education
  Marital status
 	
Family
  Income
  Family medical history
  Number of children
	Newspaper readership
	Political identification
	Previous contact with
	  drug-abuse programs
		Information:
		  correct knowledge of program
		Attitudes:
		  favorable attitude toward program
		Behavior:
		  will vote to pass the referendum

very complex, greater precision can be achieved by drawing arrows between the variables to indicate the relationships we believe may eixst. The result is a path diagram (see Figure 1.5). By charting in this way, we reveal the study's focus, enabling others to offer critiques.

Surveys invariably start as far too ambitious projects, with too many hypotheses to explore with the time and resources available. For example, think of the questions it will take to establish a family's medical history, which we might hypothesize is related to previous contact with drug-abuse programs, and which together might predict voting for the referendum.

Cutting out variables is a painful process, because we must decide which of many good ideas have the highest potential. This always involves some guessing,

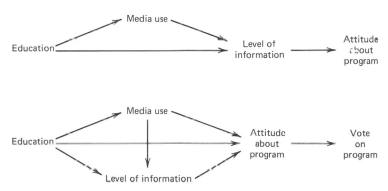

Figure 1.5. Path diagram of possible relationships among study variables.

although pilot surveys may give more reliable guidance. Some hypotheses will be cut out because they are self-evident—they need no further documentation. We will cut others that prove too complicated to measure well. Some are thrown out because they may tap overly sensitive areas that could jeopardize completing the survey. But we must always keep those that promise to speak directly to the needs of the user of the survey data.

Direction of Hypotheses. Beyond merely listing the variables and how they relate to each other, we must state clearly the *direction* of the relationships we expect to find among variables.

Examples of the kinds of directional hypotheses we might state from Figure 1.5 are:

- Older people are less likely than younger people to show interest in the drug-abuse referendum.
- Members of minority groups are more likely than nonmembers to favor passing the drug-abuse referendum.
- The higher the cost of health care in the family, the lower the level of knowledge about the drug-abuse referendum.
- The more likely people are to have voted in the Model City election, the more likely they are to say they are going to vote in this special election.

These hypotheses show how increases (or decreases) in the independent variables are associated with increases (or decreases) in the dependent variables. The role of the intervening variables can be seen in such directional hypotheses as the following:

- As education increases, newspaper readership increases; and, as newspaper readership increases, the level of information about the drug-abuse program increases.
- Families with teenage children are more likely than families without teenagers to have previous contact with drug-abuse programs; and, those with previous contact with drug-abuse programs are more likely than those with no contact to favor passing the referendum.

A table recording the directions of some of the hypotheses for our Model Survey is shown in Figure 1.6. The table lists the dependent variables across the top and the independent (and intervening) variables down the left margin. A positive (+) directional relationship is shown when the two increase together— when some respondents are "higher" on both and others are "lower" on both. The directional symbol is negative (−) when those respondents who are high on the independent variable are low on the dependent variable, and vice versa. The symbol (0) means we don't know what relationship to expect.

Figure 1.6. Summarizing hypotheses, with expected direction shown[a]

Independent Variables	Program Information	Program Attitude	Will Vote for Referendum
+ age	−	−	−
+ male	0	0	−
+ minority member	−	+	+
+ education	+	+	+
+ married/widowed	−	−	+
+ children	+	+	+
+ income	+	−	0

[a] The plus (+) sign next to each variable name (e.g., + age) is used to show the presence of a nominal characteristic (e.g., male, minority, married) or the higher degree of a continuous characteristic (e.g., level of education, number of children, amount of program information). The minus (−) sign shows the absence of the characteristic or a lower degree. The zero (0) indicates we don't know what to expect.

For example, part of the table could be read this way: "The higher their income (+), the more program information respondents will have (+), but the less likely they will be to favor the program (−); yet we don't know whether they will be more or less likely to vote for it at the referendum (0)."

Once we have completed such a table we will have sharpened our focus on what are the most important aspects of our study. If they make the questionnaire too long, promising hypotheses should be dropped, along with the variables involved. For the items that remain, the directional symbols will enable us to assign number codes to response categories that are ordered in the direction of the hypotheses (see Chapters 4 and 6).

At this stage of the study we can begin the planning of how to display the data once it has been collected. Ultimately we will want to look at a table that addresses each hypothesis. To make sure this happens, we lay out dummy tables with pairs of variables just as they would appear in a report (Figure 1.7).

Figure 1.7. Dummy table layout to plan hypothesis testing

Intended Vote on Referendum	Family composition	
	Parents with teenagers	Parents without teenagers
Favor		
Oppose		

   If we are unable to make a table for each hypothesis, it must mean that we don't have the needed variable, or that the direction of the relationship has not been expressed. What we try to avoid is discovering at the analysis stage that we can't investigate a relationship that might shed light on the problem because we don't have the data, or because the measurement isn't such as to enable the test of the hypothesis, or because we simply haven't thought through what we hoped to find out.

   Dummy tables will serve another purpose also. They will serve as instructions to the data processors and programmers, telling them what we require, and will also show us the amount of output we must plan for.

Data Structure

At this stage we also begin to think about how the data that will be gathered is to be organized. Many items of information will be discovered about each respondent. Think of these items being stored in a large pigeonhole structure, with the names of the data items (the variables) listed across the top. The whole first row of boxes will be reserved for the information from the first respondent, the second row for that from the second respondent, and so on.

   In chart form, as in Figure 1.8, this two-dimensional scheme of organization is the data matrix of a one-time survey. Once the data is all in place, we can sum-

	Variable A	Variable B	Variable C	Variable D	Variable E	etc.
Respondent 1						
Respondent 2						
Respondent 3						
Respondent 4						
Respondent 5						
etc.						

Figure 1.8. Two-dimensional data structure.[a]

[a]These diagrams are adapted from John A. Sonquist and William C. Dunkelberg, *Survey and Opinion Research* (Englewood Cliffs: Prentice-Hall, 1977), Chapter 2.

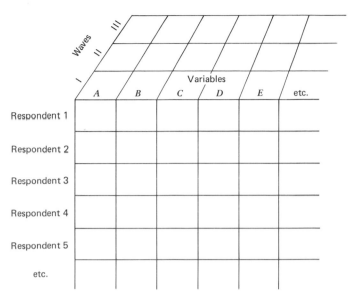

Figure 1.9. Three-dimensional data structure.

marize the contents of the whole first column of boxes—a single type of information—from all the respondents to discover how they vary. Then again, we will want to sum across one respondent's row at least a few of the variables, so we can give him or her a score for, say, media use. Also, we will want to see how several pairs of variables relate in single individuals, preparatory to summing those combinations for all respondents to discover frequent similarities.

For a panel study (in which the same individuals are interviewed a second time on the same subjects), we would add another stack of boxes behind the one already in place, into which we would sort the information received in the reinterview. The data matrix would now be three-dimensional, as in Figure 1.9, with the third dimension labeled by time of interviewing. With this data in hand, it would be possible to go through one line of pigeonholes from front to back to see how a single respondent changed on a single variable over time (for example, his or her likelihood to favor a certain candidate at several points during a campaign).

DESIGNING SURVEYS

We already know that the research design is the set of theory and procedures for carrying out a study. While our theory may be sound and our procedures practical, the research we do may not solve our problems. The information we get may be inadequate, untrustworthy, irrelevant. We must worry about basic quality questions right at the start.

Special Concerns

The concerns we have in designing surveys are shown in Checklist 4. All of these questions are important to answer. Of particular, immediate concern are questions of survey validity, reliability, and bias, and these will be discussed first. The subjects of resources and clearance are the last topics in this chapter. Other questions are taken up in later chapters.

CHECKLIST 4

Concerns in the Design of a Survey

1. Is the information *valid?* Have we asked relevant questions in relevant ways?
2. Is the information *reliable?* Is it trustworthy, consistent, stable? Would we get the same results if we did the study again?
3. How *precise* is the information? How much risk due to sampling error is involved in using the information for making decisions?
4. Does it *generalize?* Which populations and conditions does the information describe?
5. In what ways is the information *biased?* How have human errors been introduced by faulty procedures, by weak questions, and by intervention of interviewers?
6. How *accurate* is the information? What is the total amount of error due to sampling and due to the biases introduced by interviewers and other human elements in the survey?
7. Can we *extrapolate* the information? How safe is it to use the information to describe the characteristics of populations or conditions that are different from those we studied?
8. Do we have sufficient *resources?* Are skilled staff, supplies, and facilities adequate to do a worthwhile survey?
9. Will we get *clearance* to do the study? Is permission necessary before we can go into the field?
10. How *useful* will the results be? Who needs the information, and precisely how will they need the results to help them make decisions?

Validity. Just because we say we are interested in studying people's attitudes toward city services does not mean we are certain to learn them. Unless valid, our measures might instead tap people's general antipathy toward government at any level.

The time to challenge the likely validity of our measures is at the stage of hypothesizing. Usually we say that research is valid if it measures what it is supposed to measure—if we learn what we want to learn. But the question of validity has other important dimensions:

Is It Relevant? Is the information important for understanding the problem at hand? In other words, are we measuring the right variables, and are we measuring them in the right way? Thorough backgrounding, including contact with knowledgeable experts and intimate knowledge of existing research, is important for improving the relevance of our measures.

Is It Useful? How useful is the information for solving the problem? Research is valid if it helps us to solve the problem at hand. This is the predictive aspect of validity: information predicts solutions. Correctly predicting the outcome of an election is an indication of the validity of our survey data. Thus, one way to measure validity is by checking our information against some outcome in the past, or in the period immediately following field work. Another way to measure validity is to check our information against some existing yardstick, for example, examining official voting records is a validity check on people's self-claims of having voted in the past election.

Why Is It Useful? What explains the usefulness of our information? Knowing that information is useful may not tell us why it is useful. We must check the theory underlying the information in order to use the information for problems in other contexts. Most of the theoretical checks of validity are statistical. For example, we can analyze the relationship between our measures of a concept and other variables known to be related to the concept, such as seeing whether self-claimed voting is related to the respondent's education, interest in public affairs, and membership in community groups, which other studies have shown to be related to voting.

Reliability. Human behavior is changeable—it varies. In a one-time survey, we take a quick measurement, from many respondents, of aspects of a behavior. What we hope is that our *measure* of that behavior is stable enough so that we don't report variability where it doesn't exist, or fail to see it where it does exist. But our measures of human behavior are error prone, because we can never know all aspects of any behavior at a single time. Reliability is a measure of consistency, the dependability of information from one respondent to another, and for a single respondent from one time to another. Reliability is the degree to which the same (or similar) measures obtained in the same way from the same population will produce the same results at different times. Reliability can be affected by the *external* conditions in which the measures were obtained as well as by the *internal* consistency of each part of the measurement.

In practice we usually measure reliability by going back to some (a sample) of the people interviewed previously and obtaining some (a sample) of the same information as before. Comparing the differences, or errors, between the two sets shows the consistency of the information over time.

The things that affect reliability are:

- *Random variation*—There are natural differences (variations) in the study population. Thus there is always some error in our measure of human behavior.
- *Unequivalent respondents*—The sample of persons interviewed a second time is not always representative of the larger initial sample.
- *Unequivalent conditions*—Personal situations change over time. Respondents' conditions may be different. Also, new interviewers may affect respondents differently from the original interviewers.
- *Memory*—People may remember their previous answers and change them for variety, or feel compelled to stick with them despite a change in views.
- *Motive*—Depending on their previous experience and their perceptions of the reasons for the second interview, people may choose to give different information.
- *Type of information*—Personal characteristics such as income, religion, size of family, political party identification do not change readily in a short time. Opinions and attitudes, on the other hand, are less consistent over time.

Bias. Bias is distortion, a skewing or prejudicing of the results of a measurement. A properly administered scientific study will not knowingly be slanted, but there is human bias at every stage. The study design itself incorporates biases based on the researcher's own interest, discipline of study, competency, and so on. Sampling contains biases. The questions inevitably introduce bias, not by wording alone, but also by forcing people into categories either before or after the questions are asked. And each additional worker adds new biases—those of the interviewers, the coders, the supervisors, the statisticians, the programmers.

A major source of bias is the investigator's expectations of what respondents will know, think, and do in relation to the study problem. The tendency of investigators to find what they expect or hope to find is illustrated in every close election; often, commercial polls for opposing candidates will each find their own client ahead. As researchers, we must recognize our personal biases, but confession is not enough. We cannot afford to produce and use contaminated data. The job of survey management is to identify and reduce these extraneous sources of bias by selection and training of competent assistants, ever-present supervision, and adherence to accepted practices. A good research design can identify in advance our biases and inadequacies and plan ahead how to deal with them—how to control, measure, and reduce them.

Design of the Model Survey

As mentioned several times, this book uses a Model Survey undertaken in Model City for the purpose of demonstrating how surveys may be done. Some of the features of the Model Survey are evident already. Other features are described in later chapters. Checklist 5 summarizes the key elements of the research design of the Model Survey. Each point represents a choice among alternatives mentioned in this chapter so far, or, in some instances, in chapters yet to come. As always, the Model merely illustrates the process. A reader doing an actual survey should go through the checklist and make a decision on which alternatives are appropriate for his or her own study.

CHECKLIST 5

Key Features of the Model Survey Design

1. **OBJECTIVE:** The purpose of gathering the data is both theoretical and practical: (a) We are testing hypotheses for the purpose of contributing to theories of human behavior. (b) We are providing information to the Model City Council on citizens' feelings about certain social services.

2. **PRIMARY DATA:** The desired information does not exist in usable form. It must be gathered in original form from the field.

3. **SETTING:** The information exists in the community, that is, a residential, not an institutional, setting.

4. **RESPONDENTS:** The people to study are those affected by municipal services and those of voting age, so that they can be mobilized for legal, effective action on election day. Thus respondents must be city residents and must either be registered voters or be 18 years of age or older and likely to register.

5. **SELF-REPORTED DATA:** We seek data on people's information level, attitudes, and activities related to civic affairs and the political process. This is information most efficiently obtained from the people themselves, not from knowledgeable observers, secondary sources, or by observation.

6. **GENERALIZATION:** We want to describe the population of registered voters in the city—to generalize about them. But we don't have the resources to study all of them; we must rely on a sample.

7. **SURVEY:** We will do a survey because, if properly done, it can provide community-wide generalizations based on a sample of people.

8. **FACE-TO-FACE INTERVIEWING:** Since we are particularly interested in having sufficient numbers of various population subgroups, who we know from other research are more difficult to reach by telephone and mail, we will talk to people in their homes. Also, we have certain visual materials about which we want people's reactions.

9. **PROBABILITY SAMPLE:** We will draw a random-type sample called a probability sample, which means selection is made according to chance, because we do not want our own feelings to affect the selection of people for the study. Only from random-type samples can we generalize to the study population.

10. SINGLE-TIME SURVEY: We are interested only in describing people at the present time as a basis for knowing their feelings and predicting their behavior at a future time. Because of limited resources, we cannot do multiple-time surveys to measure changes over a time period.

11. SAMPLE SIZE: We will try to interview 600 people. This will enable us to estimate the population characteristics with an acceptable degree of precision and with an acceptable degree of confidence in the value of the estimates.

12. INTERVIEWERS: We will hire professional interviewers and give them special training for this survey. We will employ 15 interviewers, who combined will complete 600 20-minute interviews, each averaging 5 to 6 completions per day.

13. TIMING: Most of the interviewing will be completed within 7 days—from Saturday (*date, month*) through Friday (*date, month, year*), with an extra 2 days for cleaning-up operations.

14. VERIFICATION: We will check a 10 percent sample of respondents by telephone to ensure they were interviewed and to check problems with questionnaire responses.

15. ANALYSIS: We will process the data by computer, using the Statistical Package for the Social Sciences (SPSS) data analysis routines (see Chapter 6).

16. RESOURCES: We require $58,000 for staff, offices, facilities, supplies, and equipment. We may find ways to reduce costs by substituting resources and improving our design.

The items in the checklist do not comprise all the considerations necessary for a survey, but they do illustrate the kinds of decisions involved in undertaking any kind of research. These decisions are implemented in the following chapters.

ORGANIZING THE SURVEY

Having designed the survey, we must marshal the money, personnel, and other resources to carry it out. On the practical side, we can do only the type of study that resources permit. Hence, much academic and professional time is spent seeking support for research projects. Some individuals have turned ''grantsmanship'' into an occupation, and their skills can be called on for suggested sources and techniques for finding money. At any rate, the cutting-point criterion in project planning is whether we have the staffing and funds to undertake the study as designed.

Surveys are organized around the two critical resources of staff and money.

Survey Staff

Our survey is done by the Research Department of Model State University.

Permitting ourselves the luxury of an Associate Project Director, the Model Survey requires an office staff of about 6 full- and part-time persons and a field staff of 15 interviewers, including 3 supervisors. Over a 6-month period, these staff will have the following jobs:

Project Director. The full-time director is responsible for all aspects of study planning and conduct, including: study backgrounding, hypothesizing, designing, consulting, questionnaire design, pretesting, interviewer recruitment, training, briefing, evaluation, data analysis specifications, and report writing. Because the Director must provide active guidance in each of these areas, even though portions will be handled directly by other staff, the person filling the Directorship needs familiarity with each aspect of the survey.

Associate Director. The half-time Associate Director is responsible for supervising and evaluating the conduct of each step as assigned by the Director. We hope that the Associate Director will be a creative force in designing the study, but on a day-to-day basis he or she must attend to the details of execution. Only the Associate is likely to share the same total-study perspective of the Director, although we want all staff to recognize the context in which the survey operates and the objectives it intends to serve. Special responsibilities of the Associate include: compiling maps and census-type data for the purpose of sample selection; preparing codebooks for data processing, doing preliminary analysis as the data comes in; supervising data-processing operations; and participating in data analysis and report writing.

Secretary. Often overlooked because the title sounds deceptively routine, a quality full-time secretary is vital to survey success. This person will type and duplicate all versions of the questionnaire and of the sample and field instructions as well as all training and briefing materials, correspondence, codebooks and coding instructions, news releases, and reports. The Secretary will maintain all project files and financial accounting for the State University's administration and business office. Additionally, the Secretary will prepare vouchers and payrolls and will order supplies and services. The Secretary may assist the Associate Director and Field Manager in making maps of interviewing areas and in assembling field materials. The Secretary is responsible for securely storing completed questionnaires.

Field Manager. Although the Project Director bears overall responsibility and conducts the briefing sessions, day-to-day assignments and control of interviewers can most effectively be handled by a full-time person experienced in interviewing and with skills in motivating and directing interviewers. The Field Manager secures interviewers, assists in training and briefing, assigns and monitors their work, copes with field problems and reassignments, handles routine inquiries from the field, reports on progress to the Director and Associate, and generally facilitates the flow of field work.

Interviewers and Supervisors. For this survey, 15 interviewers, including supervisors, are needed full time for 7 to 9 days of field work, as well as for 3 days of training, practice interviewing, pretesting, briefing, and debriefing.

Chapter 5 will describe the advantages and disadvantages of using different types of interviewers, such as professional interviewing services, self-employed professionals hired for this survey, staff members of a sponsoring agency, students, and volunteers. The choice of interviewers rests on the availability of money and on how we decide the type of interviewer will affect data quality.

We use supervisors at the ratio of about one to every six or seven interviewers.

Coders. Two coders are required (full-time for each would equal 6 weeks). Translating the questionnaire responses into numbers for analysis—coding—requires clerical accuracy, familiarity with the community surveyed, understanding of the subject matter, and a feel for subtleties of language. The number of coders required depends on the number of respondents, the length of the questionnaire—especially the proportion of open-ended questions—and the number of days allowed to complete the work. Generally a handful of coders, working intensively over a short period of time under close supervision, will produce the most reliable output.

Data Processors. We will use the hourly services of a keypunch operator, a computer programmer, and possibly a consultant statistician. Depending on staff skills, we might pay also for the quarter-time service of an analyst who has the survey experience and statistical training to produce meaningful tables out of the raw results. If this person has some computer programming and operating skills, and also has sufficient research experience to be familiar with the concepts and content of the study, he or she may be an important sounding board for designing analysis specifications, as well as serving as a bridge to the computer programmer and computer center staff. We will strive for overlapping skills on the study because this will enable staff to talk to each other about what each needs.

Facilities

A survey is a big-time operation. It needs space both to operate in and from. And thorough analysis of a survey requires access to data-processing equipment, usually meaning a computer.

Space. Essential is an office that has ample table space and sufficient room, so that document preparation can be done in privacy while still allowing consultation among the staff. Larger space for group activities—briefing and debriefing of interviewers, and coding—will be required for short periods. Availability of a wall large enough for maps, time schedules, and an interviewer control chart also should be considered. There should be storage space for large volumes of materials, such as stacks of questionnaires coming in and going out, and secure storage for completed questionnaires.

If a telephone survey is to be done, a separate space with at least partial sound baffles between telephones will greatly facilitate interviewing.

Computer Access. Although survey data can be hand-tabulated (see Chapter 6), detailed cross tabulations of many variables and statistical testing of results requires the assistance of a computer. Thus, access to a computer should be assured before we commit ourselves to a survey.

Universities usually have a central computer, perhaps with several access points. They assign user numbers to maintain accounts. There may be a priority system for getting time on the computer, so if there is a time pressure for computer results, special arrangements should be made. Nonuniversity users sometimes are granted access to these facilities, although usually at a somewhat higher cost than for faculty and students.

For others, commercial computer service firms sell time on their central machines, which are sometimes halfway across the continent, connected by phone lines. Potential users can either deliver their computer-ready programs and data to the office, or they often can rent terminals for their own offices that tap into the computer for short periods when needed. Self-contained desktop computers are available for rent or purchase; these usually have limited programming capacity and size of memory, but they may be adequate for a given survey.

Computer access at a large facility may be by "batch," in which the user submits cards or tapes for the permanent personnel to run through, or it may be "hands-on," in which the user feeds his or her own cards into a peripheral machine at a remote site. Or the user may have a teletype terminal that uses telephone connections to give the computer instructions and data; the same terminal can receive the computer's results, which it types out. This is an "interactive" mode.

In any event, planning for access to a computer, as well as acquiring staff experience and skills to use the device efficiently, must be a part of the initial survey design. We cannot afford to wait until the data is all in before we start negotiating for someone to do the analysis or try to learn computer analysis procedures ourselves. We consult previous users of the proposed computer facility to learn their experience with time, quality, and cost. Processing an important survey is not the time for learning the mechanics of a new system.

Survey Costs

With rapid inflation, the specific dollar costs cited below are likely to be rapidly outdated. Nevertheless, to give a concrete feel for costs, we quote actual 1981 figures from commercial sources. Costs will vary by locality and among providers. Typical commercial costs are:

- Supervisors: $20 per hour.
- Coders: $12 per hour ($5 student).
- Keypunchers and Verifiers: $15 per hour ($5 student).
- Programmer: $20 per hours ($15 student)
- Clerical: $12 per hour.
- Professional: $60 per hour.

Survey Budgets. Figure 1.10 presents a budget for the Model Survey (per the Survey specifications in Checklist 5). The budget assumes the Survey will be done using a university's facilities (called Model State University) and with direct-hire interviewers. The budget total is about $58,000. Such a figure, of course, is not

Figure 1.10. Model Survey budget [a]

Personnel		
Study Director, 6 months, 100% time	$16,000	
Associate Director, 6 months, 50% time	5,000	
Secretary, 6 months, 100% time	6,000	
Field Manager, 2½ months, 100% time	4,500	
Subtotal		31,500
Overhead @ 45%		14,175
Services		
12 Interviewers, 7 days, 6 interviews per day, and 3 Supervisor-Interviewers, 9 days, @ $60 per day	6,600	
5 Coders, 30 hours each, @ $12 per hour	1,800	
Programmer, 40 hours, @ $20 per hour	800	
48 hours Keypunching @ $15 per hour	720	
4 days Consulting @ $200 per day	800	
½ hour Computer time @ $900 per hour, 2000 pages paper @ $.03, tape $20, data storage $50	580	
Subtotal		11,300
Space, Equipment, Supplies		
Office rentals, communications, travel	750	
Office machine rentals: typewriter, calculator	400	
Paper, stencils, data cards, field supplies, office supplies	400	
Library materials, duplication of reports	200	
Subtotal		1,750
Grand total		$58,725

[a] For 6-page, 20-minute, largely structured, 4-data-card survey with 600 respondents.

very meaningful, since survey projects can vary greatly in size, sophistication, and cost accounting. Anyone doing a survey should acquire current local rate information and compare time estimates with other researchers to calculate a realistic budget.

There are many ways of reducing costs, either by doing a less ambitious survey or by substituting resources. But, for our Model Survey, we will assume everything will be paid for by the project.

Because time is money, we include pay for the Project Director's time. All of the professionals are placed on the payroll, which results in Model State University charging overhead to cover fringe benefits and a share of the supervisory and business office costs of maintaining a research enterprise. The other personnel are not considered employees, but instead we buy their services at flat rates.

Professional consulting is a wise investment for critiques of sample design, question wording, and data analysis plans.

Interviewing costs depend upon the type of interviewer used. At this writing, professional interviewers get about $6 per hour, including travel time, with an added cost for extra travel time of 20 cents per mile. This totals about $60 per day. Some interviewing services instead charge by the interview, which amounts to about $10 per 20-minute interview and which includes travel expenses. In rural areas, the interviewing rate will be closer to $25 per hour.

Computer analysis is expensive. Hourly rates are astronomical, but speed makes the final cost reasonable for a well-prepared analysis. Computer time may cost $900 per hour, but a half hour is long enough to produce all conceivable analyses. Computer costs, however, rise exponentially with poor programming skills. Experience here is a good investment. Computer paper and temporary electronic storage of data are usually billed separately from computer time. At 3 cents a sheet computer paper can be a major item for a survey needing many tables—2000 sheets is reasonable for a modest analysis. Magnetic tapes must be purchased, and the computer center probably will charge a monthly rate for storage. These additional items will add perhaps $100 to costs over the period of a month.

In addition to salaries and services, we must plan for supplies. Surveys run on paper—many versions of questions, questionnaires, codebooks, and reports, and many copies of each when the final version is ready. Interviewers need maps, notebooks, official identification. Standard office machines like word-processing stations or typewriters, and calculators are obvious necessities, but the survey office also must have access to keypunches, a counter-sorter, and a copying machine. Depending upon what kind of computer arrangements are available, the survey office may want to have its own computer portal—a remote teletype or cathode ray tube (CRT) console for interacting with the computer during data analysis. Office space may have to be rented. One telephone, where trouble calls from the field can be handled, is required. Obviously if a telephone survey is to be conducted from the office, a bank of several telephones will have to be installed.

Substitution of Resources. The very same survey can be run for a lot less money if other resources are substituted for money. This is not a "saving," however, since substitutions of time or supplies for money only disguise costs; they are "free" to the survey, but they are real costs to somebody. We are generally glad to have someone else pick up the tab, but in some situations it makes an important difference in the quality of the survey, and we may not want to pay the bigger price of a poor survey. For a political study, volunteers' time does not count against any overall legal limitation on campaign spending, making this type of staffing for surveys especially attractive.

An example of resource substitution that could be used in our Model Survey might be the Project Director who is a college professor willing to serve without pay if the University releases his or her time from other duties. Or perhaps the Director will just take on the survey as an overload, with the cost being transferred to his or her other duties or family life. A researcher can call upon colleagues for free advice instead of paying for consulting. Such substitutions alone will cut more than one-fourth off the budget. An academic department, a business, an association, or a government agency may assign secretaries to work on the survey without billing it and may contribute office supplies, space, and telephones. This reduces the outlay by another fifth. Grants of computer time are sometimes made for academic research (although paper and electronic data storage usually must be paid for), or a business will donate its computer time after hours. If we use students for coding and keypunching at $5 per hour, and have the Associate Director do the computer programming, the expense will be reduced to about $16,000.

If, in addition, student or volunteer interviewers are used, and someone is found to do the coding for the learning value and fun of taking part in research, the survey can be done with hardly any money at all! Of course, it is no longer the same survey, because of the tradeoffs in biases from using different kinds of interviewers (see Chapter 5).

Reducing Costs. Apart from substitution of resources, there are other ways survey costs can be reduced. Good design and specific information about the people being studied have no substitutes as ways of reducing costs. Field costs often depend on the quality of existing data from which the sample was drawn. Interviewer travel time is cut down if good census data and maps exist, showing current locations of intended populations. Other changes in the sampling procedure can reduce costs, but they can lower the quality of data as well.

For example, we could permit the interviewers to choose the houses at which to interview or we could decide to include only those respondents who can be contacted on the first visit to the home, but if we accept expedients such as these in order to reduce costs, we must be prepared to pay the penalty of departing from a proper probability sample (see Chapter 2). It is better that we use limited resources for another kind of study rather than waste money on a weak survey.

Other aspects of good design that can reduce costs are:

- A knowledge of population dispersion and subgroup concentration, in order to more efficiently choose the numbers of different groups (strata) in the sample.
- A familiarity with streets and highways, commercial and residential areas, and urban renewal areas, so we improve the efficiency of interviewer assignments in the field.
- The use of questions, tests, and measurements that have already been validated by previous research.
- The use of knowledgeable persons, sound library research, and thorough pretesting to sharpen the focus of the study, eliminate faulty procedures, clarify questions, and smooth out the data flow.

Fixed and Variable Costs. Some costs are *fixed;* that is, once a study is undertaken, they won't change whether the survey is big or small. These include salaries for the study director, the assistant, consultants, the field supervisor, and the secretarial help, as well as office space and machinery, and the charge for the computer terminal in the office. Fixed costs also include institutional overhead. Other than the increased time for reading extra cards, computer data analysis costs are not affected much by the number of cases, and programming costs will be the same.

Other costs are *variable,* that is, affected mostly by the size, location, and type of the sample and the length and complexity of the questionnaire. If these are reduced, there are reductions as well in numbers and costs of staff, field travel, interviewers, preparation time, training, supervision, coding, and supplies, but the reduction is not proportionate.

Because sample size and questionnaire length affect costs most dramatically, as well as being at the heart of survey quality, survey design must consider the availability of funds from the outset.

The Cost/Quality Trade-off. Precision of survey results is related to sample size. Data quality is largely dependent upon the quality of interviewing. Because these are the major variable costs of surveys, every survey decision requires hard-nosed adjustment between what is desired and what is affordable. Devotion to scientific excellence cannot be the only criterion, because costs are overriding.

If, at some early point in the study, it becomes clear that we cannot afford sufficient precision or quality to make the study worthwhile, instead of giving up the study entirely, we could switch to telephone or mail techniques.

If we can't mount a study of our own, we could combine with other researchers to run our survey "piggyback" (in the same interview), or we could put our most critical questions into a monthly "caravan" or "omnibus" poll, which are run by some commercial research firms. Such firms sell space for individual questions to clients at rates of $200 to $500 per question for a statewide survey of about 1000 respondents. Joining another survey may not be desirable if there is danger of contaminating our questions by others. Nor is it even economical if our study is lengthy. Before we go piggyback, we need precise details of the sample used (some commercial samples eliminate certain low-income families who are not considered prime consumers for the goods the market survey is dealing with), and we need to know the subject areas of the rest of the piggyback questionnaire.

If the desired survey cannot be done for the money available, perhaps additional funding can be found. If the clients want a survey badly enough, it won't seem too expensive. These are value choices for them. In business, politics, and government, managers increasingly are choosing to do more and better surveys.

Farming Out Studies. Our Model Survey will be done entirely in-house, with hired professional interviewers. But it is possible to contract with professional research firms for any or all of the steps in a survey. Sometimes a researcher may want to do the design steps, the sampling, and the questionnaire preparation but will then farm out all the field work, including supervision and the basic data-processing stage; the same researcher takes up the reins again to do the analysis. Another researcher may want to farm out the sample drawing and questionnaire design, or even an entire study.

Costs may be higher for equivalent quality at a commercial firm, but a researcher with some flexibility of scheduling may catch them between other surveys when they are happy to get another job. Prices vary among firms, as does competence and quality control. Before making a contract, we should shop for price and service, and we should inquire around about the firm's reputation to assess its strengths and weaknesses. Then contracts for the work should be let with careful specifications for every aspect of design. The Project Director should still be involved in every step of the work as it goes through the agency.

THE CLIMATE FOR SURVEY RESEARCH

Demand for the kind of decision-making information that can come only from survey research continues to grow rapidly. This provides ample opportunities for practitioners to operate in the field. But not all of these survey researchers have been scrupulously scientific in their goals, methods, or use of information. Many people at the same time are resisting intrusions into their private lives by those who seek to gather information or to manipulate public opinion.

This has created a new climate for survey research, and we must learn to operate in it.

Threats to Survey Research

Several threats to the continuation of survey research have arisen:

Credibility. Many people don't trust polls. They may find it hard to believe that sampling a small number of people could ever be accurate, or they may conclude that, since they have never been interviewed themselves, the polls could not represent their seemingly unique attitudes. Highly publicized news media polls are sometimes wrong—even the best survey is hard-pressed to predict a close race—and this usually triggers a flurry of negative comments about polling in general.

Oversaturation. Some negative reactions to surveys occur because there are so many. Most U.S. surveys are commercial in nature, not academic or even journalistic. These include studies of consumer buying habits and brand preferences. Virtually all political candidates for major office rely on political consultants who routinely prescribe polls before and during campaigns. Academics have contributed to the saturation of some areas, particularly in small communities containing a large university or with highly visible small populations like the Congress or state legislatures.

All of these polls are legitimate, but their cumulative effect may increase public antipathy toward surveys in general. And added to this is the public's resentment against ''snooping'' and ''massive invasions of privacy'' by firms and by government agencies concerned with our credit ratings, health insurance, military service, income taxes, police records. These activities have little to do with survey research, but they probably are seen as part of the Big Brother society.

Fake Polls. Sales efforts, for example of magazines, sometimes masquerade as polls. These are especially contaminating because, instead of interviewing a modest sample of people as true surveys do, salespeople tend to blanket the city with phone calls that turn out to be sales pitches, wearing people's patience to the point that they become suspicious of all attempts to contact their household.

Legislators increasingly are using polls that typically contact every mailbox owner. Sometimes these are really a campaign device, because they can give the appearance of responding to public opinion while actually building support for the legislator's own position.

Inadequate Disclosure. Another problem is misleading reports about polling methods. A poll is sometimes undertaken by a candidate primarily to trigger contributions; the campaign manager leaks only favorable results, showing his candidate ahead or at least with a reasonable chance of winning, and, without any background details on the nature of the survey, reporters may be taken in by the codeword ''survey'' and uncritically report the results. Or, in misguided overreaction, reporters may discount or even ignore all poll releases to avoid being taken in by the hucksters, instead of learning to evaluate each poll.

Some newsmedia-sponsored surveys, instead of using a carefully drawn sample, turn to street-corner interviews of whoever happens along during the lunch hour, or they talk to just 15 households on a city block in Seattle and report these findings with the same gravity as they would a properly done survey. Such actions undercut popular confidence in all survey research.

Code of Ethics

These abuses demand improved performance by survey researchers. The American Association for Public Opinion Research (AAPOR) has developed a code of ethics for the reporting of all surveys. This code requires that news reports of surveys include the following: identification of the sponsor, date of questioning, size of the sample, nature of the population sampled, type of survey, and the exact wording of the questions.[5] Compliance with this code by the major media polling organizations of the National Council on Public Polls, which polices it, is voluntary. None of these requirements can be enforced against private polls.

Government Regulation

Research abuses to human subjects led to federal restrictions on any research involving people—that is, conducted with federal funds—a restriction that is interpreted to include surveys.[6] *Prior clearance* is now required for such studies. Specifically, the federal government requires that *risk* to participants be assessed, that any risks be minimized, that the *scientific merit* of the study be weighed against the remaining risks, and that *informed consent* be obtained from the subjects before they participate. if they are underage or otherwise incompetent to make their own decisions, the consent of parents or other responsible persons is required.

All of these restrictions are subject to interpretation. The government requires that the institution sponsoring the research—whether a university, a state agency, or a federal department—have an ''institutional review board,'' a peer evaluation group which must certify to the government that the risks are nonexistent or minimal; otherwise informed consent must be obtained from potential subjects. A clearance from such a review board is required before government-sponsored research can begin.

Risks to Respondents. These stringent federal requirements arose from revelations of serious harm occurring to subjects, generally in the medical sphere; among other examples, people with disease were left untreated to serve as controls, and some subjects were administered mind-altering drugs unbeknownst to them. But the requirements now apply to every kind of research done with federal funds. Some

[5]American Association for Public Opinion Research, ''Code of Professional Ethics and Practices'' in *Directory of Members 1979–80,* Princeton, N.J., 1980.

[6]45 Code of Federal Regulations, Part 46; proposed revision *Federal Register* 44 (Aug. 14, 1979), 47688. Revision would exempt most survey research, except on sensitive topics.

universities have extended them to all research done at the institution, regardless of the source of funds.

Survey researchers, because they only talk to people instead of doing something to them, usually think of their own projects as risk-free (and thus exempt from the consent requirement). Unlike experimental projects, the only risks most surveys pose are annoyance, loss of privacy, embarrassment at not being able to answer certain questions, or discomfiture with some subject matter   nonetheless, they are risks. Techniques to provide reassurance and to reduce uneasiness are suggested in Chapters 3 and 5.

The risks to be protected against, according to the federal guidelines, are personal risks, not collective ones. That is, if a particular ethnic group objects to certain questions about racial attitudes (for example, because the aggregate results when published may hamper intergroup relations), this is not a risk in the sense of the regulation and is therefore not sufficient reason to forbid the study.

In asking for clearance to proceed, the researchers must supply their review board with a detailed description of the project's goals and methods, often including a copy of the survey's questionnaire. A review board typically might require that specific arrangements be made for safeguarding stored questionnaires ("in a locked cabinet") and for limiting access to the master list that relates names and code numbers, so that confidentiality is not breached. These administrative procedures do not have to be spelled out to the respondents, unless someone should ask.

Informed Consent. It is in the matter of informed consent that the guidelines impinge on the contact between survey researchers and potential respondents.

The federal consent requirements can be summarized by the catch phrase "mandatory/voluntary": It is now *mandatory* that human subjects be aware that their participation is *voluntary*. Suggested introductions to interviews that meet these requirements are shown in Chapter 3.

When reasonably administered, the consent requirements need not be an insurmountable obstacle to survey research. The statute and the regulations deal with weighing risks against benefits and are not meant to stifle research. No researcher has the right to, or needs to, abuse the public in the name of gathering knowledge. Ethical researchers know this and act accordingly; but the clearances require us to be more obvious in following correct procedures. It may be that researchers will need to organize to prevent overzealous administrators or groups with hidden agendas from using the human subjects regulations to impede useful and necessary research.

Defense of Survey Research

In the face of the resistance and regulation of survey research just described, we must reaffirm the necessity and desirability of continuing survey research for several reasons.

Social Understanding. In return for the community's willingness to reveal its opinions and attitudes to the researcher, surveys offer an opportunity for ordinary people to affect the course of the political, economic, and social systems of which they are a part. In the short run, decision makers have to take this opinion into account (though not necessarily follow its every nuance). In the long run, quality field research builds better theory to understand how society operates. We can ill afford to permit the clichés of out-dated research or the contradictory folk wisdom of the political clubroom to suffice for current sound knowledge.

Instrument of Democracy. Public opinion provides a continuous input of popular will in a democracy, in itself a form of government that is, by definition, expected to respond to its citizens; public opinion does the same for a free economy, which is supposed to satisfy consumers. Surveys give citizens an additional say in making government policy on specific issues; surveys supplement their crude power to replace officials in elections, which are based upon a whole parcel of issues. One could even assert that a nation-wide public opinion survey, with a 3 percent error margin, is a more accurate portrayal of public wishes than a general election in which 40 percent of the people are not heard from at all and the other 60 percent can only pick between candidates mouthing vague promises.

Surveying of government or nonprofit, private-agency clients provides an important test of whether the programs supposedly administered for the public benefit actually are perceived as such. It provides a check on officials who claim to be acting in the name of the public, showing whether their assessments of public opinion are in fact accurate. Without independent estimates of total public opinion, these officials must act on the biased reporting of staffs or organized interest groups—or they can go on making extravagant assertions about the level of public support they have for their ideas.

The right of citizens to be heard, and their right to know what their fellow citizens are thinking, are too important to give up surveying. As to abuses of access and interpretation, if more people come to understand what they should demand of surveys, they may better insulate themselves from attempts at manipulation.

It must be understood that if surveys were to be restricted or abolished, assessments of public opinion would not cease. It would only mean that candidates, public officials, and corporate managers would make claims about what the public wanted without any check on their accuracy. It would accomplish little to restrict the survey's role of providing better information.

Responsibility of Surveys. Although the climate for research may have changed, surveys are as important as ever. To earn the right to continue, however, every survey should be a serious effort to advance knowledge, and thereby to improve decision making. Moreover, every survey should be of professional quality.

This book aims to help achieve those goals.

FURTHER READING

Babbie, Earl R., *Survey Research Methods,* Wadsworth, Belmont, California, 1973. Comprehensive review, from planning through analysis.

Campbell, Donald T., and Julian C. Stanley, *Experimental and Quasi-Experimental Designs for Research,* Rand McNally, Chicago, 1966. A classic, basic introduction to experimental design in the social sciences.

Carter, Phyllis G., *U.S. Census Data for Political and Social Research,* American Political Science Assn., Washington, D.C., 1976. Resource guide and student manual.

Dillman, Don A., *Mail and Telephone Surveys: The Total Design Method,* Wiley, New York, 1978. Thorough and practical treatment.

Epstein, Irwin, and Tony Tripodi, *Research Techniques for Program Planning, Monitoring, and Evaluation,* Columbia University Press, New York, 1977. Written to assist non-researchers in planning and using research.

Fellin, Phillip, Tony Tripodi, and Henry J. Meyer, *Exemplars of Social Research,* Peacock, Itasca, Illinois, 1969. Brief, practical discussion of many research techniques, including surveys.

Groves, Robert M., and Robert L. Kahn, *Surveys by Telephone: A National Comparison with Personal Interviews,* Academic, New York, 1979.

Hursh-César, Gerald, and Prodipto Roy, editors, *Third World Surveys: Survey Research in Developing Nations,* Macmillan, New Delhi, 1976. Adaptations of methods in different cultures.

Hyman, Herbert H., *Survey Design and Analysis,* Free Press, New York, 1955. An original source.

Miller, Delbert C., *Handbook of Research Design and Social Measurement* (3rd ed.), McKay, New York, 1977. Large collection of brief suggestions for research design, grant requests, and evalutation of survey techniques.

Moursund, Janet P., *Evaluation: An Introduction to Research Design,* Brooks/Cole, Monterey, California, 1973.

Phillips, Bernard, S., *Social Research: Strategy and Tactics* (2nd ed.), Macmillan, New York, 1971. Thorough consideration of research design and measurement.

Reynolds, Paul D., *Ethical Dilemmas and Social Science Research,* Jossey-Bass, San Francisco, 1979.

Shively, W. Phillips, *The Craft of Political Research: A Primer,* Prentice-Hall, Englewood Cliffs, N.J., 1974. Precision and accuracy in thinking and measurement.

Sonquist, John A., and William C. Dunkelberg, *Survey and Opinion Research: Procedures for Processing and Analysis,* Prentice-Hall, Englewood Cliffs, N.J., 1977. Professional-level forms and procedures. Has 20-page bibliography.

Tripodi, Tony, Phillip Fellin, and Irwin Epstein, *Social Program Evaluation: Guidelines for Health, Education, and Welfare Administrators,* Peacock, Itasca, Illinois, 1971. Brief discussion of research techniques appropriate to effective program development and evaluation.

Weiss, Carol H., *Evaluation Research,* Prentice-Hall, Englewood Cliffs, New Jersey, 1972. An introduction to designing evaluation studies.

CHAPTER 2

Drawing the Sample

This chapter explains in detail one way of deciding how many people to interview in a survey, and which ones. Continuing with the device of a Model Survey, we will draw an actual sample for a particular study in fictional "Model City."

INTRODUCTION TO SAMPLING

Sampling is a highly technical aspect of survey research. As such, it employs a number of terms that should be explained as simply as possible.

What Is a Sample?

We are interested in learning about people by talking with them. In practice it is impossible to talk with all the people in our community. Fortunately, we know that we have to talk with only some of the people to get an idea of the characteristics of all of them. This is the theory of sampling.

Sampling is a procedure by which we can infer the characteristics of a large body of people (called a *population*) by talking with only a few (a *sample*). This is not an unusual concept. Every day we "sample" the opinions of others in order to learn what is going on in the world. Talking to the barber or the cab driver is how we get some idea of what others think or know about current issues.

Most of us are careful not to generalize from the opinions of only a few people.

52

Instead, we try to talk to more people in hopes of finding a wider range of opinions. But most of our everyday contacts tend to be with others who are much like ourselves, and so they tend to be individuals with whom we agree on most things. Therefore, these people probably do not accurately reflect the full range of opinions in the whole community. If instead we select people by chance, we will get a more precise measure of the real divisions of public opinion.

In survey research, we try to estimate community characteristics much more carefully than we do in our everyday encounters. It is the power of generalization that distinguishes survey research from other research approaches. For example, after interviewing a sample of 600 voters, we can generalize to all voters in the community (within a certain margin of error). Our concern is that the *number* and *kinds* of people in the sample be sufficiently representative of the whole population to enable us to make sound generalizations about that population. In other words, a proper sample of people must constitute a small-scale replica of the larger community. Generalizations are possible, however, only with a good sample, and a good sample can be drawn only with good sampling procedure.

What Is a Good Sample?

A good sample is one that is logically appropriate to the problem under study and that, in practice, is a reliable basis for decision making.

Probability. In sampling, probability means "chance"—each person's chance of being selected for the survey. We have a *probability sample* when we design the sample in a way that ensures that each person in the population has a fair chance of being selected and we can know the arithmetic value of that chance.

For most studies, a good sample must be a probability sample, that is, one based on mathematical laws of chance rather than on the researcher's personal values and judgments. Whenever our predispositions enter into the sampling process we risk biasing the data. Probability samples are designed to be free of our personal judgments. By eliminating human biases (which usually cannot be measured) in selecting sample units, only errors that occur randomly should affect the sample draw. Only in a probability sample can we measure the amount of error due to sampling.

With a probability sample we can:

- Know the size of the sample needed to achieve any desired level of precision.
- Specify the chance (known and not equal to zero) of each unit being selected.
- Estimate the amount of error (imprecision) due to sampling.
- Determine the degree of confidence we have that our estimate is within the range of precision required.

Cost. Trying to achieve an ideal sample in the field can be very expensive, and therefore it is rare. Commitment to total scientific perfection is unrealistic, because cost is a limiting concern in every study. So the task is to design a sample that balances the strict demands of theory with the practical limits of money and other resources.

An efficient sample is by practical definition one that yields the desired information, within expected but tolerable limits of sampling error, for the lowest cost. It can also be defined as a sample that, for a fixed cost, yields the desired information with the least sampling error.

For any study we use the best sample we can afford; but there are minimum standards below which we will not go. We will not undertake a community survey (whether of a single locality or an entire nation) unless: (1) the sample is large enough so that estimates of community characteristics can be made with acceptable precision, and (2) the sample is varied enough to include people who together are representative of the community. If we can't afford this minimum, we choose another method of research or abandon the study.

What Is Sampling Error?

Even the best sample will not be completely accurate. Because we are interviewing just a portion of the population, any measure we get enables us only to *estimate* characteristics of the whole population, not measure them exactly. Sampling implies some discrepancy between the actual and the estimated value (amount) of some characteristic of the population.

We may, for example, be interested in learning the number of people in the community who support enactment of a local nonsmokers' rights law. Not being able to talk with everyone, we do a sample survey, and estimate the number of supporters and opponents in the community from the number of each who turn up in the sample. The difference between the sample estimate and the number that would have been found by a 100-percent census of residents using identical procedures is called *sampling error*. Random sampling errors occur because of the unlikelihood—without counting everyone—of finding in a sample the same, precise proportion of natural variations (differences) that exist among the whole population. Two similar samples taken at the same time will also differ from each other. When estimated statistically, this variability in measurement of population characteristics is given the technical term *variance* (see Chapter 6). Samples may be inadequate because they are too small, poorly drawn, or misrepresentative of important subgroups in the population—overrepresenting some and underrepresenting others. When errors are large—when the sample is inadequate to detect natural variations in the population—we say the estimate suffers from *high variability;* it's not reliable.

Social research is the study of human characteristics. Such human conditions are subject to change; they are *variables*. They have different values in quantity, size, frequency, direction, or other qualitative values. They have different values at different points in time—a person's age. These similar terms are important for sampling:

- *Variables*—human characteristics (traits, attributes) subject to change.
- *Variation*—for the individual, the change in a variable over time; for a population, the differences in people's traits found at a single time. This is the reason for doing research.
- *Variability*—the difference in the measures of variables; thus differences between sample and population values, or between similar samples.
- *Variance*—the amount of error in estimates due to sampling.

We never really know how much sampling error we incur in our surveys of large populations, because we never really know the actual, ever-changing value of the characteristics being sampled.

Some think that an election is a good test of the sampling error of a poll that tries to predict an election. But it is not a good test if voting takes place on a different day from the poll, with intervening events and last-minute campaigning. Moreover, the stimulus of an official election ballot or voting machine card is not identical to the preelection questions in the survey. But most important, voting is *behavior* (it takes more to move our body to the polling place than it does merely to express an *opinion* to an interviewer at the door).

The amount of sampling error affects the *precision* of the sampling estimate. Precision is a measure of how close the sample value is to the "true" population value. Usually this is expressed as a margin of plus-or-minus error. For example, we might report that 53 percent of the people, plus or minus 4 percentage points, support a proposed clean-air law. This means that we believe the actual proportion of the population who supports that clean-air law to be somewhere between 49 and 57 percent of the population.

Sampling error occurs with no specific pattern; some measures will be high and some low—it is random. But the amount of random sampling error can be estimated as long as the sample is a probability sample at all stages of selection. As we shall see, we can calculate from the division of the sample on some characteristic how precisely a sample of a given size is likely to reflect that characteristic in the whole population.

What Is Accuracy?

Sampling error is not the only inaccuracy in surveys. Accuracy of a sample—how closely it reflects the population—also includes two other elements—*sampling biases* and *nonsampling biases*.

Sampling Biases. First, some procedural errors arise during sampling due to inadequate data or clerical mistakes. Since these procedural errors do not occur randomly, they are called sampling biases. Sampling bias is the difference between the sample result actually obtained and the sample result that would have been obtained if a better sampling procedure had been used.

While random sampling errors are due to the natural variations in the population, procedural errors tend to be systematic—they occur in patterns, they are repetitive—and therefore likely to distort the sample's estimate of population variations. For example, an interviewer may bias the sample by including more younger people and housewives simply by interviewing the first person who answers the doorbell at each sample household.

Artificially, sampling biases can make significant differences appear between subgroups in the sample when they are actually insignificant in the population (or the reverse), and they can make small differences appear larger (or the reverse). The extent of sampling bias usually is not measured; therefore, we seldom really know how accurate our results are. The point is: human biases, not random sampling errors, are the weaknesses of surveys.

Nonsampling Biases. Second, nonsampling biases are also present in surveys. These include procedural errors in question writing, interviewing, and interpretation. Also, mechanical and clerical errors occur in processing data—for example, the office clerk who systematically writes "4s" that look like "9s" to the keypuncher. Ironically, counting everyone's opinions by a complete census (where the sampling error would, by definition, be zero) does not guarantee that we get the "true" value either. Even without measurement biases, such a mammoth project may well suffer from more mechanical errors than would occur in a sample, owing merely to the greater amount of data being handled.

Elections provide an analogy to this. Even a complete voter census, which is what the election amounts to, cannot always give the result exactly, because nonsampling error—miscounts, misreading of ballots, loss of ballots, mistakes of election judges, and disputed registrations—may in total be larger than the difference between the candidates.[1]

To review: How closely we approximate population characteristics depends on the precision and accuracy of our sample. *Precision* is a measure of how close a sample value is to the "true" population value as measured in units of random sampling error, which can be estimated mathematically. *Accuracy* is made up of both random sampling errors and nonrandom biases in sampling and other survey procedures. Whatever magnitude they may be, they cannot be measured exactly, and they are too often entirely undetected. For this reason we rarely know the total amount of all kinds of error in sample surveys.

Techniques to reduce nonsampling errors are dealt with in subsequent chapters. For the moment our concern is with the precision of a sample.

[1]See Ronald F. Stinnett and Charles H. Backstrom, *Recount* (Washington, D.C.: National Document Publishers, Inc., 1964).

SAMPLE DESIGN

The sample design is that part of the overall research design (see Chapter 1) that tells us whom and how to sample. It provides both the theory and the procedure for drawing the sample. The design should (1) specify the random errors that will be tolerated due to sampling and (2) provide safeguards against human biases that act nonrandomly to corrupt the sampling process.

The two main categories of samples are *probability* and *nonprobability* samples, which differ according to whether researchers allow the laws of chance to pick the respondents or whether they rely upon human judgments as to whom to interview. Because precision can be measured only for probability samples, they are the only types considered for the Model Sample.

Types of Probability Samples

There are different ways of sampling people. We can choose respondents who are scattered individually all over the city, or we can choose them in groups. We might choose a separate sample of blacks and a separate sample of whites. Or, we might choose several neighborhoods and interview only at private households in those neighborhoods. As long as the choice at every level is left to chance, all of these varieties are probability samples.

Four types of probability samples are: (1) simple random samples, (2) systematic random samples, (3) stratified samples, and (4) cluster (area) samples. Their characteristics are shown in Figure 2.1 (page 58).

Simple Random Samples. Once the simple random sample is understood, all other probability samples can be described as variations of it.

The simple random sample is like a lottery. To draw a simple random sample requires that every unit in the population has a *known* and *equal* (nonzero) chance of being selected. If we know in advance the chance that any unit will be selected, we then also know the chance that any unit will *not* be selected. Therefore we can calculate the amount of error associated with drawing a sample on the basis of knowing which units turn up in the sample and which don't.

If there are 150,000 adults in a city and we draw a simple random sample of 750, each adult's chance of selection is 1/200. This is called the *sampling fraction*. The fraction is simply:

$$\frac{n}{N} = \frac{\text{size of sample}}{\text{size of population}} = \frac{750}{150,000} = \frac{1}{200}$$

Each adult in the city has a chance of selection, and it is known to be 1 out of 200. The chance of each adult is equal, because once chosen a person cannot be chosen again for the sample. It's like drawing names out of a hat without replacing

Figure 2.1. Comparison of types of probability samples

Type	When Used	How Drawn	Degree of Precision Typical for the Same Size Sample
Simple random	Units are identified, easily locatable	Lottery	High
Systematic random	Units are ordered in a list, or can be found in some order	Take every *n*th unit	High
Stratified	Relevant characteristics are known, identifiable, and locatable	Divide population on the characteristic, then pick units randomly within each subgroup	Highest
Cluster (area)	Number of units is very large or units are unidentifiable except by area	Choose groups of units randomly, then pick individual units within these areas randomly	Lowest

the name that is selected. In this way no person has a better chance than another of being selected. Further, the choosing of one person for the sample does not affect the chance of any other person getting chosen also. Thus, the true simple random sample of sufficient size is unlikely to overrepresent or underrepresent certain types of people.

While easy to describe, a true simple random sample is rarely achieved with large populations. To give every person an equal chance of selection means that each has somehow to be identified uniquely by name or serial number. This is virtually impossible with large populations, because there seldom exists a reliable list of all people in a city. The Census Bureau doesn't print names or list individual households; the smallest segment of census information published is for one city block, showing its number of people and its total number of housing units.

Such lists of people as we do have (telephone books, city directories, social security numbers) are never complete, up-to-date, fully accurate, or carefully separated by government unit boundaries that may be relevant for our study problem. Even if lists were available from which to make a random draw, the individuals selected would be so costly to locate for interviewing that other sampling strategies are more efficient.

In contrast, simple random samples can be used efficiently with small, well defined populations for which good lists exist—all city physicians, all state legislators, or all of a university's students.

Systematic Random Samples. The systematic random sample is a variation of the simple random type. To draw a systematic random sample, the population must be listed in some manner. Sampling starts from some randomly chosen point in the population list and selects every nth unit thereafter.

For example, the Model Sample uses the Census Bureau list of all 79,500 housing units in Model City, totaled by block. For the Model Sample, we wish to choose 150 clusters of housing units to locate 750 people (these numbers will be explained later). We divide the total number of housing units by 150 to get the sampling interval, which turns out to be 530:

$$\frac{79,500}{150} = 530$$

We next select at random a number between 1 and 530 as the starting point and systematically skip through the list, thereafter designating every 530th housing unit encountered after the one we randomly chose as our starting point. Suppose we randomly selected the 100th household as our starting point. We would consecutively select other numbers by adding 530 to each . . . 100, 630, 1160, 1690, 2220 . . . until exhausting the list of 79,500 households. (This procedure is explained in detail later.)

The procedure for the systematic sample has a different effect from that of the simple random sample in that once the first unit has been chosen, all the rest of the units for the sample are predetermined. That is, the choice of the first unit eliminated 529 of the 530 housing units from having a chance to get into the sample. It is still a probability sample because we know what chance each unit initially has of being selected, and we use a randomized device to start, rather than taking the 1st unit in the list, which would have meant that the 2nd through 530th units (and the 532nd through 1060th, etc.) never would have a fair chance of being drawn.

The advantage of the systematic random sample is to save the time and cost of trying to list large populations, without losing features of probability sampling. Such samples assume, however, that there is no important or cumulative way in which units are ordered in the population. If the population is ordered somehow— from rich to poor, large to small—a systematic sample can produce biased results. Suppose, for example, that people who live in corner houses have higher incomes generally than their neighbors. If a sample of each block systematically starts with a corner house, the sample will be biased upward for income.

Large cities typically have computerized voter registration systems. The registration clerk may assign voters a registration number, or at least they are serially numbered in the printed list. We could draw random registration numbers from a table and try to locate the voters who have those numbers in the list. But that is a tedious chore. Instead, it would be easier to use a systematic procedure by figuring out what proportion of the total we need (the sampling fraction—530 in the example being used), picking a random start, and taking every 530th name from the list.

Where the registration records are on cards rather than listed, a systematic procedure that avoids counting all cards is to use a ruler to measure the total length of the filed cards and then measure off the sampling interval in centimeters, pulling out the cards at that distance apart throughout the file.

Since lists of names for large populations, like the city registration file, are incomplete and generally out-dated, however, and because it is difficult and expensive to locate specific people designated by the technique just described, we usually do something even easier. We often choose city blocks in a systematic way from a census list based on the number of individuals or households located in each. When the interviewer reaches the sample block, a random procedure is used to choose the housing unit at which to interview. We do not have to know in advance who lives there. This is the technique used for the Model Sample.

Stratified Samples. Sometimes we know that certain population characteristics are important to the study, and we want to make sure of getting an adequate sample of each. One way to do this efficiently for large populations is to divide them into several subgroups called *strata* (layers) and draw a random-type sample separately from each stratum.

The purpose of stratified sampling is to produce subgroups wherein the members of each are alike in terms of one major characteristic—the study problem. The more alike they are on this characteristic, the better. But the more dissimilar they are on other characteristics, the better. In other words, except for their relationship to the study problem, each stratum should look as much like the whole population's other characteristics as possible.

This requires knowing how to divide the population meaningfully and having the required information to do it. The simple random sample, in contrast, requires only minimum identification of the units in a population in advance of selection, trusting to chance that all theoretically important characteristics of individuals will be represented in their proper proportions. Random selection is free, then, of any errors in subdividing into strata, but it may ignore pertinent information we have about the population that could improve the efficiency of sampling and the precision of sample estimates.

Suppose, for example, we want to study the television-viewing preferences of people who watch professional football games. If from TV rating services we know that 80 percent of these viewers are men, we wouldn't take a random sample of the population, in which men and women divide nearly 50-50. Obviously, we can improve sampling efficiency and precision by taking one larger sample of men and one smaller sample of women.

The stratified sample divides the population into such subgroups as men and women; blacks, whites, and Hispanics; core city, residential city, and suburban dwellers; or whatever is important for the study. Remember, the people in each subgroup are intended to be more like each other in terms of the study problem (such as television viewing) than are all the subgroups together. That is, each stratum is more *homogeneous* than is the whole population in terms of the study problem, thus reducing the variation in the population—the differences that increase sampling error.

If the stratification does not produce relatively homogeneous groups, there is no gain in its use. Of course, members of each stratum will likely be *heterogeneous* (different from each other) in terms of other characteristics—age, gender, income, family size, occupation, attitudes, political party identification. On these other characteristics, each stratum should look as much like the whole population as possible. If we are studying party identification and sample three strata— Republicans, Democrats, and Independents—we want to represent fairly the full range of income, attitudes, religions, ages, etc. that are present within each stratum.

A stratified sample is preferred when we (1) know something about the relationship of population characteristics and the study problem and (2) have the information at hand to achieve stratification. A good deal of information is needed to form homogeneous strata. Accurate lists of subgroups in a large population may be hard to find. Familiarity with the population is essential, because judgment is necessary for forming strata. Poor classification of strata may in fact increase the overall sampling error—the opposite intended effect of stratification.

Once strata are determined, each is considered a separate population and its sample is drawn independently by some random-type procedure. Separate samples assure representation of the characteristic used for stratification. Depending on the size and makeup of the different strata, the sampling fractions may be the same or different for each. The results of all strata can then be combined for a total population estimate by statistically balancing the results so that each stratum is represented in the same proportion as it is in the total population.

Cluster Samples. If accurate population lists are unavailable, we often turn to geographic boundaries for defining populations for sampling. The *cluster sample* divides the total population into geographic areas—counties, standard metropolitan areas, cities, census tracts, city blocks, or voting precincts. A random-type sample of each of these areas, called *clusters,* is much easier to draw than is one for the entire population. An initial cluster provides an advance method for locating smaller study units within it.

Cluster samples are drawn in stages. In a typical national sample, for example, Stage 1 stratifies the country by region, and Stage 2 by county (during which only some counties are selected for further subdividing); Stage 3 picks certain census tracts within the selected counties; Stage 4 chooses city blocks within the selected census tracts; Stage 5 selects households within the selected blocks; and Stage 6 designates persons within the selected households. Usually a random-type sample is drawn of units (blocks, households, people) at each stage.

Depending on the needs of the research, the size of the sample at each stage of clustering may vary from study to study. In a very large national sample, many counties will be included; in a small sample, few. Sometimes all households in each sample block are included in the sample, sometimes only a handful. The size of the sample at each stage establishes the probability of selecting the units there. All units at each stage have to be counted in order to draw a random sample to constitute the next stage. Once counted, a sample can be drawn of the units with known probabilities of selection (usually unequal because they are based upon the number of people within each). Thus despite the grouping of units in stages, the cluster sample can be a probability sample with known probabilities at all stages of selection, and thus calculations of sample precision are possible.

Cluster sampling is common in public opinion polling because the unit selection is economical. Rather than counting every person in the whole area in order to assign a unique selection opportunity to each (as for a simple random sample), the cluster sample relies on wider-area population data, such as census population of counties, for the first stage draw, then it counts the next smaller areas—tracts—for the second-stage draw only in those counties already in the sample, and so on.

As identification systems improve and become more available on computer tape—zip codes are being expanded down to block level—it will become more feasible to sample blocks directly from the complete data. Until this information is available, however, cluster sampling is a notable economy.

Cluster sample quality depends upon the accuracy of the data from which it is drawn. Errors due to differences between the actual populations of areas and the published population figures usually are assumed to be random. However, this assumption is questionable, particularly in areas in which large-scale urban renewal and migration have wiped some blocks out completely, or in which densely populated suburbs have been created where only empty land stood before. Within a metropolitan area, old census data can systematically bias the samples we draw.

As for its trustworthiness, the essential feature of the cluster sample is that the probability of selecting any person can be known. The individual's chance of being selected can be calculated by multiplying the sampling fractions at each stage.

For example, suppose that we select 125 city blocks from a total of 2500 and that we then interview 1 adult at each of 5 randomly chosen households per sample block, with an average of 60 households per block and 2 adults per household.

STAGE 1. *The chance of selecting a block is:*

$$\frac{n}{N} = \frac{\text{sample blocks}}{\text{total blocks}} = \frac{125}{2500} = \frac{1}{20}$$

STAGE 2. *The chance of selecting a household is:*

$$\frac{n}{N} = \frac{\text{sample household}}{\text{households per block}} = \frac{5}{60} = \frac{1}{12} \times \frac{1}{20} = \frac{1}{240} \quad \text{(Stage 2 } \times \text{ Stage 1)}$$

STAGE 3. *The chance of selecting an adult is:*

$$\frac{n}{N} = \frac{\text{sample adult}}{\text{adults per household}} = \frac{1}{2} \times \frac{1}{240} = \frac{1}{480} \quad \text{(Stage 3 } \times \text{ Stage 2 } \times \text{ Stage 1)}$$

These figures are usually calculated after the survey because actual numbers of households per block and adults per household may not be known in advance.

Relative Precision of Sample Types

In general, for the same level of precision, stratified samples require the fewest respondents and cluster samples the most. Random samples lie somewhere in between.

Note that the numerical examples given in the preceding discussion of sample types illustrate the difference between the chances of being selected for the cluster sample and the random sample. For the random sample, an individual's selection chances were calculated at 1/200. The chances of being selected for the cluster sample were smaller, 1/480. Clustering changed people's chances of selection, in reality introducing larger sampling errors, because the chance of being selected was not based on simply population size but on the number of stages and how many subunits there were per stage.

Stratified samples may have less sampling error than simple random samples of the same size. Dividing population into relevant strata may reduce the variation of characteristics related to the study problem—for example, dividing a population into men and women for a study of viewing of televised football games.

Choice of Sample Type

Sampling efficiency alone does not dictate the type of sampling chosen for a study. The availability of relevant information on which to draw the sample and the cost in time and travel to locate respondents must be considered in choosing a practical, achievable sample.

Sampling designs are usually combinations of random, stratified, and cluster sampling. For example, a city sample may be stratified by ethnic groups to ensure that enough Puerto Rican, black, and Chinese neighborhoods are included to make accurate observations about these groups. But, within the strata, cluster sampling will locate the housing tracts in which to interview, and systematic random samples will be used to pick both the households and the respondents within those households.

Types of Nonprobability Samples

Our discussion thus far has been about types of probability samples. But for some studies, probability samples are either not desirable or are impossible to achieve.

Nonprobability samples are samples that use human judgment in selecting respondents. Such judgmental samples have no theoretical basis for estimating population characteristics. There is no mathematical theory to stipulate the chance of any unit being selected in a sample by personal preference. Judgmental samples tend to be flawed by human biases influencing the sample uniformly in one direction or another. The use of statistics based on mathematical models is *invalid* for generalizing to populations from such nonrandom samples.

Despite their weaknesses, we often prefer nonprobability samples. For some studies we would not want to rely on chance to find respondents, especially for selecting only a miniscule number from a large population.

Assume, for example, that we wanted to study attitudes toward neighborhood improvements among apartment landlords. It's more sensible to pick a few different kinds of apartment buildings in the city and then locate the owners than it is to rely on a random sampling of all neighborhoods, hoping to find the few landlords among many renters.

If more than 20 or 30 units are involved, random-type selection is desirable because, with that many units, some conclusions or generalizations are possible; but any conclusions must depend upon probabilities provided by random-type sampling and not someone's hunches. Some common varieties of nonprobability samples are:

(1) purposive samples, (2) quota samples, (3) chunk samples, and (4) volunteer samples.

Purposive Samples. When only a few special individuals are to be contacted, it would be wasteful to draw a probability sample. Instead we need some other method of finding the people who can best serve our purpose—a *purposive* sample. We choose our respondents deliberately, by knowing the type of people they are or where they are located. Perhaps there are only a few persons of interest to us scattered throughout a large population—for example, in a study of top city leaders. We might as well pick them and go directly for interviews, because it is unlikely that we would find more than one or two such "rare birds" in a random city-wide sample.

One use for a purposive sample can be as background interviews before we employ a probability sample. We seek out people we judge to be knowledgeable about the topics in the questionnaire to get an idea of what the full range of questions should be. But, we couldn't draw conclusions about the whole population from such a select group.

Quota Samples. A quota sample relies on the judgment and ability of interviewers to select respondents according to certain categories such as age, gender, ethnic group, income, or whatever. A team of interviewers may be each instructed to find wherever they can in a given area, say, 20 respondents—5 women and 5 men under age 40 and 5 women and 5 men over 40. Often the reason for using quota sampling is to save the cost of time and travel that is required for interviewers to make callbacks and keep appointments when specifically designated respondents are not at home. With the interviewers free to fill a quota, however, we have no way of figuring the chance for each household or type of person to get into the sample. This method is therefore not a probability sample, and we know nothing of sampling error and precision of findings.

Chunk Samples. When a newspaper's Inquiring Reporter is sent out to the street corner to interview the first five people she or he meets, the aim is usually to get a few colorful comments on some current issue. The resulting *chunk* of people does not represent the whole public—not even those who happened to be on the street at that time of day.

Volunteer Samples. For certain kinds of studies it may be necessary to let respondents select themselves—to volunteer to be interviewed. Radio and television "call-in" polls, newspaper straw polls that allow anyone to mail in a questionnaire, or the "every boxholder" surveys popular with legislators are kinds of volunteer surveys. Obviously the resulting sample consists mainly of those people intensely interested in the subject, and it is probably quite unrepresentative of all listeners, readers, or constituents. As in all nonprobability samples, we cannot generalize the results of volunteer samples to whole populations.

Maintaining Probability Design

There may be good reasons for using a nonprobability sample. But unwillingness to spend the effort and money to draw an acceptable *probability* sample is most likely the reason some researchers rely on nonprobability (nontheoretical) samples. For the Model Survey, we insist upon a probability sample.

Ideally, probability samples are specified so that we can make reliable estimates of the whole population. But although we design our samples properly, most of them will break down somewhat during the selection process. Indefinite populations, unavailable or inaccurate lists, small budgets, time pressures, poor supervision, and inexperienced fieldworkers all create disruptions of sampling theory that change probability samples to nonprobability samples. Although we rarely achieve true probability sampling, we must make every effort to control the influence of personal biases along the way so that we end up as close to our probability design as possible.

SAMPLE SIZE

We generally get more precise sample estimates as the size of the sample increases. Such sample estimates come closer to true population values because they are more likely to represent all of the subgroup types in the overall population.

Irrelevance of Population Size

This does not mean that a sample must be a large proportion of its population. Usually population size is irrelevant in field surveys because the same mathematical principles of probability sampling apply to large and small populations. Moreover, the kinds of populations that we study are usually so large—consider them to be infinite and ever-changing—that a 1-percent sample would be enormous. In this way, the populations of a city, a state, and the nation may be considered to be of equivalent size for the purposes of sampling; they are all of infinite, ever-changing size.

That the size of the population does *not* have anything to do with the size of the sample is an idea that is difficult for many people to accept. To illustrate the point, suppose we have a bag of colored marbles, into which we reach and pull out a single blue marble. We would be foolish to conclude that all the marbles in the bag were blue. If we took a handful of ten marbles, of which four were blue and six red, we'd be somewhat safer in guessing that the bag contained more red than blue marbles. But if we used both hands cupped together and brought out a total of 75 red and 25 blue marbles, we could be far more certain that the bag contained about 3 red marbles for each blue one. The point is, it doesn't matter whether it is a small bag of marbles or a large bag; what makes the estimate of its contents more precise is the *size of the handful* drawn out as a sample (always assuming that the bag was well mixed and that, therefore, any handful was a true random sample).

Thus a probability sample of 1000 people from throughout the United States may give estimates about the total U.S. population as good as a survey of 1000 people in Kansas will give of the total Kansas population, or as good as sample of 1000 people in Wichita will give about Wichita's total population. The difference is that the larger populations may have more "marbles" of different colors and hues. As populations become more complex in terms of subgroups, the more difficult it becomes to describe differences among the various subgroups. However, if we are interested only in *total* population estimates, a 1000-person sample may describe each of the above three populations with equal precision.

What Dictates Sample Size

Besides sample precision, several other elements go into deciding how large a sample to use in a survey.

Homogeneity. Among the elements affecting sample size is the extent to which the population is homogeneous. Homogeneity is the degree to which people are alike with respect to the problem under study, such as their religious attitudes. The more similar people are, the smaller the sample can be. Logically, if everyone were exactly alike in every regard, a sample of one person would suffice. This never happens, but it takes fewer people to get a good sample of a fairly homogeneous population than it does to sample a heterogeneous population. Often we cannot gauge homogeneity in advance—the reason for doing a survey is to discover the extent of variation in the population. The resulting information may be helpful in subsequent studies of the same topic, if things don't change too much in the interim.

Prior Information. Another factor affecting sample size is the kind of prior information we have about the characteristics of the population, say from previous research, recent census publications, or municipal records. Suppose, for example, we want to make generalizations about voters in a recent city election. We know that only 30 percent of the eligible voters turned out in that election, as compared with 60 percent in the last presidential election. To get a large enough sample of city election voters, we could (1) draw a larger sample of the total adult population than if we were studying only presidential voters, (2) try to identify city voters at the beginning of each interview and continue interviewing only those who were voters, or (3) use voting lists to identify and sample a special stratum composed only of city voters.

For the Model Survey, we are assuming that there is little or no information available regarding how much people know about Model City issues and politics. Moreover, since we want our Model Survey to describe subgroups and to estimate a variety of other characteristics that occur in different proportions in the population, we will take a larger sample than if we were doing a study of only a few characteristics on which some information was already available.

Sampling Procedure. The kind of sampling procedure used also affects sample size. As we have mentioned, for the same level of precision, stratified samples usually require fewer people than the simple random sample, and cluster samples usually require more.

Assume that we are interested in studying voters and nonvoters in city elections. If only 30 percent of the eligible voters turn out for the city election, a random sample of 100 people should get about twice as many nonvoters (70) as voters (30). But if we are interested primarily in voters' characteristics, the random sample is wasteful.

A stratified sample would separate the groups, enabling us, because of our special interest, to take more voters (say, 45) and fewer nonvoters (say, 35). This does several things. First, by taking half again as many voters, we can study them in more depth. Second, the increased number of voters in the sample improves the precision of our estimates of voters' characteristics. Third, by halving the number of nonvoters the sample is much less wasteful in field time and costs. And, fourth, the overall sample size is reduced—from 100 to 80.

When we want to combine the strata for a total population estimate, we have to adjust the numbers of voters and nonvoters to look more like the real population. This type of adjusting by *statistical weighting* is described in Chapter 6. Basically, to make the sample look more like the population, we have to rebalance the figures by giving more weight to nonvoters (or less weight to voters) in the total results. We could increase the number of nonvoters by some factor and/or decrease the number of voters by some factor so that when they are combined their proportions are 70-30 again, regardless of the number of cases studied.

On the other hand, a cluster sample would divide the population into geographic areas, which would tend to increase sample variability, which in turn would reduce precision of estimates for the same number of cases. As opposed to the stratified sample, the cluster sample increases variability because the clusters (1) are homogeneous in many characteristics that may not be related to the study problem; and (2) are heterogeneous in characteristics related to the problem. In short, people in the same neighborhoods are alike in many ways. But if these characteristics are not related to the study problem, the effect of clustering is to reduce the precision of our city-wide estimates.

Suppose that in a few city neighborhoods most of the residents are college students, while in other neighborhoods most of the residents are not students. If we interview a person in one area and find that he or she is a student, chances are that the next person in that area will be a student too. If we followed the cluster method, we'd find out more about these areas but at the expense of getting a less accurate picture of the whole city. Thus, we usually need a larger sample to include more areas spread around the city.

In sum, cluster sample sizes become smaller and results better when each cluster is a heterogeneous mixture of many population characteristics and each is as similar to the composition of other clusters as possible. This is just the opposite of stratified sampling, which seeks homogeneity within strata and heterogeneity between them.

Resources. Quite naturally, resources such as time, cost, and personnel affect sample size in the most practical way. We might wish for great precision, but that often will remain only a wish.

If two designs specify the same sample sizes, the one producing the more reliable results typically is better. But if the cost of selecting the sample is much greater in the first design than in the second, it might be cheaper and easier to take a larger sample based on the second design, since it could offer more useful data per unit of cost. Despite its appearance of greater effort with lowered precision, concern for costs and resources often leads us to cluster sampling.

The efficiency of cluster sampling depends on how good and how recent maps and other information are about the number and location of houses in each sample area.

Number of Analysis Categories. Another factor that affects sample size is the number of categories by which we want to analyze the data. The more breakdowns needed in analysis, the larger the sample must be.

To illustrate, suppose we want to analyze the relationship between gender and voting to see if more men or women vote. Let's assume the following: (1) that men and women eligible to vote divide evenly (50-50) in the population; (2) that about 40 percent of the people will vote and 60 percent won't; (3) that male voters will be in the smallest category; and (4) that we need at least 30 cases in the smallest category (this is the minimum number that many researchers feel is necessary for meaningful analysis).

Our table showing the anticipated numbers and percentages before sampling will look like Figure 2.2 (page 70).

We know that men are expected to be about 50 percent of the sample and voters are expected to be about 40 percent; from this we can derive the remaining numbers for the rest of the table, as well as the overall sample size needed. In this example, the sample size must be 150 in order to get about 30 male voters, which is a number equal to 20 percent of the sample. To find the percentage of the total sample the male voters represent, we multiply the proportion of the sample that are voters (.40) by the proportion of the sample that is male (.50), which equals (.20).

	Men	Women	Total
Vote	($n=30$)		40%
Not Vote			60%
Total	50%	50%	100%

Figure 2.2. Estimating sample size for a two-way breakdown of respondents

The formula to compute the sample size is:

$$\text{Sample size} = \frac{n \text{ of smallest cell size needed}}{\text{its row percent} \times \text{its column percent}} = \frac{30}{(.40 \times .50)} = 150$$

But suppose that we also want to know whether the age of voting men and women is related to their candidate preferences. Let's assume that candidate preference splits about 50-50 in a close race and (from other research) that younger men will be less than half as likely to vote as older men (splitting 30-70). If we keep the same requirement of 30 cases in the smallest cell, the table before sampling looks like Figure 2.3.

Using the expected percentages to work out the sample size, the smallest cell of 30 cases is now only 3 percent of the total sample (.50 men $\times$ .40 voters $\times$ .30 younger $\times$ .50 Republican = .03). Thus we need a sample of 1000 (30/.03 = 1000) to get about 30 younger men who prefer the Republican candidate.

These examples show how rapidly sample size increases when we need to

	Men		Women		Total
	Younger	Older	Younger	Older	
Voters Republican	($n = 30$)				50%
Democratic					50%
Total voters	30%	70%			40%
Nonvoters					60%
Total	50%		50%		100%

Figure 2.3. Estimating sample size for a four-way breakdown of respondents

provide for more detailed analysis. The number of categories needed for analysis should be specified in advance of sampling to be sure that we have the sample size to meet them. Whatever might be the ideal sample size, resources quickly set the limit as to how much detail we can afford.

As a rule of thumb, when the finest breakdown is made, no cell in a table should have fewer than five cases.[2]

Geography. While not a neat rule of thumb, usually the more dispersed the population, the larger the sample size needed. Often, populations that are spread out over different geographic terrain and conditions—from the mountains to the seashore, from the sidewalks to the cornfields—have distinctive characteristics, such as differences in occupations, education levels, interests, local issues. If geography is a basis for stratification, sample size may not increase appreciably. But, particularly within rural strata, cluster sampling is a more likely choice than random sampling because of the extra travel and logistics involved.

Type of Measurement. Other factors that affect sample size are the type of measurements used in the questionnaire and the type of statistical techniques used in analysis. As will be seen in Chapter 3, some measures require *continuous* categories instead of *discrete* categories such as yes-and-no answers. Some statistical techniques also require continuous categories. Continuous measures are like points lying along a continuum—for example, degrees on a thermometer. Because there are more points for respondents to distribute themselves among on these scales, and therefore fewer respondents per point, sample size must be increased to meet the measurement needs.

Finally, population size is *not* among the factors affecting sample size. As noted before, size of population usually has no relation to sample size. Another rule of thumb is, unless a sample approaches 1 percent of the total population, the size of the population can for the purposes of sampling be considered infinitely large, and thus various sizes of different infinitely large populations will have no bearing on sample size required.

Precision of Sample Estimates

Of all elements comprising accuracy, we can know only precision in advance of the study. *Precision* is a statistical statement of how close our estimate is to the value of the characteristic in the population. Other things being equal, precision depends on sample size. In probability sampling, larger samples yield greater precision by reducing chance errors.

Precision is a measure of the risk associated with using information; it states

[2]James A. Davis, *Elementary Survey Analysis*, (New York: Prentice-Hall, 1971).

how close the sample estimate is to the true population value (parameter)—how close the generalization is to the ''truth.'' Our concern is that results be sufficiently precise that the risk of using them is acceptable for the purpose at hand.

How precise we want our information must be decided in planning the study, and the sample size set accordingly. We don't always strive for high precision; such exactness is neither necessary much of the time, nor is it practical given lack of money and other resources.

The level of precision needed depends on how much risk we are willing to take in using the data. For example, we might be willing to interview only a dozen workers to get an impression of how they like a particular plant's new vacation schedule. But we might want a sample of 400 rank-and-file members before we would be willing to conclude about the likelihood of the membership accepting a new contract, especially if we were the owners with a major commitment requiring the plant to be operating next week.

If our estimates must be able to detect very small differences, very large numbers may have to be studied in the sample. But likewise we need only the level of precision that is adequate to make the required decision based on the findings.

The question of precision involves two factors: (1) how much error we can tolerate before the estimate might lead us astray; and (2) how confident we must be that the sampling error is not greater than we specify.

How Much Error to Tolerate. How much error we tolerate depends partly on our planned use of the estimate. Suppose we want to learn how many people know the governor's name, and we decide in advance that an error of plus or minus 10 percentage points is acceptable. If the survey finds that 25 percent of the people know the governor's name, we can believe that somewhere between 15 percent and 35 percent of the population knows it. This information may be enough to be useful in making a decision: for example, to start a campaign to improve the governor's visibility, because relatively few people know who he is. Trying to get a more precise figure would simply be wasteful; our decision would have been no different if we had used a larger sample, with only a 5 percent error, and had concluded that between 20 and 30 percent knew his name.

Suppose, on the other hand, that we are trying to predict a close election. We cannot risk much error if two candidates are running neck and neck. A very large-size sample is needed to detect subtle differences between characteristics that divide nearly evenly (50-50) in the population. Even if we allow an error of only 4 percentage points and therefore must take a sample of 600 voters, we still may fail to show the likely winner correctly. If the Democrat is favored by 53 percent of the voters in the sample, the actual split in the population may range from 49 to 57 percent. The estimate is clearly not good enough to use, and we run a great risk of wrongly forecasting the election. The maximum error we would wish to risk in this case might be plus or minus 2 percent. This would require a sample size of 2500 voters; then a 53-percent estimation of the Democrat's support would have a narrower error margin of between 51 and 55 percent. We might feel this is good enough to predict a winner. But not even a survey sampling 2500 voters would be enough to predict a closer election, because if our sample showed the Democrat to be favored by 51 percent, the true number could just as likely be 49 percent, a crucial difference.

How much error we will tolerate depends on a second factor: the expected occurrence of the population characteristic being estimated. Not all characteristics divide nearly evenly (50-50) as, say, the number of men and women. But when they do, we have the greatest difficulty in trying to show differences between them. The chances of *absolute error* (which one is the majority) are highest when about half the population has a characteristic and half does not. Small samples will show roughly equal proportions (50-50) of men and women, but it takes a much larger sample to improve our ability to detect the 49-51 division that may actually exist. In small samples the addition of just a few respondents on one side or the other can lead us to the wrong conclusion about population characteristics that are almost evenly divided.

Once we set sample size, absolute error due to sampling decreases as the value of the characteristic being estimated moves farther away from a 50-50 split. Suppose we set a sample size of 600. Table 2.1 shows what happens to the amount of sampling error associated with a characteristic when it tends to divide more evenly in the population (50-50 or 60-40) and when it becomes increasingly unevenly divided (80-20 and 90-10)

Unfortunately we usually don't have accurate information about the occurrence of many of the characteristics we study. Also, in a single study we usually estimate several characteristics. For these reasons, in our Model we are assuming that the population divides about 50-50 for at least one major characteristic we are studying, and we compute the sample size accordingly.

Although the absolute error is higher when populations are fairly evenly divided, as seen in Table 2.1, the *relative error* is least when the values are nearly even, and becomes greater when the characteristic becomes more unevenly divided.

Table 2.1. Amount of Sampling Error for Characteristics of Various Proportions
(Sample size — 600)

Division of a "Yes/No" Characteristic in the Sample	*Sampling Error*	*The Value of "Yes" in the Population Lies Between*
50 – 50	5%	45 – 55
60 – 40	5%	55 – 65
70 – 30	5%	65 – 75
80 – 20	4%	76 – 84
90 – 10	3%	87 – 93

The more rare a characteristic is in a population the more likely we are to miss it in a sample.

Suppose, for example, we are estimating a close election in which Republican and Democratic candidates share the vote nearly equally but only a paltry number of votes are cast for the Socialist Workers candidate. Almost any sample would yield about equal numbers of Democratic and Republican voters, but it could easily miss Socialist Workers voters entirely. So we can conclude with little chance of being wrong that the Socialist Workers candidate will not get 50 percent of the votes (absolute error is low), but we could not accurately estimate that candidate's actual vote (relative error is high). On the other hand, while we would have great difficulty predicting which of the major parties will get over 50 percent (absolute error is high), our estimate for each party may be very close to what they actually get (relative error is low).

If a very small number of people have a characteristic, a small sample will almost surely miss it; and even a large community sample may miss it. This shows that a general population sample is a wasteful way to try to study uncommon traits in the population. To study Socialist Workers we need a more selective strategy to locate them—for example, a list of their campaign supporters.

Setting the Level of Confidence. Deciding how much error to tolerate is only half of our concern for precision. Sampling precision indicates how close our estimate is to the true population value. But how sure are we that the true value really does lie within the plus-or-minus error range tolerated for the sample estimate? How confident can we be that our results are as precise as we plan for? We need a *statement of confidence* that the error due to sampling is not greater than that specified.

Despite careful work, it's always possible that by chance alone we can draw a bad sample. So our concern is, if we were to repeat the sampling again and again, how likely are we to get the same result—4 times out of 5, 9 out of 10, 99 out of 100?

Although we can never be absolutely sure that the population value is not outside the range of tolerated error, we can mathematically state to what degree we are confident that the estimate is a good one. Based on the tables of mathematical probabilities, we can state our certainty that the population value will be within the accepted error range of 95 out of 100 samples identical to ours (or 99 out of 100—if we choose a higher level of confidence). In other words, we are confident that the risk of being wrong in our sample estimate is no worse than 5 out of 100 (or 1 out of 100).

In reporting findings, we report levels of both precision and confidence, for example:

> Our estimate that 60 percent of Model City's adults
> agree with this question is subject to a sampling error
> of 4 percentage points in either direction, meaning

it could be as much as 64 or as little as 56 percent.
And chances are 95 out of 100 that an identical
sample would produce a result within this range.
(Or) There's only a 5 percent chance that the
sample estimate is farther than 4 percentage points
in either direction.

As a convention in most social science research, we accept our findings as sufficiently reliable if chances are not less than 95 out of 100 (the probability is less than .05) that a different result would be found. For other kinds of research, involving matters of life and death, such as side-effect danger from drugs, we might require our confidence levels to be 999 out of 1000, or even higher.

As we would expect, assuming the tolerated error is the same, the sample size needed to be 99 percent confident of getting a reliable estimate is much greater than the sample size needed to be only 95 percent confident.

Computing Sample Size

Table 2.2 shows the simple random sample sizes needed to produce sample estimates within various limits of error (from 1 percent to 7 percent) and for two levels of confidence (95 percent and 99 percent) The table shows clearly in terms of larger sample sizes the great price that is paid for increased precision and confidence.

To accept an estimate of a characteristic shared 50-50 in a population, with ± 6 percent error, and at a confidence level of 95 percent, requires a sample of 267 people. If we demand a confidence level of 99 percent, the sample increases to 461 people. If we leave the confidence level at 95 percent but increase the precision to ± 3 percent (halve the error), the sample will have to include 1067 people. Although increasing the sample size lowers tolerated error and/or raises confidence limits, the improvement is not proportional to the increase in sample size required.

The table is figured for simple random samples. We haven't shown a similar table

Table 2.2.   Simple Random Sample Size for Several Degrees of Precision

| | Confidence Levels ||
Tolerated Error	95 samples in 100	99 samples in 100
1%	9,604	16,587
2%	2,401	4,147
3%	1,067	1,843
4%	600	1,037
5%	384	663
6%	267	461
7%	196	339

for cluster samples, because we can specify only roughly in advance of the selection the chances that each person has of being in the sample. In the Model Survey procedure, the probabilities of selecting people are not calculated until after the sampling plan has been carried out in the field. To know these probabilities, we have to know the number of adults in each sample household, something we rarely know from advance information.

The Model Sample described in the remainder of this chapter is a cluster sample at the first (household) stage. As it only approximates a simple random sample, the sample sizes in the table should be considered minimum for each level of precision. Perhaps the sample size needed for a cluster sample might be half again more than what is shown in the table for any level of precision. Increasing sample size to account for increased error due to clustering does not automatically mean that our precision will be as we plan for; rather it's likely that with the larger sample we may improve precision somewhat.

Representativeness of the Sample

Thus far we have talked mainly of sample size; whether the sample will look like the population it comes from is a separate question. Merely having a big sample does not guarantee representativeness. Once size is fixed, rigorous procedures are required to ensure that each household or person selected is chosen without bias. If the sampling procedure is biased (for example, skipping over inner-city Hispanics, who are more likely to have been left out of the census data), increasing the size of the sample will only magnify the bias in terms of representing the community accurately. The Model Sample described below illustrates how a sample can be made as representative as possible by use of appropriate information and careful attention to detail.

Our concern is that the sample should represent the population from which it is drawn. We are equally concerned that generalizations from the sample are applied only to that population. As defined in Chapter 1, a *generalization* is a statement, within statistical limits of precision and confidence, describing people and conditions similar to those studied. But we cannot use the same kinds of statistical inference for extrapolations from our sample.

An *extrapolation* is not a generalization, but a statement describing people and conditions that are not necessarily similar to those studied. Because we can't study everything everywhere, we tend to seize upon the data we get from one sample and extrapolate to other populations. After sampling the opinions of teenage girls in New York public schools on abortion, we may be tempted to extrapolate their feelings about abortion to girls in other schools, to boys in private schools, perhaps even to their families. Just as there is no probability for a nonprobability sample, there is no mathematical theory for extrapolations from a probability sample. Extrapolations are judgments—often wisely and necessarily rendered in the conduct of business, government, and academics. But we must be extremely wary of applying findings to societal conditions from the dissimilar conditions found in unrepresentative samples.

Our ability to generalize from samples rests on other factors than precision and confidence. Of great significance is the number and importance of subgroups in the population. The more varied (heterogeneous) the subgroups are, the more difficult to generalize—and the more our generalizations tend to become extrapolations.

SELECTING THE MODEL SAMPLE

The Model Sample is a probability sample. Like all large-scale samples of human populations, however, it does not achieve the ideal features of a completely random selection. We have to rely on published census population data and on other records to ascertain the numbers of people and households, records which cannot be perfectly exact or up-to-date. Inevitably, some persons are not properly counted; their chances of selection are therefore not known or are misrepresented.

The Model Sample makes certain concessions to the reality of limited funds, incomplete population statistics, and restrictions on time as well as other resources. But once these conditions are accepted, we keep our personal values and the values of others (such as interviewers) out of decisions about who is selected in the sample. To the extent humanly possible, we guard against the biases of human judgment that can flaw the sample design.

Preview of the Model Sample

The Model Sample is a two-stage cluster sample. First, it selects a sample of housing units, and second, a sample of adults 18 years or older. The sample relies on census and other published data for knowing the populations of both housing units and adults. Not included in the population base are adults who are not living in housing units. Housing units are defined as apartments, duplexes, row houses, or detached single homes.

The sampling procedure starts with a list of all the city's housing units, in the order of city blocks and as numbered by the Census Bureau. This amounts to arranging the population geographically, since the blocks are sequenced in serpentine or zig-zag patterns usually extending from north to south and then from west to east, within relatively small neighborhood areas called *tracts*. If desired, geographic strata could be formed based on this ordering, but we will not draw a stratified sample.

The Model does *not* sample blocks. We use blocks only for their housing unit totals. From the block list we draw a systematic random sample of clusters consisting of *five housing units per cluster*. Within each cluster we sample one adult per household. A household is composed of the people living in one housing unit.

Which adult is chosen in each household depends upon the number, gender, and ages of all adults there. The selection is made by the interviewer in the field according to a fixed random-type procedure that cannot be altered. It leaves no room for personal judgment by the interviewer in selecting respondents.

Since each household and each respondent within a household is chosen by a random-type procedure, the model is a probability sample. But it is not a simple random sample. Rather, because the sample does not draw people directly but chooses households first, the selection is in two stages.

The chance of any housing unit being selected in the first stage can be expressed in a ratio:

$$\frac{5}{\text{(total number of housing units in the city)}}$$

The number 5 is the arbitrary number of housing units we decided would be visited at each sampling point. The chance of any adult being chosen in the second stage can be expressed in another ratio:

$$\frac{1}{\text{(number of adults in the household)}}$$

The probabilities of selection can be known in advance for the first stage, but they cannot be known for the second stage. However, the probabilities can be determined after fieldwork is completed, when we know the actual sizes of households selected; then estimates of sampling error can be made.

The Model Sample illustrates the problems of limited funds and incomplete population data, which are at the core of the design of any survey. We want to accurately represent the full range of people in the community, but we can't afford simple random sampling that sends interviewers all over the city after designated individual respondents. We decide to group respondents in some way that can reduce field costs. Since we don't have lists of individuals by which to cluster them, we use available housing unit data as a basis for clustering. It is much easier to identify, say, the 31st, 32nd, 33rd, 34th, and 35th *housing units* in a block than it is to identify the 31st, 32nd, 33rd, 34th, and 35th *adults* living in that block.

Using housing units instead of individuals in drawing the sample does not bias its representativeness. As long as we interview the same number of adults (one per household) each household has equal representation.

Any alteration of the simple random sample design affects precision. In the Model, increase in sampling error comes from two sources: (1) from sampling clusters of housing units rather than separate units, and (2) from sampling housing units instead of individuals.

The first source of increased sampling error arises from sampling housing units in *clusters* rather than individually. Often next-door neighbors are much alike in their personal characteristics—at least compared to folks across town. Because of economic and ethnic concentrations, people on one block are likely to be quite homogeneous with respect to a study problem. Since the number of household clusters selected is only one-fifth of the number of households that would be selected by a simple random sample, we risk higher errors by overrepresenting or underrepresenting certain neighborhoods in the city. As we've said before about cluster sampling, the more each cluster is like the whole population, the closer the sample is to the simple random model—hence the lower the sampling error.

Sampling in clusters of five is a good compromise between the demand for sampling precision and the restriction of funds. As the number of units per cluster increases, precision decreases. So, given our limits of time, money and other resources, we opt for five housing units per cluster, using as many clusters as sample size permits. Whatever the risks, interviewing in clusters saves so much interviewer travel time that we accept the likely sampling error.

The second source of increased sampling error comes from sampling housing units rather than individual adults. We are allowing one person to represent the views and characteristics of all others in the household. We do this for practical reasons. Members of one household are likely to have fairly similar views on many matters. At least they are more like each other than like their neighbors or people elsewhere in the city. It would not, therefore, be efficient to interview everyone in one household because it would take too many interviews before we could get enough dispersion around the city to represent all views. But since each member of the household does not have exactly identical characteristics, allowing one person to represent all others does increase our error. Locating individuals by households suppresses some of the natural differences in the population that would be represented by a simple random sample of persons.

In summary, the Model Survey is based on a sample of housing units, with one adult interviewed per sample household.

Data for Drawing the Sample

To draw the sample, we need basic information on Model City, such as shown in Table 2.3.

Defining the Household. As defined by the U.S. Census Bureau, a housing unit is a living place with a separate entrance (even though through a hall) or with separate

Table 2.3.   Model City Characteristics

Basic Data	
Population	250,000
Population 18 and over	175,000
Housing units	79,500
Census tracts	50
Blocks	2,500

kitchen facilities not shared by another group. The housing unit is not necessarily a discrete structure, because apartments are counted separately within their building. The people living in a housing unit are a household. Here we will use the terms more or less interchangeably, though we will try to use the term housing unit when referring to the physical place.

A housing unit is distinguished from a "group quarters," which is a place where six or more *unrelated* people live together, such as in prisons, hospitals, nursing homes, college dormitories and fraternities, military barracks, communes, and the like.

Distinctions between households and group quarters are less easy to make as living styles change. Thus, co-ed buildings, 24-hour open-door visiting policies, and optional cafeterias make college dormitories more like apartments than institutions. Many homes for the aged are closer to apartments than to hospital-like nursing homes, although residents may be able to move between levels of institutional care in the same complex as their needs change. Ordinary houses may contain large communal "families" consisting of couples and singles unrelated by marriage or kinship.

These people are usually excluded from household samples using the census definition; the Model follows this rule. Other surveys may wish to make adjustments to include some group quarters. This is fairly easy to do because published census data shows by blocks the total population, the group quarters population, and the proportion of 18-years-and-older population. Field inspection reports and other public data can identify such group quarters as hotels, prisons, hospitals, and other inmate quarters, all of which can reasonably be excluded from a public affairs study because the residents' participation in public affairs is restricted. But such an inspection can also identify college dorms and apartment-like senior citizen homes that have residents who should be part of the study population. Special interviewer procedures have to be created to select respondents from these group quarters, because in these cases the number of people at a single address is too great to pick only one individual to interview, and yet the group may be too interactive to treat each room as a separate housing unit. Perhaps each administrative wing, floor, or "house" could be treated as a unit.

Sources of Housing Unit Data. To draw a sample of housing units we need data on their number and location. Checklist 6 shows possible sources.

CHECKLIST 6

Sources of Housing Unit Data

1. *Block Statistics,* published by U.S. Census Bureau for metropolitan areas.
2. Enumeration District computer tapes, available from U.S. Census Bureau for all areas.

3. City planning department (studies and maps).
4. City building permit department (single family home, apartments).
5. City or county tax assessor (number, type, and value of buildings).
6. City water department (meters).
7. Electric power company (meter connections).
8. Gas company (meter connections).
9. School district clerks (school census, bus route pick-up points).
10. City directory (residence lists by street address—R. L. Polk company's publications).
11. Telephone company directory (listed subscribers).
12. City clerk or voter registration office (registrants' addresses).
13. County or state highway departments (maps often show the location of every structure).
14. Agricultural extension agents and conservation districts (aerial photographs).
15. U.S. Geological Survey (maps).
16. Newspapers (delivery addresses).
17. Advertising and marketing agencies (direct mail addresses; have survey operations of their own or have them available as users of surveys).
18. Major food and consumer goods industries (market survey operations).
19. Package delivery firms (home locations).

Block Statistics. The U.S. census counts all housing units as a part of its effort to count 100 percent of all persons. Numbers of housing units per block are printed in publications called *Block Statistics.*[3] One is published for the urbanized part of each metropolitan area, termed a "Standard Metropolitan Statistical Area," which is the census name for a large city and the several counties that surround it and are economically tied to it. Sometimes block data are printed for cities that are not large enough to be called metropolitan areas.[4] An area booklet costs about $5 for a metropolitan area of 250,000 and is accompanied by detailed large-scale maps.

In cities with published block figures it is a straightforward process to draw a sample of housing units. We can use the housing unit figures just as they are printed, because they are ordered systematically according to the boundaries of each city in the area.

Blocks are identified within *census tracts,* which are neighborhood-sized areas by which the Census Bureau reports much of its data. Tracts are seldom changed over the years, because of the Bureau's desire to detect historical population trends. When new areas are settled or population increases drastically, the tract may be split (001 becoming 001A and 001B) rather than giving it a new number that is out of

---

[3] Also referred to by the code HC(3), which stands for "Housing Characteristics, Third Count;" a state number is also added.

[4] This data is published as *Block Statistics; Selected Areas* [State name].

series. Some block numbers on the map will be missing from the printed list because there are no people living there.

Minor Civil Divisions. The housing unit data for places outside of urbanized areas is published not by blocks but by Minor Civil Divisions (MCDs), the census term for any unit below the county level that has a local government—a village, city, town, or rural township. MCDs are printed alphabetically by county, not geographically, so to draw a sample from this list we rearrange the units geographically to safeguard against choosing units—say, Anadama, Multigrain, and Zwieback—which, although alphabetically separated, may actually be adjacent townships and thus will not give the geographical spread desired in the sample.

Enumeration Districts. The Census Bureau makes available a Master Enumeration District List (MEDLIST) for each state. The list identifies census areas by location codes; thus, the areas can be rearranged in any desired order for the sample draw.

The census enumeration district (ED) is an administrative division smaller than the Minor Civil Division. The ED is a convenient geographic area for data collection that can be assigned to a single census enumerator.

In rural parts of the state, the ED may be the same as the MCD township, and therefore adds no new data detail. But for cities without block data, the ED is especially useful. The equivalent of ED data in metropolitan areas is the block group (BG). One block group consists of all the blocks in one census tract with the same first digit (all 100s, all 200s, etc.). Moreover, block groups are identified by geographic proximity; for example, all blocks numbered in the 100s are close together, and all blocks in the 200s form another small clump. This is useful for obtaining a geographical spread of the sample.

Enumeration district totals are not published but are available to the public on computer tape. The tape containing the enumeration district data for an entire state, called the "first count summary tape," can be purchased for about $80 a reel, but the user must have the computer capacity to extract data from it (the public cannot have access to the individual household responses). The Census Bureau has deposited the tapes around the country at various universities, at state, regional or city planning agencies, and at private organizations called Summary Tape Processing Centers, from whom tapes can be borrowed or copied, or who will themselves extract data at a charge.

A nationwide user's organization called DUALabs in Alexandria, Virginia, also services users with census data. The Census Bureau itself will provide unpublished materials, but charges substantially for special analyses.[5]

Before purchasing ED data tapes, we should find out if someone else already

---

[5]Potential users should contact the Data Users Service Division, U.S. Census Bureau, Washington, D.C., 20233.

has obtained the data—planning agencies may have bought detailed housing unit counts for their cities.

Other Sources. Housing unit data often can be found locally. City planning departments increasingly are collecting detailed housing data. Other sources of housing data are city directory services and the electric power company.

The smaller the geographical units, the less likely will there be full-time governments, and the less likely will formal housing unit data be available. But higher-level units, such as county or state highway departments, may have remarkably detailed maps of the small units, often showing individual rural dwellings.

The alternative sources of housing unit data are useful in all areas for updating published census housing unit data. Census counts go out of date rapidly. If the long-promised mid-decade censuses are begun, the currency of census data will improve greatly. But the problem of obsolete census counts will never be completely solved, due to rapid replacement of city housing, increases in the number of new apartments and condominiums, and construction of individual homes at the urban fringe. Thus, every census-based sample will be founded to some extent on out-of-date, hence unrepresentative, data.

In addition to updating census lists with current sources, we periodically cruise Model City looking for signs of urban renewal, new construction, and other changes in neighborhoods. This eyeball data, when added to reports from interviewers in previous surveys, gives us a better population base for drawing samples.

Equipment and Materials. Besides the list of housing units for drawing the Model Sample, we need tabulation sheets with at least 11 columns, a calculator or adding machine, a random numbers table, pencils, and maps.[6]

Many of the calculations described here are easier to do by computer—if a computer tape is available having all housing units on all blocks in the city. We can put the population data into the computer ourselves, of course, by punching the tract and block numbers and housing unit totals onto cards for all blocks in the city; but this would usually be an inordinate expense unless we were going to re-use the data many times to draw other samples.

Computer installations typically have a random number generator that produces as many random numbers as the user wants in any set range. Some data-handling packages even have the capacity to draw random samples automatically.

For our Model, however, we assume census computer tapes and programs are not available, so we use published housing unit lists and a hand calculator. Moreover, going through the theoretical and mechanical steps involved in drawing the

---

[6]Random number tables are found in most statistics text books, or see Herbert Arkin and Raymond R. Colton, *Tables for Statisticians,* 2nd ed. College Outline Series No. 75, (New York: Barnes and Noble, 1963).

sample will be instructive and will help us design or use computer programs intelligently in the future.

Steps in Drawing a Sample

Our aim is to draw a sample of households and respondents in a way that eliminates us (the researchers) and the interviewers as sources of bias. The Model Sample even picks the respondents by a mathematical procedure, so that no decisions are left to interviewers as to whom to interview.

The steps in the whole sample draw are outlined in Checklist 7. Since the checklist is not likely to be self-explanatory, detailed explanations follow with actual numbers from the Model Sample. At first reading the process may seem complex, but each step is simple, though sometimes tedious to execute properly. The instructions are presented as though we were talking directly to (you) our Associate Project Director.

CHECKLIST 7

Steps in Drawing a Cluster Sample

1. Review study needs and resources available. Decide the size of completed sample desired.
2. Increase sample size by a percentage, which is an estimate of the rate of noncompletions that will occur.
3. Decide the number of housing units per cluster.
4. Divide the sample size by the number of housing units per cluster to get the number of sample clusters.
5. Divide the total number of housing units in the city by the number of clusters to get the sampling interval, which will be used to systematically skip through the housing unit list to indicate sample units to be sampled. Each sample unit in this list corresponds to one household in a cluster of five (in the Model) to be interviewed.
6. Pick a random start not larger than the sampling interval. This is the first sampling unit.
7. Add the sampling interval repeatedly; first add it to the random start to find the value of the second sampling unit, then add it to the second unit to find the third, etc., until there is a number for each cluster in the sample.
8. Go through the column of block housing unit totals in the block statistics publication, adding their numbers. Each time the accumulated total exceeds the value of a designated sampling unit (Step 7), mark that block number and tract number as the place where the sample unit will be found.
9. Record the cumulative housing unit total for the block in which the sample unit is found.

10. Continue adding (without clearing the calculator) and marking the blocks containing sample housing units until the list is exhausted. The total number of sample units should equal the number of clusters in Step 4.

11. Within each indicated block, locate the relative position of the first unit in the cluster to be sampled by figuring how far back into the block the designated unit is: in other words, how much less the designated sample unit is than the accumulated total at that block.

12. By a random procedure designate the starting corner of the block in which each sample unit is located.

13. Figure the closest direction and the count required for the interviewer to arrive at the designated unit. Indicate the next units as the other units in the cluster.

14. Indicate the person to be interviewed at each housing unit by the use of different versions of a respondent-selection key that is based on how many adult women are in each household.

Setting Actual Sample Size. The Model Sample size is 600. Because we never get as many respondents as we intend, we assign more than 600 cases to the interviewers. The Model design does not permit substitution of other respondents or households for those assigned but not reached, for example ineligible households (aliens, no adults), vacancies, not-at-homes, refusals. Instead, we add a cushion to the desired sample size. The formula for figuring the number of interviews to attempt is this:

$$\frac{\text{desired sample size}}{1 - \text{estimated noncompletion rate}} = \text{attempted sample size}$$

The Model assumes a 20 percent noncompletion rate. Substituting in the formula,

$$\frac{600}{1 - .20} = 750$$

we therefore increase the attempted sample size to 750 units, anticipating that this will yield about 600 completed interviews. We will of course complete the sample, attempting to interview all 750 rather than stopping when we get 600 completed interviews, to avoid risking bias.

Fixing the Number of Sample Clusters. Having set the Model cluster size at five households per cluster, calculate the number of sample clusters needed by dividing sample size by cluster size ($750 \div 5 = 150$).

Calculating the Sampling Interval. To get the sampling interval, divide the total number of housing units in Model City (79,500) by the number of sampling clusters (150). The sampling interval is 530 ($79,500 \div 150 = 530$), and it means that we are going to have to pick every 530th housing unit as a sampling point. Remember, the sampling interval is used to skip through the city's list of housing units to designate those blocks on which sample clusters are located. Since blocks are listed geographically, the sampling interval ensures that clusters are chosen all over the city. The sampling interval is like a measuring stick, which is laid out repeatedly along a long line that passes through all housing units in the city, indicating at each measurement a unit picked for the sample.

The interval is based on the total number of units rather than the number of blocks in the city, because there are great variations in the number of city housing units per block. Apartment areas may contain hundreds of housing units on one block, while other blocks may have just a handful of fancy homes, a few shacks backing up against the railroad tracks, or no units at all. It would be a serious error to select every, say, sixteenth block in the city, or even to choose blocks randomly. We are sampling *housing units,* not *blocks.* The block enters the selection process only because it is the smallest area for which we can know the total number of housing units, as well as being a relatively easy way to locate housing units in the field.

Picking a Starting Point. Using a table of random numbers, randomly pick a three-digit number between 001 and 530—the range of numbers in the sampling interval. This allows all 530 units in the interval an equal chance of getting into the sample. If we started with designating the 530th housing unit in Model City (the full sampling interval) and located the first cluster there, units 1 through 529 would have no chance to be selected; neither would any other unit that was exactly 530 units farther down the list. Moreover, every researcher who chose an attempted sample size of 750 would end up sampling the exact same housing units in the city. We want to be sure that each sample drawn is independent of any others.

Select a random number from any page in the random numbers table. Looking away and placing the point of a pencil on the page, take the closest 3-digit number between 001 and 530. Figure 2.4 shows that we picked the number 161. This means that the 161st housing unit in the city census list is the designated unit of the first sample cluster. The number 161 is recorded in Column B on a tabulating sheet (see Figure 2.5, pages 88–89) beside the cluster number 001 in Column A. This sheet serves as the *master control sheet* for the study.

Now that we have all numbers needed for finding the first sample cluster, we are ready to go through the mechanical steps of drawing the entire sample.

Selecting the Sample Clusters. Using a calculator, enter the sampling interval into the memory or as a constant. Then enter the random start number (161), retrieve the sampling interval (530) from the memory, and add. The sum is 691 (161 + 530 = 691). Record this as the designated housing unit of the second cluster. Add in the interval again to get a total now of 1221 (691 + 530 = 1221), which is the

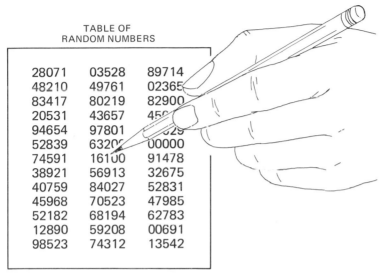

TABLE OF
RANDOM NUMBERS

28071	03528	89714
48210	49761	02365
83417	80219	82900
20531	43657	45
94654	97801	
52839	6320	00000
74591	16100	91478
38921	56913	32675
40759	84027	52831
45968	70523	47985
52182	68194	62783
12890	59208	00691
98523	74312	13542

Figure 2.4. Picking a random start from a table of random numbers.

designated unit of the third cluster, and record it. Continue this process until all clusters (150 in the Model) have a designated unit. To check the work, the number of the final designated unit should be the sampling interval times one less than the number of clusters plus the random start (in this example $530 \times 149 + 161 = 79,131$), of necessity slightly less than the total number of housing units in the sampling site (79,500) because the random start was partway through a full sampling interval.

Locating the Sample Clusters. The numbers in Column B of the master control sheet are designated housing units of the sample clusters, counting from the first housing unit in the city. We next have to find out which blocks they are on. This is done by cumulating the housing block units throughout the city, block by block, as found in Column 4 of the *Block Statistics* book. (We use the total number of year-round housing units—a more permanent observation—rather than the temporary occupancy status on the long-past date of the census.)

To cumulate housing units, clear the calculator and enter the number of housing units in the first block. Add to it the number of units in the second block, then the number of units on the third block, and so on. It's best to record each cumulated total in the *Block Statistics* book, even though there's not much room (see Figure 2.6, p. 90).

The first time the cumulated total exceeds the first designated housing unit, stop. That is the block on which the designated housing unit is located. Record the cumulated total, including this block, in Column C of the tabulating sheet (Figure

Figure 2.5. Master control sheet

A	B	C	D		E	F				
			Location of Sample Cluster			Location of Housing Units in Block				
Cluster Number	Designated Housing Unit in Cluster	Cumulated Housing Units Total	Census Tract	Block Number	Number of Housing Units in Block	1st Unit (Column C minus Column B)	2nd Unit	3rd Unit	4th Unit	5th Unit
001	161	163	MC-1	105	21	2	3	4	5	6
002	691	708	MC-1	305	27	17	18	19	20	21
003	1221	1276	MC-2	104	78	55	56	57	58	59
004	1751	1915	MC-2	202	474	164	165	166	167	168
005	2281	2294	MC-3	421	45	13	14	15	16	17
006	2811	3835	MC-5	101	98	24	25	26	27	28
007	3341	3344	MC-5	322	7	3	4	5	6	7
*	*	*	*	*	*	*	*	*	*	*
149	78,601	78,641	MC-50	324	221	40	41	42	43	44
150	79,131	79,192	MC-50	403	67	61	62	63	64	65

G Corner Start		H Counting Direction	I Actual Count To Find Units In Cluster	J Case Numbers	K Interviewer Name
Code	Corner				
7 =	NE				
3 =	SE				
0 =	SW				
9 =	NW				
0	SW	clockwise	2, 3, 4, 5, 6	0001, 0002, 0003, 0004, 0005	_____
3	SE	counterclockwise	7, 8, 9, 10, 11	0006, 0007, 0008, 0009, 0010	_____
0	SW	counterclockwise	20, 21, 22, 23, 24	0011, 0012, 0013, 0014, 0015	_____
9	NW	clockwise	164, 165, 166, 167, 168	0016, 0017, 0018, 0019, 0020	_____
7	NE	clockwise	13, 14, 15, 16, 17	0021, 0022, 0023, 0024, 0025	_____
9	NW	clockwise	24, 25, 26, 27, 28	0026, 0027, 0028, 0029, 0030	_____
7	NE	clockwise	3, 4, 5, 6, 7	0031, 0032, 0033, 0034, 0035	_____
*	*	*	*	*	*
7	NE	clockwise	40, 41, 40, 43, 44	0741, 0742, 0743, 0744, 0745	_____
0	SW	counterclockwise	3, 4, 5, 6, 7	0746, 0747, 0748, 0749, 0750	_____

Blocks Within Census Tract	Total Housing Units	Cumulation of Units	Designated Housing Unit in Cluster
MC-1 (tract total)	(747)		
101	35	35	
102	45	80	
103	33	113	
104	29	142	
105	21	163 ✓	161 (1st cluster)
106	23	186	+_530_ (sampling interval)
201	49	235	
202	121	356	
203	111	467	
301	140	607	
302	32	639	
304	42	681	
305	27	708 ✓	=691 (2nd cluster)
306	58	766	+_530_ (sampling interval)
306	28	582	
(Tract 1 cumulation)	(747)		
MC-2 (tract total)	(1,089)		
101	202	968	
102	118	1086	
103	112	1198	
104	78	1276 ✓	=1221 (3rd cluster)
201	153	1429	+_530_ (sampling interval)
*	*	*	*
MC-50 (partial)			
323	118	78,420	
324	221	78,641 ✓	=78,601 (149th cluster)
325	157	78,798	+_530_ (sampling interval)
401	185	78,983	
402	142	79,125	
403	67	79,192 ✓	=79,131 (150th cluster)
502	228	79,420	
503	80	79,500	
(Tract 1-50 cumulation)	(79,500)		150 clusters designated

Figure 2.6. Housing unit cumulation and block designation process (using U.S. Census _Block Statistics_ book)

2.5) for later use, and record the tract and block number in Column D. Record also. in Column E, the number of housing units in that block, also for later use.

Without clearing the calculator, continue to add housing unit totals for the subsequent blocks, recording the cumulated total that exceeds the designated unit for each of the clusters along with the tract and block number and the number of housing units in that block. The cumulated total for the last block in the city should equal the total number of housing units in the city (see Figure 2.6).

In a large city this cumulation process will involve thousands of entries. Thus there are thousands of opportunities for making a mistake on the calculator, even wiping out the total. It's wise before beginning the block cumulation to go through the book and cumulate and record the housing unit totals printed for each *tract*, as Figure 2.6 shows. Then when cumulating blocks, these will serve as check points—places to verify the running block totals against cumulated tract totals, rather than waiting till the very end and having to re-do all the work if the totals don't match. If at the end of any tract there is a discrepancy between the totals, or if you should accidentally clear the cumulation at any time, you need go back only to the end of the last correct tract cumulation total to start.

In *Block Statistics*, the total housing units in each tract are shown at the *beginning* of the block listings for that tract. Unfortunately, this figure is not contained in parentheses (as we have added in Figure 2.6) nor are the individual block totals that follow indented. We must be careful not to add this tract total into the cumulation of blocks, or the total of housing units in the city will be doubled. To avoid this danger, run a highlighting pen through the tract totals as a reminder to skip over them.

Locating the Sample Households on the Block. The block statistics book is now no longer needed. Turn to the master control sheet (Figure 2.5) and ascertain which housing units on the block constitute the cluster. To do this subtract the number of the designated housing unit (Column B) from the cumulated housing unit total that includes that block (Column C). Because the numbers are inclusive this will give the unit adjacent to the designated unit the position of the first unit of the cluster. Enter it, and the next four higher numbers, in Column F ("Location of housing units on the block"). The first cluster therefore consists of the second, third, fourth, fifth, and sixth units on the block ($163 - 161 = 2$, followed by four more units). For the second cluster, the sample housing units are the 17th, 18th, 19th, 20th, and 21st units ($496 - 479 = 17$, followed by four more). Perform this subtraction for all clusters.

Designating the Interviewer's Starting Corner. We designate which corner of each block interviewers are to start counting housing units in order to find which unit is the 2nd (in cluster 001) or the 17th (cluster 002) on these blocks. Again, the corner choice is random.

Using the random number table again, find four separate one-digit numbers—for the Model these were 7, 3, 0, 9. Let these digits represent, respectively, the northeast, southeast, southwest, and northwest corners of blocks. Continuing down a column in the random numbers table, record each of these four digits in the order they appear, until 250 digits—one per sample cluster—have been chosen. These starting corner numbers are written in Column G of the master control sheet. Then go back and translate those numbers into compass directions (0 becomes southwest, 9 becomes northwest, etc.).

Selecting the Interviewer's Direction. Now figure the most efficient way for the interviewer to get to the first unit in the cluster from the starting corner of the block. Normally, as for Cluster 001, the interviewer proceeds in a clockwise direction and counts to the units designated in Column F (units 2, 3, 4, 5, and 6). Just copy the same numbers into Column I. But if the first designated unit is more than half way around the block—comparing Column F with Column E—save the interviewers time by directing them to go counterclockwise around the block.

When going counterclockwise is indicated, subtracting the *fourth unit* in the cluster (in Column F) from the total number of housing units in the block (Column E) will give the first unit in the cluster the interviewer will come to. Indicate the next four housing units also (for the Model cluster 002: $27 - 20 = 7$, followed by 8, 9, 10, and 11). Enter these figures into Column I.

To verify that this procedure will indicate the very same housing units in the cluster either way the interviewer goes around the block, examine Figure 2.7. Note that for Cluster 002 the 17th, 18th, 19th, 20th, and 21st units counting clockwise are the same as the 7th, 8th, 9th, 10th, and 11th units counting counterclockwise.

In like manner, fill in columns H and I for the entire sample.

In reality, walking clockwise and counterclockwise may not always result in choosing the same housing units. Besides counting errors by interviewers, housing units may have been added or destroyed since the census enumeration. These changes don't worry us too much because the random starting corner reduces the effects of bias against including new units or excluding destroyed units. Also, reversing directions reduces the counting (thus chance for error) that interviewers have to do.

Counting is tiring, especially in four-story walk-ups. In some neighborhoods the housing units are hard to see. Some have rear access only; others are separate units, but, since they are in one structure with only one outside door and one mailbox showing, they are hard to spot. In that interviewer direction is a matter of convenience and not of sample design, exceptions can be made. When it is apparent from the map that the block abuts a lake, railroad tracks, or the bear pit at the zoo, there may be no choice in which way the interviewer will have to count.

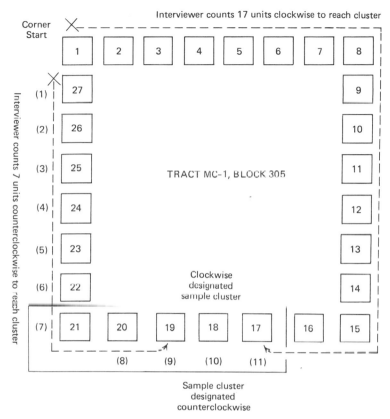

Figure 2 7 Counting housing units in a clockwise or counterclockwise direction to reach the same sample cluster. (Data from Cluster 002, Figure 2.5)

Choosing the Specific Person to be Interviewed

The last step in sampling is done at the door of the housing unit, where we select the specific person in that household to interview. Again, no discretion is left to the interviewer. Instead, the model uses a random procedure that gives all adult family members—men and women of various ages—a known chance (probability) of being interviewed. If interviewers were allowed any discretion in choosing respondents, we would not get true probability samples, because, as another function of bias, experience has shown that interviewers are more likely to interview certain types of men and women, excluding others.

All adults must be allowed the same, known chance of getting into the sample in order to keep the sample's probability design intact.

To give *any* adult a known probability of being interviewed, the Model uses a *respondent-selection key* that—with two eligibility questions—tells the interviewer whom to interview in each specific household.[7] Who is interviewed depends on how many adults are living in the household and how many of them are women.

The Model uses six versions of the respondent-selection key. A different version is printed on the front page of each questionnaire in rotation, starting randomly with any version. Thus each of the six versions is assigned to one-sixth of the respondents in a systemically random manner.

Ideally, within any household each adult has the same chance to be interviewed as any other adult there. In our Model, this ideal works for households of one, two, and three adults (18 years or older); more than two-thirds of all households in the United States fit in this pattern.[8] In households with four or more adults, the respondent-selection keys are designed to overrepresent the youngest and oldest persons in four kinds of households but to underrepresent them in two other kinds. This makes the altered randomness of their chances of being selected an insubstantial effect.

For households with five, six, or more adults, the respondent-selection key approximates an equal chance of selection for all adults. But with only six versions it cannot give an exactly equal chance to all in such households. The proportion of households with six or more adults is, however, very small. The bias introduced by the selection key is known and is considered negligible. One way of reassuring ourselves that we haven't introduced a problem is to compare respondents in such households against respondents in smaller households.

It would be possible, of course, to generate a version of the respondent-selection key for every possible situation. A computer could be programmed to yield all of these, even printing all front pages of the questionnaire and inserting each version of the respondent-selection key in rotation. For our purposes, however, six versions are adequate.

The procedure for selecting respondents may seem complicated, but in the field it works very easily. Figure 2.8 shows the six versions of the respondent-selection key.

Consider Version 1, and imagine the interviewer confronting a woman who has just opened the door. As part of the introduction the interviewer asks, "How many persons 18 years or older presently are living in this household?" She answers, "Three." At the top of the key, the interviewer circles "3 adults" and draws a line down through that column. Then the interviewer asks, "And how many of these adults are women?" She answers, "Two." The interviewer circles "2 women" at the left side of the table and draws a line across that row.

---

[7]Respondent-selection procedure is adapted from a scheme devised by Verling C. Troldahl and Roy E. Carter, Jr., which was based on Leslie Kish, "A Procedure of Objective Respondent Selection Within the Household," *Journal of the American Statistical Association, 44*, 380–387 (1949).

[8]From U.S. Bureau of Census Publication 291 (P-20 series), February 1976, p. 77. For a given city this data can be found in *Annual Housing Survey*, H-150 series.

Figure 2.8. Six versions of the respondent-selection key
Version 1 (as marked by interviewer at the door)

Number of Adults in Housing Unit

		1 Adult	2 Adults	3 Adults	4 or more
0 Women	01	Adult	03 Oldest Man	06 Oldest Man	10 Youngest Man
1 Woman	02	Adult	04 Man	07 Youngest Man	11 Woman
2 Women			05 Youngest Woman	08 Youngest Woman	12 Youngest Man
3 Women				09 Oldest Woman	13 Man or Youngest Man
4 Women					14 Youngest Woman

Number of Women

Version 2

Number of Adults in Housing Unit

		1 Adult	2 Adults	3 Adults	4 or more
0 Women	01	Adult	03 Oldest Man	06 Youngest Man	10 Youngest Man
1 Woman	02	Adult	04 Woman	07 Woman	11 Oldest Man
2 Women			05 Oldest Woman	08 Youngest Woman	12 Youngest Woman
3 Women				09 Youngest Woman	13 Oldest Woman
4 Women					14 Oldest Woman

Number of Women

Figure 2.8. (*continued*)
Version 3

Number of Adults in Housing Unit

	1 Adult	2 Adults	3 Adults	4 or more
0 Women	Adult 01	Youngest Man 03	Youngest Man 06	Oldest Man 10
1 Woman	Adult 02	Woman 04	Oldest Man 07	Woman 11
2 Women		Oldest Woman 05	Man 08	Oldest Man 12
3 Women			Youngest Woman 09	Man or Oldest Man 13
4 Women				Oldest Woman 14

Number of Women

Version 4

Number of Adults in Housing Unit

	1 Adult	2 Adults	3 Adults	4 or more
0 Women	Adult 01	Youngest Man 03	Oldest Man 06	Oldest Man 10
1 Woman	Adult 02	Man 04	Woman 07	Youngest Man 11
2 Women		Youngest Woman 05	Oldest Woman 08	Oldest Woman 12
3 Women			Oldest Woman 09	Youngest Woman 13
4 Women				Youngest Woman 14

Number of Women

Figure 2.8. (*continued*)
Version 5

Number of Adults in Housing Unit

Number of Women	1 Adult	2 Adults	3 Adults	4 or more
0 Women	Adult 01	Oldest Man 03	Middle Man 06	2d Oldest Man 10
1 Woman	Adult 02	Woman 04	Youngest Man 07	Middle Man 11
2 Women		Youngest Woman 05	Oldest woman 08	Oldest or Youngest Man 12
3 Women			Middle Woman 09	Middle Woman 13
4 Women				2d Youngest Woman 14

Version 6

Number of Adults in Housing Unit

Number of Women	1 Adult	2 Adults	3 Adults	4 or more
0 Women	Adult 01	Youngest Man 03	Middle Man 06	2d Oldest Man 10
1 Woman	Adult 02	Man 04	Oldest Man 07	Middle Man 11
2 Women		Oldest Woman 05	Man 08	Oldest or Youngest Woman 12
3 Women			Middle Woman 09	Middle Woman 13
4 Women				2d Oldest Woman 14

Where the two lines intersect, the key designates which person (here the youngest woman) is to be interviewed. The interviewer says, "I am supposed to interview the youngest woman in this household. Would that be you?" If the person nods or says yes, the interviewer begins the questioning. If not, the interviewer says, "Would you please call her to the door?"

The rest of Figure 2.8 shows all other versions of the respondent-selection key used in the Model. Comparing how the versions would work for the same household illustrates how other adults would be selected at other households with the same composition. For example, if Version 2 had been used, the result would have been the same—the younger woman would have been chosen. But Versions 4 and 5 would have picked the oldest woman, and Versions 3 and 6 would select the man. Thus each person in the household has two chances in six (one in three) of being interviewed.

Achieving the Sample

This section explains the practical aspects of getting an interviewer to the right door and to the right person. We will first discuss office control of assignments, interviewers' actions in the field, and supervision.

Office Control. The Model Sample leaves no discretion to interviewers. Every possible preparation is done in the office ahead of time for successful gathering of the sample.

Assigning Case Numbers. A four-digit case number (see Chapter 4) should be assigned consecutively to all housing units at which interviews will be attempted in the study—for the Model, beginning with 0001 and ending with 0750. The numbers are entered in Column J on the master control sheet (Figure 2.5) and also written onto blank questionnaires so that they are associated with a particular questionnaire from the beginning. For judging sampling efficiency, we need a questionnaire for each attempted interview, even if incompleted.

Interviewers are required to report progress daily to their supervisors. All sample clusters and their associated case numbers are plotted on a *master control map* in the office. This aids quick, visual understanding of how fieldwork is progressing. Different color codes can be used to show completed, untried, and incompleted interviews. The map shows very quickly where problems are developing, both by neighborhood areas and by interviewers. It is a good idea to place a transparent overlay on the map and write in codes with different-colored grease pencils; this saves valuable maps for other surveys.

On the interviewers' large-scale street maps, we mark the direction for their coverage of each cluster. As Figure 2.9 shows, we use an *X* to indicate the corner intersection from which the interviewer is to start counting houses. An arrow shows

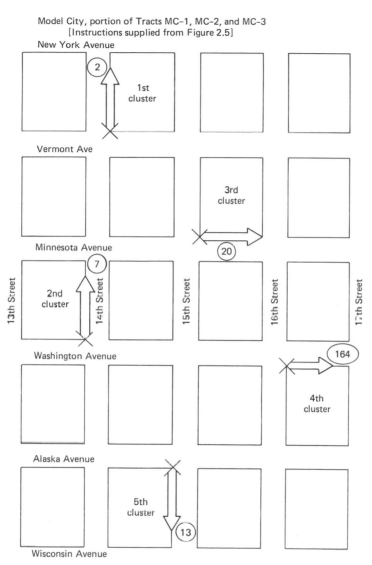

Model City, portion of Tracts MC–1, MC–2, and MC–3
[Instructions supplied from Figure 2.5]

Figure 2.9. Interviewer field instruction map.
X = starting point; ⇒ = direction of travel; (13) = count to first housing units.
(Data from Figure 2.5)

the street and direction in which to start counting. The map shows the interviewer the interviewing pattern graphically, instead of giving confusing compass directions like, "Go to the northeast corner of the intersection of Vermont Avenue and 14th Street and proceed in a northerly direction." The map also shows with a circled number the amount to count to find the first unit in the cluster. We don't clutter the field map with needless information like census block and tract numbers, which bear no relationship to anything the interviewer will see.

The maps that come with the *Block Statistics* book may be in a suitable scale for interviewers, and these can be cut (or a copy of them cut) into usable sizes for each interviewing area. Trying to use the same maps for master control is not very practical. For a large city it would take a huge wall to fit all the block maps together into one map.

Interviewers will also need a tourist-type auto map of the city to guide them to their areas.

Assigning Interviewers. Once all cases are plotted on the master map, interviewer assignments can be made keeping several considerations in mind, including: reducing travel time and costs; assigning specific interviewers to areas requiring special people (such as minority interviewers to work in areas with a large minority population); putting experienced and inexperienced interviewers close to each other; and distributing the supervisors' work evenly.

The last column on the master control sheet is for indicating by name which interviewer has been assigned to which cluster.

Interviewer Action. Checklist 8 is in the form of a handout to interviewers, giving instructions about how to find starting points and count housing units. Although most of those instructions are sufficiently detailed to be self-explanatory, the reasons for some of them, as well as special guidance for handling certain critical situations, are presented here.

CHECKLIST 8

Locating Respondents

TO: All Interviewers
FROM: Project Director
RE: Locating Respondents.

Welcome to the study. This handout is for your use in locating respondents in the field.

1. Each of you has been assigned a number of interviews to complete. Be sure each questionnaire is numbered with the proper case number and cluster number before

taking it into the field. Five consecutive case numbers constitute one cluster of interviews to be completed in one area. You will be assigned more than one cluster to interview

2. Using your city map, plan your route to cover the clusters in an efficient way. You should obviously try to complete all five interviews in a cluster at one time to save travel time.

3. Your detail map shows at which corner of a specified block you are to begin counting. When you arrive at the indicated intersection, orient your map to the street pattern. Make sure you are on the correct corner of that intersection and headed in the right direction. An arrow shows in which direction you are to count, and a circled number shows at which housing unit, counting from the starting corner, you are to get your first interview. You have no choice of housing units at which to interview.

4. Count housing units beginning with the first structure facing the street on which you are directed to travel. But count each *housing unit,* not just each house or structure. A single structure may be a double bungalow, having two housing units. A housing unit is a living area with either a separate entrance—from the outside or through a hall—or separate cooking facilities. Thus individual apartments are counted one by one. Count the apartments in a large building by the numbers on mailboxes, if they are all by the main door. Or, if not numbered, count by the names as you come to them on the boxes or on the doors, beginning with the first floor each time. Triplexes count as three housing units, fourplexes as four, and so on. Count trailers, tents, boats, and even railroad cars, if they are meant to be occupied as a housing unit rather than as extra space or vacation quarters.

5. While counting housing units, skip obvious "group quarters," since the sample is drawn on a population that excludes them. Group quarters are institutions, hospitals, nursing homes with hospital-like rooms or a common dining room (not residence complexes for the elderly where they have separate apartments), rooming-houses, military barracks, college dormitories, fraternity and sorority houses, convents, and monasteries. Despite this rule, you inevitably will find yourself counting another kind of group quarters—a house or apartment shared by six or more unrelated people. Such quarters cannot easily be distinguished from actual housing units counted by the census, since you have no way of knowing how many live there without asking. If the housing unit turns out to be group quarters, go on to the next housing unit, since group quarters are not included in the population for the Model Survey and would be skipped if you could identify them as such before knocking at the door. Remember, if six or more unrelated individuals share the premises, they live in group quarters. Five working women sharing an apartment, on the other hand, constitute a housing unit.

6. Count housing units even if they are vacant—the sample includes them. If a vacant housing unit is indicated for an interview, mark the questionnaire "vac-

ant'' (after checking with the neighbors to be sure of nonoccupancy). You are not allowed to substitute an occupied unit for the vacant one.

7. Counting housing units is not always easy. Many structures will contain several separate living quarters without this being apparent from the street. Check around the side and back for stairs and other entrances. Go into halls and upstairs to see if there are any living quarters without separate house numbers or mailboxes. Building custodians may be of help, but frequently they are suspicious of you and protective of their tenants. Obscure units cannot be skipped in your count, as would be easy to do because they are likely to be found in less desirable neighborhoods. If any such systematic neglect were introduced into the sample, a major flaw in the data would result.

8. If you exhaust all units on a block before completing your count, first check that you haven't missed hard-to-see units, such as basement or rear-entry places. If you are confident you counted correctly, continue counting around the same block—past where you started to count and recounting units you counted previously—until you arrive at the housing unit matching the circled figure, and make a note on page 1 of the questionnaire of what you had to do. Do *not* go to another block to interview.

9. Once you have counted to find the first designated unit and have completed an interview there, go on to the very next housing unit (even if it is the next apartment in the same building) to get the second interview in the cluster. Then go to the very next units after that for the third, fourth, and fifth interviews in the cluster. The ''next'' housing unit may not necessarily be adjacent to the previous one in the cluster. If the first unit was the last apartment in a building, you must go on to the next building to find the second unit in the cluster. Between units in the cluster there may be several empty lots or group quarters you are to skip. You just keep moving and counting in the same direction to designate the second and third housing unit in that cluster. No other housing unit can be substituted for the five indicated by your count. Stay on the same block to complete your cluster, even if you must count past your original starting point.

10. On the front page of each questionnaire is a respondent-selection key that tells you which person in a housing unit you are to interview. You ask a short series of questions to learn the number of qualified adults in that household. Circle the number of adults and draw a line down that column. Then ask the number of those adults who are women. Circle the number at the left and draw a horizontal line across that row. Ask for the individual described in the box where the lines intersect. You must interview the specific respondent designated in the key for that housing unit. You cannot substitute respondents.

11. If the respondent you need is not at home, make an appointment to interview him or her, or arrange to call and make an appointment (this is the only time you will use the phone to make appointments). Always keep this appointment yourself. If no one is at home on your first attempt, return at a different period of the day or on

a different day of the week. You must call back at least two times to try to complete the interview. Meeting an appointment made on your third attempt is not considered an extra callback.

12. In the disposition block at the bottom of the front page of the questionnaire, record your various attempts to contact the respondent, your appointments where necessary, and the ultimate result—successful interview, ineligible respondent, not-at-home, refusal.

13. As you begin each interview, note the time. After you have successfully completed each interview, enter the time it ends. Write your signature, and place your interviewer number in the space provided.

Handling Vacancies and Ineligibles. If an interviewer finds a vacant housing unit or one with ineligible occupants (all residents are alien, or all under 18), the interview is written off as lost. New respondents are *not* substituted in the Model Sample because there is no probability for their inclusion. By substitution we mean interviewing someone in another household who was not drawn as part of the sample, to make up for a household where no one could be reached; or it can be interviewing someone else in an assigned household in place of the respondent designated by the respondent-selection key. Instead of allowing interviewers to substitute respondents, we inflated the sample by 20 percent partially to cover just such a situation. In Model City, usually only 3 to 4 percent of the housing units are vacant at any one time, but in 10 to 20 percent of the households even professional interviewers will not be able to get an interview because of refusal or because the designated respondent could not be reached despite repeated efforts.

Handling Not-at-Homes. About half of the time, the person who answers the door is not the person designated to be interviewed by the respondent-selection key. So the interviewer asks for the correct respondent and interviews that person. If that person is not at home, an appointment is made to come back at a specific time. If an appointment cannot be set, the interviewer obtains the respondent's telephone number to call for an appointment. In the Model Survey we do not let interviewers use the telephone to contact respondents in any other instance. The first contact is always attempted in person, to reduce respondent's preparation for the interview. The exception is made for not-at-homes in order to reduce fruitless callback efforts.

If no one is at home, the interviewer inquires of the neighbors when the people are likely to be at home—whether the house is vacant, the family is on vacation, or the people work everyday at that time.

The Model requires as many as two additional callbacks to attempt to interview the proper respondent. It is extremely expensive to try to interview through callbacks every person selected for the sample who was not at home on the first call. If no callbacks are made, however, the sample will disproportionately reflect people who are home most of the time, such as homemakers or retired persons. Compensating by further inflating the sample to avoid callbacks will not suffice. This only aggravates the bias in the direction of the easily obtained respondent.

The respondent-selection procedure selects men and women from different age groups in much the same proportion as they occur in the whole population. Unless the designated people are interviewed, the sample will not be representative. Any deviation from the procedure, such as allowing substitutions by the interviewers, is undesirable. Our initial inflation of the attempted sample provides an automatic random-type situation for original respondents who are unavailable. Interviewers, on the other hand, find it easier to change the rules for substituting respondents than for selecting original respondents. So we give them no rules for substitution. The ultimate reason for this structure is that the probability of substituted respondents coming into the sample is not known, thus substitutions destroy the probability basis of the sample.

Since callbacks dramatically increase costs, the decision about how many are feasible presents the Project Director with a real-world compromise between quality and resources. If the interview cannot be completed or scheduled after two callbacks, it is considered lost. The inflation of attempted sample size offsets some of these losses. All interviewers must observe the same limits on callbacks, to avoid bias.

Handling Refusals. Experienced interviewers have lower refusal rates than inexperienced ones. Chapter 5 gives hints on interviewer training and special techniques to increase the rate of successful completion. But despite all efforts, some people simply will not participate. Again, no substitutions are made.

The Model assumes that those who refuse or cannot be reached for interviews are similar to those who are successfully interviewed, and therefore that the sample is not biased. Naturally, we check this assumption. If possible, the interviewer marks down some of the obvious characteristics of the person who refused and makes notes on the general situation surrounding the interview. Or, if our interest requires it, the interviewer may go to the neighbors and ask simple questions about the characteristics of the nonresponding household. Remember, this information is used to check the sample, not as substitute data. This information helps the study director to learn if a certain type of respondent is more likely to refuse.

Discrepancies Between Map and Territory. Despite the great efforts of the Census Bureau and local planning agencies, interviewers will find discrepancies between maps and instructions and the actual blocks. The Census Bureau itself estimates that, in the 1970 census, there was an 8 percent error rate in coding the block data correctly.[9]

Where interviewers find fewer housing units on the block than were shown in

---

[9]U.S. Bureau of the Census, *Reference Manual on Population and Housing Statistics,* March 1977, p. 44.

the census book, they may circle completely around a block without coming to the housing unit indicated by the count. City blocks can change fairly rapidly—due to urban renewal, freeway construction, fire, rezoning, changing prices. If there are not enough units to fulfill the count, the interviewer should follow the system described in Checklist 8: continue counting around the block, past the starting point again, until the correct number of housing units have been counted. The justification for this is that a housing unit cluster was once on that block, according to the census data. We must take our cluster from the units that are left. Interviewers are not allowed to go into a different block because they would not know which is the next block on the list, and we would therefore not know the probabilities of new areas entering the sample.

To help avoid surprises like this in future studies, we ask interviewers to make notes of discrepancies they find in their areas.

Supervision. Although interviewers are allowed no discretion in fulfilling the sample, the diligence, competence, and integrity of their work determine the sample's success. But achieving quality work is not left to good intentions. Instead, field supervisors ride herd on the interviewers.

Before the study begins, training of the interviewers stresses the importance of proper sampling procedure. After the study, the interviewers' sampling procedure is checked for accuracy by redoing a subsample of their work. During the study, the interviewers report daily to supervisors about rates of not-at-homes, refusals, appointments, callbacks, and other problems. Supervisors make sure that no substituting is occurring. If deviations are discovered, corrective action is taken at once.

Supervisors also do field checking, making sure interviewers are in the right areas at the right hours, and even spot-checking housing counts to be sure none are being skipped. As interviewers hand in their questionnaires, they are debriefed on their experience with the sampling devices.

Evaluating the Sample

We cannot rest with the assumption that we have a good sample just because we did everything right in drawing and achieving it. The proof is in the result. Before we analyze the results of the questions, we evaluate the achieved sample against the larger population from which it was drawn.

Disposition Codes. Each questionnaire is assigned a disposition code as it is returned to the study office. The code, written in a ''Disposition'' schematic at the bottom of the first page (see Figure 4.2, page 193), shows that the interview was completed, how many callbacks were necessary, if an appointment was made, or, if the interview was not completed, the reason—refusal, not-at-home, respondent illness, etc.

These dispositions are tabulated to figure success rates, partly for costing future studies, but primarily to examine whether the nonrespondents came more often from a single area or type of area, which would raise the suspicion of possible geographic bias. If nonresponses are higher from a particular interviewer, retraining or replacement is indicated. For interviews that got as far as respondent selection, we can discern if a certain age or gender of respondents was missed more often than others or if interviewer bias was a factor in selecting certain types of households or respondents instead of the ones designated by the key.

Verification. To verify that the sample really contains data from the people who were supposed to be interviewed, we check on interviewers by recontacting a subsample of respondents by phone or with a double postcard, asking each if they were really interviewed. The age and gender of the proper respondent from the respondent-selection key of this questionnaire is copied onto the card.

Other modes of verification, for checking accuracy of data from the more substantive questions in the questionnaire, are described in Chapter 5.

Matching with the Population. The sample is also checked against known characteristics of the population from which it was drawn. Comparisons are made of such demographic characteristics as people's age, gender, education, income, ethnic background, place of residence, religious affiliation, union membership, political party identification, and marital status.

First, comparisons are made between the total sample and total population. Then the sample is divided into men and women, and their demographic characteristics are compared to men and women in the population.[10]

Weighting. This subject is taken up in detail in Chapter 6 but deserves brief mention here. Since we often design samples knowing that certain population groups will be hard to find, in some surveys we intentionally *oversample* such groups. That is, we interview more of them than would be expected in the population by chance. But overrepresentation of groups can be dangerous if we succeed in interviewing only easy-to-find members. We must be careful to check these respondents to avoid bias in the sample.

In other surveys, if we end up with an underrepresented group we simply adjust the numbers so that their proportions in the sample are the same as their proportions in

[10]State and city breakdowns of age, gender, race, marital status, and relationship to head of household are found in Census reports PC(1)-B. General social and economic characteristics are printed in PC(1)-C, and detailed characteristics are cross-tabulated by age, race, and other characteristics in PC(1)-D (large cities only). Individual city summaries appear in the front of Tract reports PHC(1). In addition, the *County and City Data Book* published for 1977 (and every five years thereafter) contains census materials and other figures such as presidential vote that are useful in checking sample findings. Publication number: C56.243/2: C83/[year]. Beyond census data, other local sources are consulted for religious, political, and economic totals.

the population. Usually this means that we give more *weight* to certain respondents than to others, which has the effect of increasing their numbers in the sample (see Chapter 6). This kind of sample balancing can be dangerous if we get an unrepresentative handful of the hard-to-find respondents and then weight their numbers upward. For example, suppose we get only 6 Hispanic respondents in the sample but treat them as though they have the statistical weight of 60 respondents. If the 6 are a bad sample of Hispanics (for example, representing only middle-class, long-term residents), weighting them only magnifies the bias in the result.

Reporting. Whatever the result, the degree of sample-to-population correspondence is reported with the findings. Write, for example:

> Only 10 percent of the sample consists of people
> 18 to 25 years of age, while the Census Bureau
> reports the city to have 20 percent of this younger
> group.

Summary of Model Sample

The steps in drawing the Model Sample illustrate a cardinal rule: leave as much as possible to chance, that is, to known probabilities. When we let flip-of-the-coin philosophy dictate every move, we ensure that, no matter what happens, the sample is devoid of our personal biases. In sampling, almost anything we *decide* to do— rather than letting blind, unbiased mathematics do the deciding—is a contamination of the survey.

SAMPLING FOR OTHER SURVEYS

As mentioned, in each chapter we will show how some features of the Model Survey change when they are adapted to other kinds of surveys. The following looks at some changes required in sampling if the survey is a different type of face-to-face study or if it is done by telephone or mail.

Panel Studies

The panel study is a survey of the *same respondents* at two or more times. The purpose of reinterviewing the same people is to trace changes *in individuals* over time, as opposed to changes *in groups* (i.e., men or blacks), which may be estimated by two independent samples at different times.

A sample for a panel study of Model City residents may be drawn in exactly the same way as was described for the single-time survey. There is no difference in sampling regardless of the number of times we intend to interview. We will, however, have to increase the sample size for the panel study, because there is always a loss of respondents between the first and second (or subsequent) interviews.

People drop out of the study for many reasons. The most important reason (called sample attrition) is that it is hard to locate the same respondents. Residence patterns continually change: perhaps 1 or 2 percent of the population will move in one month's time, and 10 percent in six months. It is difficult and expensive to trace respondents, especially if they have left town. Other original respondents will simply be absent—gone to conferences, off on vacation, or ill in the hospital. People's status changes over time. For that matter, some of the respondents we could not get in the first survey could now be found at home, but it is too late to include them. For these reasons we must start with a larger sample.

Panel studies can sometimes be designed to reinterview respondents four times or more, for example, during election campaigns to try to detect shifts in people's voting intentions. If several reinterviews are planned, we may draw a huge initial sample and randomly divide it into several subgroups. The purpose of this is to offset the biases possible in reinterviewing the same people, who may act differently (unnaturally) simply due to their awareness of being studied.

A way of measuring bias due to reinterviewing is needed. One way is to include a small, never-before-interviewed sample of respondents each time for comparison. By comparing the responses of the "new" and "old" respondents we can see the effects of reinterviewing.

Suppose we are doing a panel study in which respondents are interviewed four times. We have to include a new comparison group for each new wave of interviewing, so we can see the effects of being reinterviewed once, twice, or three times. Because of limited resources we cannot afford just to keep adding more respondents and expanding the sample. Instead, we subtract some respondents each time as well. That is, each time we add a new subsample, we subtract an equal subsample, as shown in Figure 2.10.

What we have done in this example is to take a very large sample of the population and divide it randomly into several identical and equal-sized subsamples (A to G). We randomly choose four subsamples (A–D) for the first interview. For the second interview, we randomly subtract one subsample (A) and randomly add another (E) in its place. We do the same on each successive wave.

The result is that subsamples A and G are measured only once, and are thus free of reinterviewing biases. Since A was measured early in time and G late, differences between them show natural changes in the population over time. Comparing subsamples B, C, and D with E shows the effects of one-time reinterviewing; comparing C and D with F shows two-time reinterviewing effects; and comparing D with G shows three-time effects. On the other hand, comparing B and F shows the effects of reinterviewing early and later in the campaign.

All comparisons are based on the assumption that the subsamples are identical

	Wave of Interviewing				
	1st	*2nd*	*3rd*	*4th*	*Times interviewed*
Original Subsamples					
A	x				One time
B	x	x			Two times
C	x	x	x		Three times
D	x	x	x	x	Four times
New Subsamples					
E		x	x	x	Three times
F			x	x	Two times
G				x	One time

Figuro 2.10. Adding and subtracting subsamples in a four-wave panel study (x indicates inclusion in the wave)

in all respects. Since they were selected randomly from a larger sample, they should be equal in all ways except for minor random variations.

The vastly greater cost of careful panel studies should be obvious.

Intercept Surveys

Confronting people on the streets has been a popular form of surveying for many years. Today the "mall intercept"—interviewing shoppers in permanent stations at shopping malls—is a huge business. Of interest to us here are election-day intercept surveys, which also are becoming common.

The mass media sponsor election-day ("exit") surveys. They usually refrain from projecting winners based on these exit polls (instead using actual results phoned in from sample precincts after the polls close, for that purpose). Survey data is needed, in contrast, to report what *types* of people are voting for whom, and why. Since we have so little time to find people who have voted, and since voting rates in the United States are typically low, it would be inefficient to try to find voters in person at home or by telephone to ask how they voted. Instead, we send interviewers to the polling place to interview a sample of persons immediately after they have voted. So long as the interviewers keep a legal distance from the voting place, they can carry out their assignment.

Selecting Precincts. Whether known as precincts, beats, or boxes, our problem is to select a probability sample of the places at which people cast their votes. Using past election returns and our knowledge of Model City, we may stratify precincts by Democratic/Republican voting and by other characteristics that may be important for voting behavior, such as geographic location, ethnic mix.

Suppose, for example, we stratify precincts by Republican/Democratic voting tradition and by geographical sections of the city. The precinct sample will look something like Figure 2.11. Three different geographical types of precincts are shown in the figure. Within each type, precincts are arranged by party strength so as to have the first precinct of each stratum as similar as possible to the precinct just before it. Each precinct is listed with its identification and size (number of voters). A sample of precincts is taken within each stratum by a systematic skip procedure much like that described for the Model; that is, we cumulate the number of voters in the direction of the arrow and measure off the sampling interval successively through all of the other precincts in the city to identify sample precincts.

Just as in the in-the-home Model Sample we did not sample *blocks,* because precincts differ so much in size, we do not want to draw a sample of *precincts* (which would yield too many small ones); instead, we allow precincts to get into the sample proportionate to the number of voters they contain. Large precincts will have a better chance than smaller precincts of being in the sample. The size of precincts is irrelevant to their voting behavior as long as some geographic stratification is done to overcome any bias of small precincts being disproportionately located in certain parts of the city.

The purpose of stratifying the sample is to ensure that we get a thorough mixture of precincts—by geography, voting traditions, income level, or whatever may be relevant for the analysis.

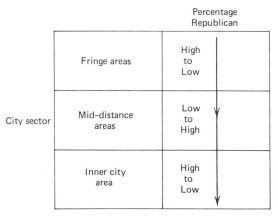

Figure 2.11. Stratification of precincts.

Selecting Respondents. The cost of interviewing depends much more on the number of precincts than on the number of respondents, because interviewers work all day at each polling place regardless of the number of respondents they get. This is necessary because different types of people vote at different times of the day. To get a proper sample, therefore, we have to be present at all times of the day to interview, for example, office workers who are more likely to vote before going to work, homemakers and retired people who are more likely to vote during the day, and blue-collar workers who tend to vote in the evening after returning from work.

Rather than interviewing just a few voters at each of many precincts, which would be very costly, we interview a large number of voters at each of relatively few precincts. We do need enough precincts to get a reasonably representative sample of the area—perhaps 25 for a large city and 50 for a state—depending upon the heterogeneity of the population. If we were trying to *predict* the election outcome, we might draw a sample of 70 to 100 precincts for a state, whereas 25 to 50 is sufficient if we're only describing voters' general characteristics as background "color" for analyzing vote returns. In general, the more precincts, the better, because the population of precincts is small and finite.

The total sample size depends as always upon how precise we wish our estimates to be and whether we will try to draw conclusions about subsampled areas as well as the whole population.

Because the precincts were drawn proportionate to size of vote, each represents an equal part of the whole population—in our example, 1/25 of the voters in the city. Therefore, we will try to intercept about the same number of people in each precinct. The sampling interval (here, the number of voters the interviewer lets pass before stopping the intended respondent) will differ for each precinct, depending on the expected voter turnout. In very large precincts, the sampling interval will also be large. For example, in a 1000-vote precinct, interviewers may be instructed to intercept every tenth voter to get a sample of 100; in a precinct of 500, every fifth voter to get 100; in a precinct of 100 or less; they will intercept every voter. Interviewing rates are always specified exactly, say, as every thirteenth or every seventh voter, depending on the precinct, and are set by the study director before election day—the interviewers exercise no judgment.

The success of the sample depends upon the accuracy of the turnout forecast. Generally, there is a close relationship between the estimated voter turnout for a current election and the turnout for an equivalent earlier election. Comparing equivalent elections is important. If this survey is for a city election, a past city election is a better estimate of turnout than is a presidential election, even if the latter is more recent. Of course, any unusual voter trends in this year's campaign should be taken into account to ensure getting adequate numbers.

All interviewing rates are set to produce approximately the same number of respondents to insure fair representation for each precinct—but not so many that they overload the interviewing and reporting capacity of the interviewing team. The number of respondents per precinct depends, therefore, partly on how long each interview will last. We suggest using a very short "ballot" that the respondents themselves fill out (see Chapters 3 and 4).

Some precincts will have experienced a growth or decline in the number of voters since the base election year on which the sample was drawn. We will accept the more-than-expected or less-than-expected numbers and the sampling rate will turn up in these instances as truly reflecting change in the distribution of the electorate throughout the city or state. But, some voters will refuse to be interviewed, and the refusal rate will vary among precincts. Whatever the resulting number of interviews in this last instance, they must be weighted during the analysis up to the full number that precinct's sampling rate would have delivered if no one had refused. Small sample precincts will have to be weighted up to full equality during analysis because they were drawn to represent an equal fraction of the total voters in the city (see Chapter 6).

There are two main problems in doing intercept surveys: keeping the correct sampling rate, and covering the exit of voters from the building. It is essential that a supervisor visit the polling place before election day to diagram the exits and assigns a pattern of shifting coverage of each exit in turn during the day.

The mechanics of respondent selection operate as follows: The interviewers work in pairs (with a third person as back-up). The two interviewers on duty cover the same exit at any given time. One has a mechanical hand counter to count each voter exiting the polls. If the sampling interval is every tenth voter, the other interviewer will stop the tenth person and hand out the interview "ballot," while the first interviewer goes on counting to identify the twentieth voter, the thirtieth, and so on.

This counting procedure is supposed to prevent interviewers from making any judgments about which voters to intercept for the survey. In reality, however, interviewers do not always keep the assigned rates. Sometimes they are simply overwhelmed by larger numbers of voters emerging from the polls than expected. Other times there are more exits to cover than planned for, or the turnout estimate was wrong. Specific instructions have to be provided to tell interviewers how to deal with these problems, or they may have to call in for directions. However, sometimes interviewers disregard their voter count and select respondents they anticipate will be more receptive because of gender, ethnic match, or other appearance clue. This obviously biases the sample. Good training, strong motivation, and close supervision of interviewers is essential in order to get reliable samples.

Telephone Surveys

Although telephone samples are popular, they are not nearly as easy to draw as they might seem, since they involve more than simply picking phone numbers at random out of a directory.

Selecting the Sample Phone Numbers. About 90 percent of the 75 million households in the United States have telephones. But about one-fourth (28 percent) of all residential phones have unlisted numbers. Moreover, about 20 percent of all families change address in any given year. We never know exactly which families are moving and which have unlisted numbers. Worse yet, some households have two or more phones with different numbers, thus increasing their probability of selection. Many residential listings (i.e., in the white pages) are actually commercial/business numbers, not households at all. And different phone books in the same geographical area often have duplicate numbers.

To try to draw a national sample from telephone directories is enormously complicated. There are about 4700 directories. Only a handful of commercial companies can readily undertake the collecting and updating of all directories, keeping clean files on some 54 million telephone listings. These make special efforts to eliminate most commercial listings and duplicate numbers.

For a survey of Model City, the telephone book may be a useful sampling frame because the area is small. Nonetheless, the book is probably at least 6 months out of date, meaning perhaps 10 percent of all households have moved and may have changed numbers. One-fourth of all phone numbers are unlisted, and an unknown percentage are not working—that is, the numbers have not yet been assigned to any subscriber.

One way to overcome the bias of unlisted numbers is to select numbers with a computerized random number generator. Called "random digit dialing" (RDD), the procedure generates random numbers of the proper length—10 digits, including area code, a 3-digit "exchange" (the numbers before the dash), and the 4-digit specific number. If RDD were used on every conceivable number, however, nearly three-quarters of the calls would be wasted, since that's the proportion of all possible numbers not in service. Therefore, we start the computer program with only the area codes and telephone exchanges *known to be working.*[11]

Of these, the computer prepares a list of all possible first 8-digit combinations as sampling units; the computer randomly adds two digits to each, and the number is dialed. If it is a commercial number, the whole 8-digit sampling unit is dropped because the telephone company assigns commercial numbers to special blocks, and all other numbers in that 8-digit sequence will most likely be commercial numbers.

From all 8-digit residential sampling units remaining, several small random

[11]We use a technique developed by Thomas Danbury (Survey Sampling, Inc.) and reported in "Alternative Sampling Models for Random Digit Dialing Surveys," a paper presented to the Advertising Research Foundation (New York, October 1975.)

The Danbury model stratifies numbers and samples randomly within strata. A clustered design is reported by Joseph Waksberg in "Sampling Methods for Random Digit Dialing," *Journal of the American Statistical Association,* 73 (March 1978), 40–46.

The major features of the two models are compared by Robert M. Groves in "An Empirical Comparison of Two Telephone Sample Designs," *Journal of Marketing Research,* Vol. 15 (November 1978), 622–31.

samples are drawn that together add up to the total sample size desired for the study. The samples are "replicates" of each other—they are the same size and are drawn in the same way from the total population of the residential units. They are sub-samples of the total sample.

The purpose of replicating the subsamples (as many times as judged to be needed) is that systematically slicing the total sample into subsamples assures that the entire geographic area and time zones are contacted evenly at any point in time. When the total number of desired interviews is obtained, or even if the study is interrupted, the phone numbers throughout the population will have been con-tacted evenly so that there is no biasing against certain telephone exchanges or time zones. We instruct interviewers and supervisors to complete their efforts to reach each number in each replicate before trying the numbers in a new replicate subsample.

Replicate sampling is also used in door-to-door interviewing and mail surveys, also with the aim of assuring fairly equal coverage of an area and population at any point in time. And, whether for personal, telephone, or mail surveys, sampling errors can be calculated for each replicate in a way that helps us to identify the different components of the overall error due to sampling.

The great virtue of the RDD draw, compared to pulling numbers from a directory, is that unlisted numbers will turn up in the sample in the same proportion they exist in that exchange.

If we cannot start with only working, residential numbers, we must inflate our attempted sample size to yield enough actual numbers to achieve the desired sample size—and prepare the interviewers for much frustration in calling nonworking or commercial numbers.

Another way to draw a telephone sample is to pick residential numbers ran-domly or systematically from a telephone directory, feed those numbers into a computer, and have it generate an equal-size sample of numbers with only the last 2 digits randomly substituted. This would pick up unlisted numbers in the proportion they exist.

Sampling Problems. There are a number of other sampling problems in telephone surveys. We will examine several, including: representativeness, time of calling, phones that are busy or do not answer, and completion rates.

Representativeness. Of the 1 out of every 10 households that do not have a phone, most tend to be lower-income households, including retired persons, minority families, and single-parent families. In social research, such people are often impor-tant subgroups. Thus we frequently make special efforts to include them. We can try to *oversample* such groups if we can attach an income characteristic to telephone numbers. For example, zip codes can be matched with telephone exchanges. Since zips are geographically based, they often distinguish population groups and can be related to census income classifications. Some companies sell customized telephone samples, which can be drawn for any of 3000 counties, 265 metropolitan areas, 35,000 residential zip codes, or other types of areas. The sample also can be crudely stratified by median census tract income level or by auto ownership, which is highly related to income.

If we cannot oversample low-income groups in designing the study, we can *overweight* their number in the final results; or we can send interviewers out to known low-income areas to collect personal interview data. In the latter instance, we have to check for differences between telephone and in-person data.

Time of Calling. Different people are home at different times of the day and different days of the week. If we are studying homemakers' food-buying habits, we concentrate our calls mainly on weekday mornings after 9 A.M. But for a public affairs survey, phone calls must be spread over a more representative period of time to get all types of people. Weekends are productive interviewing days (so are holidays, surprisingly). Saturday calls are made between the 9 A.M. and 9 P.M., while Sunday calls start after 10 A.M. Weekday calls extend from 6 P.M. to 9 P.M. If we are doing a national study from a central telephone office, we can start working at 6 P.M. Eastern Time and continue until midnight for Pacific Time numbers, where it will be 9 P.M. Sample numbers are identified by time zone and distributed to interviewers during appropriate call periods.

No Answer/Busy. Callbacks in a telephone survey are much cheaper than those for face-to-face surveys. Nonetheless we don't keep calling back endlessly. About 85 percent of all completed interviews are obtained on the first call (not counting busy signals); about 95 percent are obtained within three calls. After three callbacks, dialing becomes inefficient: five or six callbacks will produce only a 2 to 3 percent increase in completed interviews. Even using WATS lines ("wide area telephone service," which offers a fixed monthly charge for any number of calls), calling is expensive if it produces only negligible results. (At approximate 1981 prices, commercial survey agencies charge $13 to $15 per hour for WATS interviewing.) Firm rules for callbacks should be set to keep the practice uniform (see Chapter 5).

Completion Rates. As with in-person interviewing, about 98 percent of all telephone refusals come at the point of introducing the study. Very few people break off the interview once begun. The Census Bureau gathers two-thirds of its annual Current Population Survey by telephone interviewing. With government auspices, census studies have little difficulty getting people's cooperation—only 1 to 2 percent refuse. Commercial and academic researchers have more difficulty. Depending on the study, about 10 to 30 percent of all persons contacted will refuse.

Despite all efforts, no sample is ever completely free of problems associated with commercial, duplicated, nonworking, and unanswered numbers. Estimates vary, but a figure of 60 percent "good" numbers is often considered an efficient sample. However, if 80 percent of the people contacted cooperate, and if 65 percent of the sample numbers are good, the effective size of the sample still is only about half of the number intended ($.80 \times .65 = .52$). If there are biases in the way numbers were drawn, or if bias is a factor among those who refuse, the sample could seriously misrepresent the intended population. Special follow-up efforts should be made to learn whether such biases exist.

New Sampling Technology. Many people, particularly those with unlisted numbers, get irritated by telephone calls. Commercial firms have added to the annoyance by employing advanced computer technology that not only makes "junk calls" more efficient but heightens the aggravation. To initiate computerized calls, a sample of numbers is loaded into the computer, which dials the numbers, and the pitch starts if someone answers—all without human operators. If no one answers, the machine terminates the call and dials a new number.

This procedure can be incorporated into legitimate surveys that sample only limited numbers of people. Phone numbers can be put on cassette tape and inserted into a cathode ray tube (CRT) console, which then dials the numbers and displays the questionnaire to the interviewer for electronic recording of answers. Busy and no-answer numbers are automatically recalled by the machine, thus avoiding possible dialing biases, and interviewers only read the questions as they appear on the CRT and electronically record the answers. These devices can be made portable so that interviewers can work in their home areas and call at local rates.

Mail Surveys

As in every other survey, the quality of a mail survey depends on the completeness of the information we have about the population being sampled and the degree of representativeness the returned questionnaires bear to that population.

Sources of Mailing Lists. Almost any mailbox on any day will show that direct mail advertising and fund soliciting is big business. This snowstorm of mail reaches people for no other reason than that someone was located at that mailbox before.

Mail surveys are popular because they are relatively inexpensive. Also, their geographic and population reach is as extensive as the U.S. Postal Service itself, which accepts mailings to "Resident" or "Boxholder" addresses for delivery or forwarding (for first-class) to any address on all streets and rural routes in the country.

Despite this apparent comprehensiveness, not all families in our highly mobile society can be contacted by this means. Big cities have floating populations. Some persons purposefully try to avoid being located by society, and therefore they can be ignored for a voter study. However, if the study is trying to estimate the effectiveness of health or social services, the absence of important clients will seriously bias the results.

Professional mailing services develop lists from such sources as telephone and city directories, automobile registrations, and other sources. One firm has 64 million household names and addresses in its file. Of course, a major source of irritation to many is becoming a ''junk mail'' name on some firm's mailing list as a result of applying for a credit card, buying a home, entering a contest, applying for health insurance coverage, getting a job, or contributing to a charity. There is big money in ''bootleg'' mailing lists, too, which are acquired by advertisers from such sources as club memberships, medical files, hotel registrations, political party contributions, department store sales receipts, druggists prescription forms, and other seemingly private sources.

Commercial firms often make money from direct mail sales or advertising campaigns as well as from marketing studies. The lists they use typically are weighted in favor of higher-income families. Thus, they may reach only 75 percent of all households but have evidence that those households do 90 percent of the buying.[12]

Cities and counties with computer capacity are putting their voter registration records in electronic form, and printouts and tapes can be bought, usually for cost. Loaded with a tape, a computer can even print mailing labels.

Sampling from Mailing Lists. Drawing a sample from a mailing list presents no new principles. A sampling interval must be selected that is large enough to compensate for the typically low response rate; every *n*th name is then drawn.

Many mail surveys target specific persons who are known by name as well as by address. These are most efficient in terms of cost. However, some surveys are done on the basis of addresses alone.

Since the Post Office will not count mailboxes and drop a sample questionnaire to ever one hundredth ''Resident,'' any attempted sample of this type must be by size of population in whole geographic areas.

Professional mailing firms sell samples from their lists. In addition to ''every *n*th name'' samples, they may have categorized names on their lists by income level, by other census characteristics, or by auto registration. That means such lists can provide stratified samples, such as sampling ''affluent'' people only. Since these characteristics are attributed to individual families on the basis of the median for the census tract or enumeration district in which they live, however, the individual data is not wholly reliable.

Response Rates. Charities hope for a 1 to 3 percent response to mailings. On the other hand, the Census Bureau expects a 99 percent response to its decennial mail-in

[12] *Probability Sampling Service Users Manual* (New York: Reuben H. Donnelly, 1975), p. 2.

forms. Depending on the type of survey, mail returns will be as low as 10 percent for a general population sample and as high as 80 percent for a well-motivated subsampling of the population. A 70 percent completion is extraordinary.

Sending out twice the number of letters in order to double the size of the return does not provide useful information if the doubled responses only double the bias of the sample. Members of Congress often claim to vote on the basis of returns they get from every-resident surveys. This may be sound, if they realize that they are hearing from only those people who are particularly motivated to speak out about political issues; this population segment might be a factor in a reelection contest, but the sample returns are not likely to be a fair sample of the whole constituency.

Once the letters are mailed, we have less control over the response rates than with any other type of survey, primarily because there is no trained interviewer to encourage the respondent to participate. The letter must do it all. Several techniques to improve response rates, such as personalized letters and financial incentives, are discussed in later chapters.

FURTHER READING

Chein, Isidor, "An Introduction to Sampling," Appendix A, in Claire Selltiz, Lawrence S. Wrightsman, and Stuart W. Cook, *Research Methods in Social Relations* (3rd ed.) Holt, Rinehart & Winston, 1976. Basics of probability and nonprobability sampling.

Dillman, Don A., *Mail and Telephone Surveys: The Total Design Method,* Wiley, New York, 1978. Suggestions for increasing mail response.

Hansen, Maurice H., William N. Hurwitz, and William G. Madow, *Sample Survey Methods and Theory,* Wiley, New York, 1953. A standard work of classic dimensions.

Kish, Leslie, *Survey Sampling,* Wiley, New York, 1967. Mathematical basis of sampling.

Mendenhall, William, Lyman Ott, and R. L. Scheaffer, *Elementary Survey Sampling,* Wadsworth, Belmont, California, 1971.

Raj, Des, *The Design of Sample Surveys,* McGraw-Hill, New York, 1972. Practical and simple to read.

Sudman, Seymour, *Applied Sampling,* Academic, New York, 1978. Gives the basics.

Wiseman, Frederick, and Philip McDonald, *The Nonresponse Problem in Consumer Telephone Surveys,* Marketing Science Institute, Cambridge, Massachusetts, November 1978, Report No. 78-116. Gives a good idea of sample completion rates.

CHAPTER 3

Writing Questions

Once we know whom we are going to interview, we set about to frame the questions we will ask them. Other aspects of survey research are more technical, but writing the questions is a combination of art and science, an understanding of subject matter and the specific population blended with experience in the subtleties of communication.

We want to be sure to ask the right questions in the right way. To do this, we must think through the logic of each question, from its textbook theory to its use in the field. Otherwise, we won't be truly precise about which problems we are studying, nor will we know whether they can be studied in the way we have planned, whether the questions will accurately measure what we intend, and what possible uses can be made of the findings.

This process is called *operationalizing* the questions. It forces us to confront the logic of the questions, and it specifies the interviewers' tasks and the data-processing requirements. Equally important, detailing the operational form of study variables enables clients to evaluate the sense and realism of our effort.

In Chapter 1 we discussed defining the objectives of the study, that is, stating each objective in terms of the specific information we want to obtain in the field. Now we must state the objective as a measurement—a question that will evoke responses to fulfill the requirements of the study. Checklist 9 gives some criteria for judging whether hypotheses have been successfully translated into operational questions and answers.

CHECKLIST 9

Judging Whether Questions Do the Job

A question belongs in the study if:

1. Researchers and clients agree the measure is relevant to the problem and is important to study.
2. Researchers and interviewers agree unambiguously on the meaning of the question and responses.
3. Interviewers and respondents agree unambiguously on the meaning of the question and responses.
4. While each respondent shares the same understanding, each may answer the question differently—that is, the question uncovers variability in the population (what good is a question to which everyone says yes?).
5. Its response categories exhaust all meaningful answers that can be possibly anticipated.
6. Its response categories classify respondents as respondents would classify themselves, and interviewers can record the classification without hesitation or reservation.
7. Numbers can be assigned to responses that will distinguish respondents in meaningful ways as different by type or by degree.
8. There is a specific hypothesis and a specific plan for statistical analysis for the question that dictates how the numbers are assigned to responses.
9. The question and responses have no wording problems.
10. The question and responses are in a format that interviewers can readily learn and manage efficiently in the interview.
11. The question and responses are in a format that data-processing staff (coders, keypunchers) can master and proceed through efficiently.
12. The wording of the question and responses is the same as any measure it attempts to replicate (e.g., the same question taken from another study).
13. The wording of the questions and responses is the same or equivalent to any measure with which it intends to make a comparison.
14. The question and the responses are, to the extent humanly possible, known to be valid measures of the problem under study: either based on sound theory or "validated" by other research, by other types of measures, and by experts' judgment and clients' experience.
15. Responses are consistent with previous research, consistent with study hypotheses, or consistent with other related measures. (This is not mandatory, because there sometimes are good reasons for abandoning a weak measure. But the review is a good exercise for justifying a change.)
16. The measure survives the pretest and is improved by it.

PROBLEMS OF GETTING ACCURATE ANSWERS

The questions we ask determine the answers we get. This seems like an obviously true statement. But recently a state-wide sample of people was told the following before the questioning began:

> The next series of questions has to do with your possible interest in further education for yourself—*education that could help you in your job or in other ways help make your life more satisfying or productive* [emphasis added]. First, are you in fact engaged at the present time in any kind of education beyond high school?

The questions that followed such an injection of bias could never claim to give a fair estimate of people's preexisting views about life-long education.

Even where conscious or unconscious bias does not appear in a question, answers may not be accurate. People often give answers they think are more popular, socially acceptable, or prestigious. They will falsify, evade, exaggerate, misperceive, or otherwise distort answers to preserve their self-image in the presence of the interviewer.

That people exaggerate their educational status is common. Telling them, as the survey just quoted did, that education helps careers and promotes a satisfying, productive life made a bad problem worse.

Prestige bias is encountered in post-election surveys, which invariably find more people who say they voted than the actual number who did. In addition, proportionately more will also say they voted for the winner than in fact did. Some of this discrepancy can be blamed on sampling problems, because very low-income, mobile nonvoters are easier for an interviewer to overlook in getting the sample. But largely, it is due to inaccurate answers: People will exaggerate their income, dress up their job titles, claim to watch television less and go to symphonies more than they in fact do. Older people often shave a few years off their ages; and people will affirm that they know and care about an important issue, yet show complete ignorance in follow-up questions seeking greater detail. Later we will describe special techniques of interviewing that can reduce some of these problems (see Chapter 5).

Interviewing is a complex art. It depends almost entirely on the interviewers' skill in eliciting information from many different kinds of people, in different cultural and economic circumstances, with different values, beliefs, and backgrounds, all trying to agree on the content and meaning of questions. Before we send our interviewers out, we must be sure that our questions are worded and arranged in the way most likely to elicit reliable information.

Question Consistency

To maximize the chance that a question will have the same meaning for all respondents, both its wording and the way it is asked must be uniform. Survey generalizations rest on the uniformity, or *standardization,* of questions and procedures. This means that the same (identically worded) question is asked of everyone in exactly the same way. Interviewers are trained never to add anything to or subtract anything from the question as it appears in the questionnaire, because that would vary the meaning. And we insist that interviewers ask the questions in the sequence written. They must do this regardless of whether they personally think the question is good or the sequence logical. To accomplish this, we must be sure the questions are eminently askable.

As researchers writing questions, we must keep in mind that communication is a two-person game. We must select words that get across our meaning, but we must also consider how people respond—not only what they are likely to hear, but also what motives they will have for answering. Chapter 1 described a basic limitation of survey data: the reliance on self-reporting. Writing questions that skirt around the traps of self-image requires knowledge about how people perceive and relate to the world, as well as requiring practical experience with certain words and forms of questions that seem to work best.

Respondent Motives

Regardless of how tactfully worded, questions sometimes fail to produce the desired results. For self-reported information, questions must be meaningful—questions people are *able* to answer—and questions must not be inimical to people's self-interests—questions they are *willing* to answer. For example:

```
In the election for mayor, are you supporting Mr.
Taco or Mr. Bagel?
```

Respondent	*Response*
a. Unable to answer:	"What election for mayor?"
b. Able but unwilling:	"That's none of your business."
c. Able and willing:	"Mr. Taco, he's the conservative."

Sometimes we can't get answers because people don't know the answers, either from ignorance or because the subject matter is below their threshold of consciousness. But when people are able to answer questions truthfully, why don't they? Respondents have varying motives for failing to answer or for answering falsely. Although they are hard to separate from each other, the following presents some of these motives.

Prestige—the "Self-lifting" Bias. People give answers that they feel will elevate them in the eyes of the interviewer: "I read six nonfiction books a month."

Acceptability—The "Conformity" or "Popularity" Bias. People give answers that they feel are most popular or are most typical of a social group with which they identify. In effect, they give the answer they think their friends would give: "I think our society is too wasteful."

Saving Face—The "Ego-threat" Bias. This is simply the fear of embarrassment, of appearing uninformed or otherwise inadequate. This motive produces answers that defend self-image: "Of course, I vote in every election."

Reaction—The "Halo-effect" Bias. Some people answer questions they've never even considered before, simply because they're asked: "Why, yes, I think the ICBM is as efficient a weapons system as the SRBM or the MRBM systems you've asked about." Here the act of measurement has impact on the behavior being measured. The survey question manufactures an "opinion" where none existed before.

Courtesy—The "Si, Senor" Bias. Respondents answer anything just to appease the interviewer. People just don't like to hurt someone else's feelings. Older people, in particular, will make up answers because the interviewer "is such a nice person," and "works so hard," and, therefore, deserves more than a "don't know" to the questions.

Bandwagon—The "Underdog/Overdog" Bias. Even when they have no intention of voting, some people will say they will vote for the underdog candidate who is behind in the polls and others say they will vote for the opponent who is ahead. Perhaps the two groups cancel each other out—we really don't know enough about bandwagon biases. When a public official goes sour, a "hearse" effect appears. After President Richard Nixon was disgraced by Watergate it was hard to locate all of the 64 percent who voted for him in 1972.

Partisan—The "Don't Hassle" Bias. People give the answer that they perceive (correctly or not) the interviewer will favor. They sense interviewers' partisan feelings and give the answers least likely to cause conflict between them.

Response Set—The "Habit" Bias. People may answer repeatedly that they "agree" to a series of questions without considering each one on its own merits.

Irrelevance—The "Too Tired to Care" Bias. People give any answer just to get the interview over with. They have the courage neither to push the interviewer out the door nor to point-blank refuse the questions, so they just answer randomly.

Each of the foregoing motives is fairly harmless in its intent but destructive to accurate measurement. There are other, more deliberate motives prompting respondents to distort their answers. One is distrust of the interviewer's sponsor or intentions. If the interviewer is well trained in rapport-building techniques, distrust can be overcome. Maliciousness is not as easy to handle. Some people are abusive and intentionally misleading out of sheer cussedness. However, this group is never more than a tiny fraction of respondents. Typically they will break off the interview at some early point.

This Chapter introduces question-wording aids to deal with some of these problems. Chapter 5 deals with developing counteractive interviewing techniques.

KINDS OF QUESTIONS

The Model questionnaire uses four types of questions: questions of fact, of information, of attitudes, and of behavior.

Fact Questions

Asking a factual question does not guarantee a factual answer. Questions of fact are called *demographic* questions; they ask people to describe their own personal socioeconomic characteristics and perhaps those of other family members. Some of the demographic items frequently obtained in surveys are shown in Checklist 10, later in this chapter.

Such demographic characteristics are used to check the representativeness of the sample by comparing, say, the proportions of men to women or whites to nonwhites identified in our study against the same characteristics of the larger population, usually as found in U.S. Census reports. The data is also used to compare responses to substantive questions from different groups—men versus women, young versus old, Democrats versus Republicans. This is one of the principal uses of the survey tool: to detect similarities and differences between important societal subgroups and to make generalizations. Our hypotheses are often based on the assumption that people of the same social grouping tend to behave more like the people of that group than of other groups (for example, women are more likely than men to support Equal Rights legislation, and younger women are more so than older women). As samples become larger, statements about specific groups can be refined: 80 percent of the Republican Catholics who voted for Democratic Mayor Morris Meyer live in west-side neighborhoods, are college-educated, have incomes of less than $22,000 per year, and voted for Republican Governor Scoopa Spumoni in 1978.

(Technically, a collection of people who share some human characteristic, say, being 25 years old, are called a "cohort group" or a "classification," rather than "group members," because the latter term is reserved for people who actually interact in some way—say, as churchgoers—or who at least share some psychological identity, such as thinking of themselves as Democrats.)

We tend to analyze demographic data in terms of either of two aspects: (1) presence/absence of characteristics, and (2) more/less or high/low degrees of possession. For example, we might analyze different white and nonwhite respondents who have grade school, high school, and college levels of education.

Opinion and Attitude Questions

Opinion and attitude questions deal with the feelings, beliefs, ideas, predispositions, and values related to the topic under study. We distinguish opinion from attitude in that opinion is focused and expressed. Questions about *opinions* try to learn what people think or feel at a particular point in time about a particular subject. Their thoughts and feelings are, however, the fruits of an underlying, deeply ingrained attitude system. Questions about *attitudes,* then, tap the respondent's basic personality orientation acquired through years of experience. Both types of questions look something like this:

```
What do you think of the mayor's proposal to . . . ?

How important is it that the water supply be . . . ?

Do you favor or oppose the city government's decision to . . . ?

Would you agree or disagree that young people today . . . ?

Is it or is it not your belief that prayer . . . ?

Would you say that most people are for or against the . . . ?

Do you accept or reject the police department's explanation . . . ?

What is your opinion of the city council's plan to . . . ?

How strongly do you feel about the new law against . . . ?

As far as you're concerned, what is the most important . . . ?
```

Opinion and Attitude Questions

We try to distinguish opinions from attitudes. For example, if we're asking people their "opinions" of two candidates for mayor, we might be tapping *attitudes* toward Candidate A, a Democrat, and Candidate B, a Republican. That is, their opinions of the candidates are shaped by their party attitudes. Of course, even deeper attitudes underlie such affiliations. Additional probes into the reasons behind answers and the intensity with which they are held may be necessary.

We typically analyze opinions and attitudes in terms of: (1) presence/absence of them; (2) structured/unstructured focus; (3) positive/negative direction of expression; and (4) high/low degree of intensity. For example, we might find that many people have very intense, negative feelings about public officials, wanting to "throw the rascals out," but lack a clearly structured reason for their feelings.

Information Questions

We ask *information* questions to find out what people know, how much or how little, from which sources, and when they first learned about current events. For example:

```
What, if anything, have you heard or read about the . . . ?

Do you happen to know when the election for . . . ?

As best you recall, what did the Governor say about . . . ?

What do you understand by the term "circuit breaker" in . . . ?

Who is the congressional representative from . . . ?

Which of the following candidates recently said . . . ?

When did you change your party identification to . . . ?

In how many neighborhoods would you say . . . ?
```

Information Questions

People's knowledge of any subject is related to their attitudes. This is the principle of selective behavior. People selectively *expose* themselves to information (mostly information they agree with). They selectively *perceive* its meaning (understand what they want to understand). They selectively *remember* parts of it (what is helpful to them). Despite these relationships, information level can be measured even when attitudes are contrary or vague. Regardless of their feelings, we can learn how much people know accurately about something—candidates, for example.

Responses to information questions are analyzed in terms of: (1) presence/absence of knowledge; (2) vague/specific command of detail or high/low level of knowledge; and (3) correct/incorrect knowledge. For example, we might find that most respondents can identify both of this year's mayoral candidates, as well as their correct party affiliations, but incorrectly attribute a pro-welfare position to the Democrat and an anti-welfare position to the Republican.

Behavior Questions

Surveys usually ask people to describe their own behavior in relation to others. As we have seen, self-reporting is grounded in self-perception. Accounts of behavior may be accounts of how people think they should behave: the man who fancies himself a gourmet is likely to remember going out to French supper clubs more times than he actually did last year. People see themselves as they want to be in relation to others. As such, their reported behavior sometimes is more "should be" than "is." Examples of questions that cause self-image problems for respondents are:

```
Do you ever go to the library to take out books?

Did you happen to vote in the last election?

In the past week has anyone asked your opinion about . . . ?

How many television programs did you watch during . . . ?

Are you taller, shorter, or the same height as . . . ?

How much alcohol do you drink during an average . . . ?

Have you ever traveled abroad?

Do you know how to drive a car?
```

Behavior Questions

We look for consistency and patterns of relationships among reported behaviors in order to gain confidence that the behavior described is actual. We may check self-reports against other measures in the same survey and/or against external sources. For example, if a person claims to have voted the "straight Republican ticket," the answers to specific candidate-choice questions should be consistent with that party affiliation. Sometimes, with additional effort, we can check some of a respondent's claims with outside data; for example, we might check a respondent's claim to have voted against poll records or asserted party identification against party registration records at City Hall.

We usually analyze behavior in terms of: (1) presence/absence of the behavior; (2) regular/irregular frequency of occurrence; (3) degree of complete/incomplete performance; and (4) high/low degree of importance. For example, a man who reads the newspaper every day may actually read only the headlines, sports, and comics. However, if he claims that he "couldn't start the day" without the paper, since it's an important part of his routine, it would be easy to misinterpret this information. Therefore we try to ask questions that probe beyond the superficial response.

Constructs

Not all of the topics we are studying can be tapped directly through a single question. These variables we will have to construct later from responses to several specific questions. As an example, the idea of "socioeconomic status" can be a combination of occupation, income, and educational level. Or, a "ticket splitter" can be someone who votes for one party's candidate for president and the other party's candidate for senator.

FORM OF QUESTIONS

Questions can be classified either as *fixed-response* (structured or closed-end) or as *free-response* (unstructured or open-end) questions. A fixed-response question gives the respondent a choice of specific answer categories already printed on the questionnaire. A free-response question invites respondents to compose their own answers because there are no preset categories. A hybrid variety, the *semistructured* question does not have preset categories, but it narrows the range of likely responses and is not, therefore, completely free or unstructured (see Chapter 4).

Considering various kinds of studies, researchers disagree about the amount of freedom to give interviewers in asking questions and to give respondents in answering. Unstructured questioning, described in Chapter 1, is a useful tool of anthropologists and psychiatrists. It is like a conversation. The interviewer has topics in mind, but the ebb and flow of talk follows the inclinations of the respondent. This form may also be useful with a highly knowledgeable population, allowing them the liberty of stating their precise perception of a situation. But since the reliability of survey generalizations rests on the consistency of questions, survey questions must follow the inclinations of the researcher, not the interviewer or the respondent.

The Model Survey favors a questionnaire in which all but a few questions are structured, so that neither the respondent nor the interviewer can deviate wantonly from the intentions of any question. And even those unstructured questions that are used are unstructured only in their response categories, not in the question wording. Thus, every question in the survey is asked identically, and in only a few instances do respondents have complete freedom of response.

Unstructured Questions

Unstructured, or free-response, questions invite people to talk freely and at length. Such questions are used when trying to discover, say, people's reasons for voting as they do:

```
All things considered, what were the most important
reasons you had for voting for Senator Snort?
```

Pros. The free-response question is especially useful under the following circumstances: (1) when we have limited knowledge about the kinds of answers a question is likely to provoke; (2) when we anticipate a great range of responses; (3) when we are trying in the pretest to develop answer categories for structured questions in the main study; (4) when we're interested in what people will volunteer before specific prompting about a subject; (5) when we want to dig deeper into people's motivations; and (6) when we want verbatim remarkes to add "color" to our report statistics.

Cons. Despite some good uses of unstructured questions, their disadvantages prohibit heavy reliance on them in the Model Survey.

First, free-response questions are unwieldly because, as best they can, interviewers must record answers verbatim. This is time-consuming, and limits the number of questions that can be asked before respondents grow weary of the burden. Success depends on the interviewer's skill. In the worst instances, awkward lags occur as the interviewer struggles to keep up with the verbal barrage. The respondent becomes uncertain, begins to repeat answers, grows erratic, and begins to drift out of the interviewing mood. As the interviewer's fingers cramp around the pen, recorded answers become more sketchy and handwriting less legible, and we often do not in fact capture the depth we hoped for.

Second, free-response questions take up much space in the questionnaire. This limits the number that can be used if ample space is to be allotted for recording answers. This is not a trivial consideration, because interviewers tend to fill exactly the amount of space provided on the page. Two lines get a two-line answer; four lines double the answer. Since the purpose of this type of question is to get an in-depth answer, a one-line space defeats the purpose. The Model questionnaire does include some free-response items, and these are expanded with additional "probe" questions to encourage answers in depth, which takes even more space. For example:

```
In your opinion, what are some of the most important
problems facing the people of Model City today?
(PROBE:   What other problems are important?) (PROBE:
What other problems are there?)


    _____

    _____

    _____

    PROBE:_____

    _____

    PROBE:_____

    _____
```

Free-Response Question

Third, free-response questions may give the deceptive impression that we are exploring complex motivations. But the survey is not a substitute for "depth" research.

Just asking a *why* question does not mean we really learn much about people's motivations. Usually, interpretation of free-responses provides no more than a picture of what people *say* are their motivations. We can, for example, try a projective technique designed to dig beneath surface responses, hoping to reveal what a particular respondent thinks by what he or she attributes to others:

```
Would you say people living around here would ..
or would not object to someone from another race
moving into this neighborhood?
```

But the survey works best when it presents people with questions they are able and willing to answer. This includes certain structured questions that are designed to tap attitudes, which we'll discuss momentarily.

Fourth, to analyze verbatim comments after the field work, it is necessary to devise a category system by which comments can be grouped meaningfully. But how? And how many? Too few categories may sacrifice subtle meanings of the data—the flavor and intensity of responses may be lost by combining them too broadly. Too many categories, on the other hand, will be cumbersome to work with, will introduce artificial divisions between logically similar responses, and, by splitting up the respondents into too many groups, will disable us from making safe generalizations about types of people holding particular views.

Suppose, for example, we ask people why they voted for or against an incumbent alderman. They might give 50 different reasons that could range from personal dislike to mere name identification to ideological agreement. Analysis of all reasons is meaningless because we cannot generalize from the few respondents offering each reason. On the other hand, if we group all reasons simply as "positive" or "negative," what can we say about the election outcome that is much better than knowing the raw vote? Here the generalization is too broad to be useful.

One compromise is to organize most of the free-response data into perhaps a half-dozen or so basic themes, each which is mentioned by enough respondents for meaningful analysis (see Chapter 6). For more complicated questions, a two-step categorization can be developed that enables either broad or specific analysis. But this *post hoc* grouping into manageable categories will not save us from the basic weakness of analyzing unstructured responses, namely, that *we* classify the responses. Given the chance, respondents might classify themselves differently. A well-designed structured question, on the other hand, would present all respondents with an identical stimulus and a set of plausible responses (based on the findings of the pretest), and all the interviewers then have to do is check off what they say.

Lastly, relying on volunteered responses may not elicit specific data. If we want to know whether people voted for a candidate because of his stand on urban redevelopment, we must ask not only an unstructured "What are your reasons?" question but also a question about urban development directly and get a yes or no response (i.e., structured question).

To decide the proper mix of structured and open-ended questions we must consider our study objectives as well as whether we have the space on our questionnaire and the staff to process them.

Structured Questions

The *structured* question is one that gives fixed-response alternatives. The question is worded in a way that induces respondents to answer only in terms of the few alternatives given. For example:

```
As mayor, do you think Randall Harrison is doing
an excellent job . . a good job . . only a fair job
. . or a poor job as mayor?

        1--excellent

        2--good

        3--only fair

        4--poor

        5--other (SPECIFY:_____ )
```

Structured Question

Pros. Structured questions are easy to use in the field because interviewers simply check off or circle the answer they hear. Such questions are also easy to work with in data processing and analysis because they are precoded—each question and answer is assigned a unique number in advance that identifies it in analysis. It is then fairly simple for keypunch operators to transfer (punch) the codes from the questionnaire to machine data cards (described in Chapter 6).

A questionnaire must be comprehensive, providing a structured question for each point on which we are seeking information, to ensure getting complete data. A respondent may actually have a well-formed view on a subject but, until triggered to respond by the mention of a specific item in a follow-up question, may not focus on the point at issue. For example:

```
What do you think are the most important problems
facing Model City today?
        Crimes
        Taxes

How about air pollution . . do you think air pollution
is a big problem, not so big a problem, or hardly a
problem at all in Model City?

        1--big problem

        2--not so big

        3--hardly a problem at all
```

Cons. A disadvantage of structured questions is that we sacrifice the personal flavor of respondents' answers. But we are willing to lose some of the *qualitative* "feeling" of the data for the advantage of generalizing what is meaningful to us about people's reactions to a specific problem. Although fixed responses force people to decide how they stand in terms of our criteria, at least they classify *themselves,* and we don't have to guess later which subsequently formed category they should be placed in. Still, because we rely on interviewers to classify the responses they hear and to mark the codes during the interview, we lack direct control over the classification being done uniformly and correctly.

Critics feel that fixing a few response alternatives to complicated issues creates flawed data, since it: (1) glosses over important details; (2) smooths out key nuances distinguishing responses; (3) manufactures a "coalition" or summary position that encompasses different if not conflicting views; and (4) forces people to make unnatural choices they wouldn't make in the real world. But many decisions in life have severe yes or no alternatives: whether to vote or not, whether to vote for the Democrat or for the Republican. To stay sane, people generally compress the subtleties of complex conflicts into a few choices. And despite the simplification, we find that only a few respondents resist answering questions about their views in terms of yes or no, favor or oppose, agree or disagree.

In summary, we use structured questions because they are convenient, because we have hypotheses that say the preset alternatives are meaningful, and because we seek to generalize from the number of respondents attracted to each alternative.

Lest diehard critics dismiss questions with structured responses as artificial, we hasten to remind that we develop the final categories out of extensive reading, unstructured interviews with knowledgeable respondents, and pretesting with typical respondents.

Types of Structured Questions. There are two basic types of structured questions. The yes/no question offers a *dichotomous* choice (this category also includes good/bad, true/false, right/wrong questions, and so on). The *multiple-choice* question offers several fixed alternatives—for example, "Do you think the new downtown traffic control plan is a very good plan, a good plan, a bad plan, or a very bad plan?" Some variations of these two structured question types are described below.

It is standard to use numbers (1, 2, 3, etc.) in the coding of all responses. But numbers can represent quite different meanings, which must be distinguished.

Nominal. Some questions yield *nominal* responses. Nominal measurement, the simplest form, shows only the name of a classification that distinguishes one person from another—male or female, black or white. Answers are mutually exclusive. Since the responses are merely labels, a respondent can be either one thing or the other, not both. The precoded numbers assigned to nominal responses only identify the presence of a certain answer. They cannot be mathematically compared—cannot be added or subtracted. No category is bigger or smaller than another; they are only different. Thus we can assign the number 1 to a lawyer and 2 to a truckdriver and imply nothing more than that they are different. However, "1 plus 2" does not equal "3," a salesperson. Here is an example of nominal categories asked in a questionnaire:

> Now I'm going to read you some words that sometimes are used to describe political parties. As I read each word, just tell me which political party or group . . the Democrats, the Republicans, or the Independents . . it best describes:

Word:	Democrats	Independents	Republicans
a. conservative	1	2	3
b. spendthrift	1	2	3
c. war-mongers	1	2	3
d. trustworthy	1	2	3

Nominal Categories

Ordinal. In contrast, if we structure a question so that the numbers of the response categories mean that one response is bigger than another, we have increased the vigor of measurement. This next step above the nominal measure is *ordinal* measurement. Ordinal measures enable us to *rank* data in some kind of *order*. The ordinal measure permits us to say that a given response is greater than, equal to, or less than other responses. For example, if a respondent thinks that the first priority for the new Model City budget is more police patrols, the second, filling potholes in the streets, and the third, building a new Civic Center, we know that increased police have more priority than new building. However, we don't know by how much the respondent prefers the one to the others, or how strongly the respondent feels on any of the possibilities.

One ordinal method common to surveys is *subject ranking*. If, for example, we wanted to know who people think are the most influential members of the City Council, we might present a random listing of Council members and ask respondents to rank each in descending order of influence. Thus, if 1 is the highest rank and 4 the lowest, a respondent might rank council members in this manner:

> 4 Brown
>
> 1 Green
>
> 3 White
>
> 2 Black

Subject Ranking

A comparison of all respondents' rankings then reveals the influence ''pecking order'' as seen by city adults. A bias can be introduced to rankings like this when only a single version of the list of alternatives is presented to all respondents. People often gravitate to one end of the list or the other. In the illustrated list, Brown and Black may get higher ratings than they would if positioned in the middle of the list. One safeguard is to use two or more versions of the question, each with a different random ordering of the items to be ranked:

```
Which of the four candidates for the school board
would you say is best qualified for the job? . .
Which is next best qualified? . . Next? . . And
which is least qualified?
```

Random Version A   *Random Version B*

____Greeley   ____Dewey

____Webster   ____Webster

____Dewey   ____Conant

____Conant   ____Greeley

Randomized Responses

Another type of ranking is the *paired-comparison* method. Here respondents compare several alternatives, in pairs: A versus B, B versus C, and C versus A. Suppose we were comparing sources of information about federal involvement in Model City:

```
For getting information about the United States
national government involvement in local city
affairs, which do you generally find more reliable:

   (1)   newspapers......or......(2)   magazines?

   (2)   magazines.......or......(3)   television?

   (3)   television......or......(1)   newspapers?
```

Paired Comparisons

When each item is compared with every other item, the result is an overall ranking of, in this example, media reliability. An advantage of paired comparisons over straight numerical ranking is that focusing respondents' attention on separate pairs of items is easier and probably more exact. It's difficult to rank ten issues by first choice, second choice . . . all the way to a tenth choice. This can be so frustrating it confuses and annoys respondents and produces capricious rankings. On the other hand, comparing 10 items in pairs would require 44 separate comparisons. This, too, is out of the question.

If a larger number of items need ranking than a list can handle, the respondent can *sort* a deck of cards—each with one item on it, such as a photo, a drawing, a phrase. We ask the respondent to make a gross sort into three piles, which might be categories such as "likes the most," "likes the least," and "so-so" (ambivalent). Then the respondent sorts the "likes most" pile, setting out the two liked best, the next four, and so on, eventually refining his or her choice into a single order. The "likes least" pile is then sorted in the opposite direction.[1] Later, the interviewer records the order of the rearranged deck, marking the number 1 by the response on the questionnaire that matches the top card, marking 2 for the next, and so on.

Regardless of which method is used, the number of rankings must be realistic. Choice of method depends on the problem and the interviewing situation. The straight subject-ranking method has a logistical advantage, since it requires less space on the questionnaire page, doesn't require keeping track of cards, and is easier to process, to analyze, and to report.

Interval. A weakness of ordinal measures is that they don't tell us the degree of difference between numbers in the ranking. We don't know if the distance between first place and second place is the same as between second and third. Although the numerical interval between each rank is the same (one number), we cannot say that the intervals are equal.

An *interval* measure is, in contrast, one that indicates the distance between responses. On it, numerically equal intervals represent equal degrees or distance along a continuum of measurement. Some common interval scales are temperature degrees, kilometers and miles, hours, etc. Such measures show both order and distance between any points on the scale. It's the same distance between 60° and 70° as it is between 50° and 60°F, so we can add and subtract these numbers.

Ratio. If, in addition, we know the zero point of an interval scale, it becomes a *ratio* measurement. Such numbers can be directly compared: a person with an income of $10,000 has twice as much as one earning $5,000. With the numbers in this measure, we can divide, multiple, and perform other calculations.

Scale. One type of structured question uses *scaled responses* to measure the intensity of feelings.[2] Scaled responses are alternative answers, each having a different "weight" attached to it. The weight is a measure of psychological distance (intensity) between each response. Research indicates that, say, the qualifying phrase "very strongly" has a greater positive weight than "strongly," and this provides the basis for interpreting scaled responses. Weighted scale responses add more exactness to our survey measures because they indicate how much difference there

[1]Jum C. Nunnally, *Psychometric Methods* (New York: McGraw-Hill, 1957), pp. 544–46.

[2]For a general introduction to scaling methods and theory, see: William A. Scott, "Attitude Measurement," in Gardner Lindzey and Elliot Aronson, eds., *Handbook of Social Psychology,* (Cambridge: Addison-Wesley, 1968).

is among structured responses, for example:

```
Would you say it's very important, fairly important,
not too important, or not important at all that
elected government officials publicly disclose their
private sources of income?
```
                                                    (Weight)

                    5--very important   (8)

                    4--fairly important   (7)

                    3--don't know/not sure   (5)

                    2--not too important   (3)

                    1--not important at all   (2)

Scaled Responses

The questionnaire codes (1 to 5) have equal intervals. The "weights" at the right of the responses have different intervals that have been validated by research on such scales.[3] They would not appear on a real questionnaire, but they would be the known weights used in analysis. Notice that even the "don't know/not sure" response has a weighted value (at the midpoint) on this scale. ("Don't know" responses are discussed further in Chapter 4.)

Another type of structured question uses the *rating scale.* This scale presents respondents with a word, a phrase, or a statement and asks them to indicate the extent to which it describes their feelings. There are several variations on the rating scale.

A *Likert scale,* for example, presents five (or sometimes six) degrees of possible agreement:[4]

Disagree strongly	Disagree moderately	Disagree mildly	Agree mildly	Agree moderately	Agree strongly

A card printed with these statements is usually given to the respondent because the responses are too complicated to be kept in mind. Respondents look at the card as we read them a series of items to react to.

One of the best-known techniques is the seven-step rating scale anchored by opposite adjectives, which is called the *semantic differential.*[5]

---

[3]Stuart Carter Dodd and Thomas R. Gerbrick, *Word Scales for Degrees of Opinion* (Seattle: Washington Public Opinion Laboratory, 1956).

[4]Gardner Murphy and Rensis Likert, "A Technique for the Measurement of Attitudes," *Archives of Psychology,* No. 140 (1932).

[5]Charles E. Osgood, George J. Suci, and Percy H. Tannenbaum, *The Measurement of Meaning* (Urbana: University of Illinois, 1957).

How would you describe Mayor Meyer of Model City:

Bad _____ Good
     (1) (2) (3) (4) (5) (6) (7)

Strong _____ Weak
        (7) (6) (5) (4) (3) (2) (1)

Dishonest _____ Honest
           (1) (2) (3) (4) (5) (6) (7)

Semantic Differential

The respondent is handed a card like that above. He or she marks an X on each line at the point that indicates the person's feeling about the subject. Normally the numbers shown here would not appear on the card but would be on the questionnaire as a precode. (For an explanation of how the blanks are numbered, see Chapter 4).

Another rating scale, discerning agreement with *phrases or statements,* could be used instead of word pairs, for example:

The ideal mayor of this city: Agree | 1 | 2 | 3 | 4 | 5 | Disagree

Should be tough-minded ....

Must be able to control the city council.

Ought to have a college education ....

Scaled Responses to Phrases

On this scale, the numbers (1 to 5) represent positions on a continuum from strong agreement to strong disagreement. The matrix—the grid of response blanks—is a convenient way of handling responses, and is explained in Chapter 4.

Deciding how many points we should have on a scale is a trade-off. We would like the maximum detail without confusing the respondent. Generally, we believe that discrimination levels off at seven steps, with no gain at all after eleven.[6]

Using an odd number of steps permits a "neutral" or "neither" response at the midpoint, but an even number pushes people off this dead center and probably gives a more accurate reading of their attitude.[7]

Another type of structured question uses a series of agree/disagree statements, which, when added together, form a *summed index scale.* Such attitude scales may show the degree to which people are, say, dogmatic, conservative, or authoritarian (on separate scales, of course). For example, to identify people who are typically "conservative," a series of statements is read to respondents, who indicate their simple agreement or disagreement (i.e., without indicating intensity) to each:

[6]Nunnally, *op. cit.,* p. 521.
[7]Nunnally, *op. cit.,* p. 522.

```
All groups can live in harmony in this country
without changing the system in any way..........Agree  Disagree

You can usually depend on a man more if he
owns property than if he does not...............Agree  Disagree
```

Attitude Scale

The number of agreements determines each person's "conservatism" score. The person who develops such a scale must validate with research that it does indeed distinguish respondents on some characteristic and then must assert what that characteristic is.

The *cumulative scale* (or Guttman scale) is used in structured questions when we believe there is a single rank-order continuum underlying the responses given. This scale usually presents a series of statements with which respondents may agree or disagree. Whether apparent to respondents or not, the statements range from very *un*favorable to very favorable expressions. So, if thought of as being like the steps of a ladder, the bottom step is the least favorable statement and the top step is the most favorable.

Suppose we are measuring people's attitudes toward the Republican party. The cumulative scale assumes that only the most staunch Republicans will agree with all statements. The higher up the ladder we go, the more difficult it is for everyone— except the strongest Republicans—to agree with each item. And, as we go down the ladder, the easier it is for everyone—even Democrats—to agree with the statements. The following scale runs from an easy item that even fanatical Democrats may agree with to a hard item that only rock-ribbed Republicans may accept:

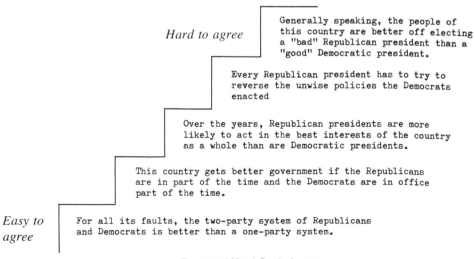

Hard to agree

```
Generally speaking, the people of
this country are better off electing
a "bad" Republican president than a
"good" Democratic president.
```

```
Every Republican president has to try to
reverse the unwise policies the Democrats
enacted
```

```
Over the years, Republican presidents are more
likely to act in the best interests of the country
as a whole than are Democratic presidents.
```

```
This country gets better government if the Republicans
are in part of the time and the Democrats are in office
part of the time.
```

Easy to agree

```
For all its faults, the two-party system of Republicans
and Democrats is better than a one-party system.
```

Easy and Hard Scale Items

	Least Favorable Item				Most Favorable Item	Agreement Score	Respondent's Rank
	(1)	(2)	(3)	(4)	(5)		
Respondent 1	A	A	A	A	A	5	1 (most favorable)
Respondent 2	A	A	A	A	D	4	2
Respondent 3	A	A	A	D	D	3	3
Respondent 4	A	A	D	D	D	2	4
Respondent 5	A	D	D	D	D	1	5
Respondent 6	D	D	D	D	D	0	6 (least favorable)

Figure 3.1. A perfect agree/disagree scale pattern

A respondent's final position on the ladder is reached at the highest step at which he or she gives a favorable answer. Determining from this final point, the scale assumes that the respondent has agreed with all items on the lower steps and has disagreed with all items on the higher steps. Suppose there are five items on a scale ranging from 1 (least favorable) to 5 (most favorable). If there really is a single, step-wise continuum for the attitude being measured, a final score of 3 indicates that the individual agrees with items 1, 2, and 3 and disagrees with items 4 and 5. Of course, scale patterns in reality are seldom so perfect.

An example of a perfect agree/disagree scale pattern for five items is shown in Figure 3.1. Respondents' scores (0 to 5) in the pattern tell how many and which items they answered favorably and unfavorably. In addition, the cumulative scale gives a rank ordering of respondents, ranking them (1 to 6) by their favorability toward a given subject.[8]

To make the concept of intensity understandable to the average respondent, one useful aid is a "feeling" thermometer," showing 10° marks between 0 and 100, which is put on a card. It is handed to respondents, who call off the number that indicates the "warmth" of their feeling about the persons, words, or phrases that the interviewer reads in turn.

Considerations of the many problems involved in actually developing attitude scales are beyond the scope of this book. We should therefore make this caution: seek more information from the literature before using scaled-response and ranking methods in order to understand their assumptions and limitations.

---

[8]Louis Guttman, "The Basis for Scalogram Analysis," in Samuel Stouffer, ed., *Measurement and Prediction* (New Jersey: Princeton, 1950).

CONTENT OF QUESTIONS

Some researchers worry that there are limits to the kinds of issues that can be safely brought up to respondents. More correctly, the real limits are on the *ways* in which issues are brought up. Each year hundreds of thousands of people are asked rather intimate questions about a very wide variety of topics. If approached properly by well-trained interviewers, people usually will answer even very personal questions about income, education, age, etc. For example, the figures in Table 3.1, on page 141, show the *average* percentage of people in four national telephone surveys who would *not* answer personal questions.[9]

The job of the questionnaire (and the interviewer administering it) is to build and maintain rapport with respondents so that emotionally charged issues—politics, religion, personal health—can be broached without discomfort. To achieve a painless exchange of questions and answers, questions must be constructed with several considerations in mind. The most complex of these is the actual wording of the questions. Question wording affects the responses that are given. Questions that are loaded, misperceived, or ambiguous can seriously distort answers.

Loaded Questions

The atmosphere in which questions are asked must be neutral. A question is *loaded* when something about it suggests to respondents that one response is more desirable than another. There are many ways that an interviewer's manner of asking questions can influence answers, but for the moment we are concerned with the biases that occur with faulty question wording. Below, we will look at some "bad" (improperly worded) questions and, where appropriate, suggest some possible improvements in their construction.

Unfair Alternatives. When a question provides unfair alternatives, it fails the test of impartiality. In the first example, the bad question asks people to agree with a statement that contains a strong implication: too much money is being spent on education. The "improved" version gives respondents the comparative basis they require to answer the question:

> *Bad:* Some people say that Model City is spending too much on building new public schools. Do you agree or disagree?

> *Improved:* Some people say that Model City is spending too much on building public schools . . and others say the City is not spending enough. Which opinion do you agree with?

[9]Gerald Hursh-César unpublished memo, CBS News Election Unit, New York, 1970.

Table 3.1. Not Answering Personal Questions

Questions Asked About:	Percent of All People Not Answering
Age	3.3
Marital status	0.0
Race	1.2
Religion	0.4
Education	0.7
Occupation	0.0
Income	4.0[a]
Political party affiliation	3.9[b]
Voting registration	0.7
Presidential election vote	10.8[c]
Listed/unlisted telephones in house	0.4
Name	8.4

[a] Income nonresponse includes 3.1% "don't know" and 0.9% refusals.
[b] Party affiliation nonresponse includes all "don't know," 0% refusals.
[c] Presidential vote nonresponse includes 4.3% "don't know," 6.5% refusals.

Maligns the Other Side. A question that presents only one side of an issue and tends to coerce agreement is maligning the other alternative. In the bad version, the respondent has no alternative but to take a stand against urban renewal:

> *Bad:* Do you think the government should spend any more of our tax money on tearing down the slums in Model City?
>
> *Improved:* Do you think the government should spend more . . or less money on replacing the slum neighborhoods in Model City with new housing projects?

Damns with Faint Praise. More subtle is the question that seems to present alternatives but in reality presents one side negatively:

> *Bad:* Some people say that the Mayor's plan is a poor plan to solve garbage removal problems in Model City. Others say it will do for now until a better solution is found. What do you think . . is it a good plan or a poor plan?
>
> *Improved:* Some people favor . . and some oppose the plan for combined garbage and trash removal by the city. Do you think the plan is a good solution . . or a poor solution to the garbage removal problem?

Omits Names. Loading questions by omitting names is a standard trick of phony campaign polls, which is done to inveigle contributions for a seemingly sure-win campaign.

> *Bad:* Hello . . I'm conducting a poll for Irving
> Hotcross, a candidate for mayor of Model
> City. If the election were held today, who
> would you vote for . . Mr. Hotcross, or
> one of the other candidates?

Varying Titles. A bit less obvious but an equally sure-fire way of biasing responses is to omit or vary titles and initials. Who would you vote for?

> *Bad:* State Attorney General Jason P. Bagel is
> running for governor this year against
> Henry Lox. Which man, Bagel or Lox, is
> best qualified to be governor?

> *Improved:* Jason P. Bagel and Henry R. Lox are running
> for governor this year. Which man, Lox or
> Bagel, is best qualified to be governor?

Personalities. Linking personalities to issues may alter responses. Answers may be considerably different—in either direction—if people are asked about a program that is named for a prominent official:

> *Bad:* Would you say that Governor Burnett's energy program
> for promoting solar heating of private homes has been
> very effective, fairly effective, not too effective,
> or not effective at all?

> *Improved:* Would you say that the state energy program for
> promoting solar heating of private homes has been
> very effective, fairly effective, not too effective,
> or not effective at all?

Institutions. Similarly, questions can be loaded by linking issues to institutions. A question about "federal government" programs will get a different set of responses than one about "national" programs:

> *Bad:* Would you say that the federal government's
> program for controlling air pollution is
> working very well, fairly well, or not too
> well?

> *Improved:* Would you say that the national government's
> program for controlling air pollution is
> working very well, fairly well, or not too well?

It may, of course, be necessary to link an institution to a program: if the response to that linkage is what we are trying to measure.

Emotionally Charged Words. Emotionally charged words can distort the meaning of questions. In the next example, the use of the phrase "defrauding the voters" is so powerful that respondents may envision real crime, failing to recognize standard campaign rhetoric:

> *Bad:* Congressman Logroll has been accused of
> defrauding the voters of this district.
> Do you agree or disagree with that charge?

> *Improved:* One of the issues in this campaign is how
> well Congressman Logroll has carried out
> his campaign promises. Do you think that
> Logroll has done an excellent, good, poor,
> or very poor job of doing what he said
> he would do?

Stereotypes. Thoughtless use of stereotypes can *create* rather than reflect public opinion, as this rather obvious example suggests:

> *Bad:* Frederick Trout, an official of the Communist
> Party, is scheduled to speak to a group of
> local school children. The Model City Society
> for Motherhood opposes his appearance here.
> Do you approve or disapprove of the stand
> taken by the Motherhood Society?

Words like "communist," "school children," and "motherhood" are so laden with moral, spiritual, and ideological values that linking them in a question impairs respondents' ability to answer honestly.

Conditioned by Context. This example illustrates a second principle: answers can be conditioned by other content in the question or by other parts of the questionnaire. Early in this chapter we showed how being conditioned by introductory comments extolling the value of education for the good life could affect people's support for certain educational programs. In the less obvious example that follows, people's personal feelings about the mayor will condition their responses to the second question about the duties of the office.

> Q1: Morris Meyer is mayor of Model City. In your
> opinion is he doing a good . . or poor job as
> mayor?

> Q2: As you understand it, what are the mayor's
> principal duties in office?

If we are interested in learning about what people understand of the functions prescribed for the office of mayor, we will have to change the *sequence* of the questions. Otherwise, we may learn that those who feel the mayor is doing a "poor" job think his principal duties are kissing babies and giving away keys to the city. A complete section on sequence of questions is presented later in this chapter.

Embarrassing Questions. Questions about voting, religion, income, and the like, when bluntly asked, can cause anxiety; this can pressure some people into giving false answers. If put on the spot, respondents who cannot answer a question honestly or accurately may refuse to answer. But since refusing to answer can itself be embarrassing, they may invent or distort answers as repayment for the tension created. To be embarrassing, a question does not have to be terribly personal. It simply has to imply that the respondent is outstripped by others. A question like "Did you vote in the city election last month?" is bound to produce a higher percentage of "voters" than there actually were, because voting is virtuous civic duty.

No matter how innocuous they may seem to us, all questions must be considered carefully for their potential embarrassment. A question that jeopardizes the respondent's ego jeopardizes the study. Care should be taken to provide *face-saving alternatives,* as these examples suggest:

> *Bad:* How much time did you spend reading the
> newspaper yesterday?
>
> *Improved:* Did you have a chance to read the newspaper
> yesterday? (IF YES: About how much time
> did you spend reading the newspaper yesterday?)
>
> *Bad:* What is your religion?
>
> *Improved:* Do you happen to have a religious
> preference? (IF YES: What is your
> religious preference?)
>
> *Bad:* Did you vote in the city election last month?
>
> *Improved:* Did you happen to vote in the city election
> last month, or didn't you have a chance to
> vote?

Misperceived Questions

Problems with word choice—jargon, technical words—with grammar, and with logic can result in respondents hearing something other than what we mean to ask.

Outside Respondent's Experience. Words that lie outside a respondent's experience have no fixed meaning, so they are misperceived—they take on meanings according to the needs of the respondent, not of the researcher. Consider the irrelevance of "precinct captains" to many rural voters. Sometimes we let jargon creep into our surveys because we're too close to the study and too far from the respondents. First-hand contact with typical respondents, common sense, and independent critique are our best safeguards against using words outside respondents' experience:

> *Interviewer asked:* Generally, do you think that precinct captains get involved in politics for egocentric or altruistic reasons?
>
> *Respondent said:* "I don't care what their financial reasons are, policemen should keep out of politics."

Technical Words. To get comparable data, words must mean the same thing to everyone. To meet this requirement we must avoid technical words that can be misperceived because they have specialized meanings. "Electoral college" suggests an educational body to the ill-informed, a convention of election judges to the near-informed, and adulterated democracy to the sophisticated:

> *Interviewer asked:* Do you think we should change the present system of the electoral college?
>
> *Respondent said:* "No, the universities are all right. It's just one bunch of smart-aleck kids making all the trouble."
>
> *Interviewer asked.* Do you favor giving more power to election judges?
>
> *Respondent said:* "No, they shouldn't have any more power than appointed judges."

Context. The context in which words appear alters their meaning. Words have a way of latching on to each other, and people hear the particular combinations that seem most logical.

> *Interviewer asked:* In challenging his opponent, the mayor demanded a dual meeting and debate on the issues ....
>
> *Respondent said:* "Dueling . . in this day and age?"

Overfamiliarity. Somewhere between the extremes of complete inexperience and overfamiliarity, each question must be worded so that it has just one meaning for all respondents no matter how they differ by education, occupation, or residence.

Extreme familiarity with some words may lead respondents to misperceive other, alike-sounding words; we hear what we know—for example:

Interviewer asked:	Do you ever read <u>foreign</u> news?
Farmer said:	"Sure, I read the <u>farm</u> news every day."
Interviewer asked:	Do you favor government control of <u>profits</u>?
Religious fundamentalist said:	"No, <u>prophets</u> are controlled only by the Lord."
Interviewer asked:	What are the important <u>social aspects</u> of medicine?
Doctor said:	"<u>Socialized</u> medicine is a terrible threat to this country."

Violate Idiom. Misperception also occurs when we violate idiom. A question worded contrary to language custom will often be misheard: "You can fight city hall" is likely to get the answer, "You're right, you can't." We try to be natural in question wording but not "folksy" to the point of using slang or colloquialisms. *Colloquialisms* change their meaning over time and from family to family. The use of *slang* detracts from the interviewers' professional veneer and the seriousness of the study. Using slang and colloquialisms also can affect motives for answering questions and load individual questions as well.

Being natural and avoiding stilted language means to *write as people talk*—the questionnaire, after all, will be *spoken* by the interviewer. Without wanton violations of the principles of good grammar, some suggested variations are:

<u>Who</u> did you vote for in that election?

Which of the two plans do you think is best <u>to effectively combat</u> the rising crime rate?

Is that something you, yourself, believe <u>in</u> or not?

Would you agree or disagree that your parents have strong moral principles, but <u>they</u> don't always act on <u>them</u>?

Hello . . <u>I'm</u> an interviewer for a public opinion survey. <u>We're</u> doing a study of some of the things people are talking about these days.

Splitting infinitives, using contractions, even mixing antecedents, can be effective ways of achieving a natural questionnaire language. But *double negatives* and other grammatical gymnastics can be highly confusing when questions are spoken deliberately, as they are in the field setting:

> *Bad:* `Do you agree or disagree that there is`
> `no situation in which the FBI is not`
> `justified in breaking laws in order to`
> `protect our national security?`

> *Improved:* `Do you agree . . or disagree . . that`
> `there are some situations in which the`
> `FBI is justified in breaking laws in`
> `order to protect our national security?`

Illogical Sentence Construction. Sentences that don't read logically cause problems for interviewers, because they have developed reading habits based on conventional word order and punctuation. As the interviewer falters, so will the respondents' comprehension. *Lengthy* questions pose difficulties for both. Interviewers may try to solve their problem by paraphrasing the question, thereby losing our uniform stimulus. Respondents, on their part, become taxed and quickly impatient, thereby imperiling subsequent questions.

When questions are *labored,* people may anticipate and misperceive the point. Overelaborate questions antagonize people by talking down to them. And, by anticipating a question's point, respondents may in fact miss it. In the example here, respondents will probably answer "excellent" or "very poor" before the interviewer completes the full range of alternatives. The result is to push ratings artificially toward the extremes, because people don't consider all alternatives:

> *Bad:* `Some people say that Senator Chuckley`
> `Snort is doing an excellent job in`
> `office, and some people say he is doing`
> `a very poor job. What kind of job do`
> `you think Senator Snort is doing . .`
> `excellent, good, poor, or very poor?`

> *Improved:* `Would you say that Chuckley Snort is`
> `doing an excellent, good, poor, or very`
> `poor job as United States Senator?`

Two-part Questions

A two-part question introduces two subjects and asks one question. This is a mistake because it is impossible, upon analysis, to decide which part of the question the answer applies to. In this next example, does yes mean that Mayor Meyer should run again or that he is not the strongest Democratic candidate?

> *Bad:* Do you think that Mayor Meyer should run
> for re-election this year, or could the
> Democrats find a stronger candidate?

> *Improved:* Do you think that Mayor Meyer should
> or should not run for re-election this
> year?

> *And:* Do you think that the Democrats could or
> could not find a stronger candidate
> than Mayor Meyer this year?

Assumes Knowledge

As the previous examples of technical and esoteric words indicated, a common error of researchers is to *assume too much knowledge*. By this, we do not mean to imply the time-worn cliché that the public has a fourth-grade intelligence, but we do want to caution clients and researchers, who are so close to their subject matter, that they should not assume others share their deep concern and familiarity with it.

Newspaper polls, recognizing the superficiality of knowledge most people have on any given subject, avoid deep probing. But where a study requires it, techniques must be employed that can fulfill two goals: (1) to avoid overburdening the less well-informed respondents, and (2) to distinguish between those respondents who speak from seasoned thinking on the topic and those who had never considered it before being asked.

Filter Questions. These two goals are met by using *filter* questions to determine which respondents are knowledgeable on a topic and therefore eligible for more in-depth questions. Even then, to overcome mental interia, wording must be concise, to-the-point, and easy to grasp. Below is an example of a filter question, which selectively leads in to two follow-up questions.

> Q.37:   Have you happened to hear about any legal
> problems some of the Model City aldermen have
> been having?
>
>   1--No   (IF NO: SKIP TO Q.38)
>
>   2--Yes (IF YES: ASK Q.37a)
>
>   Q.37a: What have you heard?
>   1--(CORRECT) Indictment for campaign
>   contributions; liquor scandal
> (IF INCORRECT   2--Other (SPECIFY:_____)
> SKIP TO Q.38)   3--Don't know
>
>   Q.37b: Do you think the indictment of
>   the aldermen will . . or will
>   not harm their chances for
>   re-election?

Frame of Reference. Another way to guard against question misperception is to provide a frame of reference. Since people often are not familiar enough with an issue to offer an opinion, questions may provide a minimum of background in a brief introductory statement. Here is an example of leading respondents through a step-by-step educational process with a series of questions:

Q.38:   What does the term "affirmative action" in city
        hiring mean to you?

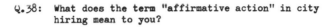

Q.39:   Affirmative action in hiring means the city
        would actively seek out and encourage certain
        minority people, handicapped, and women to
        apply for city jobs, and hire more of them.
        Do you think it would be a good idea to try
        this . . or not?

Q.40:   Some say that because women, the handicapped,
        and minority people have been discriminated
        against in hiring in the past, they should now be
        given special consideration for city jobs.
        Others say this would be unfair to others also
        seeking jobs. Do you believe that women, the
        handicapped, and minorities should be given
        special consideration for city jobs . . or not?

Unlike the previous example, where the filter question weeded out the unknowledgeables from further questioning, in this example all respondents are asked all questions. Even those respondents who already understood the term being investigated are read the explanation in the second question, to be sure everyone is operating on exactly the same information, and to avoid having the interviewers make a judgment on the correctness of answers about a complex issue.

Although providing a frame of reference is an acceptable tactic for getting crude divisions of public opinion for a newspaper poll, it has questionable value for making serious decisions based on survey findings. Such briefing does not give ill-informed and well-informed people truly comparable understanding. Rather, the ill-informed are still compelled to render snap judgments, and their answers are thus more likely to reflect attitudes than to reflect understanding based on information. In the analysis, respondents should be distinguished by their response to the filter question or weighted differently in drawing conclusions from the survey.

Ambiguous Questions

A question loses its validity when its subtleties are lost upon the respondent. Questions that are exact in their meaning are easier to answer correctly than are those that are incomplete, imprecise, or indefinite.

Incomplete. "Did you vote in the last election" is an incomplete question. It is confusing because some people are concerned only with presidential elections. Even if the question were qualified to ask: "Did you vote in the last city election?" people are still likely to answer in terms of the last campaign (whether mayoral, gubernatorial, or presidential) that was important to them—don't all these elections take place in their city? To clear up the ambiguity, better question wording is needed:

> *Bad:* Did you vote in the last election?
>
> *Improved:* Did you vote in the Model City election
> for Mayor last June?

Imprecise. An imprecise question conveys an unreal meaning or suggests an inaccurate measure. The statement "Model City now has to redistrict its ward boundaries..." can give an erroneous introduction to the question because it implies everyone in the city has to take action. More precisely a majority vote in the City Council with the approval of the mayor will determine new ward boundaries, not the city electorate.

Consider also:

> *Bad:* How concerned are you that 8 percent of the
> people in this area are presently unemployed?

This question is imprecise in several ways. First, 8 percent of which people? Does this include the hospitalized, the retired, transients, college students, housewives, teenagers, or only those seeking work? Second, is 8 percent unemployment high or low for this area? Is some unemployment good, bad, or indifferent? Third, what is "this area"? The core city, suburbs, urban fringe, all area within commuting distance, or what?

> *Improved:* Do you think the lack of summer jobs for
> teenagers in Model City is . . a very big
> problem, somewhat of a problem, or not
> much of a problem at all?

Indefinite in Time. Words are hazy if they are indefinite in time. Use of words like "frequently," "often," and "usually" is more likely to produce reports of self-image than of actual behavior. Further, the word "often" will have different meanings to different people. Questions like, "How often do you vote?" may yield such noncomparable answers as "Whenever I can," "Always," "Never," "Twice a year," "Only once per election," or "For what?"

Rather than risk inaccurate self-measurement of typical behavior, it's better to pin down specific instances of separate behavior, add them together for a single respondent, and then classify all respondents during analysis by frequency of the behavior. For example, ask respondents about participation in several specific elections and, at the same time, learn the candidates they voted for:

> Q.42: Did you happen to vote last November in the election for United States Senator between Barbara Pole and Chuck Drill . . or didn't you have a chance to vote in that election?
>
>> Q.42a: (IF VOTED, ASK: Which person, Drill or Pole . . did you vote for, or did you vote for another candidate?
>
> Q.43: Now thinking back to the presidential election of 1980 . . when Ronald Reagan ran against Jimmy Carter . . do you recall if you voted for Reagan . . or Carter . . or didn't you have a chance to vote in that election?

However, we can't press people to recall too far back, and answers will be influenced by the bandwagon effect, inflating the reported vote of the winner.

A vague question such as "How often do you usually vote?" might have a place in an attitude scale or some general index of social behavior but would be meaningless in a study where we are really interested in voting behavior patterns, such as frequency and consistency of voting, straight- and split-ticket voting, etc.

Here is an example of another kind of problem:

> *Bad:* **Among your circle of friends are you regularly asked for your opinions or advice on voting?**
>
> *Improved:* **During the past two or three days has anyone . . among your circle of friends . . asked for your opinions or advice on which candidates to vote for in the city election next month?**

Recent, more specific behavior is easier to recall without straining the memory. Again, the "bad" question may sometimes be used as part of a general scale of, in this case, opinion leadership, but it is worthless for describing actual behavior.

Obviously, focusing on a single, recent incident—what happened "yesterday"—may catch atypical behavior. That is, a person who usually gives advice might have given none on the day about which we inquire, or a person who usually seeks advice might happen to have been asked for his or her opinion for the first time that day. In analysis, we can deal with atypical behavior in individuals by using several measures of opinion leadership for each respondent. But suppose the study only wants to describe the relative occurrence of opinion leadership in the total population or in a few broad groups. In such situations, one measure might suffice, because those who are always asked for advice *except* yesterday will be cancelled out by those who are never asked *except* yesterday.

Indefinite Comparisons. Ambiguity results when indefinite comparisons are made. If we ask if something is "fair," respondents are justified in answering, "Yes, it's about average." Others might correctly wonder what are the standards of comparison. If "fair" in our question deals with justice, it must be further defined or exemplified.

> *Bad:* Do you think that the Model City welfare
>   program is fair?

> *Improved:* In terms of the number of food stamps
>   given to low-income families each month,
>   do you think that the public welfare
>   program in your state is fair or unfair?

Indefinite Persons or Places. The ambiguity of indefinite persons or places is illustrated by questions like:

> *Bad:* Are there many voters living around here?

In this question "any" could mean all, some, or one; "voters" could mean people of voting age, registered voters, or those who voted in some past election; "around here" could mean next door, in this neighborhood, across the whole town, or in the whole metropolitan area; and "living" could mean a person either not in the cemetary yet or in residence at this time. And even if all the words meant the same thing to everyone, people still could not answer the question meaningfully. If we want to know who lives or votes in the neighborhood, we should sample the neighborhood. If we want to know who knows whom and what they know about them, we should define the limits of the neighborhood or let them define it and then ask how many people the respondents personally know to be registered voters, Puerto Ricans, school teachers, or whatever.

> *Improved:* Of the people you personally know living on
>   Apple Street between 34th and 35th Avenues,
>   about how many do you know to be registered
>   to vote . . would you say nearly all, maybe
>   about three-quarters, about half . . or less
>   than half?

Such line of questioning assumes that we will obtain census block estimates of the number of households in each sample neighborhood, as well as voter registration bureau figures on actual registration and voter turnout, so we will have a comparative basis for checking public awareness of voting eligibility.

Indefinite Concepts. The word "living" in the example above actually illustrated the ambiguity of indefinite *concepts*. Here is another example:

> *Bad:* Do you think government officials in this country
>   should publicize their feelings about world affairs?

Here "government" can imply city, county, state, national, or foreign governments. "Officials" can be dogcatchers, judges, mayors, presidents, and all other kinds of elected, appointed, and even civil service officers. "In this country" could imply United States or foreign officials just passing through; "country" itself can mean either the nation or just this neck of the woods; "publicize" may mean leaking a position paper, telling more than one person, addressing a crowd, appearing on "Meet the Press," or writing a magazine article; and "world affairs" can mean any and all politcal events or only international events.

Consider again the earlier questions about opinion leadership; we often see research reports dealing with "public affairs" opinion leaders—the persons others go to for opinions or advice about something. But about what? Those whose advice people seek on state property taxes are not likely to be the same as those they ask about the political situation in the Middle East. For the concept to be useful, it must be specifically defined:

> *Bad:* Among your circle of friends, is there
> anyone whose opinions or advice you
> frequently ask about the public affairs
> issues of the day?

> *Improved:* Among your circle of friends is there anyone
> whose opinions or advice you frequently
> ask . . about such issues as the energy
> crisis and conservation of natural resources?

Deliberate Ambiguity. The ambiguous word "frequently" was purposely used in the last question, because we are interested in knowing whether an opinion leader exists at all, not in knowing the regularity of the behavior, which would be determined by asking specifically about "yesterday."

Despite our warning about using ambiguous words, sometimes we use them deliberately. Without specification of generalizations such as "most," "low-income," and "Democrats," how can we interpret answers to the question: "Do you believe that most low-income people are Democrats?" Such a question alone may be useless for problem solving, but it may be useful with a series of related items that together form some kind of attitude scale regarding political party image.

We occasionally use ambiguous wording for other reasons. To start people thinking generally about a content area, the first question in a series may be broadly phrased. Such vague questions give respondents a frame of reference, but without cueing them to prepare answers for particular topics. For example, before asking people specifically about the subjects of their political conversations, we might first ask: "In talking with your friends or relatives, do you ever discuss current events . . . like politics, or that sort of thing?" "Friends," "current events," "politics," and other such vague image words may serve to bridge the gap between different sections of the questionnaire, to filter out "nontalkers" from further questions, and to give the rest an idea of what's coming.

SEQUENCE OF QUESTIONS

Throughout this chapter we have described various ways in which either the content or sequence of questions can condition, or bias, answers to them. Question sequence may do more than bias a single response; it may determine whether an interview is successfully completed. To work best, the model questionnaire is designed in four ordered parts: the introduction, warm-up questions, main study questions, and demographic questions.

The Introduction

Six principles guide the writing of a successful introduction to a questionnaire:

- The introduction must be *short*. Don't waste time! The purpose of the introduction is to identify the sponsor and the broad nature of the study without fuss. To sound natural, the introduction must be easy to memorize. Nothing kills an interview as quickly as hearing an interviewer awkwardly read ''Hello'' from the questionnaire.
- The introduction must be *realistically worded*. Stilted wording is harder to memorize than simple phrases. Interviewers will flounder for substitute words or deliberately change the introduction to make it more natural, if the original doesn't meet this standard.
- The introduction must be *nonthreatening*. Doors close quickly when interviewers announce their intentions to talk about religion, politics, or income. Emotion-laden items should come later in the interview. A different kind of threat arises when the interviewer appears to represent a commercial interest, such as a magazine publisher. People have been aggravated to the point of hostility by sales gimmicks that are used to get the door open or the phone answered in preparation for a sales pitch.
- The introduction must be *serious*. A light-hearted approach tells people the study is too frivolous to warrant their time. On the other hand, the introduction can be too heavy and scare people off. To avoid being too much of either, the introduction should say very little except to identify the sponsor and to convey that it is the responsible undertaking of a trustworthy agency in the community. Teachers who identify their studies as ''class projects'' make a mistake, because student activities lack a sense of urgency or importance. Studies identified with a university as a whole, however, have credibility because people generally respect science and academia.
- The introduction must be *neutral*. If there appears to be any partisan interest involved, respondents can be either openly suspicious or overly receptive—depending on the point of view they think is being represented. Either way, answers will be colored by perceptions of the sponsor's objectives.

- Finally, the introduction must be pleasantly *firm*. Interviewers should speak decisively, but without bullying. If the study is conducted with federal government funds, it is mandatory that people be advised of the voluntary nature of their participation. Nonetheless, it is essential that interviewers *do not ask permission* to interview. The most successful introduction is matter-of-fact. Novice interviewers invite rejection by adding a verbal question mark to the introduction, which invites respondents to decline. Although interviewers must not be impudent or ignorant of legalities, they must exude confidence and assume the respondent's cooperation from the start.

Contact. The introduction for our Model Survey is in two parts: initial contact and respondent eligibility. Here is an example of the first part that combines some of the favorable characteristics mentioned above:

```
Hello .. I'm an interviewer for a public opinion survey.
We're doing a study of some of the things people in Model
City are talking about these days.
```

Here, the specific sponsor is not mentioned because the name may be unfamiliar, or it might seem partisan or frivolous. If this were a government-funded project, however, the sponsor's name would have to be given. Although "public opinion survey" may sound corny, it works. People know about surveys and favorably distinguish them from door-to-door sales. Another example:

```
Hello .. I'm from the Research Department at the State
University. The Department is doing a study of how the
people have been getting the news during the Model City
newspaper strike.
```

Again the credible and prestigious source is identified, and the purpose of the study is indicated in nonthreatening terms.

After this initial contact, in an ordinary survey the interviewer moves directly into the next part of the introduction without pause for reaction. We make the assumption that respondents are willing to continue because they allow it to continue and that, if at some point they no longer wish to continue the interview, they will break it off.

Informed Consent. United States government-sponsored research now requires a more formal consent from the intended respondent, if the respondent is at risk (see Chapter 1). Approving agencies (Institutional Review Boards) are often carried away in their urge to protect respondents from what are truly innocuous questionnaires; they tend to require too long and too detailed statements, which themselves may arouse suspicion and fear among the respondents. Thus, although we would not choose to introduce a study at this length, we might be required to use something like this:

```
Hello .. I'm from the Research Department of the
State University. We're doing a study of how people
find out about what government programs are available
to them. You were selected for interviewing by a
computer method for randomly picking households.
Your answers will be put together with a lot of other
people's, so you will not be identified in any way
in the overall results. If there are any questions
you don't care to answer, we'll just pass over them,
and you are free to stop the interview at any time.
```

These actually are standard replies an interviewer would give if questioned by a respondent (see Chapter 5), but here the information must be included in the introduction.

Under any circumstance, we avoid long, overly detailed statements of the *content* of the study, to avoid biasing the results. If the questions indeed deal with attitudes toward public affairs and reports of everyday activity, there is essentially no risk to respondents (except perhaps embarrassment for ignorance), the danger the federal regulations were designed to deal with. With very low-risk questionnaires, the implied consent the respondent gives by continuing the interview will be adequate.

If, on the other hand, a study does involve matters of personal delicacy or possible illegal activity, or if it requires respondents actually to perform some task other than responding, more risk is involved, and more formal consent procedures may be required by the committee set up to clear the research project.

As a part of consent, no undue benefits can be promised to subjects to elicit their cooperation. We can make generalized statements of benefit, such as increasing knowledge:

```
Your cooperation with this study will help us know
how to improve the services of this agency.
```

But we can't promise dramatic improvements in their lives that are to result sometime from the study. Small gratuities or realistic compensation for time to complete lengthy or repeated interviews are permissible. If the subject matter of the survey is of particular interest to a specialized group, we offer to mail them a copy of the study.

In situations in which respondents are receiving treatments or benefits connected with the study, it must be explained to them that they may withdraw from the study at any point without prejudice to any services they may be getting or subsequently entitled to. This can be said as simply as:

```
Of course, you don't have to answer any question
you don't wish to, and if you decide later you
do not want to continue, you may withdraw without
affecting your treatments (services, benefits)
in any way.
```

For truly risky research, a review board will require signed consent forms to indicate that respondents understand what they are being asked to do. Also, federal regulations are more protective of special populations, such as children, the retarded, or prisoners. For these, parents or other responsible officials also have to give consent. Interviewing of any institutional population—schools, hospitals, prisons—also requires the consent of those in charge.

Since any language in the introduction that appears to invite people to choose not to be interviewed will in fact reduce the response rate, we thereby risk biasing the results of the study by losing certain kinds of respondents from the sample.

Eligibility. The second part of the introduction identifies the correct respondent in the housing unit according to: (1) the interviewer's respondent-selection procedure, and (2) our definition of the study population—voters, permanent residents, newspapers readers, or whatever. If no one in the household qualifies by the standards set for the study, the interview is quickly but pleasantly terminated.

As explained in Chapter 2, the Model Survey is *not* a candidate study. If it were, the number of eligible voters in the household would be part of the respondent-selection key (changing ''number of women'' to ''number of registered female voters''), or it would be part of the warm-up section. A screening procedure that is used to determine eligible voters is described in a later section.

The Model Survey, instead, is a study of adult residents who are of voting age and who are United States citizens. Since aliens and nonresidents are excluded from the survey population of Model City adults, it is necessary to eliminate them in the selection process. This is done with three eligibility questions:

> How many people . . 18 years or older . . presently
> are living in your household?
>
> How many of these people are citizens of the
> United States?
>
> How many of these are residents of Model City?

The number of eligible adults is not known until the third question. When there are two or more adults in the household, the next question—''How many of them are women?''—is used with the respondent-selection key to establish which person is to be interviewed (see Figure 2.8). If there is only one adult, the question about the number of women is obviously unnecessary.

If the person at the door is not an adult or clearly is not the designated respondent, say (do not ask):

> According to the research method used in this survey,
> I have to ask a few questions of the (woman) (youngest
> man) (etc.) in your household. Would you please call
> (him) (her) to the door.

If the person at the door could be the correct respondent, say:

> According to the research method used in this survey,
> I have to ask a few questions of the (man) (oldest
> woman) (etc.) in your household. Would that be you?

When the correct respondent appears—now, or later by appointment—the introduction is repeated. Then the interviewer moves right into the warm-up questions.

Warm-up Questions

The eligibility questions are innocuous, but they serve to start building respondent rapport. Furthering the warm-up process, questions about a respondent's residence are useful because they are specific, nonthreatening, and relevant to the analysis:

> About how long have you lived in Model City.

> About how long have you lived at this address.

The next rapport-building question asks respondents to talk about some relatively "safe" subject allied to the topic being studied. Even if our survey is interested in the attention respondents pay to political news in the mass media, it's best to make no reference to newspapers, magazines, or television yet, because it may sound suspiciously like a sales pitch. Instead, try:

> Judging by your own experience, or by what you
> read or hear, what do you think are two or three
> of the <u>most</u> important problems facing Model City
> today?

With the latitude given, respondents find this an easy question. Also, it prepares the ground for specific questions to follow, since respondents may raise some of the topics themselves that the interviewer will cover later, which will underscore the salience of those topics to the respondent when they eventually come up.

The next question in the series should begin to direct attention to specific but still safe subjects, such as traffic congestion, recreation, or city services. In the Model we ask:

> A new subway system is being built in Model City.
> Do you think the subway will help solve traffic
> congestion, will not help solve traffic congestion,
> or won't make any difference?

Of course, no questions are wasted in the warm-up process. Each must be important to the analysis, or its use is unwarranted.

Main Questions

Once respondents are sufficiently warmed to the task, we can tackle specific issues. Questions now may concern efficiency in government, public employee strikes, bond issues, candidate personalities, taxes, farm price supports, law enforcement, public welfare, respondent political participation, or whatever is being studied.

Order. However good specific questions may be, the *sequence* of these questions is of critical concern. As the interview builds, respondents will become more aware of its specific topics. This will focus attention on the general theme, and therefore may unduly cue them to overemphasize the role of the topic in their lives. Because each question adds information, they must proceed from general to specific and from one aspect of the subject to the next in a well-thought-out pattern. Thus the following order might be advisable for this sequence:

```
What do you think are the most serious problems
facing Model City today?

As a problem, would you say that crime in Model City
is very serious, pretty serious, or not very serious?

Would you say that air pollution in Model City is a
very serious problem, pretty serious, or not a very
serious problem?

Do you think automobiles cause most of the air pollution
in this city, quite a bit of it, a little pollution,
or not much at all?

Do you think driving automobiles should . . or should not
be prohibited in the center city area when air pollution
is high?
```

Looking back over this group of questions we see that asking the later questions before the earlier ones would have biased the result of the ultimate answers. If the specific-problem question on the seriousness of air pollution were asked before the general questions, pollution would show up more often in the respondents' own identification of problems. If the first mention of air pollution were not buried among some questions on other problems, it would have revealed to respondents too early that this was to be the main topic of interest. If the proposed policy—prohibition of driving—was raised before a judgment about the relative contribution of cars to the problem, the respondent's evaluation would be changed.

Likewise, sequence is important in candidate studies:

```
What do you think are the ideal qualities a United
States senator ought to have?

Do you happen to know who is running for the United
States Senate seat from this state in the election
next fall?

Well, the present senator who is running is Phil
Ibuster . . From what you have heard, how would
you rate Ibuster as to how much he has done for the
people of this state?

How would you rate him as to how much he's influenced
by labor unions?  (etc.)
```

```
As you may know, Gus Challenger is also running
for the Senate seat against Phil Ibuster . .
How would you rate Gus Challenger on how much
he's likely to do for the people of this state?

How would you rate Challenger as to how much he's
influenced by labor unions?  (etc.)

If the election were being held tomorrow, would
you probably vote for Ibuster or Challenger?
```

Again, if the questions were asked in a different order, different results would be forthcoming. Of course, since *any* order is going to affect results, trade-offs must be made. We simply wish to avoid unanticipated effects by making a reasoned decision on which order the questions should take to be most effective—or least harmful—for the purpose of the study being done.

Demographic Questions

The final section of the questionnaire contains personal items. As mentioned earlier, people readily answer questions about age, income, religion, and political affiliation. But positioned early in the questionnaire these items might scare respondents off, since they might think that prying into these things is the purpose of the study, rather than recognizing that personal data is gathered merely to analyze other substantive questions. By the time the interview reaches its final stage, answers to personal questions come easily and naturally.

Although there is no set formula for getting such data, some practical suggestions are offered here for various demographic items commonly asked in surveys. As always, we would choose for any survey only those questions that have a plausible utility for analysis. A glance at Checklist 10 before completing the questionnaire will ensure that we don't miss a significant item, one that might be critical to the description of respondents who answer a certain way on the main topic under study. The following discussion doesn't go into depth on any item but does give at least one suggestion per item that has proved useful. Each could be the basis of a methodological study in its own right.

CHECKLIST 10

Demographic Items

1. Home Ownership
2. Household Composition
3. Principal Wage Earner
4. Marital Status
5. Education

   6.   Occupation
   7.   Spouse's Occupation
   8.   Income
   9.   Group Membership
   10. Union Membership
   11. Political Affiliation
   12. Voting Participation
   13. Candidate Preferences
   14. Religion
   15. Ethnic Group and Race
   16. Languages Spoken
   17. Age
   18. Gender
   19. Name, Address, and Phone Number(s)

Home Ownership. The interviewer should ask: "Do you own your own home, or are you renting it?" Those paying on mortgages are considered to be owners. Some people may be living with relatives, or may be unrelated lodgers, and residential businesses, parsonages, and welfare homes are also occasionally found. People in apartments may own them—as cooperatives or condominiums. Of renters ask: "How much rent do you pay each month?"

Household Composition. To learn the number of people in the household, ask: "How many people, including yourself, live at this address?" However, parents will sometimes include children who are really away in the armed forces or at college as "living" at that address. So if you want only actual residents, first ask: "Are there any children living here?" (IF "YES" ASK: "How many?"). The respondent-selection key will have already ascertained the total number of adults, so you need ask only about children living there. If you wish to know the total number of children born into the family, another question to that effect is needed.

Principal Wage Earner. Formerly we asked, "Who is the head of this household?" It was common, especially in lower-income families to find female household heads. Now, with many multiple-earner families, we may be more interested to know who makes the most money or who makes most decisions. Ask: "Who is the main wage earner in this household," and, if it is not the respondent, "What is your relationship to him/her?"

Marital Status. Because of rapid changes in life styles, we can't assume we know the respondent's marital status. Ask: "What is your marital status?" This avoids emotional words, such as: "Are you married, single, widowed, divorced, separated, or what?'' You may use this latter question as a probe to help anyone who doesn't understand ''marital status.'' Don't actually ask, but you can determine who fits the category ''unmarried, living with others'' from information about household composition in the respondent-selection part of the introduction. This avoids a frontal assault on the exact nature of the relationship, unless that in fact is of importance to the analysis.

Education. An efficient way of learning respondents' education is to ask first: ''What is the name of the last school you attended?'' You may decide not to analyze the answers, but determining the last school attended usually indicates the highest possible grade level. This inhibits respondents from inflating education. Then ask: ''What was the last grade you completed in school?'' Asking for the last completed grade reduces the tendency to include partial years in high school or college. The stress is on grade level and not education per se. This avoids the patronizing question ''How much education did you have?''

If the questionnaire does not use exact numbers of years (0–16+) to measure years of education, suggested categories are:

0–8	years—grade school
9–11	years—some high school
12	years—completed high school
	other—post-high-school training
13–15	years—some college
16	years—completed college
16+	years—graduate or professional school

With the spread of vocational and technical education and subprofessional training schools, it is no longer sufficient to ask only about formal or traditional classroom learning. Therefore, ask as a probe: ''Have you ever enrolled in any other kind of vocational or professional training school?'' Or, ''Have you ever had any other kind of schooling or job training?'' (IF ''YES'': ''What kind of school or course was it?'' ''How many months or years did you attend?'' and ''Did you get a diploma or certificate?'' Classify this data as ''other''—beyond high school but not college level.

Occupation. With more than half the married women in the United States employed outside the home, we no longer are interested only in the husband's job. Therefore we use a duplicate section of the questionnaire for the spouse. If a young respondent living with parents is primarily a student, we will want to classify him/her as such, but we will also want to record the main occupation of the household.

Getting a meaningful description of occupations is most difficult. There are thousands of different job classifications, and workers often use cryptic job titles. Moreover, one spouse is often vague about the other's work. Interviewers aren't familiar enough with the argots of different vocations to code responses accurately in the field. The best we can do is ask, ''What is your job . . . your occupation?'' and instruct interviewers to probe for at least a two- or three-word description to determine the actual nature of the work. Sometimes it is necessary to learn the place of work (stockyards), so a confusing job title (''sticker'') can be associated with the probable nature of the work. If a respondent specifies only a place of work (''highway department''), the interviewer will have to probe by asking, ''Just what do you do?'' in order to ascertain the skill level involved. The ''specification probe'' used to describe occupations is illustrated in Chapter 5.

It might be useful in some studies to know what industry the particular job is in. Thus, in a study about attitudes on energy conservation, a secretary in a university may have different attitudes from one working in the mining industry.

In the survey office, coders classify occupations according to some scheme. Checklist 11 is a simplified version of the U.S. Census job classification system used in the Model Survey.

CHECKLIST 11

Census Occupational Classification [a]

1. *Executive, Administrative, and Managerial*—Chief executives and public administrators; financial, personnel, purchasing, and marketing managers; educational administrators; health, property, mining, construction, food service, and entertainment managers; management-related occupations: accountants, labor relations specialists, and government inspectors.

2. *Professional Specialties*—Architects, engineers, computer scientists, natural and social scientists, health diagnosticians and treatment specialists, teachers, librarians, lawyers, writers, artists, entertainers, and athletes.

3. *Technical, Sales, and Administrative Support*—Health technologists; engineering and science technicians; airline pilots, computer programmers, and legal assistants; sales supervisors and salespeople in mining, manufacturing, wholesale, retail, real estate, insurance, advertising, and personal goods and services; cashiers, door-to-door salesworkers, models, auctioneers, office supervisors, secretaries, interviewers, ticket agents, order clerks, file clerks, bookkeepers, telephone operators, mail handlers, messengers, dispatchers, meter readers, adjustors, bank tellers, and teachers' aides.

4. *Service*—Private household occupations: cooks and child care workers; protective service occupations: firefighters, police, and guards; food preparers, bartenders, waiters, cooks, dental assistants, nursing aides, janitors, barbers, hair dressers, ushers, and public child care workers.

[a] *Source:* U.S. Bureau of Census, *Classified Index of Industries and Occupations* (Washington, 1980). *See also, Alphabetic Index of Industries and Occupations.* The Census uses a 3-digit code for each job and industry.

5. *Agricultural, Forestry, and Fishing*—Farm operators and managers, farm workers, nursery workers, animal caretakers, product graders, forestry workers, and fishers.

6. *Precision Production, Craft and Repair*—Mechanics and repairers of automotive, electrical, heating, and office machines; construction supervisors and tradeworkers; miners, tool and die makers, machinists, engravers, sheet metal workers, cabinetmakers, press operators, dressmakers, optical goods makers, dental appliance technicians, electrical assemblers, butchers, and bakers; gas, electrical, water, and sewage plant operators.

7. *Operators, Fabricators, and Laborers*—Lathe, milling, punch, stamping, and rolling machine operators; metal molding, casting, and plating machine operators; sawing, sanding, and tacking machine operators; typesetters; knitting, sewing, laundry, packaging, cooling, painting, washing, and furnace machine operators; projectionists; fabricators and welders; hand-cutting, trimming, and grinding workers; production inspectors; motor vehicle operators, railroad conductors, engineers, ship captains and sailors, and longshore equipment operators; grader, dozer, and industrial truck operators; helpers, garbage collectors, stevedores, garage and service station workers, and laborers.

The Model Survey adds these categories:

8. Students.
9. Homemakers not employed outside the home.
0. Retired, unemployed.

From these categories we code and analyze whatever detail of occupation suits the needs of our study.

A more specific (2-digit) code has been developed to distinguish among jobs in the major classifications, although based on the major subdivisions of the 1970 Census.[10]

For a study specifically about occupations, we would use the Department of Labor's more systematic 9-digit code.[11]

Actually, the census classifications may not be adequate if our study deals with

[10]John A. Sonquist and William C. Dunkelberg, *Survey and Opinion Research: Procedures for Processing and Analysis* (New York: Prentice-Hall, 1977).

[11]*Dictionary of Occupational Titles,* 4th ed., Department of Labor, 1977. The 9-digit code system works as follows: The first 3 digits are codes for general occupations. The first digit represents the occupational category, the second digit is the occupation titles, and the third digit is an industry code. Thus, in the code 526 the 5 stands for processing occupations, the 2 is processors of food, and the 6 is cooking and baking occupations.

The fourth, fifth, and sixth digits are a classification of worker functions, the fourth having to do with data, the fifth with people, and the sixth with things. Thus if our worker is a 526.437, he or she would be dealing with computing data, supervising people, and handling things, all in the cooking or baking occupation. The seventh, eighth, and ninth digits represent the actual alphabetical title of the job.

the socioeconomic status aspect of occupations. There is little correlation between the professional and skill levels of the Census and the status accorded the various occupations by the public. Researchers have classified occupations by status, probably the best indicator of social class. One of these is shown as Checklist 12. The higher the number the greater the status.

CHECKLIST 12

Occupation Status Levels [a]

Code

90–96	Architects, lawyers, doctors.
85–89	Industrial engineers, managers, bankers, self-proprietors.
80–84	College professors, editors and reporters, electrical engineers, pharmacists, public administrators.
75–79	Accountants and auditors, manufacturing managers, insurance and real estate salespeople.
70–74	Designers, teachers, store buyers, auto dealers, stock salespeople.
65–69	Artists, draftspersons, clothing proprietors, advertising sales representatives, foremen.
60–64	Librarians, sports officials, postmasters, construction managers.
55–59	Funeral directors, railroad conductors, locomotive engineers.
50–54	Clergy, musicians, local officials, food store managers, mail carriers, toolmakers.
45–49	Surveyors, auto repair managers, office machine operators, linemen, airplane mechanics.
40–44	Cashiers, clerical workers, electricians, construction foremen, police officers.
35–39	Restaurant managers, retail sales clerks, radio and TV repairers, firefighters.
30–34	Building managers, service station owners, machinists, plumbers, deliverypersons.
25–30	Messengers, newsvendors, brickmasons, plasterers, ushers.
20–24	Shipping clerks, bakers, cabinetmakers, road machine operators, tailors.
15–20	Blacksmiths, carpenters, auto mechanics, painters, parking attendants.
10–14	Farmers, shoemakers, taxi drivers, hospital attendants, fishers.
5–9	Hucksters and peddlers, weavers, janitors, farm laborers, steel mill workers.
0–4	Coal miners, fabric mill operators, porters.

[a]Selected and adapted from Otis Dudley Duncan, ''A Socioeconomic Index for All Occupations,'' in Albert J. Reiss, Jr., et al., *Occupations and Social Status,* Free Press of Glencoe, 1961, pp 109–138. For a seven-point scale, compare W. Lloyd Warner, Marcia Meeker, and Kenneth Eells, ''Revised Scale for Rating Occupations,'' in Delbert C. Miller, *Handbook of Research Design and Social Measurement* 3d ed., (New York: McKay, 1977). The Census Bureau also classified occupations into a socioeconomic status score based on education and income of 1960 jobholders. U.S. Bureau of Census, *Socioeconomic Status* (Washington, D.C.: U.S. Government Printing Office, 1967).

The Center for Political Studies of the University of Michigan Institute for Social Research codes its election surveys by the Census detailed codes and both prestige indices.[12]

Income. Because financial status is a somewhat guarded item, a card showing different income groups is handed to the respondent. The categories are broad enough to permit some exaggeration, as will happen, but are specific enough for analysis, because the idea is to get respondents distributed into several groups relatively, whatever the specific value of each category might be. Since income is prestigious, we avoid direct reference to the amount of money brought home each week by saying:

> Here is a card showing different income groups
> (HAND RESPONDENT INCOME CARD). In terms of total
> family income each year, what is the letter of
> the group your family is in.

CARD
YEARLY INCOME OF FAMILY
(Confidential)

A--under $ 5,000

B--$ 5,000 - $ 7,999

C--$ 8,000 - $10,999

D--$11,000 - $13,999

E--$14,000 - $16,999

F--$17,000 - $19,999

G--$20,000 - $24,999

H--$25,000 - $29,999

I--$30,000 and over

As inflation and real income grow, the upper limits must be divided enough to separate respondents who don't really belong together in economic life style. It could be expected that this change in income categories over the years would make the groups noncomparable between surveys, but raising the figures and making an adjustment to reflect cost-of-living changes during analysis compensates.

Getting only the chief wage earner's income often does not tell the full income story, what with working women's income, unmarried couples pooling expenses, cooperative living, and employed children contributing to the family weal. In order to make sure of getting the full family figure, we ask: "Does anyone else living here contribute money to your family income?" If yes, either ask about each person individually, or be sure the respondent includes all such persons in the answer about

---

[12]See: 1972, 1974, 1976 *American National Election Series: Codebook,* (Ann Arbor: University of Michigan, 1976).

family income by using this form of the question:

> **Here is a card showing different income groups.**
> **(HAND RESPONDENT INCOME CARD). Including all**
> **sources of income, what is the letter of the group**
> **your family is in.**

Remember, though, that one or a few income questions will not reveal the family's discretionary income. First, the income reported may include only wages and salaries, while they may actually have other sources of income through inheritance, royalties, dividends, rentals, stocks, pensions, welfare payments, etc. Second, economic worth is not measured by cash flow alone. Personal possessions and property are other indicators of socioeconomic status. Farm families, by living partly off the land, may enjoy a higher level of living than their dollar income indicates. And, finally, on what and how a family spends its money varies. For example, a family in which both husband and wife work may actually have less discretionary income than a single-earner family, because of the expenses of child care or other dependents.

The distinction between gross income and net income must be addressed if farmers and other self-employed individuals are to be included in comparable data with employees.

Group Membership. To establish group activity, we ask: "Do you belong to any organizations . . . that is, groups like the PTA, or civic groups, clubs, professional associations, church groups, veterans organizations, and the like?" Then probe further, asking, "Any other? . . . bowling leagues? garden clubs?" In the Model, groups are classified according to the categories in Checklist 13. To obtain the degree of group participation, we can ask about the number of meetings attended during the last year, or what positions were held.

CHECKLIST 13

Group Classification

1. *Fraternal/Social*—Masons, Elks, Moose, Rotary, Optimist, Shrine, Toastmasters, Eastern Star, alumni associations, country clubs, and fraternities and sororities.
2. *Professional*—American Medical Association, American Association of University Professors, National Office-Manager Association, Radio-TV News Directors Association, American Institute of Banking.
3. *Public Affairs*—League of Women Voters, citizens leagues, American Civil Liberties Union, Parent-Teachers Association, NAACP, neighborhood improvement associations, citizens advisory councils, Common Cause.
4. *Public Service*—Red Cross, Civil Defense, Scout leaders, volunteer rescue squad, Sierra Club, Planned Parenthood.

5. *Business*—Chamber of Commerce, Goodwill Industries, development associations.
6. *Farm*—Farm Bureau Federation, National Farmers Union, National Farm Organization.
7. *Church or Religious* (apart from basic church affiliation)—Knights of Columbus, Ladies Aid and Guild, choir.
8. *Veteran/Patriotic*—American Legion, Veterans of Foreign Wars, National Guard, Reserve Officers Association.
9. *Cultural/Esthetic*—great books clubs, little theater groups, symphony associations.
0. *Hobby/Sports*—garden clubs, bridge clubs, dance groups, classic car clubs, golf clubs, bowling leagues.

Familiarity with community groups is necessary to classify the incredible variety of group names turned up in a survey. Interviewers should write down all of the group names mentioned for classification back in the survey office.

Note that in the Model Survey political party identification, trade-union membership, and religious affiliation are relevant enough to warrant separate questions.

Union Membership. Group membership questions will not always turn up union members. Because some people are sensitive to union membership questions, we do not ask bluntly, "Do you belong to a union?" Also, being in a union family, even if the respondent is not actually a union member, may be significant to attitudes. We ask: "Has anyone in this household ever been a member of a union?" (IF "YES":) "Is that person a member now?" and "Would that be you?"

Political Affiliation. To most people an inquiry about party affiliation is routine. To put the question in a nonthreatening form, we ask: "In politics, do you consider yourself a Democrat, a Republican, or a member of some other party?" People find it easy to say what they *consider* themselves to be. Adding "or a member of some other party" offers an escape hatch for those who like the feeling that other choices are available.

Including the alternative of Independent increases to unrealistic levels the number of people identifying themselves that way or claiming they "vote for the man and not the party." Being an Independent is a civically more prestigious alternative. Thus, we do not suggest it in the main question. When we encounter a volunteered "Independent" response, we add a *leaning* question: "Well, do you tend to lean more toward the Republicans or toward the Democrats?" Those who persist as "Independent" are so recorded. Based on responses to other voting questions, we should reserve a separate category for those respondents who are apolitical, rather than lumping them as Independents.

We usually want to know the strength of party affiliation:

```
"Would you call yourself a strong (Democrat)
(Republican) or a not very strong (Democrat)
(Republican)?"
```

Chapter 4 offers a suggested format for this question (see p. 206).

Voting Behavior. Voting behavior is a separate matter from party identification; many professed Republicans and Democrats cross party lines, and many Independents vote for the same party year after year. If the study centers on political participation, voting questions might appear in the body of the questionnaire. In a candidate survey, voting questions might appear in the introduction to eliminate probable nonvoters from the survey. But voting questions could well be included as routine demographic questions in a study less centrally focused on politics.

There are two decisions citizens must make about voting—whether to vote at all, and for whom to vote. Both of these need to be investigated. The Model Survey interviews nonvoters as well as voters, so rather than use questions about voting as a filter or screen for eliminating people from the sample, it distinguishes voters from nonvoters in the analysis by whether they differ on other questions. Because of the special difficulty of ascertaining who are likely voters, we will describe here some questions that can be used either in the introductory screen or in the demographic section to deal with voting behavior.

Screening Likely Voters. Difference in the questions used in screening likely voters is one of the reasons for periodic discrepancies between findings of major polls, such as the Gallup Poll and the Harris Survey. Until there is more systematic research, it will remain a toss-up as to whether survey differences are due to screening procedures, sampling methods, question wording, dates of interviewing, response alternatives, poor interviewer selection and training, interviewer-respondent differences, or any number of other possibilities.

The Model's screening device for identifying likely voters consists of questions to determine *eligibility* to vote, *knowledge* of voting place, *interest* in the election, *certainty* in plans to vote and evidence of *past voting*.

Screening Likely Voters.
(Before an election)

a. *Ascertain whether respondents are registered or planning to register to vote:*

```
As you may know, there's going to be an election
in Model City on November 2. Right now, are you
registered . . so that you can vote in that
election, if you want to?

(IF "NO" OR "DON'T KNOW," ASK:)

Are you planning to register in time to vote
in the November 2 election, or not?
```

Note: Residents of states with at-the-polls registration would be asked:

> Are you planning to register at the polling place
> on election day?

b.   *Find out if they know where to vote:*

> If somebody wants to vote on election day, where
> around here do they go to vote . . what place?

c.   *Gauge their interest in the election:*

> Would you say you are very interested, fairly
> interested, not too interested, or not interested
> at all in this coming election for mayor?

d.   *Get a statement of their certainty to vote:*

> How certain are you to vote in this election . .
> Right now, would you say that you definitely
> will, probably will, probably will not, or
> definitely will not vote in that election?

e.   *Obtain evidence of past voting:*

> Thinking back to the election last year for
> governor, were you registered so that you could
> have voted in that election if you wanted to?
> (IF "YES" ASK:) Did you have a chance to vote
> in that election, or weren't you able to?
>
> (IF "VOTED":) Which person, Jason Bagel the
> Republican . . or Henry Lox the Democrat . .
> did you vote for for Governor . . or did you
> vote for another candidate?
>
> How about the election for United States
> Senator in 1980. Were you registered to
> vote in that election? (IF "YES") Did you
> have a chance to vote . . or weren't you
> able to?
>
> (IF "VOTED":) Which person, Barbara Pole the
> Democrat, or Chuckley Snort the Republican . .
> did you vote for . . or did you vote for another
> candidate?

Following are three groups of people who, by their answers to the screening questions, are profiled as "likely," "marginal," and "unlikely" voters:

LIKELY VOTERS
1.   Are registered to vote.
2.   Know where to vote.
3.   Are very interested in the election.

4. Say they definitely will vote.
5. Voted in previous elections for which eligible.

MARGINALLY LIKELY VOTERS

1. Registered/plan to register to vote.
2. Do/don't know where to vote.
3. Fairly interested in the election.
4. Probably will vote.
5. Voted in at least one previous election for which eligible.

UNLIKELY VOTERS

1. Don't know if they are registered/don't plan to register.
2. Don't know where to vote.
3. Are not very interested in the election.
4. Say they probably or definitely will not vote.
5. Voted in no previous election for which eligible.

There are many possible combinations of answers, each producing a different profile. (A matrix enabling the interviewer to decide which persons to classify in each way is shown in Chapter 4.) The specific profile of likely voters may differ from study to study, depending on the purpose. Some researchers use tougher criteria than others. If the screen is being used to eliminate respondents from further questioning, a good reason for using softer criteria is money. Voter turnout varies from around 25 percent of the eligible voters in local elections to 60 to 75 percent in some areas in national elections. If only one out of every two or three people encountered (who are 18-plus years of age, residents, and citizens) is likely to vote, interviewing costs increase rapidly as we become more particular about which people we're willing to include. Many candidate studies are done "piggyback" as part of commercial studies. In these studies respondents may be selected for the purposes of the commercial sponsors, so the interviewing service will be unwilling to break off a contact to look for another who will vote. For a candidate survey desiring 600 completed interviews of likely voters, this means paying for 1200 interviews, an unrealistic prospect.

Even in a candidate survey it is not wise to quit the interview immediately upon determining we have snared an unlikely voter. In this instance, the interviewer should skip to the demographic section to pick up some key items. These will tell us more about the persons the political process is not reaching and will check the representativeness of our total sample contacts—likely voters are not representative of the population.

When all is said and done, voter screening questions aren't very effective. Up to 80 percent of the respondents may pass as likely voters, far higher than subsequent turnout on election day. And some of those who are classified as *unlikely* voters will vote, turned out by some last-minute party or a candidate's appeals to vote. If, in a before-the-election survey analysis of likely and unlikely voters, the two groups show no major differences—say, on candidate preferences—there's no problem with estimating the breakdown between candidates. But often we aren't that lucky.

Obtaining Candidate Preference. The candidate preference of likely voters can be measured by asking who is favored and how strongly. For example:

a. *Introduce the candidates by saying:*

> As you may know, the two candidates for mayor of Model City are Democrat Morris Dance and Republican Roland Rock. If the election were being held today, which candidate . . Rock or Dance . . would you vote for?

b. *Test the intensity of their choice:*

> How sure are you that you'd vote for (INSERT NAME) . . very sure, fairly sure, not too sure, or not sure at all?

The reason for mentioning the party designation with the candidate is that, since it appears on the ballot, the question in this form simulates what the voters will see at the polls. In the analysis, the candidates' relative strength should be estimated by people's likelihood to vote as well as by the strength of their support.

We can get other measures of intensity and, therefore, presumably can predict the likelihood that a vote will be cast in the intended direction (as well as obtaining clues from issue questions about the nature of each candidate's support) by asking:

> How much difference would it make to you if (INSERT NAME OF OTHER CANDIDATE) were to win the election for mayor?

> Regardless of your choice, which candidate . . Dance or Rock . . do you think is likely to win the election for mayor?

We may wish to ask the preference questions of the unlikely voters as well, to see whether turnout could affect the result:

> If you were to vote, which candidate would you favor . . Dance or Rock?

Once an election is over, the questions change from *intention* to *behavior*.

(After an election)
a. *Find out if they are registered.*

> The election for mayor of Model City was held this last November 2d. Regardless whether you voted, were you registered so that you could have voted in that election . . if you wanted to?

b. *Ask if they voted.*

> Sometimes people find it hard to vote in city
> elections . . because they were ill or couldn't
> get away from work . . or something like that.
> In your own case, did you happen to vote in
> the November 2d election, or didn't you have
> a chance to?

c. *Find out who they voted for or favored to win:*

> (IF "VOTED":) Morris Dance and Roland Rock were
> the two candidates for mayor of Model City in
> the November 2d election. Which man . . Rock
> or Dance . . did you vote for, or did you decide
> not to vote for either?

> (IF "DIDN'T VOTE":) As you may recall, Morris
> Dance and Roland Rock were the two candidates
> for mayor in the November 2d election. Which
> man . . Rock or Dance . . did you favor to
> win that election?

Giving the face-saving excuse for not voting violates the general principle of not loading questions. Nonetheless, this "counterloading" works well to reduce the inflation of voting claims.

Religion. We start with either of two questions that are easy to answer: "Do you happen to have a religious preference?" or "What . . . if any . . . is your religious preference?" These make no assumption of church attendance nor do either imply that one has to have a religious preference. Further, the religion in one's background is not always the preferred religion, so we avoid that question. Asking one of our alternatives allows respondents the choice of specifying the religion with which they identify, if any.

Religious denominations can be classified in great detail or as simply as:

> Protestant
> Catholic
> Jewish
> Other
> None

Or, if the purpose of the study or the religious configuration of the community made this desirable, a probe question can be used: "What church or denomination would that be?"

If importance of church activity is relevant, ask:

> Would you say you go to (church/synagogue) every week . .
> almost every week . . once or twice a month . . a few
> times a year . . or never?

Ethnic Group and Race. Ethnic identification, including native language and race, is important in explaining attitudes. These characteristics have, however, become blurred. Nationality has become mixed with race and native language. Spanish-speaking people (''Hispanics'') are variously distinguished as ''Puerto Ricans,'' ''Latinos,'' ''Chicanos,'' ''Mexican-Americans,'' and ''Spanish-Americans.'' Sometimes a racial distinction is added: ''Hispanic-Black'' and ''Hispanic-White.''

These combined characteristics result from efforts to study significant groups in the population both more intensively and more specifically to locale. A study in Los Angeles necessarily will be concerned with people whose roots lie in Mexico. A study in New York must deal with more people whose ancestry is Puerto Rican. The Hispanic Black/White distinction mirrors the differences in treatment of such persons in our society and, thus, how they may differ in their behavior—voting, shopping, working, whatever.

The selection of ethnic/racial categories depends on the type and scope of the survey. Unless sampling many thousands of people or deliberately oversampling specific groups, a national survey of perhaps 1500 people is not likely to encounter more than three racial types and a handful of Native Americans. The approximate proportion of each group in the United States is shown in Table 3.2.

The national polls usually use the racial terms ''White'' and ''Nonwhite,'' or perhaps ''White,'' ''Black,'' and ''Other,'' because the small numbers of Orientals and Native Americans usually found do not warrant separate analysis.

Interviewers *observe* and record racial groups. Although not taboo, it usually isn't necessary to *ask* a respondent's race. If there is doubt, probe questions can be provided. Many interviewers have never had contact with some racial groups outside of stereotypic individuals and will misclassify people; for example, Pakistanis, Asiatic-Indians, Arabians, and other darker-skinned (''brown'') Caucasians are sometimes classified as Negroid. This fact alone casts doubt on the usefulness of the four racial categories for surveys dealing with social and political problems. What makes people members of any ethnic group is their perception of themselves and others' perceptions of them.

Table 3.2.   Racial Percentages of U.S. Population

Race	Percent
Caucasion	84
Negroid	12
Oriental	3
American Indian	1
Total	100

The Model Survey uses these racial/ethnic categories:

>American Indian/Native American
>Asian-American/Oriental
>Black/Afro-American/Negro
>Hispanic-black/Spanish-speaking black
>Hispanic-white/Spanish speaking white
>White/Caucasian
>Indeterminable/Other, SPECIFY:_____

We have found that interviewers are more comfortable working with these seven distinctions than with less. If too few of some categories turn up in the sample, we can combine categories during analysis.

Many times we are interested in ethnicity or nationality. Since all persons in the Model Sample are citizens, we ask: "Other than American, what is your family background . . . your nationality?" Some researchers ask the question as: "What country do your ancestors come from?" But history may not reveal how people identify themselves today. "What is the country of your national origin?" is confusing to late generations of immigrants from long ago. "What ethnic group do you belong to?" can stir resentment from those who do not think of themselves as being in a separate category. Some studies give cards to respondents and ask them to describe their background similar to this:

>Asia
>Pacific
>Indian Subcontinent
>North Africa/Mediterranean
>Africa
>North Europe
>South Europe
>East Europe
>North America
>South America

This kind of choice puts an enormous burden on respondents, because this is asking them to make distinctions we can't make ourselves. Neither is asking interviewers to judge nationality by geographic region any less foolhardy. The Model questionnaire records verbatim the countries that respondents choose to name and recodes them later in the office to fit the analysis scheme used.

Language. If the interview is being conducted in English, ask: Do members of your family usually speak any other languages besides English?" If the answer is affirmative (which sometimes will be obvious), ask: "What language is that?" Then:

"Which language . . . English or (INSERT NAME) . . . is spoken most of the time here?"

Age. The interviewer should say (not ask): "And what is your age." If the respondent hesitates to answer, the interviewer adds: "That is, your age at your last birthday." This simple alteration often gets responses from those respondents who are on the verge of refusing. If the person still balks, it's best not to ask again but simply record an estimated age with a question mark after it. Age groupings are generated at the analysis stage.

Gender. Interviewers observe and record without asking whether the respondent is male or female.

Name, Address, and Phone Number. The demographic section ends with the respondent's name, address, and phone number. These may be needed to verify interviewers' work or, possibly, to recontact respondents in a panel study. The information must be asked in a routine way, inasmuch as we have guaranteed confidentiality to respondents. Interviewers say (not ask):

```
And your name is .. (IF NECESSARY: "Your name is confidential;
it's just so my office knows I really conducted this interview.")

____ _____

Just to be sure, the address here is _____

_____  Apt._____

And the phone number is _____
```

The last words written in the questionnaire are: "Thank you very much."

IMPROVEMENT OF QUESTIONS

Once questions have been written, we submit them for testing to two diverse groups—professional critics and members of the public for whom they were written.

Critique

Reading this chapter should have made clear that no amount of forethought, intense creative thinking, and outside criticism is too much to expend on the delicate task of question wording in any survey. Any literate person—other than the drafter—can point out weaknesses in questions, but consulting an experienced survey researcher at this point is a gilt-edged investment. Subject-matter specialists can suggest changes to improve precision and can ensure that the subject has been covered completely. The client, or other data users, should also review the questionnaire, but the researcher must retain the final judgment on question wording and placement.

Pretest

The final test of the questions comes from trying them out on people just like the typical respondents. This is called a pretest (see Chapter 5). The pretest will point out weaknesses in wording and adequacy of responses. We will find countless places needing rephrasing and polishing. Some questions may have to be completely replaced, or simply junked. This is so inevitable, despite every effort at the drafting stage, that we would never let a survey go into the field without an adequate pretest.

Now, with the pretest behind us, we are satisfied the questions are good—capable of eliciting a response and reliable in measuring a concept across a diverse population. We also believe they are valid—the right questions for the problem asked in the right way, based on our first-hand familiarity with the problems and populations being studied and our thorough search of existing information.

Having met these criteria, we can be fairly certain that our questions will be properly operational: they mean what they are supposed to mean to all people; they measure what they are supposed to measure; they provide answers that the interviewers and respondents can agree on without reservation; and they produce results that researchers and clients can agree are useful for problem solving. Arranging the questions to facilitate asking them and recording the answers is the concern of Chapter 4.

QUESTIONS IN OTHER SURVEYS

The principles of question wording described above apply to other in-person, telephone, and mail surveys. The major difference is the control we gain or lose over respondents' exposure to questions. Another difference is in the handling of technical subjects and of demographic items.

As before, we will look at two other kinds of face-to-face surveys—panel studies and election-day intercept surveys at the voting place.

Panel Studies

Two difficulties that frustrate panel studies are that people drop out of the panel between waves and people's answers become conditioned by reinterviewing.

We recommended in Chapter 2 that a large, rotating sample design be used to cope with the loss of some respondents and learning by others. But panel studies have implications for questioning too. Researchers sometimes make the mistake of dropping some of the demographic questions after asking them on the first wave. This allows substituting other questions, based on the belief that information about a person's religion, income, education, and occupation is not likely to change between waves. There are, however, some reasons for keeping these original questions.

The Model asks all demographic information again at each reinterview. Several factors account for this: (1) We must establish by research whether personal characteristics in fact change, and over what period of time that happens. (2) Changes in demographic characteristics may or may not be an explanation for changes in the behavior under study. We cannot risk an unmeasured change in some independent variable being a possible explanation of new behavior. (3) Tracking demographic characteristics over time is the best check we have on sample representativeness at all waves. Doing this also enables us to pinpoint which people are dropping out of the study; we may be reinterviewing a biased subsample of the original group. And (4) it is the very assumption that demographic characteristics are least likely to change within a study period that compels us to get them on all waves, as these are our firmest estimate of the reliability (consistency) of survey data over time.

Panel questioning raises another problem, because reinterviewing influences people's answers. The effects of reinterviewing are not always the same. Some people become more sophisticated—their interest in and knowledge of the subject have been increased. Some people become strongly opinionated on the subject, although their opinions were vague or unclear before. Some tend to freeze in their answers, not wishing to change from a previously stated position, although they may actually feel differently about it now. And some expand on previous answers, even changing them to avoid seeming to repeat themselves.

One implication of all this for panel studies is the need to use more than a single measure of key concepts in any single questionnaire. This enables us to check the consistency of each measure in relation to others on a single wave, as well as consistency of each measure between waves.

Moreover, related measures of the same concept, used together, are usually more stable than any one measure alone. Reinterviewing may cause people to change answers to any given question, but it is unlikely to change the general direction of their feelings or the overall pattern of their behavior. In addition, the rotating panel design, with some first-time respondents in each wave, enables us to compare different groups of respondents to see whether and how answers are influenced by repeated interviewing.

Panel studies must employ special face-saving care to make it easy for respondents to admit *on more than one occasion* to nonprestigious or unpopular answers. If we intend to see the same people again, we have to make sure of our welcome. Embarrassing or tension-producing questions are a sure way to increase refusal rates on the next round. We may get away once with careless questions, but seldom twice with the same people. Also, we should be mindful of the conditioning impact of our subject matter. Highly emotional, controversial, or otherwise threatening subjects are more likely to be remembered over time.

Intercept Surveys

There are severe restrictions on the type and number of questions that can be asked successfully on intercept ballots. Election-day exit polls have a single objective: to report a sample vote fast and add a little color for broadcast or print commentary. Intercept studies are relatively recent at polling places, dating from the mid-1960s, but they have been around for years at supermarkets and shopping malls in the form of marketing studies.

The methods of conducting an election intercept survey are described in Chapters 1 and 2. Usually the "ballot" handed to the respondent is targeted toward learning which candidates were voted for, with a few demographics, and perhaps answers to a couple of issue questions. It also has the interviewer observe and record gender, race, and estimated age group. (For a facsimile of an encounter ballot, see Figure 4, page 228.)

Upon determining the designated respondent emerging from the voting place (see Chapter 5), the interviewer records three identifying code numbers at the top of the form; the interviewer selects them from memory, so that the complete code as shown below is not seen by the respondent.

A = *Gender*	B = *Race*	C = *Age*
1—Male	1—White	1—Under 35
2—Female	2—Black	2—35–55
	3—Oriental	3—55 and over
	4—Other	

The observation codes are subject to some error. In the quest for speedy reports—and wanting to avoid any antagonism—we accept age estimates as useful information but something less than hard data. The "4—other" race code can be assigned a specific meaning (for example, Chicano) at voting places where that will be useful for analysis.

The interviewer briefly introduces the survey verbally (i.e., the introduction is not printed on the ballot): "This is an election news poll. (HAND BALLOT TO PERSON.) Would you just mark this secret ballot the same way you voted inside, and put it into our Election News ballot box."

Besides containing blocks in which to check the candidates voted for in this election, the ballot may also inquire about candidates supported in a previous election, as well as identifying a sharply limited set of demographic categories, say, party affiliation, union membership, and income group. Sometimes the reverse side of the ballot is used to get respondents' yes/no or favor/oppose positions on a few major campaign issues.

Today's intercept survey trend is toward adding more questions, but this increases the risk of noncompletion greatly. More conventional voter surveys are also done on election day, perhaps by telephoning people after they have voted, in order to have time for a longer questionnaire. But the value of the streamlined intercept ballot is the speed and relative ease with which results can be transcribed by telephone to the newspaper city desk, to local TV stations, or to national television networks for election night commentary. Obviously, to realize this value the ballot must be kept short.

A factor that distinguishes the intercept survey from other face-to-face surveys is the lack of control over respondents and responses. Interviewing is hectic. The voting places are crowded at peak times of the day, and people are rushing to get in and get away. The interviewer has barely enough time to judge which person to interview, mark the observation codes, give a hasty introduction, push the ballot into a perhaps skeptical hand, and turn to the next respondent. This is not like an exchange over coffee in a living room typical of an in-the-home survey, and the same results should not be expected. And by turning the ballot over to the respondent to mark, the interviewer loses much control over the respondent's exposure to questions, understanding of the task, and recording of answers. A corrective in election-day intercepts is to increase the number of interviewers (and costs) to try to collect more data by personal interviewing and larger questionnaires.

Telephone Surveys

Most questions that can be asked in a personal interview can be asked as well in a telephone survey. Generally telephone surveys are briefer than personal interviews, partly because it is easier for respondents to hang up, and partly because speed and cost are usually the reasons for doing a telephone survey. Questions tend to be less complicated than in the face-to-face setting. We avoid free-response, probing questions not because of their complexity but because interviewers and respondents exchange only verbal cues. Respondents tend to talk more rapidly, with fewer pauses, and at greater length on the telephone than in person. That's because they can't see the interviewer, so they don't know their questioner is faltering in trying to keep up with writing lengthy answers.

On the other hand, we don't necessarily avoid complex questions in telephone surveys (although we don't want interviewers explaining questions on their own). If a question cannot be understood by a substantial number of respondents, it is poorly constructed and should have been corrected or discarded after the pretest. If the respondent simply cannot answer such a question, we prefer to rest with this information rather than having interviewers reinterpreting the question.

There are three important differences between telephone and face-to-face interviewing: (1) we have greater control over respondents' exposure to questions; (2) there is an additional burden on the telephone introduction; and (3) we rely more on probes for demographic questions.

Control. The respondent has no idea of the sequence of questions and can glean none by peeking at the questionnaire pages or watching the interviewer for telltale clues, giving the interviewer more control. Moreover, as discussed in Chapter 5, we can exercise greater control over the interviewers' reading of questions through monitoring their calls if interviewing is done from a central place.

Introduction. The same rules that apply to the doorstep introduction apply to the telephone introduction. However, it is easier to refuse an unseen caller than to chase someone off the doorstep. Too, the telephone call is more likely to be suspected of being a nuisance call or sales pitch. Thus the telephone introduction must grab respondents' attention immediately and hold it until we can complete the respondent-selection key process. While the telephone refusal rate is at least as low as personal interview rates, nearly all (98 percent) of the refusals occur at the point of introduction.[13]

To improve response rates, it is particularly effective to load the introduction with as much prestige as possible—always, of course, being truthful—for example:

> Hello .. I'm calling from TV News in Los Angeles. We're doing a national research study for our television news programs. Including yourself, how many people living in your household are 18 years old or older?

Here we immediately mention the prestigious, noncommercial, nonpartisan sponsor: TV News. We say that we're calling from Los Angeles because it makes an impression on people to know the city they're being called from, particularly if it's from out of state. We convey the impression of a *national* undertaking, not just some local project. We stress that it's a *research study*, not a sales pitch. It's being done for *television*, which now has the greatest credibility of any social institution. And it is for our *news programs*—therefore, serious and important.

Notice that the first part of the *respondent-selection key* is built into the introduction. There is no hesitation in getting right into the interview. We try to involve people in the enterprise before their resistance builds. Very young children, who sometimes pick up the phone, speak unintelligibly, and hang up, may present a special problem. The interviewer can only call back. We discourage interviewers, upon hearing a youngster's voice, from saying, "Hi, honey, is your mommy home?" This has caused refusals from irate 20- to 30-year-old women with

---

[13]Gerald Hursh-César, CBS News Election Unit, *op. cit.*, 1970.

youthful-sounding voices who resent being "honeyed" by strangers impugning their status.

Demographics. Mistaking adults' voices for children's illustrates the problem of getting demographic information by telephone. Unable to see their respondents, interviewers have no basis for observing racial characteristics, estimating age, counting preschool children, and sometimes even noting gender; it is impossible to describe other physical characteristics of the household and often hard to interpret whether a respondent's silence represents thoughtfulness, distraction, or ignorance.

On the other hand, with the cloak of anonymity that the telephone gives respondents, we have very few problems with refusals on demographic information. Because interviewers must rely on only verbal cues, however, we build, as a standard component, specific *probe questions* into the body of each demographic question. The following are examples of various probes used in different demographic categories.

Age. Two probes are used to get age. The interviewer uses them automatically with the first hint of hesitance:

```
And what is your age. (IF HESITANT: That is, your
age at your last birthday?) (IF NO ANSWER: Well are
you in your 20s, 30s, 40s, 50s, or what?)
```

Education. Getting people's education is less of a problem in telephone surveys. In this situation we reverse the education question, asking the grade first. If there is hesitance, rather than marking "don't know/no response," we switch to another question, and if it succeeds we repeat the first question:

```
What was the last grade you completed in school
(IF DK/NR: Well, what was the name of the last
school you attended?) (IF ANY: And what was the
last grade you completed there?)
```

Income. Since we are unable to use response cards, we have more success in obtaining respondents' income by reading a few categories that are rounded off at the 5,000s and 10,000s.

```
Is your total family income closer to $5,000,
10,000, 15, 20, . . or more than $20,000 a year
(IF DK/NR: Well, is your family income more or
less than $10,000 a year?)
```

Incidentally, the question reads aloud like this: "Is your total family income closer to five thousand, ten thousand, fifteen, twenty . . . or more than twenty thousand dollars a year?" (A format for pinning down total family income by phone is shown in Chapter 4, page 230.)

Race. We never let interviewers judge someone's race or ethnic group on the basis of voice or accent. Instead we ask a straightforward question. If there is any hesitancy, the probe is used to suggest ways people might classify themselves. As before, how many and which categories we use depends on the purpose and locale of the study:

> And, what is your race . . how do you classify
> yourself? (IF DK/NR: Well, most people classify
> themselves as black, white . . oriental,, or something
> like that. How do you classify yourself?)

The interviewer is prepared to receive alternative answers and code them, such as "Puerto Rican," "Chicano," "Native American."

Religion. It may seem silly to ask people if they are "closer" to one religion than another, but it works as a probe of religious preference:

> What .. if any .. is your religious preference?
> (IF DK/NR: Well, are you closer to being Catholic,
> Protestant, or Jewish?)

We don't specify further or ask about other faiths. They emerge in the answers.

Mail Surveys

The principles of good question wording for personal and telephone surveys apply to mail and other kinds of self-administered questionnaires. With the latter, however, we simply have no control whatsoever over respondents' exposure to, perception of, and understanding of the questions. In the typical mail survey, all aspects of question meaning, sequence, response categories, conditioning effects, unforeseen offense, etc., are out of our hands.

While mail survey questions can suffer from the same frailties as other surveys—loaded, ambiguous, and misperceived wording—at least the problem of "consistent bias" is eliminated when there is no corps of interviewers between the questionnaire and the respondents. Still remaining are the significant bias potentials of the questions and of the capacities and motives of respondents.

All of the motives that affect people's answers to personal and telephone inquiries operate in the mail situation as well. But the result is much more likely to be refusal—in the form of the wastepaper basket. A respondent who judges a mail questionnaire to be irrelevant, threatening, partisan, or embarrassing will throw it away. The same person may not slam the door on an interviewer, and the interviewer has techniques to rescue an interview that's going awry. An additional respondent motive confronted in mail surveys is the "junk mail" instinct. Some people automatically toss out mail that resembles anything other than personal or business correspondence, without opening it.

Another factor in our loss of control in mail surveys is that we cannot chose who opens the envelope, who decides if it is to be thrown away, who passes it on to the intended respondent, who fills it out, and, finally, who mails it back—if anyone. (Chapter 4 describes techniques of questionnaire design that combat the junk mail instinct.) One safeguard against unintended respondents (e. g., the secretary answering for the boss) is to adapt the questionnaire to the selective interests and skills of the intended respondent (e. g., ask the secretary about word-processing technique; ask the boss about the cost of maintenance).

Checklist 14 contains some rules of thumb for questioning in mail surveys.

CHECKLIST 14

Question Writing for Mail Surveys

1. The question has to do it all. With no interviewer to repeat the question or to probe, wording must be flawlessly specific, relevant, and understandable.

2. Questions must be concise and straightforward. There is no chance to encourage people to try answering difficult questions, although respondents do have the opportunity to review the questions and their answers if they wish.

3. Response categories must be understandable, applicable, and simple. Elaborate lists of possible answers will be bypassed.

4. Response categories must include all desired answers. There is no opportunity for probing or for writing down a response that the person cannot find in the list. Don't expect or require write-ins.

5. Wording should follow conventions for written grammar. This is not a conversation; the informality built into the face-to-face questionnaire is not appropriate on paper.

6. Technical subjects, argot, colloquialisms, and slang should be avoided in a survey of general populations.

7. The questionnaire introduction is less important, requiring only a minimum of instructions—but a covering letter is essential to grab attention, stimulate interest, and explain the mission. The cover letter must legitimize the survey, giving it credibility and urgency. If the study is federally funded, the required consent is given simply by mailing back the questionnaire. The cover letter should state that, since it is important to the study to get a complete response, a follow-up letter will be sent to nonrespondents, but that recipients wishing no further contact can avoid this by mailing back the blank questionnaire. The cover letter should state how the respondent was chosen—by computer from lists of registered voters, from membership lists of organizations, or whatever. Writing such information into the cover letter anticipates a possible challenge that would be answered in a face-to-face survey if queried by the respondent. The cover letter also states the procedures that will be followed to maintain confidentiality.

8. Respondent-selection keys cannot be used. The would-be respondent should be designated by name or by category desired: working woman, oldest man, high school student.

9. Sequence of questions should have logic, but this is not critical, since we cannot

control the order in which questions are read or answered anyway. The study design must bear this reality in mind.

10. Warm-up questions are a waste. Respondents either do or do not accept the task outlined in the cover letter. Further, any general questions are risky, as respondents are not likely to ponder vague items, and space is at a premium.

11. Free-response questions invariably are wasteful, except for a highly specialized sample. Ordinary people will not take the time and energy to write out detailed answers. Legibility and literacy are problems, and there is no ability to probe answers for more germane, complete, or meaningful content.

12. Trick questions ("sleeper" or "cheater" questions) to detect false answers are useless. Because respondents can look back through their previous answers, the items designed to check consistency may be discovered.

13. Questions that measure knowledge are not very reliable; people can look up or ask others for the answers.

14. Questions that measure reactions to timely events or that tap moods of the moment often produce meaningless data: people may set aside the questionnaire to answer much later when they have had time for reflection and analysis, or they may answer different questions at different times.

15. Questions that combine to make up an attitude scale have limited success, because juxtaposed on paper the scale often becomes self-evident. Also, people tend to resent and be a bit suspicious of peculiar questions, the kind that a good interviewer could pass off easily.

16. Questions that seek a comparison of concepts—such as a semantic differential rating of two candidates—are unproductive, because people can compare profiles against each other and manufacture a conformity or divergence that they might not have if questions were asked in sequence.

17. Demographic questions on paper are probably least threatening to those who have had extensive in-school experiences filling out forms. Even an item about whether a household is living on public welfare will be less threatening if not asked as a question. Simply list them as items.

18. Brevity is the watchword. Every required turn of the page loses another increment of respondents. For a general population sample, the questionnaire must be "doable" when it is opened. Otherwise it will be set aside and likely never returned.

FURTHER READING

Chun, Ki-Taek, Sidney Cobb, and John R. P. French, Jr., *Measures for Psychological Assessment: A Guide to 3,000 Original Sources and Their Applications,* Institute for Social Research, University of Michigan, Ann Arbor, 1976.

Jenkins, James J., W. A. Russell, and G. J. Suci, "An Atlas of Semantic profiles for 360 Words, *American Journal of Psychology, 71* (December, 1958): 688–699. Twenty scales show all important relationships.

League, Richard, *Psycholinguistic Matrices: Investigation into Osgood and Morris,* Mouton, The Hague, 1977. Essence of semantic differential.

Lindzey, Gardner and Elliot Aronson, eds., *Handbook of Social Psychology,* 2d ed., Addison-Wesley, Cambridge, MA, 1968. Comprehensive articles.

Miller, Delbert C., *Handbook of Research Design and Social Measurement* (3rd ed.), McKay, New York, 1977. Description, evaluation, and listing of numerous measurement scales.

Nunnally, Jum, *Psychometric Methods,* McGraw-Hill, New York, 1957. Detailed, sensible consideration of measurement and scaling.

Oppenheim, A. N., *Questionnaire Design and Attitude Measurement,* Basic Books, New York, 1966. Deals with question-wording problems and imaginative testing.

Robinson, John P., Jerrold G. Rusk, and Kendra B. Head, *Measurement of Political Attitudes,* Institute for Social Research, University of Michigan, Ann Arbor, 1968. Reprints hundreds of scales, with results and evaluation.

Robinson, John P., and Phillip R. Shaver, *Measures of Social Psychological Attitudes* (rev. ed.), Institute for Social Research, University of Michigan, Ann Arbor, 1973.

Robinson, John P., and Kendra Head, *Measures of Occupational Attitudes and Occupational Characteristics,* Institute for Social Research, University of Michigan, Ann Arbor, 1969.

Snider, James G., and Charles E. Osgood, eds., *Semantic Differential Technique: A Sourcebook,* Aldine, Chicago, 1969. Complete examples.

Stouffer, Samuel A., ed., *Measurement and Prediction,* Princeton University Press, Princeton, 1950. Sourcebook for Guttman and other scaling techniques.

CHAPTER 4

Designing Questionnaires

The drafts of survey questions must be compiled into a working instrument for the interviewers to use in the field. Questions can't be just patched together to fit symmetrically on a few sheets. Instead, the physical arrangement of the interview schedule, or questionnaire, must be planned in every detail so as to ensure that data is successfully obtained—more efficiently, more accurately, more completely, more usably.[1]

PRINCIPLES OF GOOD DESIGN

The questionnaire is the physical form of all theories, hypotheses, and hunches that have gone into planning the survey. The problem of questionnaire design boils down to converting "theory"—statements about what supposedly makes people operate—into simple questions and answers that can be exchanged between two nontheoreticians sitting in the living room—one holding a baby and the other balancing a coffee cup and a set of questionnaires, response cards, and a pen, while trying to hold the attention of the first.

In such situations of nonprivate, hurried, and distracted communication, we have a special obligation to ask the *right questions* in the *right way* with minimum

---

[1]We use the terms schedule and questionnaire interchangeably, although some researchers insist that the term questionnaire be restricted to forms that are self-administered.

difficulty for the interviewer. Chapter 1 dealt with asking the right questions—defining the study problem and formulating directional hypotheses about it. Chapter 3 dealt with composing the questions in the right way. We now consider how the physical form and arrangement of the questions furthers the purpose of the study.

TECHNIQUES OF GOOD DESIGN

Questionnaire design is based not on esthetics but on utility. The problems of the two principal questionnaire users—interviewer and data processor—must be taken into account at every step, and techniques must be employed to minimize them.

For the Model Survey, our questionnaire design must anticipate the needs of different staff members: Interviewers, using 8½ × 11 inch paper in notebooks, will be knocking on doors, interviewing people at the door or in the home, and recording most of their answers as circled numbers. Office staff will be logging in each questionnaire and scanning it for major errors and inconsistencies. Coders will then pore over each one, checking for missing or implausible number codes, sometimes devising new codes, and transferring codes to the side of the page or to a separate form for the keypuncher. Keypunchers will then transfer the numbers to machine data cards, which, after a series of additional checks, go to the computer. Chapter 6 contains suggestions for data processing, but the requirements of that stage must be anticipated during initial questionnaire design.

Other ways of designing and processing questionnaires are possible. For example, questionnaires may be printed directly on data cards or computer-readable, letter-size sheets of paper. Using these, interviewers, or respondents themselves, punch out holes with a stylus or darken circles with a pencil. With minor checking, these cards or forms can go into the computer without translation by clerical staff or machine operators (see Chapter 6). Even more rapid systems use no handwritten responses but enable respondents or interviewers to signal their answers with the push of a button on a remote device, which electronically flashes a code that can be perceived by the computer.

Each of these systems has advantages for different situations. Each attempts in one way or another to reduce the number of human steps in the process of gathering and computing data. But none of these is particularly suitable for the needs of the Model Survey. Some employ a technology ill-suited to field work conditions or demand greater respondent cooperation than is practical for general population surveys, although they may be suited to highly selective samples. Others may require respondents to come to a central place or to allow installation of electronic devices in their home, usually meaning a financial incentive must be offered.

The questionnaire-to-card-to-computer routine is, of course, our method here for illustrating the general principles of the physical aspect of the data gathering and recording phases of the survey process. Once we have mastered the experience-derived design techniques suggested here, they can be adapted to new methods.

General Features of Questionnaire Format

To achieve a good questionnaire format we use a four-part questionnaire, a realistic number of questions, a logical sequence of items, adequate spacing among them, and a sensible, consistent layout.

Physical Layout. The physical layout of the questionnaire has much to do with the ease with which interviewers get through an interview. Careful attention to spatial arrangement may prove the difference between good and bad interviewing. A good questionnaire format is one that uses a consistent alignment of questions and responses, a consistent set of symbols and interviewer instructions, and a consistent code-numbering scheme. It also provides ample space between items, uses colored paper stock for important pages of the questionnaire, and contains smooth transitions to help the interviewer move from one block of data to another.

But convenience to the interviewer is not the only concern. We design questionnaires also for the convenience, and therefore accuracy, of the coder who will prepare them for keypunching and for the keypunch operator who in some instances transfers the information from the questionnaire to the data card.

Space. Good format does not crowd the page. In the hurried interview situation, an interviewer's eyes move constantly from the page to the respondent to maintain rapport. Liberal spacing of items helps eye movement to and from the proper place in the question sequence. Tight spacing can lead to the interviewer missing items, meaning the respondent must be recontacted later or missing items must be thrown out of the analysis, often dragging other data along with them. Also, if a question is skipped the following question is out of context; it will make less sense to the respondent, to say nothing of presenting him or her with a different interviewing stimulus from other respondents. If the natural flow of questions is interrupted by the interviewer's awkward fumbling through the questionnaire, a respondent may become more aware of the loss of time and break off the interview. These difficulties are inexcusable when the remedy is so simple. We believe it is just as easy, once the principles are clear, to design a good questionnaire instead of a weak one.

Consistency. Good format requires being consistent. Few things are as distressing to interviewers as unnecessary changes in format makeup and style. Interviewers get accustomed to particular page arrangements as well as familiar ways of asking questions, and it's difficult to keep switching tactics. Thus we even try to keep format changes minimal between successive surveys. That means we use the same indention and alignment so that questions are almost always found in the same places on the page, and responses are aligned in the same way, enabling interviewers and coders who have worked together before to build on their skills. Consistency for the sake of interviewers is clearly important, and researchers who plan to use a commercial field service are well advised to first negotiate the questionnaire format with the agency, so that study goals are not compromised by an ill-suited, standard commercial format on the one hand or rebellious interviewers stumbling through our format on the other. The rule of thumb is: give in to the agency format except when study aims dictate something special.

Color. Questionnaires can be improved with judicious use of colored pages. Questionnaire pages typically are white 20-pound paper, because anything thinner does not stand up under constant page turning by interviewers, coders, and keypunchers. But there are practical reasons for using colored pages too. A distinctive front page—pastel pink or yellow—makes it easier to find individual questionnaires in piles and easier to count them for distribution. Different-colored front pages between studies or waves of a panel study help distinguish the proper questionnaires. Without such precaution, even the best office will make a serious mistake sometime.

In some studies more than one questionnaire version is used for experimental purposes. A color scheme helps distinguish them. A middle page may be colored to signal the interviewer where the next section begins if a respondent fails to qualify for questions in the section currently being asked. If the front page is not colored, the last (demographic) pages may be colored to set them off from the rest of the questionnaire, because these are the pages the interviewers are instructed to try to complete even when respondents threaten to break off the interview or are not eligible for interviewing—say, nonvoters in a study of voters.

Obviously, we don't want to lose the value of colored pages by overusing them—for example, with all of the uses mentioned in a single questionnaire. We do *not* use color coding to distinguish different versions of a questionnaire's front page that match different versions of the respondent-selection key (see Chapter 2); this would clue interviewers to whom they are looking for, a choice interviewers are not allowed to make.

Precoding

Precoding, the assignment of numbers to represent questions and responses, is essential to speedy data processing (see Chapter 6). By definition it must be done at the stage of questionnaire design, (i.e., *before* the study goes into the field). This advance planning ensures that responses will yield results that speak to the study's purpose, and it prepares questionnaires for data processing so that no restructuring will be needed later.

Data from the Model Survey is processed by computers and other machines. In order for it to be handled in this way, respondents' verbal answers must be transformed into numerical language that all machines can read.

Each item of data from a respondent—a variable—is assigned to a numbered "field." For the Model Survey, a field is one or more columns on a data card in which the numerical code for the particular response will be punched. We can assign column and code numbers in advance of the study, because our hypotheses tell us which questions to ask, in which order, and in which direction to code responses. Remember, if we don't know which codes to assign to response categories, we have not translated study hypotheses into proper operational form. Waiting until the data is in from the field in the hope it will somehow fall into usable shape is inviting confusion and delay.

A data card is shown in Figure 4.1. The card has 80 columns and 12 rows, of which we will use rows 0 through 9. One column (designated from C01 to C80 on the questionnaire) will usually be reserved for each question, but sometimes more than one column will be needed for a single item. On the other hand, we never put two questionnaire items into a single column. Because some questions will require more than one card column, because we don't squeeze two or more items into one column, and because identification data occupy the same block of columns in all cards, it is unlikely that the question numbers will correspond to the column numbers.

The vertical rows on the cards (usually 0 to 9 in each column) correspond to possible responses to a question. Thus the responses expected or allowed for each question will be numbered with a precoded row number that represents a *punch*

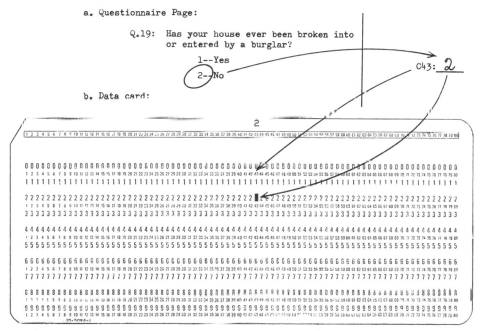

Figure 4.1. **Correspondence between precodes on questionnaire and punch on data card.**

position. These codes are printed on the questionnaire page right beside the response. The correspondence between questionnaire and data card is shown in Figure 4.1. Note that punch position 2 has been punched out of Column 43 on the card; because the respondent answered *no,* the interviewer circled the precoded *2* before *no,* the coder transferred the *2* to the right-hand margin by the column number, and the keypuncher depressed the *2* key over Column 43. (By the way, the computer reads the oblong hole in the card, not the number printed in the top margin by the keypunch machine.)

Categories for open-end questions cannot be known in advance, so that the punch positions cannot be precoded. But we do reserve adequate column numbers for those questions and print them in the questionnaire margin. This leaves space on the questionnaire and the data card for recording codes after the various answers given by respondents have been studied and we have devised a set of codes to classify them. This way all codes for the whole questionnaire can be keypunched in sequence at one time.

Identification Codes

Precoded identification data are necessary to understand what these particular data cards mean long after the interviewing period. The Model Survey precodes almost all identification data on the front page of the questionnaire and correspondingly in the first several columns on each data card. The practical reason for frontal placement is that the items are also used for office control— keeping track of the completion of assignments. Some items are repeated on all data cards for a single respondent, in order to be able to identify all data pertaining to each individual, no matter how the data is mixed together.

Standard Identification Items. Identification items used in the Model are described in Checklist 15 and are illustrated in Figure 4.2, which duplicates the front page of the Model questionnaire. The column numbers assigned to each item in the Model are shown in Checklist 15 as well. The first three items (Columns 01 to 09) are repeated in all data cards as standard identification. The same columns are reserved for this information in every study we do, so that we become habituated to looking for it there.

CHECKLIST 15

Identification Items

(*C* indicates column number on data card)

1. C01-04—*Study number.* Unique to one project. Precoded and preprinted on the questionnaire.

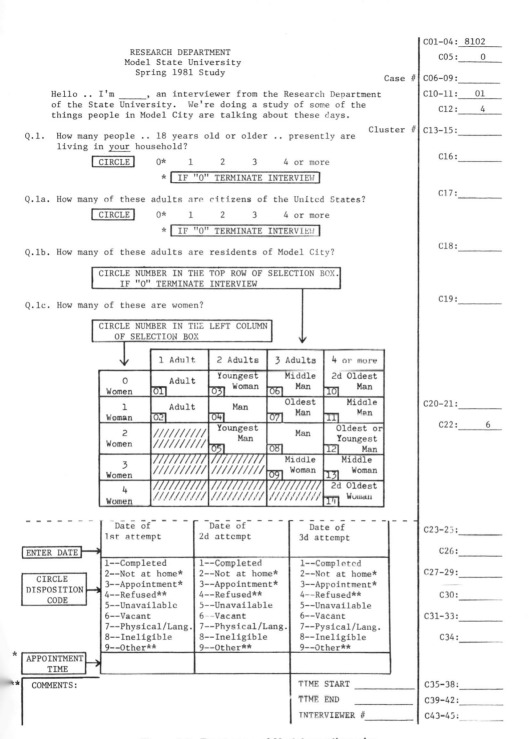

RESEARCH DEPARTMENT
Model State University
Spring 1981 Study

	C01-04: 8102
	C05: 0
Case #	C06-09: ________
	C10-11: 01
	C12: 4
Cluster #	C13-15: ________
	C16: ________
	C17: ________
	C18: ________
	C19: ________
	C20-21: ________
	C22: 6

Hello .. I'm _____, an interviewer from the Research Department of the State University. We're doing a study of some of the things people in Model City are talking about these days.

Q.1. How many people .. 18 years old or older .. presently are living in <u>your</u> household?

[CIRCLE] 0* 1 2 3 4 or more

* [IF "0" TERMINATE INTERVIEW]

Q.1a. How many of these adults are citizens of the United States?

[CIRCLE] 0* 1 2 3 4 or more

* [IF "0" TERMINATE INTERVIEW]

Q.1b. How many of these adults are residents of Model City?

[CIRCLE NUMBER IN THE TOP ROW OF SELECTION BOX. IF "0" TERMINATE INTERVIEW]

Q.1c. How many of these are women?

[CIRCLE NUMBER IN THE LEFT COLUMN OF SELECTION BOX]

	1 Adult	2 Adults	3 Adults	4 or more
0 Women	Adult 01	Youngest Woman 03	Middle Man 06	2d Oldest Man 10
1 Woman	Adult 02	Man 04	Oldest Man 07	Middle Man 11
2 Women	//////////	Youngest Man 05	Man 08	Oldest or Youngest Man 12
3 Women	//////////	//////////	Middle Woman 09	Middle Woman 13
4 Women	//////////	//////////	//////////	2d Oldest Woman 14

	Date of 1st attempt	Date of 2d attempt	Date of 3d attempt	
ENTER DATE →				C23-25: ________ C26: ________
CIRCLE DISPOSITION CODE →	1--Completed 2--Not at home* 3--Appointment* 4--Refused** 5--Unavailable 6--Vacant 7--Physical/Lang. 8--Ineligible 9--Other**	1--Completed 2--Not at home* 3--Appointment* 4--Refused** 5--Unavailable 6--Vacant 7--Physical/Lang. 8--Ineligible 9--Other**	1--Completed 2--Not at home* 3--Appointment* 4--Refused** 5--Unavailable 6--Vacant 7--Pysical/Lang. 8--Ineligible 9--Other**	C27-29: ________ C30: ________ C31-33: ________ C34: ________
* APPOINTMENT TIME →				

** COMMENTS:

TIME START	________	C35-38: ________
TIME END	________	C39-42: ________
INTERVIEWER #	________	C43-45: ________

Figure 4.2. Front page of Model questionnaire.

2. C05—*Case number prefix*. Wave number in panel study. If substitutions are allowed and this respondent is a substitute, it is coded *9;* otherwise, *0*.

3. C06-09—*Case number*. Unique to intended respondent. Prenumbered on the questionnaire.

4. C10-11—*Card number*. Serially numbered from 01 to last card needed for coding one respondent's whole questionnaire. Precoded and preprinted on questionnaire where each new card begins.

5. C12—*Cluster number prefix*. Residence code indicating rural or urban. Precoded and prenumbered on the questionnaire from the sample draw.

6. C13-15—*Cluster number*. Designated by sample draw. Prenumbered on the questionnaire by office staff.

7. C16, C17—*Eligibility*. Number of adult citizens in the household.

8. C18, C19—*Household composition*. Number of resident adults and women for respondent designation.

9. C20-21—*Designated respondent number*. Precoded in cells of respondent-selection key.

10. C22—*Respondent-selection key version*. Rotates systematically among the case numbers. Precoded; preprinted to match the version of the key on this front page.

11. C23-25—*Date* of first attempted interview. Interviewer records; coded by 365-day calendar (e.g., June 30 = 181).

12. C26—*Outcome* of interview attempt. Precoded.

13. C27-29—*Date* of second interview attempt, if necessary.

14. C30—*Outcome* of second interview attempt, if necessary.

15. C31-33—*Date* of third interview attempt, if necessary.

16. C34—*Outcome* of third interview attempt, if necessary.

17. C35-38—*Time* interview began. Coded by 24-hour clock.

18. C39-42—*Time* interview ended. Coded by 24-hour clock.

19. C43-45—*Interviewer number*. Assigned by field supervisor; entered prior to going into the field.

These are the basic identification items used in the Model Survey. Notice that the rule to follow is to make the office responsible for the assignment of as many of these codes as possible. This cuts down the potential for errors, such as duplicate, missing, or incorrect numbers. Interviewers have enough to do without having recording of identification codes added to their burden.

Other Identification Codes. The foregoing items are used in all surveys. But each study also has unique features that may require additional identification codes. For example:

Census Area Codes. The U.S. Census has identifying numbers for states, congressional districts, counties, and minor civil divisions (municipalities and townships) within counties. Beyond this, a location code identifies the parts of a given municipality that are divided by county lines. In state-wide studies, a governmental sub-division code on each questionnaire permits us during analysis to combine respondents into regional groups for demographic comparisons with Census data for the same area, say, by congressional districts. Likewise, a national study will use state or regional codes to group respondents (e.g., a state code would be necessary to group all those who are in states with presidential primaries, or those who correctly identified their senate candidates).

Other Place Codes. States and municipalities themselves prescribe codes for city wards and voting precincts, school or judicial districts, vocational training areas, industrial zones, mosquito control districts, sanitation and watershed areas, and so on. Regional coding has become official with growth of intermunicipal and inter-county consolidated services under various associations of governments. There are even "catchment areas" that designate the sharing of state-provided facilities for mental health, education, and computer services. Moreover, both private firms and public utilities—gas, electricity, water—have regional and area codes that might be valuable for surveys dealing with energy, ecology, and related environmental problems.

Institution Codes. State governments, university research centers, regional planning bureaus, and every major department of the federal government have assigned codes to institutions, (e.g., hospitals, colleges, day-care centers, job-training programs, nursing homes, prisons, industries, farm cooperatives). We often study people in association with institutions and services. When we do, we have to have the ability to compare institutional data too.

Weight

Sometimes a study will deliberately *oversample* a certain part of the territory, say, a rural area or a minority ghetto, in order to get enough respondents of that type to analyze. To avoid having these extra people bias the overall sample totals, it will be necessary to weight them down, or (more usually) to weight up the undersampled group. If the weights are known in advance, these can be precoded on the appropriate questionnaires. Thus a weight of 1 might be assigned to the oversampled part, and a weight of 2 to the rest to bring them up to their true relative proportions of the total population. This deliberate weighting would be figured in advance and pre-printed on the questionnaires assigned to the respective areas. Three columns will be necessary in case of a decimal fraction weight. (The use of weighting is described in Chapter 6.)

Disposition Codes

The box at the bottom of the questionnaire's front page (Figure 4.2) contains a number of codes showing what happens to the questionnaire in the field, the dates and times of interviewing, the number of interview attempts, and whether the interview is completed, incompleted (due to respondent unavailability), refused, or pending by appointment (see Chapter 5).

DESIGN OF QUESTIONS AND RESPONSES

The general principle in designing format for questions and response categories is *consistent alignment*. It is not always possible, of course, but once we establish a page format we deviate from it only as necessary, reducing the chance for interviewer errors.

Each page has a vertical line segregating the right margin from the rest of the page. This margin space contains preprinted column numbers assigned to each question. Where we already know the code number to be punched in a column, we preprint this too (as with some identification items such as card numbers). The rest of the column numbers are followed by a colon and a short blank. After the questionnaires are returned, coders will transfer the response number circled by the interviewer for each question to its corresponding column blank in the right margin. Keypunchers may then read directly down the margin and punch the numbers into the indicated columns on the data cards.

Vertical Alignment

Each main question is *indented* the same distance from the margin. Response categories are indented to about the middle of the page, starting two lines below the question and usually in *vertical alignment,* 1½ typewriter lines apart. This is a convenient format for the interviewer to follow, with enough room to circle the numbers for responses. Single-line spaces on the typewriter are too close together to permit accurate, rapid recording by hand:

Q.24. **Do you agree or disagree with the mayor's decision to ask for the resignation of Patrick Mundane, the Chief of Police?**

            1--agree   C40:____
            2--don't know
            3--disagree

Note that a dash (two hyphens in typing) connects the code number with the response. If we preferred to have the interviewer use an *X* mark, an underlined blank would be used instead to allow space for the *X*. These *X* marks (and especially check marks) are less satisfactory in a relatively small space than circles, because they can get big and sloppy and, therefore, imprecise as to where they belong.

Horizontal Alignment

Vertical alignment of response categories is not always practical. Suppose we ask how many radio news programs a respondent listened to yesterday, and we wish to know the actual number up to seven programs (only a very few answers will exceed seven). Here we can list the responses as numbers running horizontally and instruct the interviewer to circle the appropriate number:

Q.38.   About how many times . . if any . . did you
        happen to listen to news on the radio yesterday?

| CIRCLE | 0 1 2 3 4 5 6 7 or more times   C49:____

If interviewers were to use X marks, the categories would have to be boxed to provide a better aiming point for the mark. Blank spaces for checking would be confusing, because it would be hard to tell if the blank went with the the preceding or the following code.

Sometimes response categories are arranged horizontally and separated by a vertical line to show that different types of answers lead to different follow-up questions:

Q.25.   Do you favor or oppose the plan to change
        the city's school attendance boundaries?

*1--favor	**2--oppose	**3--don't know	C41:____
*Which particular schools should have their attendance boundaries changed?	**Are there any schools whose attendance boundaries you think should be changed?		

There are other ways of handling the same problem. One is to put boxes around response categories:

Q.25.   Do you favor or oppose the plan to change
        the city's school attendance boundaries?

1--favor	2--oppose 3--don't know	C41:____
Which particular schools should have their attendance boundaries changed?	Are there any schools whose attendance boundaries you think should be changed?	

Another way to make categories distinctive on the page is using arrow-directed paths:

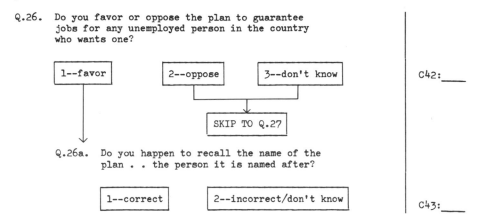

The object of this design is instant, continuous, mistake-proof progression by the interviewer with only momentary glances at the page. While boxing response categories is distinctive, a page with many boxed-in responses looks busy and can bewilder interviewers. Boxing works best with one- or two-word responses. It doesn't work well with lengthy answers or long lists of responses.

Blanks

The Model Survey uses preestablished categories many times for income, education, and other continuous variables. Categories are somewhat less threatening to respondents, they save coding time, and may best serve the kinds of analysis desired in the survey report. We usually recommend, however, getting actual figures, such as exact age, specific thousands of dollars of income, last grade in school, number of years resident in the community, actual number of radio newscasts heard, etc. Actual numbers have advantages over categories in that, first, they improve the strength of certain statistical analyses and, second, as raw data they can later be categorized in different ways for different purposes. This is especially important to give us the ability to compare our data with data for any other studies of the same populations.

The theoretical issue is whether we should report data by categories *we* later form on the basis of the actual data collected; or require respondents to *classify themselves* by categories we know or assume in advance to be representative of the population. For the Model, we think it best to use precategorization based on current Census data and other survey data based on appropriate categories. The typical survey user is not likely to have the time or resources to do extensive recategorization.

If exact figures are to be written down, then a single, slightly longer answer blank will be provided that is without response numbers. More column numbers will have to be designated in the right margin—two for age (lump those 100 and over with the 99 year olds), and three for income (no need to code the last two zeros).

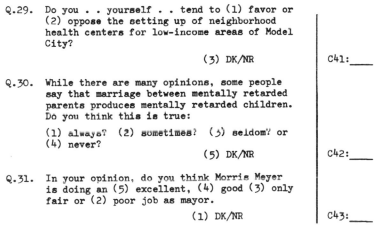

Q.48.   And what is the annual family income
        of this household.

             (INSERT FIGURE) $_____   C73-75____

Q.49.   Your age at your last birthday.

             (INSERT ACTUAL YEARS)_____   C76-77____

Categories Within Text

To conserve space it is possible to incorporate response categories *within the body of the question* and let the interviewer circle the code there. This is an efficient format for interviewers to follow, although it requires somewhat closer attention to the page. We recommend it only if most of the questionnaire, or at least substantial blocks of questions, can be arranged in this way. Otherwise, the interviewer is forced to go back and forth between different formats.

Q.29.   Do you . . yourself . . tend to (1) favor or
        (2) oppose the setting up of neighborhood
        health centers for low-income areas of Model
        City?

                           (3) DK/NR   C41:____

Q.30.   While there are many opinions, some people
        say that marriage between mentally retarded
        parents produces mentally retarded children.
        Do you think this is true:

        (1) always? (2) sometimes? (3) seldom? or
        (4) never?

                           (5) DK/NR   C42:____

Q.31.   In your opinion, do you think Morris Meyer
        is doing an (5) excellent, (4) good (3) only
        fair or (2) poor job as mayor.

                           (1) DK/NR   C43:____

Here we see that the response categories appear only once and are read as part of the question. Interviewers usually require extra training with this format. They must learn to read the categories wherever they appear (for example, notice the difference in where categories appear for Q.30 in contrast to the others). They must learn *not* to read the "don't know/no response" category, although it is accepted as a legitimate response when the respondent cannot or will not answer the question. And they must remember to circle the code number that *precedes* the answer given by the respondent.

Directional Coding

Oftentimes we want to measure something by rank ordering or by degrees of intensity (or psychological distance) between responses. As mentioned earlier (see Chapter 1), the study hypotheses indicate the positive or negative direction of the relationship expected for any two variables. The hypotheses tell us, in other words, the order in which we should assign codes to response categories. For example, suppose we are trying to measure "permissive" attitudes with a series of agree/disagree attitude questions. To prevent respondents from falling into a habit of answering only "agree," we word some of the items so that "agree" is the most permissive attitude and word others so that "disagree" is the most permissive.

By sacrificing the mere *appearance* of consistency in the position of the code numbers on the questionnaire, we seek real consistency for the interviewer, the coder, the keypuncher, and the analyst. We put all the "agree" responses, whatever they mean, in the same relative position on the questionnaire so that the interviewer doesn't have to jump around.

Consider this example:

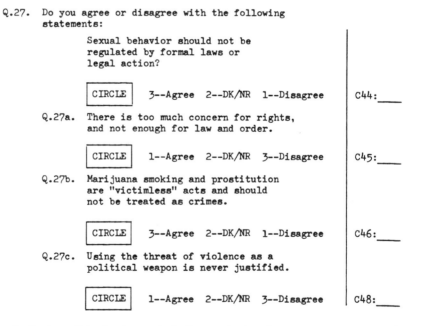

```
Q.27.   Do you agree or disagree with the following
        statements:

                   Sexual behavior should not be
                   regulated by formal laws or
                   legal action?

           CIRCLE      3--Agree  2--DK/NR  1--Disagree      C44:____

Q.27a.  There is too much concern for rights,
        and not enough for law and order.

           CIRCLE      1--Agree  2--DK/NR  3--Disagree      C45:____

Q.27b.  Marijuana smoking and prostitution
        are "victimless" acts and should
        not be treated as crimes.

           CIRCLE      3--Agree  2--DK/NR  1--Disagree      C46:____

Q.27c.  Using the threat of violence as a
        political weapon is never justified.

           CIRCLE      1--Agree  2--DK/NR  3--Disagree      C48:____
```

A nearly foolproof device is created. Respondents who want to appear consistent must think through each question; they cannot simply fall into the rut of answering with the same word. Because "agree" is always on the left, the interviewer can keep eye contact with the respondent while locating the correct response to circle by "muscle memory"; this way the interviewer is less likely to communicate a bias by reacting to a set pattern of answers because there won't be time to analyze the answers. Since we have already assigned the highest code to the permissive response to each question, the coder merely has to copy the numbers into the right margin as always without having to translate meanings by referring to a master sheet. And the analyst can call for a ''permissiveness'' score based on the simple sum of the codes for the four questions.

In the example, the answers assumed to be permissive are (a) agree, (b) disagree, (c) agree, and (d) disagree. Each has been precoded as ''3.'' A respondent like the one who answered the question in the example would have a score of 12 and would be identified with the ''most permissive'' group. Respondents with scores of 4 would be classified as ''least permissive.'' Significantly, people who can't decide, who are truly neutral, or who aren't willing to participate cannot be erroneously classified, as would happen if code 0 were used for ''don't know'' (which would compute as less permissive) or, on the other extreme, if—following one convention—8 were used instead of ''don't know'' (computing as more permissive).

A single study has many hypotheses. To decide the direction of coding, let the *core hypothesis*—the expectation about the most important dependent variable—determine the direction of the codes. Looking back to Figure 1.6 (page 31) for another example, the most important dependent variable is ''Support for the Referendum.'' Determining this factor is the reason for the study. Measures of those who know about the referendum, who talk about it, who are favorably disposed toward it, and so on, are all indications of support for it. The critical question—even more important than who will vote a month from now in the election—is who supports passage of the referendum. This, therefore, is the variable we use to code all responses as ''high'' or ''low,'' positive or negative.

The Model uses directional coding because we believe the burden should be on the researcher to make a reasonable guess in advance of printing the questionnaire about how individual responses fit study goals and to number them accordingly. This makes all subsequent steps purely mechanical, lessening the risk of errors. Not all research organizations agree that coding should be directional. Since many people use their data for different purposes, the Inter-University Consortium for Political Research recommends that, regardless of the meaning for the study, code 1 be used consistently for ''yes,'' ''agree strongly,'' ''good,'' or ''most positive'' responses; that code 5 be used for ''no,'' ''disagree strongly,'' ''bad,'' or ''least positive'' responses; that code 2 should indicate ''agree, but not strongly''; that 3 be ''not sure''; and that 4 be ''disagree, but not strongly.''[2]

If this convention is followed, it is necessary during analysis to *recode* these

---

[2]*Policies and Standards for Coding Data* (mimeo), Technical Services Division, Inter-University Consortium for Political Research, Ann Arbor (undated).

responses (change the numbers) in the direction of the hypotheses if two or more questions are to be combined or used together in some procedure.

Don't Know/No Response

The letters DK/NR (''don't know/no response) can mean *can't answer* (ignorance) or *won't answer* (refusal). Sometimes the distinction is important, and in these instances we provide separate codes for them. In the Model Survey we use the DK/NR convention for all items unless we have reason to expect unusual rates of ignorance or resistance that would be meaningful to analyze. (Many researchers use DK/NA, the NA standing for ''no answer.'' However, the Model reserves NA to mean ''not ascertained,'' which signifies interviewer failure—that is, the interviewer either didn't ask the question, didn't record the response, or received a response that was unintelligible or unresponsive to the question. Note how this differs from ''don't know'' or ''refusal,'' which are responses that the interviewer recorded.)

In the foregoing example of directional coding the DK/NR code is set physically and numerically between the ''agree'' and ''disagree'' responses. This is intentional. For some purposes, DK/NR is ''missing'' information—we don't know whether the person really did agree or disagree. For other purposes, DK/NR is simply a point psychologically somewhere between agreement and disagreement— the respondent is undecided or firmly neutral. Since we can't say DK/NR is higher than ''agree'' or lower than ''disagree,'' we put it in the middle. As an estimate of how the respondent really would have answered our question under other circumstances, the middle position is the one of least error. That is, in a series of three numbers the middle number (2) is only one removed from either of the others. If we were to guess the respondent's likely answer and to put it at one of the extremes in the series (as 1 or 3) it would be two numbers removed from the number at the other extreme—and thus a larger error, if the other extreme were in fact the respondent's true feelings. Some researchers assign a consistent code 8 for all ''don't know'' responses, and then eliminate them from the analysis. This results in a loss of data where the respondent was merely undecided.

In the Model, DK/NR is coded in the middle position of any ordinal or interval scale. With nominal data—''Is any person in this family a member of a labor union''— there is no meaning to high or low numbering. Therefore coding an 8 for DK, and ignoring this respondent where union membership is concerned, would be appropriate.

Reserved Codes

Some thought must be given in advance to questions that will end up without responses, either because the interviewer was directed to skip the question for certain respondents, or because of interviewer failure. We don't precode for these, because we don't want to distract interviewers or lead them to think that unanswered questions are acceptable, which might lessen their efforts. But Chapter 6 suggests that code 0 be saved for legitimate skips and code 9 for failure by the interviewer to get a response where one was called for. Therefore we try to avoid using them as codes for other responses.

Symbols

Various symbols guide interviewers through the questionnaire. Checklist 16 lists these, but some will be explained further here.

CHECKLIST 16

Interviewing Symbols and Instructions

Q.6.	Question number. Shows where interviewer begins reading again after being told to skip some questions. Used as label in the report to tie it to location in questionnaire.
C37:___	Column numbers on each data card. Aligned in ruled-off right margin of page. Interviewers ignore these, but coders transfer circled response codes to these blanks before keypunching begins.
1--yes 2--DK/NR 3--no	Precoded numbers in front of response categories represent punch positions (usually 0 to 9) in one column on a data card. Unless instructed to the contrary, interviewers never read numbers to respondent but simply circle the number of the response given.
. .	Two spaced dots within the question indicates a slight pause in reading the question.
<u>you</u>	Any word, series of words, or part of a word that is underlined should be emphasized in reading.
CIRCLE	Interviewer instructions are printed in CAPITAL LETTERS. These are not read to the respondent.
CIRCLE	Such instructions are usually enclosed in a box.
(IF "YES")	Instructions enclosed in parentheses usually indicate some follow-up action that is one of various alternatives entirely dependent on the previous response given. Other examples are:
(HAND PINK INCOME CARD)	This instruction within the body of the question tells the interviewer to give a response card to the

	respondent at this point in the reading of the question.
(SKIP TO Q.19)	This tells the interviewer that the respondent's answer disqualifies her or him from further questioning on the topic and to move ahead to the next section of questions. An instruction of this nature is always placed next to the response category that triggers it.
(INSERT NAME)	This instruction tells the interviewer to insert a name in a follow-up question that the respondent mentioned in the previous question.
(IF "YES" ASK:)	From a designated response to the previous question the interviewer is told to ask a specific follow-up question. Otherwise it is not asked.
(REPEAT)	This tells the interviewer to repeat the same categories for a lengthy series of questions, but to keep repeating them only until the respondent has them clearly in mind and can respond without having the categories read.
PROBE:	This tells the interviewer to continue questioning the respondent to get a complete, specific, and meaningful answer.
SPECIFY:	This means that a particular answer must be clarified or added to. It acts as a probe to make a general answer more precise.
CIRCLE	The most common instruction, it tells the interviewer to circle the code number of the response given. Only *one* code can be accepted.
MULTIPLE ANSWER	Only when this symbol appears does the interviewer accept more than one answer to a fixed-response question and circles all of the appropriate codes.
DK/NR	This is an abbreviation for "don't know/no response." It is accepted when the respondent cannot or will not give an answer that fits any of the other categories. This response is never read to the respondents as a choice they have.
$\longrightarrow$	Arrows and other lines (vertical and horizontal) guide the interviewer from question to question when there are alternatives to follow up in different ways.

Symbols also adapt written questions to conversational form and help to ensure that all interviewers are presenting the questions identically. Use enough symbols to preclude any hesitation in reading the questionnaire, and use them consistently, so that they become second nature to the interviewers. But don't overuse symbols, because then they become gimmicky and distracting.

Series of dots. Within the body of the question, two spaced periods indicate a slight pause in reading:

```
It has been suggested that the Model City Housing
Authority set the rents that can be charged on
private dwellings . . instead of letting landlords
set the rents.  Do you think this is a good . .
or a bad idea?
```

Asterisks. An asterisk before a response code tells the interviewer that such a response now leads to another question or question series. The follow-up question is also marked with an asterisk:

```
Q.4.  Do you think that landlords in this city . .
      in general . . have been acting fairly . .
      or unfairly in setting rents on private
      dwellings?

              1--fairly

              2--DK/NR

             *3--unfairly
```

* | IF "UNFAIRLY," ASK Q.4a. |

```
Q.4a.  *Without naming anyone, do you personally
        know someone who is being charged unfair
        rent by his or her landlord?
```

Underscoring. Any word, series of words, or part of a word that is _underlined_ should be stressed in reading the question. Although interviewers are instructed to read questions impartially, and without dramatics, words sometimes must be stressed to clarify meanings:

```
Sometimes political parties mail out sample ballots
showing the candidates they endorse.  Has anyone here
received a sample ballot at your home?
```

Arrows. Arrows are used like traffic signs directing interviewers to unusual tasks. In the next example, the arrows make the alternatives pretty clear:

Q.52.   In politics . . do you consider yourself a Republican,
        a Democrat, or a member of some other party?

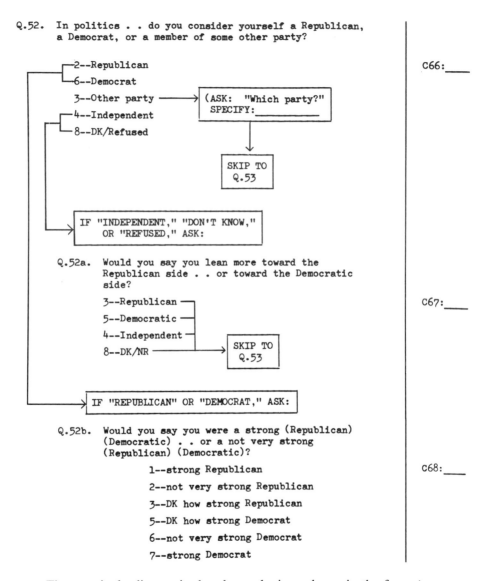

C66:____

C67:____

C68:____

Q.52a. Would you say you lean more toward the
        Republican side . . or toward the Democratic
        side?

Q.52b. Would you say you were a strong (Republican)
        (Democratic) . . or a not very strong
        (Republican) (Democratic)?

            1--strong Republican

            2--not very strong Republican

            3--DK how strong Republican

            5--DK how strong Democrat

            6--not very strong Democrat

            7--strong Democrat

The seemingly disorganized code-numbering scheme in the foregoing questions is for the purpose of setting up a new variable that summarizes party identification into a spectrum: (1) strong Republican; (2) weak Republican; (3) leaning
Republican; (4) persistent Independent; (5) leaning Democrat; (6) weak Democrat;
and (7) strong Democrat; with (8) don't know, didn't answer, and refused; and with
(9) used to mean someone affiliated with a minor party. We reserve the next card

column (here C69) for this new variable, called "extended party identification," if we ask coders to make the summary. Otherwise we later recode the data from the three example questions by computer in a new variable without saving a column for it (see Chapter 6), while preserving all the original information we gathered in Columns 66 to 68.

Vertical Lines. Vertical lines sometimes distinguish alternative question series following various responses. But a vertical line may also set off and tie together a series of follow-up questions:

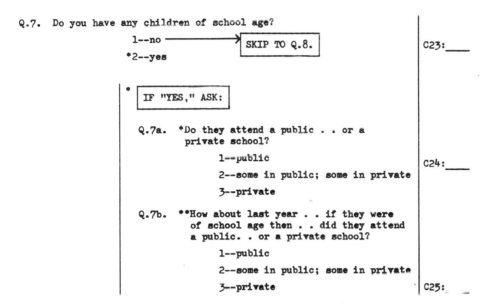

Sections. Sometimes neither arrows nor vertical lines are as clear to the interviewer as simply separating follow-up responses into different sections below the main question:

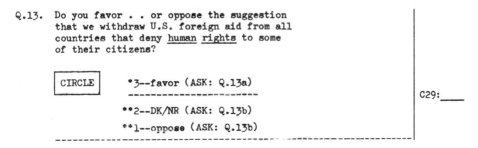

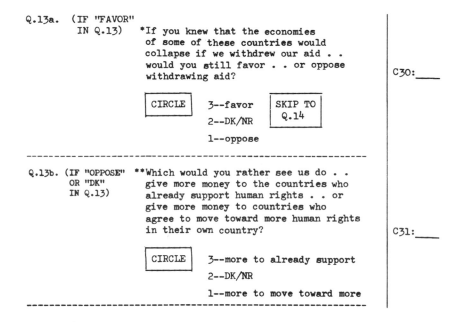

Q.13a. (IF "FAVOR" IN Q.13) *If you knew that the economies of some of these countries would collapse if we withdrew our aid . . would you still favor . . or oppose withdrawing aid?

C30:____

CIRCLE   3--favor   SKIP TO Q.14
          2--DK/NR
          1--oppose

Q.13b. (IF "OPPOSE" OR "DK" IN Q.13) **Which would you rather see us do . . give more money to the countries who already support human rights . . or give more money to countries who agree to move toward more human rights in their own country?

C31:____

CIRCLE   3--more to already support
          2--DK/NR
          1--more to move toward more

Interviewer Instructions

Good physical layout of the questionnaire is not enough to ensure that questions will be asked properly. Instructions for coping with many different situations must be written in a form that interviewers cannot ignore. *All* instructions are written in CAPITAL LETTERS and usually set in a *box:*

IF "DON'T KNOW," SKIP TO Q.44.

When previous responses appear in the interviewers' instructions, they are set off by *quotation marks* as above. When a follow-up question is included in the instructions, it is set off by quotations and written in capital and lower case letters, following the word "ASK":

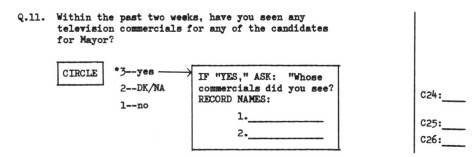

Q.11. Within the past two weeks, have you seen any television commercials for any of the candidates for Mayor?

CIRCLE   *3--yes ——→ IF "YES," ASK: "Whose commercials did you see? RECORD NAMES:
          2--DK/NA
          1--no   1._____
                                   2._____

C24:____
C25:____
C26:____

Interviewer instructions in the body of the question are set off by capital letters *enclosed in parentheses:*

Q.52.   **Here's a card showing different income groups (HAND RESPONDENT INCOME CARD). Just tell me the _letter_ of the group your family is in.**

> | RECORD LETTER | _____

C79: _____

Special Questions

The formats described thus far will fit most questions. But some questions require different treatment.

Free-Response Questions. Too often we defeat the purpose of free-response questions by failing to give incentive to the interviewer to keep digging for complete answers. Either we cramp the space allowed for writing verbatim comments or we give no directions to keep probing. As noted earlier, interviewers have a talent for filling up just the amount of space allotted for answers. If we want fuller answers, we must be willing to sacrifice the amount of interviewing time and page space that good free-response questions require. It is particularly important to allow ample writing space for pretest questioning, for these will give us a better idea of how much space is needed.

To encourage probing, we don't have to ask separate questions but can build them right into the initial question:

> Q.48.   **What were the main reasons you decided to vote for (INSERT NAME) for mayor? (PROBE: What other reasons did you have?) (Any other reasons?)**

Or we build the probe questions into the answer space as a more timely reminder to the interviewer:

Q.48.   **What were the main reasons you decided to vote for (INSERT NAME) for mayor?**

_____   C65: _____

_____   C66: _____

_____   C67: _____

                                                C68: _____
PROBE: What other reasons? _____

_____   C69: _____

Any other reasons? _____   C70: _____

A variation builds probes into the question when meaningful initial answers are given. If the initial answer is empty, the interviewer gets special instructions to alter the question slightly:

Q.52. And . . what has the President done in foreign affairs
that you particularly <u>like</u>? (PROBE: What else has he
done that you like?) (What else?)

> IF "DK/NR" ASK: "Is there anything he's
> done that you like?"

C74:_____

_____ C75:_____

PROBE:_____ C76:_____
                                        etc.

The underlined spaces for writing are double-spaced, aligned flush with the question, and run almost to the right-ruled margin. Indention shows that the response to one question may lead to a further question:

Q.16. What have you heard or read about the plan to
create groups called "<u>neighborhood corporations</u>"
in different areas of the city?

_____ C38:_____

_____ C39:_____

_____ C40:_____
                                        etc.

> IF "DK/NR," SKIP TO Q.17. OTHERWISE ASK Q.16a.

Q.16a. As best <u>you</u> know, what are the "Corporations"
supposed to do for their neighborhoods?

_____ C41:_____

_____ C42:_____

_____ C43:_____

PROBE: What else would they do?_____ C44:_____

_____ C45:_____

Anything else?_____ C46:_____

Semistructured Questions. Some free-response questions do not require verbatim answers in great detail. These "semistructured" questions are asked open-ended—we don't know what people are going to say. Intensive probing is encouraged, but the responses may be paraphrased. They are listed topically by the interviewer in the order given, so that analysis can differentiate between first and subsequent answers:

Q.1.   In your opinion what are the most important problems
       facing the people of Model City today?
       (PROBE: What other problems are important?)
       (Any other problems?)

       | SPECIFY: | 1st problem:_____   C21-22:____

                      2nd problem:____   _____   C23-24:____

                      3rd problem:_____   C25-26:____

   Although a numbered list to code answers to semistructured questions will need
to be developed later (and probably could be done after the pretest), we would not
want to print this long list on the questionnaire and have the interviewer pore
through it looking for the responses given.

   Asking people's occupations is a good example of a semistructured question.
Since the U.S. Census offers some 20,000 different job classifications, it is impossible to list them on the questionnaire page. Instead, we provide spaces for the
specific job title, the industry, and a description of the work done in case the job title
is cryptic.

Q.98. What is your job . . your occupation?

       | SPECIFY: | Job title:_____   C21-22:____

                      Place of work:_____

                      Type of work:_____

(See Chapter 3 for a description of the special problems of ascertaining occupation,
and Chapter 5 for general techniques of probing semistructured questions).

   Another form of the semistructured question anticipates most responses with
coded categories but allows for others that don't fit into the coding scheme:

Q.54. What would you rather see us do: (3) prosecute all
       campaign abuses now, no matter which Senators and
       Congress members may be punished . . or (1) bury   C25:____
       the past and toughen the laws so such abuses cannot
       happen in the future?   (2--DK/NR)

       OTHER ANSWERS:_____

       _____

   Questions that combine fixed- and free-responses are jeopardized by interviewers' nonrandom recording errors, a nice way of saying that when there is a
choice between writing answers longhand and circling a code, interviewers selectively tend to "hear" more precoded answers than actually are given.

We sometimes press respondents for more exact information even in fixed-response questions. In the example questions on party identification (see p. 206), people who said they belonged to the "Other Party" category were asked to *specify* which one by name. "Independents," and those who didn't claim an affiliation, were asked to specify whether they leaned toward either of the two major parties. And, those who said "Republican" or "Democrat" were asked to specify the intensity of their affiliation. As a result, we came away with a much more rigorous and, therefore, more meaningful classification.

Filter Questions. As we have seen, sometimes further information is wanted on a subject that does not apply to all respondents. To know whom to ask which questions, we first use one or two "filter" or "screen" questions. Such questions retain some people for follow-up and let others skip to the next subject. For example, we learn first who has voted in the election before asking about specific candidates supported. Or we learn who knows about the polluted city drinking water before asking opinions about what should be done about it.

In the following example, it would be absurd to ask further questions about job discrimination of people who say no to the first one. Note the use of indention to set the follow-up questions off from the main path of interviewing:

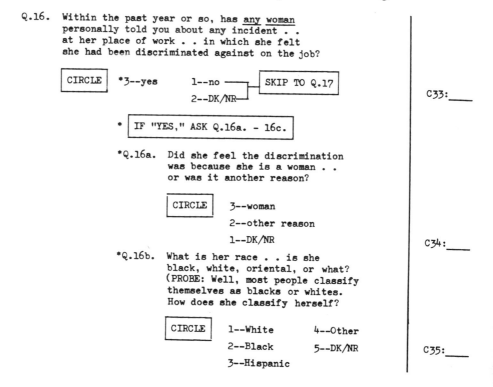

Q.16. Within the past year or so, has <u>any woman</u>
       personally told you about any incident . .
       at her place of work . . in which she felt
       she had been discriminated against on the job?

       | CIRCLE | *3--yes   1--no ──→ | SKIP TO Q.17 | C33:____
                     2--DK/NR─┘

       * | IF "YES," ASK Q.16a. - 16c. |

       *Q.16a. Did she feel the discrimination
                was because she is a woman . .
                or was it another reason?

                | CIRCLE | 3--woman
                             2--other reason
                             1--DK/NR   C34:____

       *Q.16b. What is her race . . is she
                black, white, oriental, or what?
                (PROBE: Well, most people classify
                themselves as blacks or whites.
                How does she classify herself?

                | CIRCLE | 1--White   4--Other
                             2--Black   5--DK/NR   C35:____
                             3--Hispanic

*Q.16c. What kind of discrimination
was it . . what did she complain
about?

CIRCLE 1--less pay for equal work
2--less chance for promotion
3--demeaning jobs
4--personal harassment or abuse
5--other, SPECIFY_____

C36:____

We do not always use the filter to eliminate people from further questioning on the same subject. We will sometimes want the opinion of people about an issue even though they don't know anything about it yet. In this circumstance we use the filter question later during analysis to distinguish those who are more knowledgeable and, therefore, may have thought about the issue longer. If we wish a response from everyone, we ensure the same stimulus by giving a brief summary of the situation —even to those who know it already.

Q.14. Have you heard or read anything about proposed
changes in the local property tax system?

C43:____

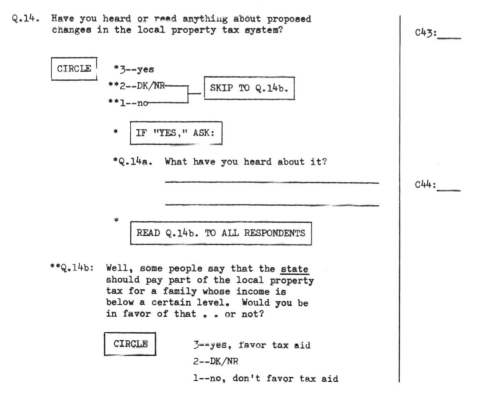

CIRCLE *3--yes
**2--DK/NR ── SKIP TO Q.14b.
**1--no

* IF "YES," ASK:

*Q.14a. What have you heard about it?

_____

_____

C44:____

* READ Q.14b. TO ALL RESPONDENTS

**Q.14b: Well, some people say that the state
should pay part of the local property
tax for a family whose income is
below a certain level. Would you be
in favor of that . . or not?

CIRCLE 3--yes, favor tax aid
2--DK/NR
1--no, don't favor tax aid

Repeat Categories. Much questionnaire space can be saved by using one introduction and the same response categories for several related questions. For example, with a series of good/bad questions rating several bills passed by the state legislature, the (REPEAT) symbol is used, written into the body of the question. It tells the interviewer that after introducing the question series once, they need not repeat the introduction. Instead, the interviewer repeats only the response categories as the way of asking successive questions.

Q.4.   Now, how would you rate the quality of the following
       laws passed this past session by the state legislature
       in Capital City. (REPEAT) Would you rate as <u>very good</u>,
       <u>good</u>, <u>bad</u>, or <u>very</u> <u>bad</u>:

REPEAT CATEGORIES AS NEEDED FOR EACH QUESTION		CIRCLE ONE CODE PER QUESTION			
	Very Good	Good	(DK/NR)	Bad	Very Bad
Q.4. the law that a house-buyer must be given a statement of energy use for that house?...................	5	4	(3)	2	1	C28:____
Q.4a. the law that reduces property taxes for low-income people?.......	5	4	(3)	2	1	C29:____
Q.4b. the law that requires shutting down an industrial plant that pollutes the air or water?...........	5	4	(3)	2	1	C30:____
Q.4c. the law that reimposes the death penalty for murder?	1	2	(3)	4	5	C31:____

When certain that the respondent has learned the categories and can respond to each question without verbal prompting, the interviewer may stop reading them and just glance up for the answer. If the list is very long, the interviewer might repeat the categories near the end anyway, just to make sure the respondent is still alert.

Notice in the previous example the use of directional coding. The researcher had a hypothesis about the reaction to laws by people of various ideologies. Thus 5 represents the supposed ''liberal'' position and 1 the ''conservative'' position. If the hypothesis had instead been support for the legislature regardless of content, all ''very goods'' would have been coded 5.

Schematics. Boxes, matrices, and other schematics are used for economy of space and neatness. The schematic is recommended when several identical responses are used for a series of items. As the previous example shows, a special format can save page space and speed up questioning when several questions have a *common intro-*

duction. To reduce clerical and keypunching error, however, we prefer to put the response codes into boxes rather than leaving them hanging in the air.

In one format, the first question is included in the body of the introduction. This schematic reminds the interviewer of how succeeding questions are read:

Q.41.   I'm going to read some statements that may . . or
        may not . . describe Mayor Morris Meyer. As I read
        each statement, just tell me if you agree . . or
        disagree with the statement. For example (REPEAT)
        do you **agree** . . **disagree** that: the mayor is too
        old for the job.

REPEAT CATEGORIES AS NEEDED PER QUESTION	CIRCLE ONE CODE PER QUESTION			
	Agree	(DK/NR)	Disagree	
Q.41. (The mayor is too old for the job) ...	1	(2)	3	C62:____
Q.41a. Is one of the best mayors the city ever had	3	(2)	1	C63:____
Q.41b. Has underworld connections	1	(2)	3	C64:____
Q.41c. Has too many cronies on his payroll ..	1	(2)	3	C65:____
Q.41d. Has made Model City a more desirable place to live	3	(2)	1	C66:____
Q.41e. **Agree** or **disagree** . . he should be re-elected	3	(2)	1	C67:____

Another schematic repeats a shortened version of the main question, inserting a different word or phrase with each repetition:

Q.8.   Compared with other members of the City Council,
        how would you rate Scoupa Opumoni on leadership
        . . would you rate him as an excellent, good, only
        fair, or poor leader? (REPEAT) How would you rate
        him as **____** . . excellent, good, only fair, or poor?

** ASK EACH WORD	CIRCLE ONE CODE PER QUESTION					
	Excell	Good	(DK/NR)	Only Fair	Poor	
Q.8. (a leader)	5	4	(3)	2	1	C27:___
Q.8a. an intellectual	5	4	(3)	2	1	C28:___
Q.8b. an honest person ...	5	4	(3)	2	1	C29:___
Q.8c. a hard worker	5	4	(3)	2	1	C30:___
Q.8d. an effective person.	5	4	(3)	2	1	C31:___
Q.8e. a family man	5	4	(3)	2	1	C32:___

Checklist 17 presents hints for effective schematics, though they obviously cannot apply to all situations.

CHECKLIST 17

Designing Schematics

1. Put only related material into a schematic. Each should constitute a substantial subpart of the survey. Don't use a schematic for only two or three questions.
2. Write the first question of the series into the body of the introductory statement to show the interviewer how to read each successive question.
3. Use the (REPEAT) symbol to tell the interviewer to repeat the response categories for each question in the series until the respondent has learned the kinds of answers wanted.
4. As needed in the middle or toward the end of the series, have the interviewer repeat the response categories just to be sure the respondent still has them in mind.
5. Use a consistent format for all schematics in the questionnaire, and for successive surveys if possible, to keep interviewer surprises to a minimum.
6. Provide clear interviewer instructions with each schematic: REPEAT CATEGORIES AS NEEDED, CIRCLE ONE CODE PER QUESTION, etc.
7. Assign each item in the schematic to a separate column of a data card; the items are really separate questions but just arranged efficiently.
8. Precode the response alternatives. Code in the direction of the hypotheses, that is, not necessarily uniformly in the schematic.
9. Instruct interviewers to circle codes, not check boxes (or cells).
10. Enclose (DN/NR) in parentheses and instruct interviewers never to read this as a permitted response.
11. Keep shapes and sizes of the cells (boxes) within the schematic as uniform as possible. Don't let it be easier for an interviewer to find and circle a response code just because it is in a bigger space.
12. Connect each question with a series of dots to its row in the schematic.
13. Use schematics only when their use reduces wasted space and neatens the page for a substantial number of questions that have a common introduction or response categories.

Combination Questions. Different kinds of questions may be asked in combination about the same topic. Depending on what we are trying to learn, we may: ask a free-response or fixed-response question; filter out people by their lack of knowledge; ask a scaled-response question about the intensity of attitudes; and ask a dichotomous question about behavior. A slight indention with a vertical line down the left side could tie these together. How elaborate we get depends on the degree of our interest and how long we think we can sustain respondents' attention. For example, suppose we were trying to get an in-depth notion of public response to a new interest group active in city affairs, called the "Citizens Movement." We might use this combination:

Simple Awareness.

Q.5. Have you heard or read anything about a group
called the "Citizens Movement"?

CIRCLE *3--yes 1--no SKIP TO Q.7

2--DK/NR

C29:____

General Knowledge. A free-response question with two probes taps prevailing knowledge among those saying yes to Q.5:

*Q.5a. From what you've heard, what is the Citizens
Movement . . what kind of group is it? (PROBE:
What else have you heard?) (What else?)

_____ C30:____

PROBE:_____ C31:____
etc.

General Opinion. A structured multiple-choice question to get reactions to the group:

Q.5b. Do you think that the "Citizens Movement" will
make a lot of changes, some changes . . or really
no changes in the politics and government of this
city?

CIRCLE *4--a lot of changes

*3--some changes

2--DK/NR ——— SKIP TO Q.5

**1--no changes

C32:____

Specific Opinion. A semistructured question tries to elicit some particulars from those respondents who said in Q.5b that the Citizens Movement would make "a lot" or "some" changes:

*Q.5c. What are two or three changes . . that you feel
the Citizens Movement will make in our political
or governmental system? (PROBE: What other changes
will it make?) (Any others?)

SPECIFY: 1st change_____ C33:____

_____

2nd change_____ C34:____

_____ C35:____
etc.

Intensity of Feeling. Now a scaled-response question tries to determine strength of feeling in those people who responded to Q.5c, regardless of whether it was "a lot of changes" or "no changes":

```
**Q.5d. How strongly do you believe that the Citizens
        Movement will make (INSERT ANSWER TO Q.5c) in our
        political or governmental system . . very strongly,
        quite strongly, not too strongly, or not strongly
        at all?
```

CIRCLE	
	5--very strongly
	4--quite strongly
	3--DK/NR
	2--not too strongly
	1--not strongly at all

C36:____

Specific Behavior. Finally, we use a schematic to investigate what amount and type of actual contact people have had with the Citizens Movement. This is asked of all respondents who said yes to Q.5:

```
Q.6. In the last year or so, how has the Citizens
     Movement come to your attention . . for example:
     have you seen any news programs about them?
```

ASK EACH QUESTION	CIRCLE ONE CODE PER Q.			
	Yes	DK/NR	No	
Q.6. Have you seen any news programs about them?...............	3	(2)	1	C37:____
Q.6a. Have you attended any of their rallies?	3	(2)	1	C38:____
Q.6b. Have you talked to any Citizens Movement Members?............	3	(2)	1	C39:____
Q.6c. Have you read any of their newspaper advertisements?......	3	(2)	1	C40:____
Q.6d. Have you contributed any money to them?...	3	(2)	1	C41:____
Q.6e. Have you become a member of the Citizens Movement?............	3	(2)	1	C42:____

Sleeper. In a long list of questions we might slip in a question to check on a person's earlier answers. This is called a *sleeper* because it seems innocuous but is a measure of consistency. In a voting study we might ask late in the questioning: ''By the way, where do people vote around here?'' If the person doesn't know and has lived at the same address long enough, this could cast doubt on his or her previous answers about voting in the past election. Upon analysis, we would separate these people from other ''voters.''

Response Cards

In certain situations we may give a card to the respondent on which precoded responses are listed, rather than reading the responses.

Sensitive Subjects. A sensitive question or one that is subject to response inflation may be handled in this way. For example, to find family income the respondent is handed a card and asked to give the *letter* corresponding to the family's income group. This lets the respondent avoid mentioning a specific income figure, thus reducing the sensitivity about revealing personal information as well as reducing the temptation to give a better-sounding dollar figure. Letters are used on response cards rather than numbers, because numbers have high and low values that themselves may lead to inflated responses. The questionnaire page has precoded numbers to match the letters of the income categories on the card. These numbers, not the letters, will be coded into the right margin to be keypunched into the data cards.

Complicated Response Categories. A response card is also used when a lengthy series of questions has *complicated response categories*. To help in remembering the categories, a card is given to the respondent and the interviewer says:

```
I'm going to read you some statements. As I read each
statement, use this card (HAND RESPONDENT GREEN CARD)
to tell me if you agree strongly, agree moderately . .
disagree moderately, or disagree strongly with the
statement.
```

Since these categories are more complicated than usual and are a mouthful for the interviewer to keep repeating, a card eases the interviewer's task and focuses the respondent's attention. In the example, neither letters or numbers were used. Yet there are occasions for using numbers, as when the problem specifically calls for a high/low rating. For example, we might use a card depicting a 7-step rating scale:

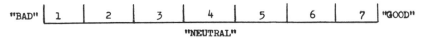

With each of several questions, the respondent is asked to give the number that comes closest to describing his or her feeling:

```
Here is a card (HAND YELLOW CARD) showing seven numbers. The
lowest number, "1," means "Bad." The highest number, "7," means
```

```
"Good." The middle number, "4," is neutral . . it means neither
good nor bad. As I read each of the following statements, just
tell me which number . . from 1 to 7 . . best describes your
feelings about cigarette smoking and health.
     The next statement is . . .
```

As mentioned in Chapter 1, some researchers use a diagram of a thermometer with the numbers 0, 10, 20 . . . up to 100 to help respondents express their relative warmth of feeling toward certain subjects. When this device is used in the Model questionnaire, each question has a scale printed under it, where the interviewer marks the number that the respondent gives.

Lengthy List. A third use of response cards is when respondents are asked to select answers from a lengthy list or to rate choices of several items. Suppose we were asking people to rate the "effectiveness" of seven city officials in "getting things done for the city." The respondents are given a card listing officials' names, and the interviewer asks: "Which person on the list do you think has been most effective in getting things done for Model City?" This is followed by the questions: "Which person would you say is in *second* place in getting things done? Which one is in *third* place? Using the name-list card makes sense if it aids recognition of names respondents may have seen or heard in the media, which may be more realistic than having them try unaided to recall names out of the blue.[3] The questionnaire has codes from 1 to 7 printed beside each name. The interviewer finds the name of the person mentioned as being first in influence and circles 1 after the name and then does the same for the rest of the rankings.

The response card has the pitfall of any fixed-response question: the categories must exhaust all possible or acceptable answers. If the answers can only be "yes" or "no," a response card is not needed. More complicated categories must be adequately tested to make sure that respondents will be able to answer within the alternatives given. On the other hand, a large array of alternatives may suggest more answers than people may have in their minds, so the card provides a convenient source of new information from which satisfactory answers may happily (unhappily for the researcher) be chosen.

When using response-list cards we make more than one version because this may offset the tendency some people have to pick the response at the top (or bottom) of the list. Determine the response order for different cards randomly, but randomize the cards *among* interviewers; don't burden one interviewer with more than one card version for the same question.

However useful cards may be, there is a practical limit on the number of cards

---

[3] Whether and when to use "aided recall" or "unaided recall" questions is a subject of much debate. Prompting respondents' recall with a list tends to lead to overreporting. Letting them answer without prompting leads to underreporting. We often use the two techniques in combination, first asking an open-ended (unaided recall) question, followed by a card list (aided recall).

the respondent can be asked to read or the interviewer can keep track of. Color coding the cards and including a storage envelope stapled to the notebook will save the interviewer from awkward fishing for the right card; a reminder in the questionnaire to TAKE BACK CARDS will ensure that there is something to hand to the next respondent.

Sorting. Cards used in a different way can facilitate rating by use of a *sorting* technique. Researchers who want to know what aspects of community life are most important to residents might prepare a deck of small cards that each feature one "good" quality "Nearness to public transportation," "Neighborhood police patrols," "Good schools," "Low taxes," etc. At the proper point in the questionnaire, the interviewer would ask the respondent to arrange the cards on a flat surface in order of importance. The interviewer records the identifying letters on the cards in the order they are placed.

Other Devices

Other visual aids to questioning include photographs, drawings, or written materials. For example, we might show the pictures of five candidates to see which ones people can identify, or we might show a facsimile of a candidate's billboard—perhaps with the name unreadable—to see if people recognize it. Sometimes we show respondents several advertising slogans and ask their preferences.

The questionnaire may have a separate pull-out section of questions. We give these to respondents, asking them to complete them on the spot. They often include personal questions that people may be reluctant to talk about openly, such as abortions or use of drugs. Candidate preferences can be identified by including a separate ballot form; people mark them and deposit them in a slotted box carried by the interviewer, which assures similar privacy. Of course, in order to permit analysis with other information on the questionnaire, these separate forms must carry the case number of the respondent. That is why information received in this manner is *confidential* rather than *anonymous.*

Commercial surveys may carry packages and products for respondents to identify or sample. Interviewers may even carry cassette tape recorders that play jingles, theme music, etc., and try to learn which have caught the public ear.

All these imaginative devices maximize the advantage of doing face-to-face interviews.

Voting Screen

Questions that gauge people's inclination to vote can be used in different studies for different purposes as another characteristic by which to analyze their responses, or to eliminate unlikely voters from the sample at an early stage. The Model Survey is interested in learning about all different kinds of people, while a candidate survey needs to learn about only those who will influence the candidate's success.

In the early part of a campaign year, newspaper polls typically combine political and other kinds of content in the same study. They might employ voting-screen questions and report only candidate preferences of likely voters, but they don't eliminate respondents with the screen, both because a good population sample will contain many nonvoters and because the extra time and cost of finding and surveying only people who may vote is wasteful. Toward the end of the campaign, the polls are more likely to concentrate on political prediction; they therefore reject unlikely voters for interviewing as extraneous, or at least they will make prodigious efforts to report on likely voters only.

No voter screen is flawless. Our knowledge of voter behavior is never fully complete. Last-minute appeals and campaign turnout efforts can have a marginal effect. Turnout in a presidential year varies between 40 and 70 percent; turnout in presidential primaries can range from 10 to 40 percent; off-year elections seldom exceed 40 percent nationally, and local and school board elections are often far lower. These figures mean that a voter screen must identify the more than half of the sample who will be discarded. Gallup claims their voter screen, verified by checks with registration officials about actual voting by respondents after the election, gives a "likely voter" sample of which 87 percent actually vote.[4]

Formerly, the question "Are you registered to vote, if you want to?" was thought adequate to determine likely voters, particularly as election day drew closer. People who take the trouble to register are indeed more likely to vote, but, because registration requirements vary (from periodic reregistration to "permanent" registration [your name stays on the rolls if you vote once within a stipulated time period]), many people do not actually know their registration status. Moreover, some states now allow registration at the polls on election day itself, meaning that a last-minute appeal can transform the hitherto unlikely voter into a bonafide registrant and voting participant, whom only an election-day intercept survey would detect.

Here we present a six-question voting screen used in the Model Survey (see Figure 4.3). Our procedure requires the interviewer to complete all questions and determine likely voters on the basis of all answers. We do this because, first, we don't know for sure which questions and answers will predict voting and cannot take the risk of terminating interviews at the point a person gives one unacceptable answer. For example, we don't quit because someone says she is "not very interested" in the election; instead we allow her to be "saved" if she resembles a voter on some other criteria. Second, we want answers to all questions so that we can continue research (say, by

[4]Harold Mendelsohn and Irving Crespi, *Polls, Television, and the New Politics*, (Scranton: Chandler, 1972) page 75.

Q.1. As you may know, there's going to be an election in Model City on June 27th. Right now, are you registered . . so that you can vote in this election if you want to?

    IF "NO" /"DK" ASK: Are you planning to register in time to vote in the June 27th election, or have you decided not to register?

      CIRCLE   3--yes, registered

                2--not registered, but plan to

                |1|-not registered; don't plan to

C21:____

Q.2. If you want to vote on election day, where would you go to vote . . what place?

      ENTER PLACE   _____

      CIRCLE   2-- correct place *Fire Station #19*

                |1|- DK/NR/incorrect place

C22:____

Q.3. Would you say you are very interested, fairly interested, not too interested, or not interested at all in that election?

      CIRCLE   5--very interested |3|-DK/NR

                4--fairly interested |2|-not too interested

                                  |1|-not interested at all

C23:____

Q.4. Right now, would you say that you definitely will, probably will .. probably will not, or definitely will not vote in that election?

      CIRCLE   5--definitely will |3|-DK/NR

                4--probably will |2|-probably not

                                  |1|-definitely not

C24:____

Q.5. Thinking back to the election last year for governor . . were you registered so that you could have voted in that election if you wanted to?

    IF "YES" ASK: Did you have a chance to vote in that election, or weren't you able to?

      CIRCLE   4--voted |2|-registered/didn't vote

                3--ineligible |1|-DK/NR/not registered

C25:____

Q.6. What about the 1980 election for President . . were you registered to vote in that election?

    IF "YES" ASK: Did you have a chance to vote . . or weren't you able to?

      CIRCLE   4--voted |2|-registered/didn't vote

                3--ineligible |1|-DK/NR/not registered

C26:____

UNACCEPTABLE ANSWERS	
NUMBER ACTUAL	
NUMBER ALLOWED	2

→ IF ACTUAL IS GREATER THAN ALLOWED SKIP TO DEMOGRAPHICS, PAGE 5

Figure 4.3. Voting screen.

panel studies) during and after the campaign, trying to improve knowledge of which questions predict voting behavior.

The Model procedure requires interviewers to ask all questions, obtaining both "qualifying" and "nonqualifying" answers. Qualifying answers are those that fit the "likely voter" profile for the study at hand; they may change for another study. As shown in Figure 4.3, nonqualifying answers are preprinted with boxed-in codes on the page. Interviewers circle responses to each question. At the end of the series, interviewers quickly count the number of times they got a nonqualifying answer and write this in a summary box at the bottom of the page. If the number of nonqualifying answers actually obtained is larger than the number allowed for this study, the interviewer would skip to the last page of the questionnaire and ask some key demographic questions (for sample-to-census checks) before closing off the interview. The candidate-survey voting screen shown in Figure 4.3 allows two nonqualifying answers without termination. This number is preprinted on the page. In scanning the six questions, the interviewer looks for the nonqualifying response boxes that are marked. This is a quick visual process and is the only calculation (besides the respondent-selection key) that we ask interviewers to do in the field. Recording the number of marked boxes as "NUMBER ACTUAL," the interviewer compares the two numbers. Suppose the respondent disqualifies on three questions. Since NUMBER ACTUAL, 3, is larger than NUMBER ALLOWED, 2, the interviewer skips to the demographics page.

Other studies may relax the criteria for qualifying answers. For example, in a presidential election study we may accept people who are "registered, but didn't vote in the election for governor" (Choice 2 on Question 5), since many people are in fact off-year abstainers. Contrarily, in another study we might allow fewer answers to qualify. For example, we could box in "not registered, but plans to" (Choice 2 on Question 1), especially in a state without election-day registration, on the grounds that most of those people will not get around to registering before the cutoff date.

Note that the whole voting screen is boxed-in, to show it is a unit, and that it occupies only one page, so that the interviewer does not have to flip pages to add up the nonqualifying responses.

Transitions

The four parts of the questionnaire should hang together naturally in the interview. The smoothness with which the respondent is led through the introduction, warmed up to the questioning process, exposed to the major issues, and classified by various demographic characteristics depends on the *transitional devices* used to weave each section into a whole. Transition is best achieved when question sequence is logical. As in a normal conversation, one question should lead to another, and ultimately a variety of seemingly unrelated topics should be covered without pause.

At times, however, it is best to break a chain of thought deliberately in order to dispel boredom or to prevent respondents from falling into stereotypic answer patterns. During a sequence in which questions and answers are much alike, variety will liven things up. In other instances, a "fog" question with new content is introduced to help people forget previous answers.

It is amazing how a subject like defense against nuclear war can change without pause into prenatal maternal care merely with the aid of such simple phrases as: "Now, here's a different kind of question . . ." or "Turning to another subject now . . ." or "Well, that was interesting. Now what do you think about . . . ." Of course, an interviewer's deliberate voice inflection can also indicate subject change: "Yes . . *well* now . . and what would you say about . . . ."

These marvelously simple, effective transitions stitch topics together like a patchwork quilt. The thread that moves from core issues to demographic questions is a casual remark that assures the respondent the interview will soon be over: "Now here's a few final questions." (This purposeful grammatical lapse somehow gives just the right conversational flow at this critical juncture.)

QUESTION SEQUENCE

Providing proper question order is not merely a mechanical or technical challenge, but one of substance. The location of each question must be considered as to how it will affect following questions. Once names or topics are mentioned, an information-level question is useless. Once alternatives have been suggested, free-response is influenced. Once the subject matter focus of the interview is clear, the salience of this topic to the respondents will rise. Once sensitive areas are touched, some respondents will not be as cooperative.

Since everything cannot be saved for last, the questionnaire designer will have to trade off some benefits against other risks. No arrangement should be haphazard; rather each location must be defensibly reasoned. Pretesting will reveal some unanticipated interactions between questions that may then be reassessed.

DESIGNING FOR OTHER SURVEYS

It is in questionnaire design that we find the greatest differences between survey types. The one exception may be panel studies; since they are merely face-to-face studies that reinterview some of the same individuals, they require the least adaptations.

Panel Studies

Some adjustments are necessary in questionnaire format to allow for recontacting respondents in panel studies.

Identifying Change. Perhaps the key issue for panel questionnaire design arises in the earliest days of study planning and hypothesizing. Panel studies attempt to identify and make conclusions about changes in people's opinions; we have all seen examples of how artificial such conclusions can be. For instance, the election study late in the campaign that finds people more knowledgeable than earlier and concludes that the candidate's strategy is working. Here, the entire election process— including historical coincidences—is operating. In designing panel measures, we have to specify what changes we expect should occur, and from what causes, and set precise criteria for judging those changes and all possible components that could explain them.

Measuring change in opinion over time has its hazards, too. One of the routine questions of public affairs surveys asks: "What are the most important problems facing the people of Model City today?" Just as snowstorms are seasonal, issues are topical. During the winter, the typical Model Citian replies that the most important problems are snow removal, traffic congestion, physical health, and heating costs. During the summer, he or she complains about lack of leisure time, panhandlers on the sidewalks, crime in the streets, again traffic congestion, and the rise in gasoline costs. In the six months between surveys, Model City didn't change—the weather did. Obviously, different problems are important at different times, reacting to factors such as the weather, the fiscal year, the holiday season, the school break during summer, seasonal employment, to name a few.

Attitudinal measures have special implications for panel studies. When we use an attitude scale (see Chapter 3) we must be sure it has been validated: that there is previous research showing that it truly measures the attitude under study. Without validation, it's risky to conclude about the results of such scales.

It's common practice in surveys to ask a series of agree/disagree questions for which we add up agreements and get a total attitude score. Certain people are "conservative," we might say, because they agree with most of 16 statements about the role in society of the federal government, the church, schools, family, and the mass media. Then, because we want to ask other questions on the next wave of the panel study without adding to the length of the interview, we drop some of the 16 items—keeping a group that is representative of the scale. In analyzing the second wave, we may find that some conservatives are now liberals and some liberals, conservatives. Obviously, people are likely to shift positions on a few items. But if we use the entire 16-item scale, there is likely to be a pretty good correspondence between each individual's *total score* on the two waves. Although answers may flip-flop on a specific statement (e.g., about the church or the government), the overall pattern of ideology should be quite consistent over a short period of time.

The same problem occurs in measuring *behavior:* If we ask a 10-item index of questions to determine which respondents are public affairs activists, we have to repeat the whole index on the later waves to get the same measure of activism. Like topical issues, behavior is susceptible to cycles or periods of time. Different behaviors occur, last longer, or are more important during, for example, the football season, the last month of an election campaign, the harvesting season, holiday periods, school terms, etc. There are "natural" times for certain behaviors to occur, of which panel studies must be aware.

Panel measurements must have a capability to detect whether changes in information, attitude, and behavior are: (1) *intrinsic*—not due to topicality or cycles; (2) *real*—not artificially the results of reinterviewing; (3) *durable*—will persist after the novelty wears off; (4) *important*—something of consequence to the individual; and (5) *progressive*—not likely to fall back (regress) to previous states.

Additional Information Needed. Reinterviewing should be planned at the time of the initial questionnaire. This ensures that sufficient information will be gathered and recorded to enable relocating the same respondents. This is no easy task, for it requires full name and address, phone number, time of day and day of week contacted (therefore, suggesting a likely time for a second visit), and even hints on how to find the right door. For identification purposes, the panel number, or wave number, should be added to the standard identification numbers.

Card and Column Locations. Additional questions asked in a second wave could continue right on from the last column number used, but there is risk of mismatching respondents when we add more punches to an existing card. It is safer to start a new card for the new information; the numbering should also reflect the next card number (Card 04 if the initial survey had three cards). This card must contain the same basic identification codes (Columns 01–09) from Card 1 for that respondent to enable physical collating or electronic matching of data from the two waves.

Repeated Information. Although the first interview obtained complete demographic information, much of this should be obtained anew, (since status changes can occur, and since rechecking original information is wise anyway). But most important, we will want to interview a control group (people who have not been interviewed before), and we will want them all to have the same stimuli.

Intercept Surveys

Because intercept surveys, such as those done at the polls on election day, are conducted under many handicaps, the design and questioning must be extremely simple.

Format. Figure 4.4 (see page 228) shows an example, front and back, of a short intercept questionnaire. Brevity and privacy are the watchwords. Respondents are asked to fill out this questionnaire—like a ballot—on their own. If it seems too long or too complicated, they will simply refuse to participate. Therefore it should be small in size, yet uncrowded.

a. Front side

```
┌─────────────────────────────────────────────────────────────────────────┐
│              E L E C T I O N   N E W S   P O L L                           │
├─────────────────────────────────────────────────────────────────────────┤
│          [A]  1 2    [B]  1  2  3   [C]   1 2 3                            │
├─────────────────────────────────────────────────────────────────────────┤
│  PLEASE CHECK THE BOX(ES) OF THE CANDIDATES YOU VOTED FOR                  │
├───────────────────────────────────┬───────────────────────────────────────┤
│  [D]    SENATOR                   │  [E]    GOVERNOR                        │
├───────────────────────────────────┼───────────────────────────────────────┤
│  1.  [ ]  Gilda Lilly             │  1.  [ ]  Ada Poorperson               │
│           (Republican)            │           (Republican)                 │
│                                   │                                        │
│  2.  [ ]  Sally Forth             │  2.  [ ]  Delia Fullhouse              │
│           (Democrat)              │           (Democrat)                   │
│                                   │                                        │
│  3.  [ ]  Clara Fye               │  3.  [ ]  Cora Napple                  │
│           (Conservative)          │           (Conservative)               │
│                                   │                                        │
│  4.  [ ]  Other                   │  4.  [ ]  Other                        │
├───────────────────────────────────┴───────────────────────────────────────┤
│                   PLEASE TURN OVER TO THE BACK                             │
└─────────────────────────────────────────────────────────────────────────┘
```

b. Back side

```
┌─────────────────────────────────────────────────────────────────────────┐
│              PLEASE CHECK ONE BOX PER QUESTION                             │
├───────────────────────────────────┬───────────────────────────────────────┤
│  [F]   IS YOUR FAMILY'S           │  [G]   WHAT IS YOUR                    │
│        CHIEF WAGE EARNER          │        RELIGIOUS PREFERENCE?           │
│        PAID BY THE HOUR?          │                                        │
├───────────────────────────────────┼───────────────────────────────────────┤
│  1. [ ]  YES                      │  1. [ ]  CATHOLIC                      │
│  2. [ ]  NO                       │  2. [ ]  JEWISH                        │
│                                   │  3. [ ]  PROTESTANT/OTHER              │
├───────────────────────────────────┴───────────────────────────────────────┤
│                   THANK YOU VERY MUCH                                      │
└─────────────────────────────────────────────────────────────────────────┘
```

Figure 4.4. Intercept survey questionnaire.

The ballot's absolute essentials are on one side: (1) camouflaged demographic codes to be checked off by the interviewers before handing out the ballot; and (2) the names of the candidates, for respondents to indicate for whom they voted. A few questions on issues and group affiliation can be put on the back side of the questionnaire. Since some respondents cannot be induced to turn over the sheet, this arrangement will guarantee that at least the critical candidate-preference and demographics data will have already been obtained.

The questionnaire should not be an exact replica of the official state ballot, because respondents may think it illegal or it may trigger strong feelings of privacy violation. Yet large boxes by the candidates' names (for respondents to place Xs) will look serious enough to be credible.

Precoding. Ballot items must be precoded, even though respondents will see the numbers; the results must be phoned into headquarters in computer-ready style, and there is no time for coding large numbers of ballots and for error checking.

Telephone Surveys

The design principles for telephone surveys are much the same as for face-to-face surveys—an interviewer will again be reading from a form; but there are some restrictions.

Design Restrictions. Telephone questionnaires typically differ from face-to-face questionnaires in these ways:

- Overall questionnaire length is shorter, because feasible interviewing time is briefer.
- Individual questions must be shorter to keep the interaction between question and response high, which helps to lessen phone hang-ups.
- No cards and no visuals can be used, though a short tape could be played if there were no delays in triggering it.
- No lengthy lists of response categories can be used, and response categories cannot be complicated.
- No involved rating questions or comparisons of more than two subjects can be included.
- Additional disposition codes for times of all calls as well as additional spaces for writing time zone and appointment phone numbers are needed.

Obviously, certain restrictions on design for telephone surveys are imposed by the loss of eye contact. But there are no limitations on the types of hypotheses tested, subjects asked about, or page format. The limitations are on response categories—they must be kept few, brief, and consistent, using yes/no, agree/

disagree type choices for large blocks of questions, and be separated with other content for variety. In so doing, formats using response categories read within the text work best (a method previously discussed in this chapter).

Adaptations of Page Format. Because interviewers don't have to maintain eye contact but can keep their eyes on the questionnaire, pages do not need all the white space of the face-to-face questionnaire. Page format is of no significance whatsoever to respondents, who only *hear* the questions. Since the contact is verbal, as in face-to-face interviews, all devices of questionnaire design can and should be used in telephone surveys, including schematics, REPEAT symbols, voting screens, semistructured questions, and filters.

Since cards cannot be used, however, the sensitive detail of family income may have to be approached somewhat indirectly. The following shows a ''path'' format that pins income down:

```
Q.54:  Is the total yearly family income in your household
       under . . or over $10,000.

           1--under              7--over              C78:_____
      ┌──────────────────┐   ┌──────────────────────┐
      │ IF "UNDER $10,000" ASK* │   │ IF $10,000 or over" ASK** │
      └──────────────────┘   └──────────────────────┘

   *Is it under or over $5,000.    **Is it under or over $15,000

      2--under      3--over        5--under      6--over
                                                              C79:_____
    ┌─────────┐ ┌─────────┐     ┌─────────┐ ┌─────────┐
    │ IF "UNDER│ │ IF "OVER│     │ IF  "UNDER│ │ IF "OVER│
    │ $5,000" ASK:│ │$5,000" ASK:│     │$15,000"  │ │$15,000" ASK:│
    └─────────┘ └─────────┘     └─────────┘ └─────────┘

    Is it under .. Is it under ..                 Is it under ..
    or over $3,000. or over $8,000.                or over $20,000

    ┌────────┐  ┌────────┐      ┌────────┐   ┌────────┐
    │ CIRCLE │  │ CIRCLE │      │ CIRCLE │   │ CIRCLE │
    └────────┘  └────────┘      └────────┘   └────────┘

    1--under 3   3--under 8      5--under 15  6--under 20   C80:_____

    2--over 3    4--over 8                    7--over 20

                8--income refused, or DK even after PROBE
```

Racial identities, which were observed with no questioning in face-to-face interviewing, must be asked directly. Under no circumstances let interviewers judge a respondent's race by voice. In asking, the interviewer should avoid drawing attention to the question but should instead say it as an off-hand remark:

```
            And what is your race. (IF HESITATION, SAY:
            Well, most people refer to themselves as black,
            white, or some other racial group.)
```

The portability of the telephone offers at least two pluses. First, interviewing can be done in a central facility or at private homes. And, second, at a central calling place, supervisors and monitors can solve questionnaire problems on the spot. (But this is no excuse for skipping the pretest, because any changes necessitated during the interviewing will mean already-completed interviews will not be strictly comparable to those done following the change).

Other Questionnaire Forms. Another plus of phone interviewing is that, with less wear and tear than in field surveys, the telephone questionnaire can be more easily rendered in the form of mark-sense or optical-scan pages. Discarding the physical form altogether, the questionnaire may be displayed electronically on a special console. In the latter mode, the set-up at each interviewer's desk consists of the following:

- An operator's headset (instead of a hand-held instrument), which enables talking with respondents while keeping hands free to record responses.
- A cathode ray tube (CRT) that displays the questionnaire to the interviewer, one question at a time, with the speed controlled electronically by the respondent's progress through the interview.
- An electronic keyboard that enables the interviewer to key respondents' answers directly into the computer.
- A cassette tape that, when inserted into the console, automatically controls the entire sampling and dialing process.

With this equipment the interviewer can simply insert the sample-control cassette and sit back. The tape automatically dials predetermined sample numbers, permits a preselected number of rings, disconnects automatically if no answer, records the disposition of the number, and proceeds to dial the next sample number—all without involving the interviewer. The procedure can be tailored for use in interviewers' own homes all over the country. The nation-wide growth of a network of research firms with interviewing staffs operating such consoles from offices and homes will give impetus to the spread of localized, and therefore cheaper telephone interviewing.

Mail Surveys

We cannot control behavior at the other end of the research chain in a mail survey—that is, who opens the envelope, in what sequence questions are read, or which questions are answered. Questionnaire design here, instead of being a matter of convenience for interviewer and coder, must do everything—supply motivation, create communication, and win completion.

Design Principles. Some tips on question writing for mail surveys have already appeared in Chapter 3. Checklist 18 outlines the general rules of good mail questionnaire design.

CHECKLIST 18

Format of Mail Questionnaires

1. WHITE SPACE: Use space liberally. Don't clutter pages with precodes, identification items, disposition codes, or anything else that does not help the respondent to answer the questions. Plan ahead for such items to be added later in the office.

2. IDENTIFICATION: Use one identification number—a single case number that identifies intended respondent, address, locale, and group identification. Too many numbers will make the page look like a police dossier.

3. PHYSICAL FORM: Make the print large enough to be read by weak or failing eyes. Print black on white or black on pale yellow for best readability. If money permits, use a distinctive, colored letterhead for the covering letter, and use a print-style typeface (rather than ordinary typewriter face) for the questionnaire itself, to give it greater authority. Use a paper stock that will hold up under rough treatment—expect dogs or babies to chew the corners, as well as coffee spills. Do not use mark-sense forms or other techniques that require special pencils or that can't stand to be mutilated.

4. LANGUAGE: If there is any reason to expect mailing to non-English-speaking homes, for example, Spanish-speaking, print two versions of the questionnaire or a bilingual version.

5. LENGTH: Keep the questionnaire short. Respondents must believe they can complete it on the spot without significant effort or undue time. For a general-population survey, a format of one page—or front and back on a single page—is ideal. If it has to be longer, it should be in brochure form (4-page maximum). Sometimes a questionnaire can be prepared in slightly larger size and photo-reduced to fit on one page, but be sure to leave more space for answers so that only the questions will shrink.

6. SIMPLICITY: Almost none of the design techniques of face-to-face and telephone surveys can be used in mail questionnaires—after all, we prepared those for use by trained interviewers. Don't use respondent-selection keys, complicated schematics, scale values and weights, voting screens, open-ended questions, and other format devices that will only confuse respondents. Asterisks and other symbols help interviewers who are trained to use them, but they do not help other respondents. Keep it simple. Just proceed from one question to the next.

7. NO VARIATION: Unless truly unavoidable, do not use filter questions. Instruct respondents to answer all questions. Do not make them responsible for determining their eligibility to answer questions. Even if they must mark a "not applicable to me" category, they must have responsibility for every question to minimize skipping others by mistake. When it is essential to use a filter (say, when questions apply only to someone who is presently enrolled in college), mention this requirement in the cover letter, and repeat it at the top of the page, not in the questionnaire. Set off this requirement distinctively.

8. PAGE FORMAT: Format must be utterly consistent. If different formats and techniques are inevitable, separate them on different pages.

9. BOXES: The use of boxes and sectioning is effective for dividing questionnaire pages into different types of content or different response problems because it is a familiar form to taxpayers, students, and employees.

10. NO PRECODES: Precode numbers should ordinarily not be printed in the boxes because they mistakenly suggest to respondents that ordinal and interval measures have a high/low value. At the later coding stage, a template is put over the page showing the code for each response. The template is a clear plastic facsimile of the page with the addition of precoded numbers beside each response category (see Chapter 6).

If precoding must be used on the questionnaire, it is not wise to code responses directionally unless the codes run in the same direction for each question. People are suspicious of numbers that, for no apparent reason, run in different directions for their answers. And what they suspect, they do not fill out and return.

A mail survey designed to fit on the front and back of a single sheet is shown in Figure 4.5*a* and Figure 4.5*b*.

Note especially the questionnaire's sponsorship, its aura of legitimacy, its motivational qualities, its assurance of easy response (and the appearance that confirms this), and its tone of gratitude. No writing by the respondent is required, only blanks to check, with an attempt to get them to use X's. No precoding numbers appear. Sections make it clear there is one task per area. Response categories are spaced far enough apart so that the respondents' marks cannot be misconstrued.

The demographic items are not prying questions, but statements. While not all of the response categories read well with the stem, it is less confusing and pompous than repeatedly saying "I am a(n) . . ." If the respondents don't fit into these categories, they will either write something in without a blank being provided or skip the question. Since we can't be in their homes to record subtleties, we will sacrifice subtlety for a better return rate.

Successful data collection is all any questionnaire design is for.

Motivation. The problem of mail surveys is the low response rate. Part of the problem is the "junk mail" instinct, which rejects anything that doesn't appear to be a personal or business letter. Commercial direct-mail firms have ingenious attention-getting devices that try to get people to open the envelope. If there is an incentive—such as monetary, in-kind reward, or simply the virtuous, personal satisfaction of helping science—it cannot operate unless someone knows about it. One way is to shriek on the envelope: "OPEN ME—I'M WORTH MONEY TO YOU." A more subdued approach is to make the envelope appear as much as possible like a personal or business letter by using a first-class stamp (not metered

In order for us to get the views of more people, please complete this questionnaire at this time -- it takes only about 3 minutes. Then mail it today in the postage-paid envelope to the address on the back.

(All answers are confidential.   Your name is not required.)

PUBLIC AFFAIRS SURVEY OF CITY ACTIVITIES

- Which of the following activities of city government especially interest or concern you?

PUT AN X BY AS MANY AS YOU ARE CONCERNED ABOUT

_____Parks, recreation   _____Property tax rates

_____Library service   _____Dutch Elm disease control

_____Street repair   _____Police protection

_____Help for the needy   _____Job opportunities

_____Trash removal   _____Other:_____
                                            (write in)

- Now go back and CIRCLE the ONE SINGLE item in the list that concerns you most.

- Have you ever written, or telephoned, the Mayor or your Alderman about any problem you had with the city?

_____ YES   _____NO

- Did you get a reasonable, satisfactory response?

_____YES   _____NO

- If city services must be CUT, how much of each of the following would you prefer to see cut?

PUT AN X IN EACH LINE SHOWING HOW MUCH TO CUT

Police patrols   _____CUT MUCH   _____CUT A LITTLE   _____DON'T CUT

Neighborhood fire stations _____CUT MUCH   _____CUT A LITTLE   _____DON'T CUT

Number of school buildings _____CUT MUCH   _____CUT A LITTLE   _____DON'T CUT

Trash collection   _____CUT MUCH   _____CUT A LITTLE   _____DON'T CUT

Street repair   _____CUT MUCH   _____CUT A LITTLE   _____DON'T CUT

- NO ONE LIKES TAXES, But . . .

If more money had to be raised to keep the city services you want most, mark here how you think the city should raise that money:

_____Property tax   _____Sales tax   _____Income tax

OVER, PLEASE

Figure 4.5a. Mail survey questionnaire (front page).

I am:

☐ A homeowner

☐ A renter

I am:

☐ Male

☐ Female

I am:

☐ Married with children
       at home

☐ Married without children
       at home

☐ Single, living alone
       (includes widowed, divorced)

☐ Single, living with others

My age group is:

☐ Over 65

☐ 45-64

☐ 30-45

☐ 21-30

☐ 18-20

My family income group last year
(all earners together) was about:

☐ A ($1,000-$5,000)

☐ B ($5,000-$10,000)

☐ C ($11,000-$15,000)

☐ D ($16,000-$20,000)

☐ E ($20,000-$30,000)

☐ F (over $30,000)

I have lived in Model City about:

☐ 1 year or less

☐ 2 to 5 years

☐ 6 to 10 years

☐ more than 10 years

☐ all my life

I consider myself to be a:

☐ Republican

☐ Democrat

☐ Other party member

☐ None of the above

My occupation is:

☐ Clerical or Sales

☐ Blue collar (factory, craftsman)

☐ Managerial or business

☐ Professional person

☐ Student

☐ Homemaker

☐ Retired

☐ Unemployed

Thank you very much.

Please mail today to:

Public Affairs Survey
Box 929 University Station
Model City 99999

Figure 4.5b. Mail survey questionnaire (back page).

postage), a typewritten address (not an address label—those nasty computers can do this), and with the personal name of the would-be respondent on the address (not "occupant"). Inside we offer incentives and include a self-addressed, postpaid, return envelope. Metered mail or no-postage-required return envelopes can be used here to avoid having the stamp peeled off for personal use.

Despite these efforts, characteristically mail survey completion rates are low and samples unrepresentative of target populations. Though weighting techniques can be used to restore some balance (see Chapter 6), they are not a substitute for a good initial response. We critique, re-do our questionnaire several times, and pre-test, until it works without the slightest hesitation or irritation. For anything but a highly specialized population, this above all means brevity.

FURTHER READING

Babbie, Earl R., *Survey Research Methods* (Belmont, California: Wadsworth 1973), pp. 145–148. Brief treatment of format.

Dillman, Don A., *Mail and Telephone Surveys: The Total Design Method* (New York: Wiley, 1978). Strategies and techniques for improving response rates.

Lansing, J, and J. Morgan, *Economic Surveys* (Ann Arbor: Institute for Social Research, University of Michigan, 1971). Useful suggestions for design of survey instruments.

Oppenheim, A. N., *Questionnaire Design and Attitude Measurement* (New York: Basic Books, 1966). Illustrations of checklists, rating scales, inventories.

Warwick, Donald P., and Charles A. Lininger, *The Sample Survey: Theory and Practice,* (New York: McGraw-Hill, 1975).

5

Conducting Interviews

An interviewer in an important metropolitan attitudes survey was hustled off a farmer's property after introducing herself by saying, "Well, here I am to interview you hicks in the sticks." The survey's office heard about that one, but how many times did something almost as bad happen?

Never in the survey are we closer to truth than the point at which the interviewer *intervenes* between the intentions of the question being asked and the intentions of the response being given. Survey research is a process of people (researchers) talking to people (respondents) *through* other people (interviewers). The intentions of the researcher's question are not always conveyed accurately to the respondent. And the intentions of the respondent's answer are not always conveyed faithfully to the researcher.

The problems are human. The solutions are too. One of the solutions is to recognize the significance of the interviewer's role in the survey. On many projects, the interviewer unfortunately is treated as the lowest head on the totem pole. What a mistake! For all its brilliant planning, a survey is no better than the people carrying it out in the field. The interviewer is the critical point of failure in survey research. We cannot control interviewers' biases as we do other biases. And often the damage done in interviewing is irreparable; we can code the data twice to control coding errors, but we can't interview twice.

IMPROVING INTERVIEWING

If the survey is largely at the mercy of interviewers, then the task is to get good interviewers and to assure their professional behavior.

Finding Interviewers

There are a number of alternatives: (1) we may use the professional interviewers of a survey organization; (2) hire and supervise professionals on our own; (3) use students from a class; (4) rely on volunteers; or (5) use staff members of the organization doing the survey. A brief comparison of the various sources for obtaining interviewers will point up the advantages and disadvantages of each. This is summarized in Figure 5.1.

Commercial Interviewing Services. Using experienced interviewers can advance the study by a giant step, and having others responsible for recruiting and supervising them takes a major administrative load off the study director, but the cost may be prohibitory.

Commercial polling is big business. Professional interviewers are available throughout the country. Large field services of perhaps 1500 interviewers are maintained by national survey organizations, and almost every large city has one or more survey firms. Using such firms does not guarantee quality; not all interviewers hired by them are equally competent or supervised equally well. When contracting interviewing services, it is essential to have specific, agreed procedures which ensure that the quality of training and supervision meets the standards of the study design.

Professional excellence among commercial firms ranges greatly. At the lower levels, some bad but common practices are: overrepresenting their professional training in the social sciences; claiming larger full-time field staffs than they actually employ; using ready-made samples drawn for advertising and marketing studies in which low-income groups are purposely ignored; and running studies "piggyback"—combining two or more studies in one questionnaire—without forewarning.

Assuming we are satisfied with the quality of a firm's interviewers, however, the biggest obstacle to using professional interviewing services is cost—cost for training time, interviewing time, travel time, and transportation expenses. In addition, by yielding control over the field work, we must ask for improved quality safeguards by the interviewing firm's own supervisors, which increase costs. Added on top of this, of course, will be the overhead and profit of the firm.

Direct-hire Professionals. The Model Survey favors hiring, training, and supervising professional interviewers directly. Much money is saved by eliminating commercial overhead costs. Since polling organizations do not use all of their interviewers full-time, many of the same people are available for part-time work. By

Figure 5.1. Types of interviewers

Type	Availability	Competence	Motivation	Cost	Control	Bias
Professional	Small pool in large cities	Experienced, cocksure; no subject-matter specialization	Money; pride	High cash	Economic sanction, personal reputation	Possibly against low-income respondents
Staff	Full-time employees	Subject-matter familiarity; need interviewer training	Commitment to agency goals; self-motivated	Foregone regular agency tasks; overtime for nights and weekends	Subject to direction	Toward agency policy
Student	Captive, but part-time	Theoretically oriented; varying talent, all need training	Increase knowledge course grace	Time out from other learning	Expect instruction; peer pressure	Toward subject matter; varying interview stimuli
Volunteer	Must be recruited	Mixed; interested in study; most need training	Advance the cause; personal recognition	Free, or expenses only	Minimal, except group morale	Overmotivated to cause

239

hiring professionals, we gain the great initial advantage of their experience. And this also offers us an improved capability to control field work through selective hiring, tailor-made training, and close field supervision.

Improving control over interviewing is enormously important but not easy. Sometimes it requires retraining professional interviewers in our own preferred survey techniques. Some will have long-standing, undesirable habits that are difficult to change. As interviewers become more experienced it seems to be their occupational disease to view each survey as the same: "If you've done one, you've done them all." This is true whether hiring professionals directly or contracting with a firm. There is a difference, however: when we contract for interviewing, we may naively assume the job will be well done, but when we hire direct, we are forced to come face-to-face with the glaring weakness of survey research—the interviewers. It's a humbling education. Because some professionals are not amenable to training in new procedures, it often is easier to train inexperienced interviewers in preferred techniques than to break the old habits of experienced workers.

Students. The cost of professional interviewers usually is too great for academic researchers without a grant. College teachers often use students from their classes. Much money is saved with a captive labor supply. But, more important, sound educational objectives can be achieved. These two reasons are so compelling that the disadvantages of using students seem less forbidding, but there are real drawbacks.

Unfortunately, in most courses only limited interviewer training can be given. Even with an ideal training period students will still be too inexperienced to develop the self-confidence, naturalness, and caginess necessary to handle difficult respondents.

Yet many students can become good interviewers. The teacher-director has closer contact and control over student interviewers than does the national survey agency with headquarters in Princeton or Ann Arbor. Properly engendered, student motivation will be high—higher than among professionals working for mere money. Cheating in the form of "armchair interviewing," an unfortunate foible among footweary interviewers, can be reduced by charging up the students' morale in the classroom, by augmenting their respect for scientific self-discipline, by generating an excitement for contributing to knowledge, and ultimately by recognizing their natural and realistic fear of academic reprisal through grades and other means.

The educational advantages for students are impressive. First, they learn something about the methods of science. From interviewing they acquire a live, personal understanding of survey research impossible to get through lectures or reading. They gain a vital respect for the reliability of carefully gathered survey data, as well as a knowledge of survey limitations, shown by their own experience.

Second, students learn about the subject matter of the social sciences. In interviewing, they come nose-to-nose with an electorate completely shorn of academic euphemisms. Many students gain new social awareness when they enter for the first time a home where the family is on welfare, where strangers are met with suspicion, where no adult has ever voted, and where the world of public affairs is irrelevant to daily existence.

Finally, students learn more about themselves by discovering where their views fall in relation to the contentions of others. Too few students get the experience of fighting to remain neutral while probing attitudes hostile to their own. Such education in self-control is valuable for the headstrong or overprotected.

With these kinds of educational gains possible, students deserve to be given the experience of survey interviewing. This does not mean that surveys should be undertaken when the only objective is student learning. Nor does this excuse inadequate training or sloppy procedures—improper polling is poor pedagogy and bad science. If students are used to conduct a survey, every caution should be exercised to safeguard the quality of the data.

Volunteers. No-cost volunteers are often used to do low-cost surveys for political campaigns. The principal danger in using volunteers is the opposite of using other kinds of interviewers: in this case it is overmotivation.

Volunteers who answer a candidate's plea to help with a survey usually are highly partisan. They charge into the field with a fervor that quickly cues respondents as to what they may or may not safely tell these intense strangers. The respondents who don't plan to vote or who are committed to the opposition are poorly regarded by the volunteer. Respondents quickly sense this condemnation and, if not antagonized, seek to give the "acceptable" answers, no matter how far from the truth.

Another disadvantage is that volunteers are likely to be people with time available mostly in the daytime—homemakers with school-age children, or retired people. If this is the only period they are free to interview, they will find at home mostly other homemakers, retired people, the unemployed, and night-shift workers. This would bias the sample; we must have interviewers for evening hours also. Further, although initially well-intentioned, volunteers tend to be unreliable—they don't show up day after day. Since interviewing is neither a job nor a requirement for them and comes second to other concerns, it may mean the survey cannot be completed in the required period.

Considering the crucial decisions candidates make based on their survey data, it is questionable whether political polling with volunteers is worth the risk. Besides, volunteers are not really cost-free. Training for them must be particularly intense. On-the-job corrective instruction and close field supervision are essential. A professionally trained survey researcher is needed for this job.

Organization Staff. Another kind of interviewer is staff members drawn from the organization sponsoring the survey. Partisanship is only part of the problem with sponsor staff. By definition, they have strong, vested interests in the survey results, which may affect their jobs, salaries, and stature.

The advantages are that staff are captive labor—they can be assigned rather than recruited to the project, out-of-pocket costs are low or nil, they are familiar with the study content, and we can use the hire/fire sanction as an effective control. Disadvantages of using staff members as interviewers are that they will have to be taken off their regular work and may resent it and that they will have to be trained and may resist acquiring new skills. Even where careful interviewing has been done, an in-house survey will be suspected of bias. Therefore, using regular staff is not recommended for important surveys.

Selecting Interviewers

Some types of interviewers will be more successful than others, depending on the kind of survey. A trained female nurse will be a better interviewer than an untrained male college student for a study of women's health problems. A man experienced in agriculture will be more successful than a woman trained in sociology for a study of unionization among farmers. A black woman will be more successful than a white man in a study of shopping habits among black families.

Generally, the more closely interviewers resemble the people they interview, the more likely they are to achieve *rapport*. The higher the rapport, the more reliable the data—usually. This is a rule of thumb for general community studies, but there are exceptions. Often in closed communities, such as small towns, Indian reservations, nursing homes, or factories, outsiders are seen as having higher status than locals, and such status helps strangers to collect information that people wouldn't tell their friends or neighbors.[1]

While there are no fixed rules for deciding on how or whether to match interviewers and respondents, we usually try to assign to certain selected neighborhoods interviewers who have the appropriate characteristics. Some physical characteristics are obvious signals to others about what kind of people we are—or at least signals that help people to imagine who we are. These signals are: *physical appearance* (including language) and *personal mannerisms*.

Physical Characteristics. Gender, age, race, and language are the chief physical characteristics taken into account in selecting and in matching interviewers. In the following, we will review each in some detail.

---

[1]Gerald Hursh-César, and Prodipto Roy, *Third World Surveys: Survey Research in Developing Nations* (Delhi: MacMillan of India, 1976).

Gender. Since community studies are usually cross-sectional (about equal numbers of men and women are interviewed), gender is important for selecting interviewers but not for matching them with respondents.

For the Model Survey we use female interviewers. We do so because the Model samples the general adult population, and, for this kind of survey, women—especially mature women—are the best interviewers. Statistics show that they typically have higher completion rates, fewer refusals, and fewer problems than men. Because surveys are usually part-time work, more women are likely to be available than men. But we must be careful how we hire. City editors are finding that gender can apparently no longer be used as a criterion for matching respondents—even in a study of male athletes in the locker room. And equal-opportunity hiring laws require that we specify reasons for selecting only one gender for a job. We prefer female interviewers because they seem less threatening to most respondents than men. Women especially may be reluctant to open the door to an unfamiliar man. Male respondents too are more likely to be sympathetic to a female's request for an interview than to another man's request. Financially dispossessed people often will not open the door to someone who looks like a bill collector—and bill collectors are usually male.

Of course, men are used successfully as interviewers in certain situations, but we prefer to go with the probabilities, which favor female interviewers for general-population samples. By eliminating certain people from the sample or by affecting the responses of those obtained, the use of men seems too costly in terms of biased data.

Age. Although we don't fix limits, women between the ages of 25 and 55 typically are most successful as door-to-door interviewers in general population surveys. Interviewers cannot look so young that respondents suspect the survey is not serious. Yet, interviewers must be youthful enough to withstand the physical rigors of the job. Other than these general considerations, age might be important only in studies of specific groups; for example, we would use more mature interviewers in studies of nursing homes or retirement communities.

Race and Ethnicity. These are important matching characteristics in general population studies. Interviewers who are drawn from the racial/ethnic background to be studied are generally the most successful: blacks are more successful interviewing blacks; whites are more successful interviewing whites (and similarly, Puerto Ricans with Puerto Ricans, American Indians with American Indians, Chinese with Chinese). Where single ethnic groups are clustered in specific neighborhoods or areas, if possible interviewers are used who have matching ethnic characteristics.

Language. As quickly as the interviewer's mouth opens, *language* becomes a physical signal. With only rare exceptions, the Model Survey does not permit others to translate respondents' answers to interviewers. Therefore, whenever a survey enters a locale in which a second language is prominent, interviewers with that language ability are assigned. In the United States this is most frequently required for Spanish and most large interviewing services now have a pool of Spanish-speaking interviewers.

Other Physical Characteristics. People are more willing to talk to interviewers who are "normal-looking" than to those who have "abnormal" characteristics. Interviewers having foreign accents (and "foreign" appearance) are severely handicapped by language problems and cultural hostilities.

There are other "abnormalities" that can lead to refusals. Interviewers with speech impediments or other speaking problems have much difficulty; even those with strong regional accents (say, an Eastern accent in the rural South) may encounter problems. Those with physical afflictions may make respondents feel embarrassed, causing them to break off or hurry through the interview to end their discomfort. Similar reactions can occur with interviewers who are abnormally tall or heavy.

Other physical concerns involve *mannerisms* and *voice*. In training, we coach interviewers as we would actors to play a role of congenial unobtrusiveness—like the old-time English butler in the movies: bland but capable. Also, we specify certain apparel. Interviewers are instructed to dress for a supporting not starring role in our survey melodrama. They shouldn't go out in their Sunday best, nor should their dress be overly casual. In particular, those who appear unkempt or who dress faddishly have less success in the field.

Personal and Behavioral Characteristics. Other than physical characteristics, various personal and behavioral characteristics—among them: education, experience, personality, motivation—are also important in interviewing. Although it's difficult to make a single profile of the best interviewers, the following are interviewer characteristics that we have found to be important for successful work.

Education. "Too much" education can be a liability if it gives the interviewer a sense of social distance from respondents. Usually, however, interviewers with some college experience tend to be the most successful in general-population surveys.

Experience. Normally, interviewing experience is important for success. But like education, too much experience can be a liability. Professional interviewers often have worked with only periodic supervision and little close scrutiny, which offers them many opportunities to pick up bad habits that go undetected. For a one-shot survey, putting extra time and money into supervising professional interviewers is a wise investment. As we have mentioned, for a continuing survey operation we prefer to train novices in our system rather than struggle to break bad habits learned elsewhere.

Personality. Successful interviewers tend to be gregarious and extroverted. They are not timid or withdrawn. They are talkers, highly social people, and they usually have great curiosity about the world and other people's life styles, habits, and beliefs.

Informed and Involved. Successful interviewers tend to be interested in public affairs and to be knowledgeable about events and issues. They have above-average exposure to the news and public-affairs content of newspapers, magazines, and television. They usually are registered voters who vote in most elections. They may well belong to a number of community groups and voluntary associations.

Married with Children. The typical female interviewer is married and has children. Because of the part-time nature of most interviewing work, it especially attracts people with other activities and responsibilities.

Motivation. Interviewers usually come from the broad middle-class population. Most work to supplement family income, so much so that the economic motive may be the strongest work drive. In any event, interviewers seldom come to their work accidentally. They generally find the work intellectually stimulating. It lifts them from traditional roles, enhances their self image, offers a certain degree of economic freedom, does not have specific educational prerequisites, and can be mastered with relatively little training in a short time.

Training Interviewers

The organization that does many surveys will train interviewers in the particular research *system* of that organization. Interviewers are not trained in the same ways in different organizations; the quality and depth of training vary greatly.

Many organizations rely on the training that they assume their interviewers have gained elsewhere, but this is often only training-through-experience that amounts to little more than an accumulation of unprofessional habits. Commercial firms tend to conduct superficial training programs—often by mail—because they cannot charge clients directly for such training. Clients can be billed for training done specifically for a study but not for that done to enhance general professionalism.

Good training tries to instill both professional values and procedures, and it goes far beyond the mere technical requirements for a single study. Instead of a fixed time duration for such training, it is a continuous process of learning by doing. It is "complete" when the interviewer demonstrates mastery of skills through professional job performance. Because each survey brings new problems, however, all interviewers over time require remedial, on-the-job training to correct bad habits and reinforce good ones.

Each interviewer selectively biases survey data in his or her own ways. One of the reasons for using relatively large numbers of interviewers in a study is to reduce the impact on the overall results of the behavior of a single individual. But we want to lessen interviewer bias even further, so the general objective of training is to make interviewers as much *alike* in their field behavior as possible.

The nature of the training depends on the specific needs of the interviewers' job: (1) what *information* they need in order to understand their assignment; (2) which *attitudes* they must have to be motivated to perform professionally; and (3) which *skills* they must master in order to perform competently.

Information—What Must Interviewers Know? In addition to knowing the skills of their trade, interviewers should have a solid understanding of field conditions, basic principles of research, sampling and selection procedures, interviewer and respondent biases, the purpose of the study, and conditions of employment.

One debate about interviewer training concerns how much to tell them about study objectives. In the Model Survey we do tell interviewers the general purpose of the study, but not the purpose for asking each specific question—that is, the hypothesis being tested by that question. This is an important distinction. On the one hand, interviewers must know enough about the subject matter and purpose of the study to recognize relevant responses, to probe for more meaningful answers, and to record answers without reservation into their correct categories in a multiple-response set. This kind of information defines the limits of likely responses to any question.

We do not, on the other hand, tell interviewers which answers to expect or which answers would bear out our hypotheses. Telling them this only increases their likelihood to hear "correct" answers more often than others. Furthermore, we do not tell them the nature of attitudes being measured by any question. For example, we would not tell interviewers that certain items on the questionnaire measure people's totalitarian beliefs. Armed with such knowledge, the interviewers' own beliefs will affect their ability to record the respondents' answers without some biasing reaction. The greatest danger in using volunteers in a candidate survey lies exactly here—they know what every candidate wants to hear (*not* the truth!) and can't help providing it.

Checklist 19 summarizes the kinds of information the Model Survey gives in interviewer training.

CHECKLIST 19

Interviewer Training Information

1. THE PROBLEM: This is information on the nature of the study—why it is being undertaken, how the findings can be used, and its important implications that may benefit the people or the problem under study. Interviewers need this orientation for their motivation.

2. THE POPULATION: Training should describe the people being studied so that the interviewers know whom they will be talking to, where the people live, and any special characteristics that are important for respondent selection.

3. THE SPONSOR: It's usually not wise to identify the specific study client, because this may bias either interviewers' behavior or respondent answers (e.g., a survey of political candidates or of competing brand name products). But the organization conducting the survey will be known. In the Model Survey, however, the sponsor—the University Research Department—is scientifically prestigious and should be identified.

4. SURVEYS: Training should introduce interviewers to some of the theory and practice of survey research, as an important, valid methodology of the social sciences. Enough must be learned about the survey approach to bring interviewers to respect its capability and to believe in it, so that their standard replies to inquiries about their work are given earnestly and confidently.

5. SAMPLING: Interviewers also must know enough about sampling to understand the principles of randomness and the sources of sampling biases. They should be given exercise in drawing judgmental and random samples to understand first hand the problems of subjective sampling and to see why we avoid it in the Model Survey.

6. CONSISTENCY (STANDARDIZATION): Training must convince interviewers of the importance of standardized behavior in the field. They must understand the reasons for consistency in approaching respondents, introducing the study, asking questions, recording responses—professionalism here means doing it *our* way, not *their* way.

7. INTERVIEWER BIASES: A large part of training is devoted to showing interviewers how their own personality and characteristics can bias questionnaire data. They must learn to identify the major sources of interviewing biases, both generally and for themselves specifically, and must know the devices for protecting against their own behavior influencing respondents' answers.

8. RESPONDENT BIASES: Training should deal with respondent motives for evading or falsifying answers—not the least of which is their desire to please and their perception of interviewers' expectations. This helps interviewers to understand the humanness—hence the fragility—of their interaction with respondents.

9. SELECTION PROCEDURES: This is nuts-and-bolts field information, demonstrating how to read maps and how to follow instructions in locating interviewing areas, selecting households and apartments, selecting the correct respondents within households, and making appointments, as well as how to select substitute respondents, if permitted. The best training in selection procedures is actual practice.

10. INTERVIEWING PROCEDURES: This is practical information (and practice) on how to administer the questionnaire (e.g., familiarity with symbols, format,

colored pages, directional coding) and data recording (e.g., probing response categories, dealing with indeterminate responses, legibility, etc.).

11. SUPERVISION AND PROBLEM SOLVING: This is straightforward information about who supervises the field work, which supervisors work with which interviewers, what are their responsibilities, why they are required to carry out checking and monitoring activities, and so on. The intention is to improve interviewers' understanding of the managerial—as opposed to the ''boss''—role of the supervisor in coordinating field work; and to encourage interviewers to seek assistance from supervisors, not to hide their problems.

12. VERIFICATION: Without implying we are suspicious of our interviewers, we convey some of the criteria and procedures used for verifying interviewers' work including: recontacting respondents, supervision, debriefing, and data and records analyses.

13. SCHEDULING AND LOGISTICS: We announce the time and timing of the survey, the number of interviews each interviewer is to make, the areas of assignment, the expected completion dates, the procedures for getting assistance, and the use of field instructions and other materials and forms.

14. ADMINISTRATION: We detail the interviewers' conditions of employment— wages, tax withholding, benefits, insurance, dates of payment, administrative forms, etc.

Training Attitudes—What Must Interviewers Believe? We motivate interviewers to professional performance by helping them to understand the process and to believe in the contribution quality research can make to the common good. This presumes we are dealing with professional interviewers, not partisans who are already motivated by the purpose or sponsor of the study. Checklist 20 shows some of the attitudes we try to encourage in interviewers.

CHECKLIST 20

Interviewer Attitudes

1. *This job is important*—Stress the importance of this particular study: how it intends to contribute to the public good, solve problems, ameliorate unacceptable conditions, improve the community, aid science.

2. *I must follow instructions*—Teach the importance of following instructions, the necessity of proper field procedure, the importance of consistent biases.

3. *Biases can cripple data*—Educate about the destructive role of predispositional biases: how each interviewer's personal experiences and perceptions can color information, how biases affect data quality.

4. *Research is important*—Communicate the value of research: how research information improves our ability to make decisions, to solve problems, to contribute to the common goals of society, to save money and resources.

5. *Surveys work*—Stress that surveys can be valid, reliable measures of people's information, attitudes, and behavior; that random sampling really works—that a few selected people can reflect accurately the characteristics of many

6. *People like to be interviewed*—Help interviewers know they are not snoops nor irritants: people like to express their opinions, they know about polls, they are usually flattered to be chosen, they are curious about how it all works.

7. *I am a professional*—Each interviewer should believe: "I have a job to do: I am a professional being paid for services rendered."

8. *I am a guest in someone's home*—Each should understand that "I must respect the people whose time I am using; no matter how different the life style or the expression of opinion, I must treat all respondents with equal courtesy and respect."

9. *Randomness works*—Each should believe: "No matter what I think about who should be part of the sample, we are likely to get a better (more fairly representative) sample of the community by relying on chance, as the strict Model Survey selection procedures have, rather than personal decisions about whom to interview."

10. *The respondent is entitled to privacy*—Warn that respondents usually are more comfortable expressing themselves privately on some issues; so, interviewers must help to ensure that privacy.

Training Skills—What Must Interviewers Be Able to Do? There are two basic areas of interviewer skill: respondent-selection procedures and questionnaire administration. Whether interviewers master the desired skills can be determined only by their performance, not by tests of their knowledge. Knowledge is, of course, necessary to skill, but it is not itself an adequate measure of skill.

This is a point apparently lost on researchers who hire and "train" interviewers sight-unseen through the mail. Usually, training-by-mail is done in national surveys. Consisting of names on a mailing list, interviewers are referred from one agency to a second agency, which usually assigns regional supervisors to coordinate the flow of interviewer work in their state or metropolitan area. Sometimes supervisors are required to conduct brief (perhaps one-day) in-person training sessions at a central place to which interviewers come, but as often as not, interviewers are simply contacted by mail and sent their questionnaires, field instructions, interviewing guides, and administrative forms. This clearly is inadequate training.

Checklist 21 shows the major skills interviewers must master in order to undertake field work in the Model Survey.

CHECKLIST 21

Interviewer Skills

Respondent-Selection Procedures—Interviewer must be able to:

1. *Use maps,* street guides, other field materials.
2. *Locate study areas,* determine corner starts and direction of interviewing route.
3. *Follow the correct route* through the study area, enumerate houses without error or omissions—giving all housing units a chance to be selected.
4. *Recognize the street boundaries* of each study area and not exceed them.
5. *Follow correct house-interval skipping procedures* as required for this study; identify households as distinct from group quarters or other non-households.
6. *Explain the rights of the respondent,* as required by government-sponsored studies.
7. *Use the respondent-selection key* for ascertaining the correct person to interview based on the number of adults and females in the household.
8. *Follow correct procedure for substitution* of households or respondents, if permitted at all.
9. *Use any screening device* included with respondent-selection keys for determining respondents eligible for interviewing.
10. *Use any other eligibility criteria* built into the introduction.
11. *Secure appointments* from within the household, or from neighbors, for making callbacks to the designated respondent.

Interviewing Procedures—Interviewer must be able to:

12. *Read precodes* such as response numbers, categories within text, rating scales, and dichotomous or multiple-choice categories.
13. *Follow questionnaire format* and symbols (e.g., arrows, asterisks).
14. *Use special questions*—scales, rankings, paired comparisons.
15. Correctly probe open-end and semistructured questions, knowing how much to probe, about what, and how to recognize when an answer is complete (see Checklist 24).
16. *Use filter questions* to determine respondents' eligibility to answer successive questions.
17. *Use response cards* correctly for aided recall questions.
18. *Employ standardized replies*—the interviewers' ''stock-in-trade'': the use of certain phrases to meet respondent objections and answer inquiries about the study (see Checklist 25).

This section has summarized the basic information, attitudes, and behavior we try to impart in interviewer training.

Evaluating Interviewers

Although verifying the quality of interviewers' work is usually done after the survey is completed, interviewer evaluation is an ongoing process that must start with the beginning of the job. We evaluate our Model interviewers at several points in their selection, training, and work.

Selection. The Model is a one-time survey for which we hire and supervise our own professional staff. We first construct a *profile* of the "best" interviewer for our study. Then we try to find interviewers who most closely fit the profile. The profile is made up of various desirable background characteristics, aptitudes, personality traits, and job skills. Setting appropriate qualifications requires a careful assessment of job requirements. This *needs assessment* is also the basis for training.

Training. Even for a one-time survey, the Model has an intensive training program that lasts several days. Interviewers are paid for their time. We can expect a number of interviewers to drop out of the training program. Some will be novices with mistaken expectations about the job. Others will be professionals who feel that they have nothing to gain from further training. Tests are given both *before and after* training to determine improvements in interviewers' job skills, attitudes, and knowledge. Naturally, we will find the biggest gains in interviewers' knowledge and skills. We really can't do much to change deeply ingrained attitudes in a short period of time, but we can improve motivation in most cases.

On-the-job Training. There is no guarantee that any improvements achieved during training are real. The gains may be due more to the novelty of training, and may wear off quickly. Therefore, we do not rely on training alone to guide the interviewers' work. Study supervisors are required to maintain close, frequent contact with each interviewer, especially in the first few days. Supervisors each have mini-training kits for on-the-spot refresher training in such things as question asking, delivering the introduction, using the respondent-selection key, probing, and understanding format symbols and precodes.

   If the survey operation is a continuing one, experienced interviewers are periodically brought back to refresher training courses.

Performance Measures. The only way to judge interviewers is by their actual field performance. We measure performance in order to monitor continuing developments in the field, control quality of work, and detect problems of incompletion, delays, and interviewing misconduct.

   There are many ways of measuring performance. Usually we compare the performance of each interviewer with that of all other interviewers in the same study. If we use the same group of interviewers for several studies, we can gradually build an invaluable pool of information on interviewing time, cost, biases, and reliability.

Some of the methods for checking performance are shown here. None of these devices is foolproof. Each may be an indicator of interviewer misbehavior—errors, omissions, falsifications—but no single one is conclusive. However, misbehavior usually occurs as a pattern. Thus, where we find interviewers doing one thing improperly, there is usually supporting evidence from other indicators.

Respondent Verification. The most direct way of checking interviewers' work is to ask the designated respondents if in fact they were interviewed. Interviewers are aware that verification checks will be made, and this provides a fairly effective deterrent against "armchair interviewing"—interviewers filling out questionnaires themselves. But respondent verification will not assess the quality of the interviewers' work.

Response Verification. Details on the quality of interviewers' data can be gained by analyzing item by item each interviewer's data compared with those of all other interviewers. Verifying quality this way requires restudying a sample of each interviewer's respondents and asking a few questions a second time. As explained later, this re-interview check can show the general consistency or stability of the data over time. Unusually inconsistent or unstable responses from one time to another may be a cue to look for other interviewer problems.

Completion Rates. Over time we can establish fairly definite estimates of how many interviews can be accomplished in a given time period—say, five or six per day. Completion rates vary by questionnaire length, question complexity, language problems, ethnic area, etc. We can set expected limits—like production rates—for the purpose of examining more carefully the work of interviewers who complete fewer or more than the standard number of interviews per day.

Time and Cost Figures. Like completion rates, we learn over time how much interviewing should cost, how much traveling is required, which field expenses normally crop up, and how much time is required per interview. An interviewer who will fudge costs will fudge data as well. Comparing all interviewers, we look for those who deviate significantly in one direction or the other. If an interviewer's costs are too low, it may be due to ignorance of the full requirements of the study, or the interviewer may not be actually contacting the correct respondents. If costs are too high, the economic motive to pad expenses may have become irrepressible.

Data Response Patterns. Just as interviewers who falsify time and expenses stand out from the overall group, so do those who falsify data. It is really very difficult to cheat. People don't answer questions randomly, they answer in patterns. Interviewers similarly cheat in patterns. Random responses result in illogical inconsistencies, which might trigger us to eliminate the questionnaire from analysis as incredible or fictitious. When interviewers try to act like respondents, they invariably color the data with their own predispositions. Over several questionnaires, an unlikely similarity or stereotyping of responses will result. We therefore compare the pattern of responses for all questionnaires submitted by each interviewer against the total pattern found for all questionnaires of all other interviewers. In this way distinctive patterns of interviewer biases or falsification are often revealed.

Substitutions/Appointments. Another symptom of interviewer problems is abnormally frequent breakdowns in the respondent-selection procedure. For interviewers in general, evidence usually includes the following: interviewing the wrong persons instead of the persons designated by the selection key; encountering a high number of households in which no one is home or no one is eligible for interviewing; and making an unusually large number of appointments—particularly, if appointment questionnaires are turned back to the office to be done by others.

Type of Respondent. A breakdown in the respondent-selection procedure is easily spotted by checking the composition of each interviewer's households and the type of respondents interviewed; stereotypic patterns of cheating are usually pretty clear. An interviewer is immediately suspect when we find that almost all households have the same composition (e.g., two adults and two children) or almost always yield interviews with the same respondent type (e.g., homemakers, who are most likely to be home most hours of the day).

Refusals. Comparing all interviewers together, those with high refusal rates tend to have other problems as well. Refusals occur mostly at the point of introduction. Interviewers with abnormally high rates either require retraining or have certain personal characteristics ill-suited for this study.

Filter Questions. One tip-off to improper interviewing is an unusual pattern of respondents being disqualified from a series of questions following a filter question. Lazy interviewers will avoid work by marking filter questions in such a way that they disqualify respondents from answering follow-up questions. This is most likely to happen if the follow-up questions are open-ended ones requiring more interviewing effort.

DK/NR Responses. An unusually frequent number of DK/NR (don't know/no response) answers typically signals interviewer problems, which may include lack of interest in the work, hesitancy or fear of asking questions, or unwillingness to probe.

Missing and Inconsistent Data. Usually, when responses are missing, it is evidence of sloppy rather than dishonest interviewing. Inconsistent answers, on the other hand, more often tip off cheating—and lazy cheating at that. Although after a few legitimate interviews experienced interviewers can become pretty skillful in manufacturing questionnaire data, invariably the patterns of these responses are too patterned to be credible.

Open-end Responses. Open-end questions often trip up even the most skillful armchair interviewers. Usually those who falsify questionnaires tend to give short shrift to the free-response question, recording only minimal, sketchy remarks, which tend to all sound alike.

Legibility. When we can't read the interviewer's handwriting, either the interviewer is working under duress or is scribbling phony open-ended answers in the belief that no one looks at them anyway. This is usually the sign of a novice.

Debriefing. Interviewers who find that all study methods work well and who have no suggestions for improvement may not be sufficiently immersed in the fieldwork to see flaws. We always double-check interviewers who have no criticisms to offer.

Complaints and Problems. Interviewers who have uncommonly frequent difficulties in the field or who stir up the wrath of an unusually large number of respondents are often in trouble in other ways. Usually, they are too inexperienced or are temperamentally unsuited for the job. Interviewers who are disrespectful of respondents often abuse other features of their work as well.

Absenteeism/Tardiness. The lowest-quality interviewers typically are also those who are most unreliable—who don't show up at the times scheduled or who are chronically late to training sessions and other meetings.

Signatory Evidence. We sometimes require interviewers to bring back certain evidence of their interviews. This usually is done for valid reasons other than checking performance. For example, we might require respondents to put a ''ballot'' in a sealed envelope, or we might ask for respondents' signatures on release forms or on requests for study results.

Motivating Interviewers

Motivation among professional interviewers may pose a greater problem than among students. Professionals work mostly for commercial market-research agencies, surveying consumer preferences for brands of cake mix, beer, hand lotion, and the like. Although commercial interviewers initially are motivated mostly by their wage, we try to impress them with the unique quality of the information we seek and the contribution the findings might make to community improvement. If they come to appreciate the importance of their personal efforts, professionals may achieve true interviewing excellence.

We can only train interviewers in technique. We cannot ''teach'' ethical behavior. Through a deliberate strategy of training reinforced with practical incentives, however, we can motivate interviewers to professional behavior. The incentives are not necessarily financial.

Respect. Interviewers are our communication links to the respondents. Hence, they are the strength or the weakness of the survey. Their work is difficult and often performed under unpleasant, arduous conditions. They should be viewed with respect as compatriots, not as hirelings. How we view interviewers—our attitude toward them as professionals or as minions—is quickly conveyed. Interviewers tell us that one of their first, lasting impressions is the study director's attitude toward them. The snobbish manager who "looks down on" or who patronizes his or her staff is asking for trouble.

Simplifying. We make the interviewer's job as simple as possible. This is not mollycoddling. Our aim is to make it easier to do the job correctly than to do it incorrectly. We can reduce the incidence of slipshod or unscrupulous behavior by showing interviewers that we have carefully considered each element of their job before deciding on its final form.

Involvement. One way to demonstrate our concern for the job interviewers do is to involve them in decisions—mostly through pretesting and debriefing. As many interviewers as possible should be involved in pretesting so that: (1) we get the widest possible range of interviewer reactions; (2) we train as many interviewers as possible for the main study; and (3) we commit them emotionally to the improvements made.

Feedback. The debriefing sessions following the pretest are essential for gathering interviewers' ideas. Later, when interviewers see that their ideas have actually been used to make improvements, they need little convincing to follow the desired procedures. Over time, this kind of feedback becomes important to interviewers' morale and sense of professional responsibility. If debriefings are hurried, administered by inexperienced staff, or the findings are given little credence, interviewers regard these signs as evidence that their experiences are not valued. This kind of snub is not only bad mannered, it is irresponsible. No one on the study team knows more than the interviewer about how procedures work in the field.

Maximizing Control. We require interviewers to do only those jobs that they uniquely can do—interview a sample of people. This involves a steady stream of decisions. Our job is to free them from as much administrative detail, calculations, or recording as we can. This has several advantages. First, we save interviewers' time for what is important—and thereby save study funds. Second, we demonstrate our respect for their professional role by not burdening them with unnecessary "donkey" work. And, most importantly, we lessen the opportunities for field errors by putting as much of the field work as we can under office control, thus reducing the number and variety of decisions that interviewers are required to make. We have more ability to control our office staff and to check their work than we do with interviewers. So, we assign as many "field" tasks as possible to the office staff (e.g., drawing maps, recording case numbers, writing directions for walking to the interviewing site, fixing corner starts, determining skip-intervals, etc.).

Being Realistic. Various incentives can be built into interviewers' conditions of employment. Wages, benefits, and other conditions must be competitive with other research agencies. Beyond economic incentives, a prime motivator is our treatment of the interviewer. One aspect of our collegial role is to give interviewers no more to do than can reasonably be accomplished in the time allotted for field study. Requiring unrealistic efforts is only asking for errors. It is less costly to hire additional interviewers and distribute smaller caseloads than it is to suffer the consequences of low-quality data.

Sharing Information. We give all interviewers a summary of the study results. This accomplishes two things: first, they take pride in the evidence of their work; second, seeing the overall results provides a good perspective on their individual experiences. It enables each to balance his or her picture of the average respondent against the larger picture for all respondents. This encourages interviewers to be less hasty in the future in forming prejudgments about what respondents will answer to each question. It also helps them reflect on how their own expectations may have influenced respondents toward certain answers.

We also give interviewers a percentage summary of nonresponses (no answers and refusals) to the survey's demographic questions. This helps stress to them that the vast majority of people (usually over 95 percent) will answer personal questions about income, age, religion, etc., thus raising their confidence in being able to ask anything.

Seriousness. It is important that the interviewers see that we are very serious about trying to do a good job, and that we care very much about the quality of their work. Among other things, we inform them of some of the quality controls and respondent verifications used for evaluating their work. But additionally we seize every opportunity during the study to emphasize the significance of professional performance and adherence to study procedure. Thus, we build professionalism training objectives into each stage of contact with the interviewer: selection, training, briefing, supervision, debriefing, written evaluations, and even in the letter accompanying the study results that are mailed to them.

Sanctions. Of course, there are other, less positive ways of motivating good performance: unsatisfactory professionals can be fired, volunteers can be released, students can be flunked. The need to use such negative sanctions will decrease as interviewer feelings of professionalism increase.

A Note on Student Interviewers

Surveys that use student interviewers may be both training exercises for the students as well as bona fide means of obtaining useful data on the sociopolitical processes of the community. But surveys should never be training exercises alone. Interviewers, including students, must be fully trained and equipped for their field assignment before the survey is undertaken. Neither the pretest nor the actual survey is an appropriate occasion for the novice interviewer to learn the ropes. No responsible survey is frivolous. We cannot intrude on people's lives and time simply for the purpose of training.

If a class is being used to conduct a survey, success (by all definitions) depends on the students' motivation. Some ways to develop that motivation are presented here.

Research: Intregal to Learning. The need for doing research must grow out of the course content. Good instructors commonly point out and demonstrate how to remedy gaps and inconsistencies in our knowledge. Among the many methods, students should learn the great contribution possible through survey research.

Forewarning. Students must be fully warned of the amount of effort involved in a survey project. A survey is too much work to spring as an extra assignment. Notified early about the work ahead, students can begin planning their time so they may allot large blocks to field work when it begins. It must be clear from the beginning that the quality of their survey performance will count in grading.

Self-confidence. Students must be trained to develop self-confidence as interviewers. Most students are not sure that they will like interviewing, nor do they feel they will be good interviewers. Training engenders confidence.

Student Involvement. Students must have a part in all phases of the study. This is the best way to sustain their interest. Initially hesitant, they will soon be caught up in the excitement of the survey and the importance of the academic contribution they are making. In retrospect, virtually all will enjoy and appreciate the learning experience.

As the topic of the survey is developed in class, all students can suggest problems to be explored and try their hand at writing questions. Every student should spend some time on one of the several work committees that are necessary to produce the survey—such as sampling and coding. This lends an additional sense of participation and enables them to appreciate more fully the many tasks in conducting field surveys.

Extra Opportunities. Find the class leaders. A few especially interested class members should be constituted as a planning committee. They will meet many hours outside of class to frame the questionnaire with the Project Director. This group can benefit from what will be a seminar on survey research. They also are good candidates for supervisors and can help train the rest of the class. It's wise to give the leaders some advance interviewing experience. Their first-hand experience that interviewing is fun will be accepted more readily by other students than will all the instructor's assurances.

Reporting. Keep the class informed. Each day during the initial stages, when much is being done behind the scenes by the planning committee, progress should be reported to the class as a whole. Make students method-conscious, so they will appreciate the relation between how something is done and what is discovered. At appropriate points, the Director should emphasize the true group nature of the project—how the validity of the whole study depends peculiarly on the quality of the work of each member. Ideally, the Director will communicate his or her own convictions about the necessary objectivity in the study and the dedication to knowledge that scholars share.

Writing. Allow students to synthesize their experience. The rewards of interviewing to students and instructor are great. Students will understand and appreciate the teaching nature of the project better if, at the end of the course, they are asked to write a brief paper describing what they have learned about the study's subject and about survey research as a method of acquiring knowledge. These retrospective papers will be introspective, too.

INTERVIEWING TECHNIQUES

Most people can master the techniques of interviewing. The difference between good and bad interviewers is not skill. It is *attitude,* the interviewer's approach to the job. Without proper motivation, interviewers will stumble and fail regardless of their technical abilities.

The most important training objectives, apart from learning the specific requirements of each different study, are: (1) to acquire a healthy interviewing *attitude;* (2) to know the do's and don'ts of *personal conduct;* (3) to master specific interviewing *skills;* and (4) to be able to meet problems with *standard replies.*

Approach

Interviewers are not automatons. They cannot confront every situation or respondent in the same way. What works with one may not work with another. They learn to adapt to particular situations by being sensitive to the needs of each respondent—above all to be human, gracious, and friendly. But we also aim at helping them to achieve a general sense of *detachment* from the interview. The goal is to treat each response with equal respect, regardless of how repugnant to their own personal values.

We cannot induce humans to act as machines. But we can show interviewers how they may bias people's answers through their own idiosyncracies in asking questions and recording responses. And we can show them how their personal views on a subject, if communicated to the respondent, may distort the respondent's own true views.

Our training objectives are to raise interviewers to a professional level, at which: (1) they operate without a personal stake in the content of each interview, and (2) their views or behavior neither add to nor subtract from the research intention of any item on the questionnaire.

Checklist 22 lists various aids to developing a successful interview approach. It is presented as a training manual to be handed out to interviewers, and the approach tips in it are written as though we were talking directly to an interviewer. For simplicity, we refer to the interviewer as female and the respondent as male.

CHECKLIST 22

Interviewer Approach

Your approach should be:

1. *Neutral.* As an interviewer, you merely soak up information like a sponge without giving any of it back. Your job is to record that information, regardless of whether you think it good, bad, indifferent, boring, or exciting.

   Don't, by word or reaction, indicate surprise, pleasure, or disapproval at any answer. Even a slight intake of breath will cue a respondent that you have reacted to his answer.

   Don't attempt to influence responses in any way. The truth is all that really counts—what the person *really* thinks or feels about the subject.

   Remember: the object of the survey is to get the honest, uninfluenced opinion of each individual interviewed. You are merely the medium through which the opinion is conveyed. Nothing of *you* should be in the interview results.

2. *Confident.* You are a trained professional. You are on a professional assignment for an important purpose. There is nothing frivolous or time-wasting about your

work. Don't be apologetic. By learning more about what and how people think, you are increasing the chances that our results may directly benefit them. In exchange, all we request is a few moments of their time.

Be confident, not afraid or wary. You have been thoroughly trained in interviewing techniques, and you know they work. You are no amateur. If you convey insecurity or hesitancy to the respondent, he will immediately suspect your motives. His answers will become unsure, reluctant, suspicious. People like to give their views. You've been trained to get them. Don't make a fuss about it. No one knows your job better than you do.

3. *Impartial*. Whatever you may think of an individual or his opinion, keep it to yourself. Each interview you are asked to get, and therefore each person you speak to, is equally important.

You should be adaptable to anyone and gracious to all. Each person you approach poses different problems requiring different techniques. The important thing is to inspire the confidence of every respondent regardless of sex, age, residence, income, political affiliation, or whatever.

4. *Casual*. You are not a spy out on a secret mission. If you pursue your assignment too earnestly, too grimly, the respondent is forced to the defensive. He won't tell you what he honestly thinks.

You are not subjecting the individual to the third degree. This is not in any sense a quiz or intelligence test. He'll tell nothing if he thinks you're watching for errors or conducting an examination. Don't make him think it's a matter of life and death. Take it easy.

Approach the interview pleasurably, and let the respondent enjoy it, too. Assume that he wants to express his opinion and wants to be interviewed. You merely are giving him the chance to express himself on matters that may be important to him.

5. *Conversational*. Use an informal manner of speaking, natural to you, and aimed at putting the individual at ease. Know the questions so well that you never sound as though you're reading them formally.

Although you are conversational, never lose control of the interview. From the moment the correct respondent is present, talk him through the introduction and right into the body of the questionnaire before he reacts negatively.

Be politely firm and businesslike. Permissiveness and timidity are immediate clues to the respondent that he is dealing with a novice or someone who does not know her job.

Be ready with standard replies (see Checklist 25) to handle interruptions or objections. Give these answers in an offhand tone of voice as though you've heard the objection a hundred times, and proceed with the questions.

6. *Friendly*. A major objective is to put the respondent at ease. If he isn't relaxed, you can't make him talk. The burden of ignorance has to be lifted from the respondent's shoulders—that is, he must not be made to feel ashamed of his lack of information.

Your attitude, therefore, must be sympathetic and understanding. Emphasize that there are no correct answers. Rather, he must be made to realize that what he thinks really is what counts. An opinion can never be wrong.

If the respondent is forced to answer "I don't know" to a series of information questions, he may become embarrassed and start grasping for any answer at all. Good question wording will provide alternatives like "... or haven't you had a chance to read about that?" A sympathetic interviewer will make these alternatives seem a natural part of the question instead of making them sound like a judgment—"You don't know that either?" or something equally demoralizing.

If the individual seems confused by a question, even after repetition, record whatever answer is given. A "correct" answer is not as important as the respondent's goodwill. Or, if the respondent objects to a question, you are allowed to side with him to the extent of saying politely, "I don't know why, but that's the way my office has the question worded." Blame us, not the respondents, for questions they don't like.

Personal Conduct

Checklist 23 is a brief list of things we train interviewers (1) that they must *never* do, and (2) that they must *always* do in the Model Survey. Regardless of how much experience interviewers have, they are required to use the guidelines here. Everyone must follow the same procedures.

CHECKLIST 23

Interviewer Conduct

Never do any of the following:

1. NEVER get involved in long explanations of the study. Use the standard responses given you. Invite respondents to call your office if they remain skeptical.
2. NEVER try to explain sampling in detail. When people ask how and why they were chosen say: it's a "random sample." Or, say it's done "by scientific methods," "by the people in charge of the study," "by a computer" (if it is).
3. NEVER deviate from the study introduction provided for this survey. Do not invent your own explanation. Stick with the explanation that has been tested, proved workable, and is the one all other interviewers are using.
4. NEVER try to justify or defend what you are doing. You are only "following instructions."
5. NEVER try to explain procedures or question wording. You "don't know why" questions are written as they are, but that's the way "people in the office" did it.
6. NEVER suggest an answer and never agree or disagree with an answer. Above all, this is a survey of respondents' feelings, not yours.

7. NEVER interpret the meaning of a question. If the respondent does not understand, just repeat the question slowly, exactly as written. Remember, you don't know why questions are written as they are. They are written by "people at the office."

8. NEVER add to or subtract words from a question. Read the question exactly as written. Read distinctly, evenly, naturally, Do not give unusual inflection to words. Do not give emphasis to any one part of the question or to any response alternative.

9. NEVER change the sequence of questions. Read them exactly in the order written.

10. NEVER try to ask questions from memory. Know the questions thoroughly, of course, so you can ask them naturally. But read them exactly as written.

11. NEVER rush the respondent. Let him understand the question fully. Don't show impatience. You are more concerned with getting good data than getting out the door.

12. NEVER patronize respondents who don't speak standard English as well as you. They are probably fluent in another language or an informal dialect.

13. NEVER react to answers. Do not smile, grimace, gasp, laugh, frown, query, agree, disagree—or anything else. You are a sponge soaking up information; you give nothing back but a gracious and friendly manner.

14. NEVER do anything that suggests to the respondent that an answer is right or wrong. You have no opinions as a professional interviewer. Your only job is to learn others' opinions.

15. NEVER dominate the interview. Your job is to get information, not give it. And don't intimidate people.

16. NEVER change an answer to a finished question, if you already have gone on to other items. Note at the appropriate point that the respondent now would say something else. But usually, unless there is strong reason to make a change, we accept the first meaningful reaction to a question as the important or true one.

17. NEVER record a "don't know" answer too quickly. People say "I don't know" when stalling for time to arrange their thoughts. The phrase merely may be an introduction to a meaningful comment, so give the respondent a little time to think.

18. NEVER give the impression that what you are doing is secretive, out of the ordinary, or unusual. You are not the CIA. You are doing what countless people do every day: asking people questions about themselves.

19. NEVER let another family member sit in on the interview, unless you're collecting joint interviews in the home.

20. NEVER let another person answer for the intended respondent. If the respondent is unable to understand and cannot answer any questions, you should abandon the interview. Obviously, certain populations on whom we are collecting data (say, preschool children) may require that parents provide the information.

21. NEVER let another person interrupt the interview. Don't try to answer third-party questions or challenges. If the respondent agrees to your presence, that's all the authority you need.

22. NEVER let another person offer his or her views to the respondent. If others cut into the conversation, or if the respondent asks for their opinions, tell the respondent only his opinions are important. Gently but firmly instruct family members not to interrupt.

23. NEVER tell the respondent in advance what questions are coming up, and never let him see the questionnaire. If he knows what to expect, he's thinking ahead about what answer to give. Exception: sometimes we give a special section of the questionnaire to the respondent to fill out.

24. NEVER conduct personal interviews by telephone. You may sometimes be instructed to make appointments by phone, but always *interview* in person.

25. NEVER let another person accompany you into the home interview, unless you are specifically assigned as a team.

26. NEVER interview more than one person in the same family or the same housing unit. Members of one family are likely to share the same opinions on many subjects, and the Model sample calls for the diverse opinions of the community.

27. NEVER interview someone you know. Turn the questionnaire back into the office for reassignment. Strangers are preferred as respondents, because you'll find it easier to be objective and impartial with them.

28. NEVER let another interviewer do the work for you. If you cannot complete the work yourself, notify the study Director at once.

29. NEVER reveal the details of your job or of specific interviews to others. The information you obtain is confidential, and you must respect this.

30. NEVER correct apparent errors on someone else's advice. Instead, tell the Supervisor or the Study Director about your difficulties. *

31. NEVER falsify interviews. All work is carefully examined, and methods of detecting false information have been devised. It isn't worth the trouble to do the job poorly or wrong.

Always do each of the following:

1. ALWAYS study all questions until you know what they mean and are familiar enough with them so you can really ask the questions instead of reading them blindly.

2. ALWAYS interview yourself for practice, answering each question thoughtfully. Then interview someone else, again for practice. Of course, these interviews are not counted as part of the assigned interviews you turn in.

3. ALWAYS reread your instructions between interviews. You may pick up points you missed before or correct errors you have begun to make.

4. ALWAYS check with your supervisor whenever you encounter difficulties with

questionnaire wording or procedures. Each survey presents new problems. Rather than being a confession of weakness, asking questions is evidence that you care.

5. ALWAYS be polite. You are a guest in someone's home.

6. ALWAYS act naturally. If you force yourself unnaturally or pretend to be something you are not, people sense it very quickly and become suspicious of your motives. Your motives are good in this encounter, so don't let respondents think otherwise.

7. ALWAYS be firm about interruptions and privacy. Gently but firmly instruct third parties that your interview must be with the respondent, as instructed by your office. You are interviewing only him, not others.

8. ALWAYS be prepared to carry the point of privacy further. Even if the respondent says it is all right for another person to stay, say that your instructions are to interview in private because all other respondents in the study are being interviewed privately, and you must have all situations the same.

9. ALWAYS complete the interview at one sitting, unless the respondent really has to interrupt it.

10. ALWAYS assure confidentiality. No names can ever be identified. The questionnaire will become only numbers in the computer.

11. ALWAYS interview the person you are supposed to. You cannot substitute respondents within the household (e.g., the grandmother for the mother).

12. ALWAYS interview only at the household designated for the sample. For our purposes, interviews at households not in the sample are worthless.

13. ALWAYS use the same introduction written for the questionnaire. Do not change it.

14. ALWAYS use the same standard replies that have been written for answering people's questions. Don't be inventive. You can always invite still-skeptical respondents to call the study office for assurance of your legitimacy.

15. ALWAYS record "free-response" answers verbatim. Don't paraphrase or interpret. The exact words people use to describe feelings are important. Include the flavor of language used, instead of summarizing the contents in your own words.

16. ALWAYS write legibly. When you check over the questionnaire before leaving, be sure that your written answers can be understood and that each represents what the respondent actually said.

17. ALWAYS use the response categories provided for each question. If a person's answer doesn't seem to fit the categories, write the response verbatim and check it over for completeness before leaving the interview.

18. ALWAYS ask the questions exactly as they are worded and in the same order every time. Each interview must be done the same way, to assure uniform and reliable results.

19. ALWAYS record every answer in the correct place. A questionnaire with serious omissions or errors may have to be discarded. The analyst cannot guess later what the respondent's answers were.

20. ALWAYS repeat questions only once if the respondent does not understand or

objects to a question. Repeat it exactly as written; do not attempt to explain it or make it easier for him to understand or agree with. Any personal interpretation on your part is sure to indicate the answer that you expect from such a respondent, or that you would like to hear. If he still does not understand or objects to the question, record whatever statement he makes and go on immediately to the next question. Make no further comment about that question.

21. ALWAYS record the qualifications ("yes, if . . ." or "yes, but not . . .") that come as answers to straight yes/no questions. Write the qualifications in a space nearby. Later they may reveal something important about the question that was not anticipated.

22. ALWAYS be able to reconstruct respondents' answers. If free-response answers are lengthy and you cannot write down every word, make notes that give the sense and the style of the comment. Use abbreviations that are understandable, so in checking over the interview you can fill in the content of the answer.

23. ALWAYS get specific comments, not vague, meaningless generalities such as "I like it because it's good" or "Because it's interesting" or "It's okay." Ask "Why?" in such cases.

24. ALWAYS keep talking as you write. If probing for more information, repeat the respondent's answer or ask a follow-up question as you record the response to the first. Start the respondent thinking about a question. If you let a silence grow, he has more opportunities to become distracted, bored, resentful, or may even change his mind. Keep voice contact with the respondent, and record his answers as quickly and smoothly as possible. This is one key to the informal atmosphere essential to successful interview.

25. ALWAYS focus the respondent's attention on the questions. If he wants to talk about his new moped or the New Left, politely but firmly steer him back to the questions, saying, "That's interesting . . . now what would you say about this question . . . ?"

26. ALWAYS blame "people at the office" for anything that respondents don't like. You may appear to take their side to the point of agreeing that questions or procedures are strange and that you don't know why they are done as they are. But, you must ask the question the same way of everyone, so that the answers can be compared.

27. ALWAYS take the blame for faulty communication. If the respondent stumbles, say that perhaps you didn't read the question clearly or read it too rapidly. Don't ever let a respondent feel the questions are too difficult for him.

28. ALWAYS accept a refusal graciously and naturally. Don't react. If the person hesitates or initially refuses, simply repeat the question, saying you only want to know the respondent's feelings about that question. Stress that you only want to know how the person feels about that question today. Stress that answers may differ from day to day, and then say "but as things stand today, how do you feel about . . . ?"

29. ALWAYS be particularly careful with preschool children and pets. Don't try to be too friendly too quickly. Let the respondent relieve the child's fear of strangers. Take it easy.

30. ALWAYS be prepared for unusual home situations. You may find a respondent's kitchen is not as spotless as yours. You may find that another family has 12 more children than yours. So what? This is why we do surveys: because people are different, and differences are important to us. Do not express surprise or displeasure about anything you find. Please keep your personal feelings to yourself.

31. ALWAYS check over your questionnaire before leaving the interview. It doesn't take more than a few minutes in the home to go through the questionnaire item-by-item, checking that all questions have answers, that all answers fit the correct categories or are explained, and that all answers are legible. Say, "I'll just see if I've got everything."

Probing

The goal of closed-end questions is to elicit unambiguous responses—responses for which there is no reservation in the interviewer's mind about which questionnaire categories they fit. The goal of open-end questions is to elicit responses in depth—to get full information from the respondent, information which may combine several responses in one, all of which are relevant to the question asked. To achieve either goal, an essential skill needed is the ability to *probe* to get unambiguous, complete, and meaningful answers.

Why Probe? What is probing? Probing is the skill of stimulating conversation, of encouraging people to answer questions in full. A dictionary might define it as: "searching to the bottom; scrutinizing; examining thoroughly."

In surveys, people are often asked questions that they haven't spent much time thinking about previously. They may need time to organize their thoughts or to recall pertinent information. Yet they may respond immediately with a very general answer. The job of the interviewer is to probe such answers to get all of the respondent's relevant information or complete opinion on the subject.

How is this accomplished? Like the reporter, we ask WHO, WHAT, WHERE, WHEN, WHY, and HOW. For instance: if the questionnaire asks, "What do you think of the new solid-waste recovery plan?" and the response is, "I think it is a good plan," we really have no useful answer at all. We must begin to probe.

Probing, we might ask: "How is it a good plan?" "What makes it a good plan?" or "Why do you think it is a good plan?" We pick up the respondent's *ambiguous word* "good," and probe for the specific what, why, and how of the person's feelings. Through probing we may find that the respondent thinks: (1) "The solid-waste pick-up will keep the streets cleaner," *but* (2) "It will not really pay for itself''; and *also* (3) ''While It's a good plan, it won't work to change behavior because people won't save their recyclables anyway.'' We have come a long way from the first answer of ''It is a good plan.''

There are many words like ''good'' which have different meanings in different situations to different people. Figure 5.2 presents a list of some of these ambiguous words. For our purposes an ambiguous word is any word needing clarification. Any time they hear a respondent use ambiguous words, interviewers are trained to probe to find out exactly what the respondent means. For instance, ''frequently'' may mean twice a week to us, but to the respondent it may mean once a month. We never assume that we can interpret another person's words. We always ask the respondent what he or she means by a particular word.

How to Prove. Checklist 24 (pages 268–270) details some tips on probing. It is written as though talking directly to interviewers who are in training. Again, for simplicity, the interviewer is female and the respondent male. Other probing tips are also contained in Checklist 23 above.

Figure 5.2. Some ambiguous words to probe

good	poor	fair
bad	rich	unfair
easy	useful	better
hard	useless	worse
satisfactory	majority	fine
unsatisfactory	minority	nice
often	frequently	several
seldom	infrequently	few
quantity	occasionally	large
quality	sometimes	small
high	close	most
low	far	many
a lot	strong	some
a little	weak	much
important	before	here
unimportant	after	there
more	broad	around
less	narrow	near
likely	plenty	like
unlikely	enough	dislike
people	slightly	moderately
public	average	partially
sure	certain	superior
unsure	uncertain	inferior

CHECKLIST 24

Probing

The following are useful techniques.

1. THE ECHO PROBE: Echo the respondents exact answer (e.g., "I think it's a good plan."), but while raising your voice at the end to form a question (i.e., "You think it is a good plan?"). This is most effective if you repeat the answer as you write it down.

2. THE REQUESTION PROBE: Repeat part of the question, for example, "What else do you think about the solid-waste plan?" If you simply say "anything else?" you are inviting a no answer, so it is better to add part of the question to this type of probe, making it more of an assertion than a question.

3. THE SILENT PROBE: A short wait for further clarification while still looking at the person can be very effective, because people start talking to fill lulls in the conversation. Remember, a permissible pause should not become an embarrassing silence. How often and how long to pause varies with each respondent. As a rule, silence should be used sparingly.

4. THE RECAPITULATION PROBE: Request the respondent to rephrase his previous answer. The purpose is to give you more time to write and to let the respondent clarify his remarks and add detail. This can best be used in conjunction with the silent probe. This is done by pausing and, if there is no answer, asking for further clarification: "How would you say that another way?" or "I'm not sure I know exactly what you mean?" or "Could you explain what you mean by that?"

5. THE ENCOURAGEMENT PROBE: "Uh-huh," "yes . . . yes." "I see," and other neutral words of encouragement by the interviewer tell the respondent that his answers are acceptable and he should continue. These are very effective probes. You offer no opinion of your own while encouraging the respondent to continue talking.

6. THE NONVERBAL PROBE: Encouragement can be both verbal and nonverbal. We cue respondents to continue talking merely with a smile, a nod of the head, or an inviting gesture (such as we would make if we were beckoning someone toward us).

7. THE SPECIFICATION PROBE: Ask a question to get a more specific comment, not being satisfied with vague, meaningless generalities, such as "I like it because it's good" or "Because it's interesting" or "It's okay." Ask "Why?" in such cases. More specifically, you might probe by saying one of the following:

   "I see. Well, could you tell me what you have in mind?"

   "And just exactly why do you think that is so?"

   "Could you tell me a bit more specifically what you think?"

   "And why do you say that?"

"How do you mean that?"

"Could you tell me more about your thinking on that?"

"Just for my own understanding, what do you mean by that?"

"And what else do you think about that?"

"What other reasons do you have for feeling as you do?"

"Why do you think that is the case?"

"I'm not sure I quite understand what you have in mind."

"Would you tell me why you feel that way?"

"What other thoughts do you have about that?"

"What else do you think of when you think of that?"

"What do you have in mind?"

"Could you explain that a little more fully?"

"Would you give me an example of what you mean?"

"Would you say then that . . . (REPEAT QUESTION)."

"Yes, but . . . (REPEAT QUESTION)."

8. THE REPEAT PROBE: Whenever there is some confusion between the interviewer and the respondent, the best thing for the interviewer is to *repeat the question*. The interviewer's sanctuary, your safety, is in the body of the question itself. Whenever you become muddled or tense in an interview, simply go back to the question and repeat it exactly as written. You are only human, and people are quite willing to accept your mistakes or confusion.

People often say "I don't know" to a question almost before the words are out of the interviewer's mouth. As mentioned before, don't record that first answer too quickly; often respondents are stalling for time to arrange their thoughts. But a "don't know" answer may also have several other possible meanings, including: (1) the respondent doesn't understand the question and is trying to cover his embarrassment; (2) he is trying to evade the question because it is too sensitive, and he feels his answer may be unacceptable or too revealing; or (3) he really doesn't have an opinion on the subject. In the latter case, the "don't know" answer is entirely acceptable. But it is your responsibility to try to get an answer by repeating the question with a neutral preface. Consider the following phrases:

"Let me repeat the question . . . (REPEAT QUESTION)."

"Well, in your opinion . . . (REPEAT QUESTION)."

"Well, as things stand today, would you say . . . (REPEAT QUESTION)."

"All things considered . . . (REPEAT QUESTION)."

"Well, as you see things right now . . . (REPEAT QUESTION)."

"As far as you're concerned . . . (REPEAT QUESTION)."

"I see, but in your own view . . . (REPEAT QUESTION)."

"Well, generally speaking . . . (REPEAT QUESTION)."

"Would you say then that . . . (REPEAT QUESTION)."

"I'd just like to get your thinking on . . . (REPEAT QUESTION)."

"Would you give me your general ideas on . . . (REPEAT QUESTION)."

"Well, what is your general reaction to . . . (REPEAT QUESTION)."

"I see, but taking everything into account . . . (REPEAT QUESTION)."

"Uh-huh, but considering everything . . . (REPEAT QUESTION)."

"I didn't read that clearly, let me try again . . . (REPEAT QUESTION)."

Note that you absolutely *do not* change or adapt the question in any way but merely repeat it as written, yet the preceding phrase and the repeat gives the respondent a new try at answering it.

When To Stop Probing. An answer to a closed-end question normally requires no probing. If probing is required at all to get the information, we stop probing on a closed-end question when the respondent's clarified answer can be put without reservation into one of the response categories.

We stop probing on an open-end question when the answer is complete—that is, an answer that clarifies the specific reasons for the opinion so that we are able to record exactly what the respondent has in mind, and the range, meaning, and intensity of his or her feelings.

Probing Symbols. Most probing is done on open-end questions. Such questions appear on the questionnaire without fixed-response categories, but with a series of lines for recording comments. When we have probed, we so indicate by marking down a *probe symbol*. Some probe symbols are described below.

- When you probe an ambiguous word, such as "good," write down the word with a question mark and enclose it in parentheses. Thus, a probe such as "What do you mean when you say a good plan?" would appear in the verbatim remarks as *(Good?)* and would be followed by the respondent's answer.
- Probing with who, what, where, when, why, and how is indicated by writing the appropriate word in parentheses with a question mark. For example, the symbol *(Why?)* might be used to show that the probe question was: "Why do you think it is a good plan?"

- The probe symbol (R) is used to show that you repeated the question to encourage further conversation.
- The probe symbol *(Else?)* is used to show that you asked the respondent a general probe such as, "And what else makes you think it's a good plan?"
- The probe symbol *(Other?)* is used to show a change in topics. For example, if you are asking the respondent to describe two problems that he feels are very important and you exhaust his thinking about the first problem he mentions, (say, "high taxes,"), you would then say, "What other problems are important?" and would write in the symbol *(Other)*.
- The respondent's own answer, in parentheses with a question mark, is a probe symbol indicating a request for more detail. In the following example, the response to the question was, "Taxes are important." Then you ask "What's important about taxes?" and record *(Taxes?)* to show your probe. In this example, taxes have to be clarified because there are federal income taxes, state income taxes, city income taxes, sales taxes, property taxes, gasoline taxes, and so on.

Note that all probes are indicated with the respondent's words recorded verbatim. Always record the respondent's exact words, including slang and bad grammar, as in the following example:

> In your opinion, what are two or three of the most important problems facing the American people today? (What other problems are important?) (What others?)

PROBE: *Taxes are important. (Taxes?) They're too high, especially the sales tax. (High?) It's up to six percent. (Else?) Nothing, that's all. (Other?) Well, welfare's pretty important. (Why?) The poor people ain't getting the help they should. (Help?) You know, like food stamps and stuff like that. (Stuff?) Oh, I don't know, they should get free food stamps, that's all. (Else?) That's all I can think of. (Other?) No, just those two.*

There are two instances in which extensive probing is required but answers do not have to be written verbatim. The first: You are asked to *list* answers topically in the order in which they are given. When the answer is recorded in this manner, you continue to probe, but, as can be seen in the next example, you are allowed to paraphrase the respondent's answers, as long as they are specific enough to be meaningful.

In your opinion, what are two or three of the
most important problems facing the American
people today? (What other problems are
important?) (What others?)

LIST: 1. *Sales tax too high - up to 6%.*

2. *Welfare-poor people need more food stamps.*

3. *Nothing*

The second: For certain kinds of short-answer questions, you will be asked to
probe extensively to get a very specific answer. For instance, in order to code or
classify a respondent's occupation we must know exactly what he does in his job.
An "engineer" might be a railroad engineer, a stationary engineer, a methods
engineer, or an electrical engineer. These jobs, while having the generic name
"engineer," demand very different skills and require different kinds and levels of
education. To classify this person correctly, we must know exactly what kind of
engineer he or she is.

Since job titles can be very ambiguous, never accept a title alone as an
adequate description of a job. Probe for the company, find out the type of work
involved, and keep at it until you are absolutely sure of what people do when
on their jobs. The U.S. Census interviewers are required to obtain from respondents at least two words to describe each of the following: what is done by a
company at the respondent's location, what the respondent's job title is, and specifically what the respondent does. Consider this example:

What is your job . . your occupation?

SPECIFY: *Engineer (Type?)*
Methods. (Methods?) Efficiency expert
(Where?) Ford Motor Co. (Job?)
Assign production rates.

A different kind of specification probing is frequently used with closed-end
questions. The probe is written into the question so there is no ambiguity about how to
probe. The next example has two ways of asking for clarification of an answer to a
closed-end question. First, suppose you are to ask the respondents' ideology,
whether they are liberal or conservative, but they say something else. You are to
record the specific words by which they describe themselves. But second, if the
respondents say they consider themselves to be something else, or don't know, you
are to ask further to see which way they lean, in order to get all the information
possible.

```
In politics, do you consider yourself more of a liberal . .
or more of a conservative?

            1--Liberal

            2--Conservative

   *3--Other    SPECIFY: _____
                         WRITE IN EXACT WORDS )

  *4--DK/NR   (IF DK/NR, ASK:)

  * (IF "OTHER" OR DK/NR, ASK:)

       Well, would you say you lean more toward
       the liberal side, or more toward the
       conservative side?

            1--Lean liberal

            2--Lean conservative

            3--Other    SPECIFY_____

            4--DK/NR
```

Standard Replies

There are many problems in surveys that interviewers must solve quickly and matter-of-factly for the success of the interview. Such problems occur when respondents question the legitimacy of the study, their presence in it, the value of their opinions, or the sense of a question.

Interviewers must be prepared to deal skillfully with these situations in order to complete the interview. This section presents a number of *standard replies* that have been found to be very effective in handling respondents' questions or objections. These standard replies must be tools that are practiced by the interviewer until they become such an integral part of the interviewer's personality that they flow automatically in a natural tone of voice. In most cases, interviewers learn that using "the people in the office" and the "people in charge" as the source for question wording and procedure is an effective way of taking the side of the respondent and *shifting the burden away from themselves,* as we wish them to do.

Although they may seem simple-minded in print, general explanations work well in conversations. This is the principle of the standard replies. People will accept a brief, neutral explanation of our work, as long as we do not appear to be evasive or deceitful: "We're just doing a study of some of the things people are talking about these days." Learning these standard replies and being able to respond immediately with them eliminates the floundering, confused, ineffective, defensive, or—worse—contaminating comments that interviewers might blurt out otherwise.

Successful handling of respondents' questions or objections requires a businesslike attitude. Interviewers are trained to accept any question naturally, as though it has been asked many times already that day. The answer must be immediate and brief, not an elaborate or lengthy explanation. Generally a simple, innocuous answer will satisfy respondents' questions. We never ignore a respondent's question; instead, we parry it with the kind of standard replies described below.

Once we answer the question or meet the objection, *we do not hesitate* but continue immediately with the interview. We do not give respondents time to reconsider their objections or to debate our answer.

General Guidelines. As before, this section is written directly to the interviewer as though we were in a training session. Some general guidelines for the larger interviewing strategy are described first, followed by some standard replies, which are specific tactics.

Do Not Give Lengthy Explanations. The standard replies are your stock-in-trade for answering questions. Commit the replies to memory. Use them at will. *They are proven devices for answering questions about surveys.* In various studies, you may be questioned by many people, including officials. You have to produce good answers—spontaneously and naturally.

In ordinary conversation when someone asks, "How are you?" a complete medical history is not the expected answer. People don't really expect or want long answers to questions. People in the United States are familiar with Gallup-Poll kinds of surveys, and they don't expect you to justify what you do or to explain your procedures. Recognize this. Some of the standard replies below are built on the following proven principles:

- People sometimes ask questions of the interviewer as a way of *establishing their role* in the situation.
- Although people know about surveys, they are not likely to have been interviewed before, and 99 times out of 100 they are *flattered* to be chosen.
- Most questions people ask are *harmless by intention*—just devices to clarify relationships.
- But the *interviewers' reactions* often create a real problem, because some overreact, become defensive, and overexplain.

Relax. You can always give more information if necessary, but try to save time. When asked a simple question by the respondent (e.g., "How was my name chosen?"), give a simple answer (e.g., "I don't really know. The people in my office are in charge of such things.") and continue with your job which is asking the *respondent* questions. But this easy way of dealing naturally with questions relates to feeling natural about yourself. Really, much of the success of interviewing is based on the feeling that you are *supposed* to be doing what you are doing.

Do Not Readily Accept Refusals to Participate. Sometimes when people say they will not participate in the study, they are *willing to be asked again*. Don't accept at once when people say: "I'm too busy," "I don't have enough time," or "Come back later.'' If necessary, you'll make another specific day and time appointment to come back. But chances are, the person is only hesitant, perhaps reluctant, but is ultimately not refusing to participate unless *you make refusing easy*. Ask again, stress the importance of the study, show your identification, but do *not* shrug your shoulders and meekly walk away.

Do Not Ask for Permission to Work. The standard introduction provides a smooth transition from the first moment of contact at the door into the body of the question-naire. Questions that may arise in the respondent's mind in these early moments are likely to be in the vein of: ''What's this all about?'' ''Why was I chosen?'' ''Is this a sales pitch?'' ''What's her game?'' and so on.

Your friendly, courteous manner and the quickness with which the respondent is involved in the study often put such questions to rest wtihout being spoken. A manner that is anything less than businesslike and confident may raise doubts about your role. Do not ask for permission; asking conveys inconfidence and poses the option of refusal, which the respondent may not have consciously considered.

At the doorstep, don't ask questions to gain permission; instead *suggest* the course of action you desire. For instance, instead of asking, ''May I come in?''—to which a respondent could easily say no—say, ''I would like to come in and talk to you about this.''

The best tactic is to assume the respondent has time to be interviewed and will be willing, provided we show the desired course of action. Never encourage inter-view refusal or postponement with self-defeating questions like these:

''Do you have time?'' (''NO.'')
''I hope you're not too busy.'' (''I AM.'')
''Would you like me to come back?'' (''YES, LATER.'')
''Is this a convenient time?'' (''NO.'')
''Are you interested in things like this?'' (''NO.'')
''Could you spare a few moments?'' (''NO.'')
''Would you mind letting me interview you?'' (''YES, LEAVE ME ALONE.'')

Other, equally self-destructive things interviewers can do are to volunteer the specific nature of the study (e.g., politics and religion), the number of questions or questionnaire pages, or the specific time involved (e.g., ''This will only take 30 minutes.'').

You are asking people a lot of personal questions, and they have a right to be curious. You cannot afford to arouse their suspicions or to abuse their sensitivities by ignoring their questions, but don't encourage questions with timidity and permis-siveness. Remember: thousands of people all over the country are asked personal questions in surveys nearly every day of the year.

Do Not Use Loaded Words in Your Explanations. ''Loaded words'' are those that provoke strong feelings or mental images. The term ''federal government'' is loaded. The standard replies are written to avoid such words. It is mandatory that in all cases you use the neutral wording we provide for introducing and explaining the study. Loaded words blurted out inadvertently may cause respondents to answer differently from how they might otherwise, which biases the study.

Some of the loaded words we avoid in survey explanations include "education," "educational television," "political party," "class project," "minority children," "ethnic groups," "Department of Health and Human Services, Washington, D.C.," and other terms naming the study sponsor, its purpose, or its target population.

On the other hand, some loaded words work well in explaining the study, especially those related to science. Telling people that their names were chosen as "part of a scientific sample" is an effective answer to questions about sampling. The whole aura of scientific respectability can be used to overcome objections, reduce interruptions, and eliminate further questions.

Do Not Convince Respondents To Ignore Questions. We try not to alarm respondents about an essentially straightforward study. Federal regulations require that respondents be apprised of the voluntary nature of certain federally funded studies. Questionnaire introductions are required to inform the respondents of this fact. However, you should not state this in a manner that convinces the respondent that there are going to be some questions he/she should not answer. This makes the study seem more secretive than it is. It clues the respondent to be on guard, cautious, suspicious. You are saying there is something wrong with what you are doing. But, in fact, it is the opposite: there is plenty that is "right." We don't really deal in rights and wrongs, but if researchers for a federally sponsored study failed to prove it had a useful purpose, which they are required to do, you probably wouldn't be working on it.

Do Not Tell Respondents That Some Questions Are Sensitive. There is no such thing as a sensitive question. *People* may be sensitive. One person is sensitive about this and another about something else. Let us not try to define for our respondents what we think they may be sensitive about. Chances are we'll be very wrong.

We have been asking people for years "personal" questions about age, income, race, ethnic background, level of education, newspaper readership, television viewing, eating habits, voting behavior, sleeping attire, sexual activities, etc. But, like a self-fulfilling prophecy, if you think such questions are sensitive, you will find they are, because you will convey your insecurities to the respondent. Doing this only succeeds in making the respondent aware that you think something is "wrong." Your problem now becomes a problem for the respondent, where there was none before. And this becomes a problem for us, where there should not have been a problem at all.

Drop the notion of sensitive questions. People will often say personal things to strangers that they wouldn't even say to family or friends.

Use Standard Replies. Below are some common inquiries or objections for which you need spontaneous and natural-sounding answers. Memorize these standard replies, so that you can cope immediately and effectively with any of these situations. The key idea here is this: people really don't want or need elaborate answers.

It is impossible to describe all the problems that require standard replies in the interview situation, but each of the next four sections in Checklist 25 represents a basic *theme* of standard replies. Associating the underlying theme with the specific problems will help you learn the appropriate replies.

CHECKLIST 25

Standard Replies—How to Handle Respondent Inquiries and Objections

Theme 1: The Survey Introduction

In many situations, a simple rephrasing of the introductory remarks you first used in the interview will satisfy respondents' inquiries. Although you are not really saying anything new, you are providing an answer without adding any personal interpretations of your own. While most people are actually very willing to go ahead with the interview, many need the personal satisfaction of raising some kind of an objection, if only to assure themselves that they are not to be taken lightly and to establish that they are in control of the situation. Simply rephrasing the introduction normally satisfies this type of respondent. (Italics are respondent questions.)

- *Who's doing this study?*
  The study is being done by the Research Department of Model State University. It's a study of the things people in Model City are talking about these days.
- *Are you selling magazines or something?*
  No, I am a research interviewer for the Research Department at Model State University. We're doing a study of some of the things people in Model City are talking about these days.
- *What's this all about?*
  This is a research study being done by the Research Department of Model State University. We're doing a study of some of the things people in Model City are talking about these days.
- *Why are you doing this?*
  The Research Department does studies like this all the time . . . to learn what people think about what's going on in the city today.
- *How do I know you're from the University?*
  Here's my identification (if necessary, show other documents). If you would like, I can let you talk to one of the research supervisors in charge of the study—she'll be happy to answer your questions.

- (IF STILL NOT SATISFIED)
  Would you like me to give you the University phone number? You can call the
  Research Department and talk to my supervisors (If yes, give the "trouble" number.)

Theme 2: The Respondent's Opinion

Frequently, people must be reassured that they are not being tested for intelligence but
rather are being surveyed for their opinions. Their opinions, like their values and
beliefs, are never wrong. They may differ from your own, but neither you or they are
right or wrong—you merely hold different opinions. But when people have the fear of
being tested, you need only stress that whatever the person thinks is all that really
matters in this survey. Note that standard replies below emphasize two basic points: (1)
that this is a survey of the respondent's opinions; and (2) that what he thinks is all that
really counts.

- *What do you mean by that?*
  Whatever it means to you. Whatever comes into your mind. Whatever you usually
  think of when you think of that.
- *What's the matter, did I say something wrong?*
  No, not at all. We're only studying people's opinions, and there are no right or
  wrong answers.
- *Well, it depends. It's hard to answer that kind of question because there are so many
  considerations.*
  Yes, there are many considerations ... but as things stand today, would you
  say ... (REPEAT THE QUESTION EXACTLY AS WORDED). OR: There really
  are no right or wrong answers ... it's more about how you *feel*. What are your
  feelings about this?
  If respondent still hesitates: Well, just generally speaking, how would you tend to
  answer the question as things stand today?
  If respondent cannot answer: (Don't comment. Mark Item DK/NR And go on to the
  next question.)
- *Gee, I don't know. . . . What do you think?*
  What I think doesn't matter at all. This is a survey of your opinions, and what *you*
  think is all that really counts.
- *I'm no good at these kinds of things; I don't keep up with the news.*
  That doesn't make any difference. This isn't a test of what people know, it's only
  what you think that counts. We are just asking your opinion on various topics.
- *Let me get my wife; she knows all about these things.*
  It's not what you *know* that counts, it's *your opinion* that's really important. Since
  you were chosen by a scientific sample, *you* are the one who is important to us, and
  interviewing someone else would not be as good.
- *Why interview me? . . . Talk to my wife.*
  You were selected completely by chance according to procedures worked out by my

office. So your opinions are important and interviewing someone else wouldn't be as good.

- *My wife wants to listen. . . . You can interview both of us.*
  It's really only your opinions that count. Sometimes people in the same house have slightly different opinions, and just *your* opinions are important to us.
- *If other person interrupts:* I'd appreciate it very much if you would let (RESPONDENT) answer the questions alone. According to our research procedure, we must talk only to (HIM) (HER) in order to learn many different opinions. Interviewing someone else would not be as accurate.

Theme 3: Siding With The Respondent

Many times the respondent will shy away from or object to a question. The smart interviewer does two things: First, where appropriate, she empathizes with the respondent by agreeing generally that the questions are difficult and that the respondent has the right to his reaction. Second, she explains that she is only an interviewer and that the "people in the office" are responsible for question wording or study procedure.

Above all, if the respondent stumbles over a question or needs time to collect his thoughts, the interviewer very quickly assumes the "blame." For example, the interviewer's response might be, "Perhaps I didn't read the question clearly." Never let the respondent shoulder the blame for faulty communication. Note, too, that in this section the interviewer cites reasons of "scientific procedure" and "accuracy" in explaining why the respondent should cooperate in the study.

- *Gee, these are hard questions.*
  I have trouble answering some of them myself. But we really just want to know what you think about the questions. Any answer you give is a good answer.
- *That's a stupid question.*
  I don't know why, but that's the way my office has the questions worded . . . and we are instructed to ask them just as they are written.
- *Whoever wrote these questions doesn't know what he's talking about.*
  The people in my office wrote the questions. I don't know how or why they ask the questions they do; I'm just an interviewer.
- *I just can't answer that.*
  Well, maybe it's the way my office worded the question, but what are your feelings about the subject, the way it's worded? (REPEAT THE QUESTION.)
- *I hadn't thought much about that before.*
  Let me repeat the question, just take your time thinking about it. (REPEAT THE QUESTION.)
- *That's pretty confusing. What did you say?*
  Let me repeat the question. (REPEAT THE QUESTION EXACTLY AS WORDED, BUT SLOWER.)
- *If still confused:* I don't know why, but that's how our office has the question worded. Just answer as best you can, all we want is your opinion.

- *That's none of your business.*
  Of course you don't have to answer any questions you'd prefer not to. I'm just trying to get your opinion because our study is more accurate that way.
- *If still refuses:* (Don't comment. Mark item "refused" and go on to the next question.)
- *I don't have time . . . I'm too busy.*
  Yes, I know, people *are* busy these days. My questions will only take a few minutes, and I think you'll find them very interesting . . . I think you'll enjoy this.
- *If insists he's too busy:* The questions won't take long. You can go right on with your work, and I'll just run through these items. (BEGIN QUESTIONING IMMEDIATELY.)
- *If still insists he's too busy:* Why don't I come back in an hour or so, when you may have more time.
- *If still insistent:* What would be a better time for me to call back? Because you were chosen scientifically, it's very important that we talk to all of the people we are supposed to . . . otherwise, our information will not be as accurate.
- *He's not here right now, why don't you interview me?*
  Well, I think you *would* have very interesting answers . . . but according to the research procedure used in this survey, I have to talk to the (PERSON) in your household. What would be a good time for me to call back to talk with (HIM)(HER)?
- *If still insistent:* I know your answers would be very interesting, but (PERSON) was chosen by a scientific procedure, and our information just wouldn't be complete if we didn't talk with (HIM) (HER).
- *If pressed further:* I don't know exactly how they select the people to be interviewed . . . I'm just an interviewer. The people in charge of the study here are very strict about interviewing only the person we are told to talk to at each household. What would be a good time for me to call (HIM) (HER) at home?

Theme 4: Science and Confidentiality

As indicated in the previous section, we sometimes refer to the needs of science and accuracy as reasons for wanting to interview particular respondents. We also assure people on scientific grounds that we have no prior knowledge of them, that they are chosen at random, and that their opinions are grouped with the opinions of many others for purposes of analysis. Related to this are assurances of confidentiality.

- *How did you get my name?*
  I didn't have your name. Your household was chosen at random. According to the research procedure in this survey, I am just supposed to talk with the (PERSON) in this household . . . you.
- *Why did you come here?*
  Your household was chosen from a scientific sample of households all over the city. We are interviewing a lot of people.

- *Does this mean you'll be coming back?*
  No.
- *If necessary:* It's very unlikely you would be interviewed again, since we only select a few of all of the households in the city. OR: Houses are selected at random, and it's impossible to say which will be chosen and which won't.
- *Why do you want to know that?*
  Well . . . many people are being asked these same questions, of course, and what you say is confidential. We are interested in these questions only to see what a lot of people in Model City generally are thinking about.
- *What are you going to do with my answers?*
  Your answers are confidential. The information you give me is put together with information from a lot of people all around the city. This gives us a pretty accurate idea of what most people are thinking about these days.
- *If necessary:* We analyze the information and present the findings on reports like these (SHOW REPORT).
- *Why do you want my name; what are you going to do with it?*
  It's just so my office will know that I did conduct this interview, so they can check my work in case I made a mistake. Your name is always kept confidential.
- *If still refuses:* Well, of course, you don't have to give your name if you prefer not to. You and your answers are never identified. The research people in the office are only interested in what all of the people say . . . not any individual person.
- *What do you need my address for?*
  It's just so the people in charge of the study can check the accuracy of their sample.
- *If asked to explain:* The sample is based on addresses. The people in the office check them to be sure the sample is correct.

Summary. The standard replies in this section cover only some of the situations you will encounter in interviewing. Be prepared to use them quick and naturally. Above all, don't overexplain. Be brief. Don't hesitate for reactions; go on immediately with your interviewing. A simple reply given in a matter-of-fact, nonapologetic manner will satisfy most people. Don't evade questions; simply deal with them quickly and politely. Then go on with the questions as soon as possible in a conversational way.

Never feel embarrassed about asking any of the questions in the interview. These kinds of questions are asked every year of hundreds of thousands of people across the nation. Nor should you be hesitant about imposing on people's time. For a small portion of their time, you are trading them a chance to be more influential in public affairs. Just have a businesslike attitude that shows you are there to complete the interview. That is your business.

Safeguarding the Interviewer

There are certain perils to interviewers. Especially in central-city high-crime areas, interviewers may not feel safe in unfamiliar neighborhoods after dark. There is sufficient justification for these fears. Checklist 26 presents a number of common-sense precautions to help assure interviewers' personal security.

CHECKLIST 26

Tips for Safeguarding Interviewers

1. FIRST CONTACT: To the extent possible, schedule interviewing assignments so that most interviews in insecure areas are attempted during the daylight hours. This may require some economically inefficient juggling of caseloads, but the personal security of the interviewer is above such concerns.
2. SUCCESSIVE CONTACTS: If no one is at home and appointments cannot be made, interviewers might be instructed to try to learn from neighbors the time when the designated respondents usually are home. The Model Survey doesn't use this tactic on the first interview attempt. Too often, strangers who poke around asking strange questions about neighbors are met with suspicion and hostility. The distortions of purpose that suspicious neighbors carry back to the designated respondent can make the interviewer's subsequent visit very unpleasant. In the Model we prefer to make a callback later during the day.
3. APPOINTMENTS: Normally, we instruct interviewers to go into insecure areas after dark only for specific appointments—that is, confirmed, with the time and place set. They are not asked to walk the streets searching for unknown addresses.
4. TIME AND COSTS: Interviewing in insecure neighborhoods is generally less efficient than in, say, the suburbs, because we curtail first attempts to the daylight hours. In budgeting the survey, sampling estimates must take into account the number of respondents needed from the areas in question, and adequate resources of time and staff must be allowed to cope with the problem.
5. GUARDED ACCESS APARTMENTS: To gain access to apartment buildings having locked and guarded doors, interviewers are instructed to consult the resident managers. Interviewers should go armed with a variety of documents, which may include: (1) a personal identification card with photograph; (2) a letter of introduction from the study; (3) a signed acknowledgement from the Better Business Bureau and the Police Department; (4) newspaper clippings and other written material describing the study or the survey organization; (5) a list of "trouble" numbers that managers can call for verification of the interviewers' activities. Like confirmed appointments, these apartment buildings may be visited after dark. The interviewer is instructed to ascertain the designated apartments (and likely alternates) for interviewing attempts and to give a copy of the list to the manager before knocking on the first door.

6.   FORWARDING ADDRESSES: The interviewers are instructed to give lists of the appointments they have for a given day to their families or friends, to their field supervisors, to building managers, even to other respondents.

7.   NEIGHBORHOOD POLICE STATIONS: Interviewers are instructed to go to the closest police station in the area, explain their activities, and give a list of streets on which they will be working and at what times. Later, they might revisit the station, dropping off a list of addresses at which appointments have been made for a later time.

8.   WORKING IN TEAMS: Interviewers work together in teams of two or more in insecure neighborhoods. While we do not permit more than one interviewer to interview a single respondent, two interviewers may work in the same apartment building or on the same street. They are required to check frequently with each other and to let respondents know they are together in a team.

9.   INDIGENOUS INTERVIEWERS: Interviewers are selected who are indigenous to the cultural group in the areas under study.

10. FRIENDS AND FAMILY: While interviewers are not permitted to take other persons into respondents' homes, they will often get a friend or family member to accompany them to the address and to wait until the interview (usually an appointment) is completed.

11. SUPERVISOR CHECKS: Interviewers are required at scheduled times to check in by telephone with their supervisors. The supervisor has a list of scheduled appointments in case the check-in call is not made.

12. MALES: We often employ men as interviewers to keep evening appointments in insecure neighborhoods. Since male interviewers may pose a threat to respondents, we make sure the respondent is informed by his/her family that a male interviewer may keep the appointment.

13. THIRD PARTIES: On special occasions, we have hired males specifically to accompany interviewers to insecure neighborhoods.

14. DRESS: As a matter procedure in any situation, interviewers are instructed to dress modestly and not to wear jewelry or carry purses.

15. BADGES: To aid the interviewer's official-looking appearance, we furnish them with identification badges worn on the outer garment. The idea is that people are less likely to be disturbed by interviewers who appear to be on official business. On the other hand, interviewers may be mistaken for government officials—the police or a city inspector—and their reception may not be hospitable. It is best to forewarn respondents for whom appointments are made.

Privacy for Interviewing

Getting privacy is often difficult. Children, spouses, and in-laws all are curious about the presence of a stranger, the questions being asked, and—most important—the responses being given. Respondents' answers are, of course, often influenced by the inhibiting presence of interested third parties. Spouses and older people can be particularly destructive to respondent honesty—especially if they try to interject their views.

Adults who interrupt usually want to be interviewed themselves. The most difficult person to deal with is the one who feels he/she is more knowledgeable on the topic than the respondent. The previous section on standard replies cites some effective responses to this situation.

Interviewers are trained to politely and firmly seek privacy with their respondents up to a point: if further insistence will jeopardize their continued presence, that is the time to relent. Some of the devices for trying to secure privacy are described in Checklist 27.

CHECKLIST 27

Securing Privacy for Interviewing

Devices for securing interview privacy include:

1. DIVERSION: Ask the respondent to send the children outside to play or to run an errand.

2. IGNORE: Sometimes interlopers will lose interest and disappear when their comments are ignored by both interviewer and respondent.

3. SATISFY CURIOSITY: People will often go away after hearing a brief explanation of the study and a few warm-up questions.

4. ROLE EDUCATION: Respondents can be quickly educated about their role by explaining to them the biasing effects that others can have on their answer. We all know this is true simply from having been in two-person conversations that suddenly become three-person conferences.

5. EXPLAIN INSTRUCTIONS: Third parties seem to have more sympathy for persons *requiring* privacy than for those merely *requesting* it. The interviewer says something like this: "It's not my doing, it's my instructions. The people in my office require that each interview be private in order to be sure they are all done the same way. I'm only following instructions."

6. ENLIST AID: With role education, the respondent can be enlisted to expel third parties.

7. MOCK INTERVIEWS: Obstinate third parties who want to be interviewed can be mollified by telling them: "I have some questions to ask you, too, just as soon as I finish interviewing (RESPONDENT). Excuse us now and I'll be with you as soon as I can." This is usually pretty effective, and interviewers are given dummy questionnaires with only a few items to use in such situations. The extra questionnaires are, of course, discarded.

8. CONSENSUS QUESTIONS: Occasionally there are questions in the interview for which other family members' responses are useful and which are not tests of

respondents' knowledge, for example: physical characteristics of the community, locations of places, historical events, names of local groups and people. These "consensus" questions are used like dummy questions for the purpose of mollifying third parties. Unlike the mock interview, responses to consensus questions are included as part of the survey data.

9. CALL THE OFFICE: If the interviewer's ploys don't work, we may invite the interloper to call the survey office and talk to officials there who will explain the study and the need for privacy. This is an effective diversion—occupying (and educating) the interloper while the interview goes on.

There are other techniques for achieving privacy, not the least of which is simply insisting on the right of the respondent to express personal opinions free of the interruptions, disagreements, or influence of not-so-helpful family members. And none of the techniques alone is as effective as are several used in combination.

PREPARING FOR INTERVIEWING

Pretesting

The pretest is the most misunderstood and abused element of the survey process. As commonly used, the pretest is an early, troubleshooting phase in which we look for questionnaire weaknesses. But it should be far more than that. The pretest is an advance dress rehearsal for the main study, done under conditions identical (or very similar) to those expected for the main study. As such, it offers opportunities to test more than just respondents' understanding of individual questions.

Because interviewing is expensive, pretesting usually involves relatively few respondents(more on this shortly). Since the pretest is supposed to be a small-scale replica of the main study, however, it should supply information for decisions about all aspects of study planning, sampling, questionnaires, data processing, and logistics. The pretest can reveal, for example, problems in the following survey elements: (1) *sampling*—finding population subgroups, selecting households and respondents; (2) the *introduction*—establishing legitimacy, dealing with refusals, enhancing smoothness; (3) *questionnaire administration*—improving question sequence, wording, format, and logistical symbols; (4) *responses*—determining range of answers, detecting unexpected, inconsistent, and nonvariable responses; (5) *data processing*—setting content analysis categories and precode assignments; (6) *interviewing*—strengthening rapport techniques, spotting objectionable questions, dealing with refusals and privacy; (7) *logistics*—establishing rates of time, caseload, and cost; and (8) *data analysis*—handling response variability, confirming hypotheses.

The pretest is *not* the time to train interviewers. Although interviewers gain proficiency through training, practice, and actual experience, the pretest should not be their first interviewing experience. Because the pretest is an important time in the survey for deciding whether and how to proceed with plans and procedures, we don't want to make such critical decisions on the basis of novices getting their first exposure to the field. It is equally misguided to use only the most skillful interviewers, based on the mistaken assumption that they will know best where the flaws are in our methods.

The sensible solution is to use as many as possible of the interviewers who will be used in the main study. This has several advantages. First, we involve all interviewers in the development of the survey. This is important both for motivation and for exposure to the study. Second, rather than relying on the reactions of only a few, we learn from the experiences of many. Third, we confront the full range of problems that are liable to occur in either group—most skillful or least skillful. And, fourth, we reduce the influence of any single interviewer on our decisions to revise the survey in some way. We rely on group rather than individual experiences.

There is no set number of pretest respondents to obtain. One rule of thumb some use is to get 30 cases, the assumption being that certain types of statistics can be used with 30 or more people. This is weak logic. It is better to require each interviewer to obtain three to five interviews, which should be enough to enable each to uncover any problems with field logistics, respondent selection, or questions.

The pretest should be carried out exactly as we plan to perform the main study (only in smaller numbers). This includes training and briefing interviewers, and it includes assigning them to neighborhoods similar to those in the main sample. We do not, however, use any of the actual households drawn in the main sample for the pretest.

When interviewers return they should be debriefed individually or in small groups. We sit with them and carefully review every facet of household and respondent selection, questioning, and data recording. They are paid for this debriefing time, and it is an invaluable opportunity to go through each questionnaire looking for instances of misunderstanding, poor wording, awkward format, as well as negative reactions to subject matter or to questionnaire length.

Project Directors profit greatly by doing some of the pretest interviews themselves. More than the interviewers, the Director knows how much leeway there is for change in question wording, sequence, and format. After the pretest, we tabulate all responses and review them to see whether the questions are doing what they are supposed to do, and, indeed, if the characteristic under study is showing up at all. We rework parts of the questionnaire that are unproductive, change any confusing wording or interviewer instructions, and note the remaining problems and suggested techniques to overcome them. We use these notes in the interviewer briefing sessions for the actual study. We also use the pretest questionnaires to do preliminary (not final) coding on open-end questions and to debug the data-processing routines.

Briefing

Before going to work, even trained interviewers need thorough briefing to learn the questionnaire and respondent-selection procedures used for this survey. Briefing sessions give interviewers a chance to inspect the tool they will use in the field. This is their opportunity to draw upon their experience (or inexperience) in anticipating the difficulties posed by the questionnaire. So we encourage them to raise questions at this time.

Since the study is likely to involve many interviewers, we plan to have a series of briefing sessions at different times during the same day. A group of five to seven interviewers is maximum. Larger groups tend to get out of hand, because the interviewers are inclined to buzz among themselves and ask questions of each other rather than address the Project Director. Questionnaire problems and field procedures are described in a set of *briefing notes* prepared for each survey and cross-referenced to the questionnaire. Interviewers are required to read the notes and the corresponding questionnaire items before we discuss them in the briefing session.

Experienced interviewers sometimes are oversophisticated, thinking they have encountered every possible problem already. Nonetheless, even these "best" interviewers will commit mistakes in the field without thorough briefing.

The briefing is *not* an explanation of the study. We do not elaborate on why questions are worded as they are, or why certain items are included in the questionnaire. Pretest results, the research and consultations of others, the nature of the study, and our own experience have determined each item on every page. The interviewer's job is to administer the questionnaire as she or he finds it. We never tell interviewers what kinds of answers to expect. To reiterate, such cues become self-fulfilling prophecies—interviewers find what they expect to find. We discuss only the kinds of answers that will require special handling in the field.

Using an overhead projector is ideal for visual demonstration of the questionnaire. Acetate transparencies take only seconds to make on office copying machines. The Project Director goes through the entire questionnaire showing exactly how each item is to be read and marked on the page. The interviewers follow along in their briefing copies, making extensive notes regarding field administration.

After this initial visual demonstration, two interviewers conduct a demonstration interview in front of the group. As they act out the interview, the Director at the projector marks the responses on the transparencies, stopping at critical points to illustrate problems. The group gets in the act also, critiquing both the asking of questions and the marking of answers.

Practice Interviewing

Demonstration interviews are superb instruction. These can be done with either outsiders or fellow interviewers role-playing the "parts" of various respondents.

While the demonstrators go through their paces, the Project Director can have them stop at any point to make suggestions about asking the question or recording the answer or to call attention to an adroit maneuver by the "interviewer." Then interviewers pair off to interview and coach each other, under supervision of the Director.

For further practice, each interviewer should receive a questionnaire to try on an outsider, a family member or friend who is comfortable to work with. (Make sure these questionnaires are marked "Practice" so they don't end up in the study!)

Even after actual interviewing has begun, we continue instruction; supervisors check each interviewer's daily progress and suggest corrections for faulty techniques.

Assuming interviewers have already participated in pretesting and debriefing, Checklist 28 summarizes the steps in interviewer preparation for field work (again, written to speak directly to interviewers).

CHECKLIST 28

Preparing for Interviewing

Interviewers:

1. Check your field kit to be sure you have all supplies and materials listed on the inventory sheet.

2. Reread the briefing notes carefully. Check the notes against the questionnaire until you know the problems involved in various questions or questionnaire procedures.

3. Study the questionnaire closely. Familiarize yourself with the format and symbols. Interview yourself—try to give thoughtful answers to each question. Ask your supervisor about the pronunciation of any word that is unfamilar or about any question or procedure that is unclear. Note any problem you anticipate for the field.

4. Conduct a mock interview for practice with the interviewer next to you. Let her then interview you. To be useful, the interviews must be done seriously.

5. Memorize the introduction on the front page of the questionnaire, so that you can use the introductory remarks naturally. Then, memorize the first words of the first question, so that you can move quickly from the introduction to the heart of the study.

6. Join actively in the briefing session, offering suggestions and critique as you can. Be sure all of your questions are answered.

7. Conduct a practice interview with one or more persons you know. Be comfortable but be serious. Do not mix these questionnaires with those obtained from regular respondents.

8. If you have any further questions or concerns, contact your supervisor immediately. Do not start interviewing until you have resolved all problems.

COORDINATING FIELDWORK

Coordinating field surveys requires exact attention to details of planning and organization. Below are some suggestions written directly to project leaders.

Interviewer Kits

Each interviewer needs a handy kit to organize and facilitate the field work. Three-ring *notebooks* are ideal. Label the outside cover with the interviewer's name and number, case numbers assigned, and name and phone number of the sponsoring organization. An official-looking notebook will help in gaining access to respondents.

Inside the front cover of the notebook should be pasted a *map* of the interviewing area. This should be a large-scale map showing the blocks at which the interviewing will be done (Figure 2.9, page 99). The kit should also contain a smaller-scale city map showing how to get to the interviewing area.

When using three-ring notebooks, do not staple the questionnaire pages. Use paperclips so the interviewer can remove the clips and more easily turn the pages while in the field. She reclips the questionnaire when it is completed. Later, when the questionnaires are checked in, pages should be stapled. If clipboards are used instead of notebooks, staple the pages once at the top left before going into the field.

Include in each kit a supply of *questionnaires* equal to the number of interviews assigned, plus two for briefing and practice interviewing, and two for spoilage in the field. (There should always be enough extra questionnaires run off for briefing, practice, spoilage, and coding, as well as to use as appendices for a report, for circulation to other interested scholars, and for the files.)

In the Model Survey callbacks may be necessary to interview the respondent specified by the selection key on the questionnaire. So an *appointment form* is needed. The Model questionnaire includes spaces for appointment information right on the first page, for recording items such as name, gender, age, family relationship, address, phone number, appointment date and time, and a record of callback attempts. Also, the interviewer uses the back of the first page for describing situations that result in refusal. As questionnaires are checked in, this information helps supervisors correct interviewing techniques and alerts the Director to possible sampling biases.

To the back inside cover of the notebook we fasten a pocket to hold *cards*, such as the income card, that are used in the interview.

When using paid, professional interviewers, include an *expense sheet*. The expense sheet should provide spaces for the interviewer to show the specific number of hours spent interviewing and traveling each day, as well as the time spent in briefing sessions, in practice interviews, and in checking over completed questionnaires. Also, the sheet should indicate mileage for each day in the field and money spent for parking or bus transportation.

An official-looking badge, a letter of introduction, study authorizations, and professional credential cards are all useful in this situation. Letterhead stationery is particularly effective if some prestigious institution is involved. The letter very briefly explains the project, its scientific and impersonal nature, and invites cooperation. Interviewers seldom will need to display this item.

Supply a red ballpoint *pen* to mark the questionnaires—red for contrast with white pages and black ink, which saves time and eyestrain for coders later. Interviewer's materials are set out in Checklist 29.

CHECKLIST 29

Interviewer Materials

1. Three-ring notebook.
2. Cover identification label.
3. Case numbers assigned by clusters.
4. Block map of interviewing area.
5. City map.
6. Clipped questionnaires.
7. Extra questionnaires for briefing, practice, spoilage.
8. Letter of introduction and other credentials.
9. List of ''trouble'' numbers.
10. Income cards (and other cards if used).
11. Tips for interviewers (Checklists 20–28).
12. Expense forms for time, mileage, and parking or tokens.
13. Red ballpoint pens.

Assignments

Sending the now well-trained, well-briefed, well-motivated, and well-equipped interviewers into the field requires maximum coordination. Fortunate is the Project Director who has an able Field Manager to carry this load.

Transportation costs are reduced substantially by sending interviewers to areas near their homes, where feasible. Obviously interviewers cannot work in neighborhoods where they are known personally to respondents, because this destroys the impartiality of the interview. When students and other nonprofessionals are used, car pools may be arranged to take several interviewers in one general direction.

Draw up a master-control sheet listing interviewers' names and numbers and the sample cluster numbers and questionnaire case numbers assigned to them (see Figure 2.5, pages 88–89). Other columns on the sheet are used to keep a running account of case numbers—by completions, refusals, unavailables, substitutions, appointments, and reassignments to other interviewers. The control sheet can be prepared manually or by a computer—depending on access, cost, and size of study.

To ensure that field work progresses according to schedule, interviewers should check in at the end of each day of interviewing. We must have daily progress reports in order to know when to reassign other interviewers to incompleted areas. We cannot afford to lose every interview in a single area of the city because of inadequate field communication.

Trouble Numbers

A telephone command post maintains constant communication between interviewers and the project office. Inexperienced interviewers use the trouble number often, to handle difficulties they encounter, or sometimes simply for reassurance that they are doing all right. Since the number also is given to suspicious respondents, all calls should be answered with the official study sponsor's name, such as "Model State University Research Department. May I help you?" Different phone numbers may be used for field control or study verification.

Interviewing Period

The bulk of interviewing for one study should be done in a relatively short period of time. The Model Survey plans for five days of interviewing plus two days for clean-up, but a week plus the two weekends around it is a rule-of-thumb maximum. A short interviewing period is especially important if intervening events may contaminate data on people's knowledge of issues or events. For example, if we're asking what people think of legalized marijuana use, and halfway through the interviewing two aldermen are indicted for dealing with drug pushers, the reliability of the data is jeopardized.

Time of Interviewing

Interviewing should be done on several consecutive days, at all times of day, to increase the likelihood of locating all types of respondents.

Different types of people are at home at different times in a 24-hour day. During the mornings and afternoons, we are most likely to find at home greater numbers of the elderly, the sick and infirm, married persons, women with young children, unemployed persons, night-shift workers, low-income and minority persons, retireds, people of below-average education. The young, unmarried, mobile, employed Caucasian is particularly least likely to be home during the weekday daylight hours.

We would ordinarily interview, except by appointment, only between 9 A.M. and 9 P.M. Almost everyone is up and about during those hours. But so many households now have all adults employed that most interviewing is planned for late afternoon and early evening. Saturday and Sunday interviewing is important to get the 9 A.M. to 5 P.M. weekday workers, especially those employed out of the city. Also, although inclement weather is not pleasant for interviewing, it is the best time to find people at home.

Monitoring Fieldwork

Intensive supervision, the master-control sheet, and the trouble number are all means of keeping on top of the flow of work.

Throughout the duration of the survey we monitor the *disposition* of questionnaires—the number completed, refused, not complete due to respondent unavailability, pending appointment, and so on. We must keep abreast of the flow of work to pinpoint bottlenecks, slowdowns, and other interferences with the success of the study. Each day we check the status of fieldwork by interviewer, by cluster, by section of the city. We examine the refusals to see if these are occurring in particular neighborhood or ethnic patterns. We watch also for other clues; for example, does a specific time of day or a specific point in the interview correspond to unaccountably higher refusal rates? We check to see if new interviewers are having greater problems than experienced ones, and we consider pulling those with less success back for quick remedial training.

In addition to watching for trouble spots, we keep track of interviewers who are ahead of schedule, who might take on additional clusters, or who can be used to make callbacks or keep appointments for other interviewers.

Questionnaire Identification. As seen in Chapter 4, various items are used to identify each questionnaire, each interviewer, and each sample cluster. For example, the *case number* enables us to keep track of each interviewer's completion rate—as does the *interviewer's number*. The *cluster number* helps us to spot any problems developing in the geographical dispersion of interviews. Analysis of the *respondent type* reveals unusual patterns of people being interviewed, alerting us to possible sampling problems.

Disposition Codes. In addition to monitoring fieldwork by identification items, various codes are important for keeping abreast of the disposition of questionnaires in the field. These *disposition codes* provide a record of each interviewer's success in obtaining the correct interview, whether on the first, second, or third attempt, or not at all. They appear at the bottom of the questionnaire's first page (see Figure 4.2, page 193).

The disposition record tells us something about the cost and efficiency of interviewing. It may also be a critique of the interviewer. Moreover, callback appointments often are made with respondents who were unavailable at the time of the first call. Since some appointments are made for times at which the original interviewer will be unavailable, the disposition records are used by office staff to reassign the callback appointments.

The codes of particular interest here are those that show interviewing attempts, callbacks, appointments, substitutions, and dates and times.

Attempts. Usually about 95 percent of all completed interviews will be obtained within three attempts. The Model Survey requires at least three attempts: one original attempt and two callbacks. Determining how many attempts it takes to get an interview is important for planning survey costs and also for identifying the kinds of biases we incur by not interviewing all designated persons.

Callbacks are required to round out the sample. If no callbacks were made, the sample would yield more people who are home most of the time, such as homemakers and retired persons. The Model respondent-selection procedure designates men and women of all age groups in proportions similar to the general population. Any deviations from the procedure, such as allowing substitutions, are undesirable, because the chance of new people coming into the sample is not known—thus destroying the probability nature of the sample.

The Model Survey instructs interviewers to make two callbacks without an appointment. If no one is home at the sample household on the second attempt, the interviewer may then go to the next-door neighbors and ask what the sample household name is and what hours the residents are normally home. Neighbors are often suspicious of people asking questions about others, so identification letters and credentials are very important here. Armed with this information, the interviewer attempts a reinterview at a time when someone is likely to be home at the sample household. If no information is obtained from the neighbors, interviewers are still instructed to callback later that day or at a different time the next day, in the likely event that residents are normally absent each day at the same time.

Failing to make contact after two further attempts, the interviewer may try to telephone for an appointment—using the telephone directory if the family name is known, enlisting aid of helpful neighbors who will give the interviewer their phone number and agree to be called to learn whether the residents are home (this works in small towns or close city neighborhoods), or even leaving a business card with the interviewer's own home phone number and asking for a return call. If after three attempts and a phone call the designated respondent is not reached, the interview is considered lost, and the questionnaire is returned to the office.

Case Number. Obviously, the case number is essential for monitoring fieldwork. As noted in Chapter 4, each designated respondent is given a four-digit case number that uniquely identifies him/her among all other respondents. Each interviewer is assigned a series of case numbers to complete, such as numbers 0998 to 1023. All questionnaires have case numbers, not only for those people interviewed but also for those who refuse, who are not at home, who are substituted into the sample (if allowed), and so on.

Case numbers may be preprinted on the questionnaire or filled in by the office staff in advance of the study. The four-digit number serves a monitoring purpose. For example, the number "0056" indicates that this is the *56th person* designated in the sample for interviewing. Sometimes a fifth prefix digit will be used to identify substitutions (not permitted in the Model). For example, the number ''10056'' would indicate that this is a questionnaire from a person *substituted* for the originally selected 56th person, who was *not* interviewed. Or, if this were a panel study, ''00056'' might indicate the original interview, ''10056'' the first reinterview, and ''20056'' the second reinterview.

As suggested earlier, interviewing through callbacks is expensive. Most commercial surveys forego the expense, preferring to substitute alternative respondents. There is evidence that substitution results in getting more people in the sample than we should who are most likely to be home on weekdays—e.g., homemakers, retirees, unemployed. The Model avoids substitution, however, so that we can apply all of the statistical tests that require strict adherence to probability at every stage of sampling. Substitution, moreover, is risky, because it demands a field decision that relies on interviewers' judgment. This we try to avoid, because it becomes temptingly easy for interviewers to substitute at will instead of making greater efforts to locate the intended respondent, thus risking biasing the sample. In the Model, we compensate for not using substitutions to make up for unobtained interviews by inflating the original sample size (see Chapter 2), but this also means we endure higher field costs than surveys that allow substitution.

Checklist 30 describes some of the disposition codes used to monitor survey questionnaires. (Compare the codes with those in the box at the bottom of the questionnaire front page in Figure 4.2).

CHECKLIST 30

Questionnaire Disposition Codes

Attempts

In three identical boxes across the bottom of the questionnaire front page, the result of each interviewing attempt is recorded. This helps in planning costs, sample size, number of interviewers, etc. for later studies.

	Date of 1st attempt	Date of 2d attempt	Date of 3d attempt
ENTER DATE →	*245*	*246*	*248*
CIRCLE DISPOSITION CODE	1--Completed ②--Not at home* 3--Appointment* 4--Refused** 5--Unavailable 6--Vacant 7--Physical/Lang. 8--Ineligible 9--Other**	1--Completed 2--Not at home* ③--Appointment* 4--Refused** 5--Unavailable 6--Vacant 7--Physical/Lang. 8--Ineligible 9--Other**	①--Completed 2--Not at home 3--Appointment* 4--Refused** 5--Unavailable 6--Vacant 7--Physical/Lang. 8--Ineligible 9--Other**
APPOINTMENT TIME →	DATE: *Mon Sept 2* TIME: *6* am/⟨pm⟩	DATE: *Wed Sept 4* TIME: *7* am/⟨pm⟩	DATE: TIME: am/pm

Date

Record the date of each attempt, to separate interviews completed before or after an intervening event that disrupts the survey period. The Model Survey uses a 365-day calendar code (''244'' is September 1), but each study date's calendar code is prefigured and listed in the interviewer's instructions, so they don't have to figure it out.

Result Codes

Record the result of each interview attempt in the result column in accord with the following code scheme:

	Code	
1	Completed	Interview successfully completed; coded in the result column (at the first, second, or third attempt).
2	Not at home	No one is home; a callback attempt will be made. At neighbor's suggestions, likely times are recorded in the space for ''appointment'' at the bottom of the box.
3	Appointment	Designated respondent is unavailable, but an appointment time has been fixed (note in the bottom space).
4	Refused	Designated respondent has been contacted and has refused to be interviewed. Reasons are written in the ''comments'' space, or on the back of the page.
5	Unavailable	Designated respondent is not available during the survey period and cannot be interviewed, or no one is home during any of the three interviewing attempts.
6	Vacant	Designated housing unit is vacant.
7	Physical/ Language	Designated respondent is infirm, has a communication impairment, or is otherwise incapacitated and cannot be interviewed, or the respondent cannot converse in the language of the interviewer. Note the language for possible reassignment to another interviewer.
8	Ineligible	No one in the household is eligible for interviewing.
9	Other	All other reasons for noninterview; explain in the space for ''comments'' at the bottom.
0	Inapplicable	Interview was successfully completed already on an earlier attempt; code in second or third space of result column.

Time

Start and end times are recorded for each attempt, using 24-hour clock time. In order to plan the budget wisely for future surveys, we keep a running account of how whatever). Time is also important for showing whether certain types of respondents are more likely to be unavailable or to refuse at different times of the day. Finally, with rapid dissemination of information by mass media, it's sometimes useful to know if interviews take place before noon or after evening TV and radio news.

Interviewer Number

The three-digit number assigned to the interviewer is entered in the last space on the front page.

Clean-up Squad

All interviews are seldom completed with the initial assignment. Reasons for interviewer failures range from illness to irresponsibility. A small corps of interviewers is kept available as a clean-up squad, to be rushed to sampling areas where difficulties arise.

Checking In and Debriefing

Immediately after completing their assignments, the interviewers are *debriefed* by the Supervisor. Serious problems should be brought to the Project Director's attention. Questionnaires are carefully checked to determine that they are properly completed, that the right people in the right houses were interviewed, that each questionnaire contains the correct identification numbers and case number, the respondent's name, address, and phone number, plus interviewing time and date, and interviewer number. If for some reason supervision has been faulty, any work yet to be completed will be discovered now and the clean-up squad will be sent into action.

Completed questionnaires should be organized for editing, processing, and storage. We resist temptations to keep some out for any reason, as invariably they will get lost. Moreover, we have assured respondents their replies are confidential, which means all questionnaires should be stored away together in a locked cabinet.

After all data processing is complete (including content analyses of open-end questions), all questionnaires should be destroyed.

Verification

To verify the questionnaires means to make sure that the interviewers actually obtained the information shown on the questionnaires from the proper respondents. It must be done before respondents forget too much about the interview. If the survey is a class project, verifying should be done in time to include it as a measure of the quality of each student's contribution to the project as part of his or her final grade.

Four types of verification are described here.

Sample Verification. We check to see that interviews were attempted at the designated sample households and with the correct respondents. All questionnaires can be given a preliminary verification by using a city directory or reverse telephone directory to check names, addresses, and phone numbers. A reverse directory, obtainable from the telephone company, lists subscribers by streets rather than alphabetically. First we see whether the identification data on the questionnaire jibes with that in the directory. Then we check whether the addresses are in the assigned block and seem to fit the pattern that would follow from the first housing unit assigned for interviewing.

Where available, a commercial city directory is useful for verification. It indicates the presence of a phone—or a nearby phone—and, most important, it lists people who do not have phones, as well as those who have unlisted phone numbers. The city directory may also show the occupation of the householder and spouse, making possible a further check of the questionnaire. We do not use the directories as final proof, as there will be discrepancies in addresses. Given the fantastic mobility of the American population, perhaps one-fifth of the respondents will have moved since a year-old directory was published.

The preliminary verification is then amplified to check a random sample of completed questionnaires. If we suspect systematic error or other interviewer failure, all questionnaires from an area or from a particular interviewer must be verified.

The simplest verifying procedure is to telephone respondents to see whether they indeed were interviewed. This should be done with finesse, for respondents have a tendency to protect the interviewer, whom they now know, against the home office. (Remember, we have encouraged interviewer-respondent rapport.) Choose a woman with a businesslike though friendly phone voice to make the calls.

Ask respondents whose addresses on the questionnaires do not match those in the directories, "How long have you lived at that address?" If only a short time, ask, "What was your previous address?"

When phoning is impractical—or for an additional check when also using phone follow-ups—send a return postcard to respondents stating that "our records show you were recently interviewed by a member of our organization" and asking:

- How long did the interview take?
- How did the interviewer contact you—by phone or at home?
- How would you rate this interviewer—good, fair, or poor?

These items reveal whether an interview was conducted at that address at all, whether the contact was in person, whether all questions probably were asked, and the impression made.

Question Verification. Verification should reveal if the interviewer asked all questions. Dishonest interviewers have been known to telephone respondents and secure only demographic items, thinking these will protect them from discovery at the verification stage. In the verification phone call, after identifying the study, we mention that we believe the person was interviewed recently in our public opinion survey. The respondent should confirm the fact. Then say, "In checking over the survey form, we seem to have forgotten to write down . . ." Then either ask all questions actually left out of that questionnaire or just a portion (some innocuous questions), so that the answers can be checked against the interviewer's entries. Use items somewhere past the questionnaire's middle to make sure the interviewer got that far.

If a falsified questionnaire is suspected, all of that interviewer's respondents should be called and the interviews verified in depth, until irregularities are discovered and corrected. We keep the results of this verification for rating interviewers as well as for deciding whether these questionnaires can be counted in the survey data.

Question Reliability. Chapter 1 defined *reliability* as the consistency of responses from one time to another. To check reliability requires that a sample of each interviewer's respondents be reinterviewed, using a sample of the questions asked previously. This mini-study is done under conditions as much as possible like those of the original field conditions—although different interviewers and reduced questionnaires are used. Comparisons between answers received in the original and the follow-up interviews will give some indication of the stability—hence, trustworthiness—of the data. The issues involved in checking the reliability of survey data are complex and many. They are treated more fully elsewhere (see Chapter 6).

Question Validity. Chapter 1 defines a question as valid if it actually measures what it is intended to measure. For example, a question that asks people if they voted is invalid if a follow-up check at City Hall of their voting records reveals that most of them are lying. The question itself may be valid ("Did you vote?"), but it may fail to measure the desired behavior because other complications of the interviewer's behavior, questionnaire sequence, and respondent's perceptions of the interviewer can also affect question response.

Usually the validity of survey data is compared against other methods of getting the same data. For example, the following all check another source: check the respondent's refrigerator against respondent claims of drinking Sunbright Orange Juice; check registration files against claims of automobile ownership; check hospital records for claims of treatment; ask employers about employee claims of working; observe legislative behavior for claims of political leadership; and so on.

INTERVIEWING FOR OTHER SURVEYS

Panel Studies

Interviewing procedures for panel surveys are no different from those of one-time studies. The job is, however, more difficult, because interviewers must relocate specific individuals by name and are required to make extra effort to do so.

As noted in Chapter 2, loss of respondents from one interview to the next is a major problem in panel studies. Certain types of people are more likely than others to drop out of the sample. Serious attrition of the sample may cause it to become unrepresentative of the original population. We make extra efforts in panel interviewing to get an acceptable number of respondents each time.

Suggestions for panel-study fieldwork are itemized in the following:

- Allow more callbacks to get as many respondents of the original sample as possible.
- For the second (and successive) wave(s), plan for higher time and cost rates per completed interview. Neither substituting respondents nor inflating the sample by 25 percent to cover nonresponse applies to panel reinterviewing.
- With specific names and previous contact already established, consider using the telephone to set up appointments. Consider, as well, interviewing respondents at their place of work.
- If any appreciable time has elapsed between interviews, plan on approximately a 10-percent address change factor. Extra time and effort must be expended to track down people who move within the study area. Decisions will have to be made about trying to trace (even through telephone interviews) people who move outside the study area.
- Although it is easier to locate respondents when known by name and address, invariably much field time still is lost to inefficient travel and because appointments are more likely to be needed. This should be remembered during planning.
- Don't return the same interviewers to their previous respondents (unless necessary for reasons of matching characteristics, such as non-English-speaking respondents). Rotating interviewers reduces the chances of individual biases affecting the interview.
- Anticipate respondents' fears. If a respondent's first interview was an unpleasant, perhaps fatiguing, experience or led the respondent to express unpopular or emotional views, he or she will be reluctant to repeat such an experience. In other cases, respondents may fear that they will forever be pestered by this survey. Assuaging these fears requires confidence and tact. Interviewers require supreme belief in the value of their work to do this well.
- Expect a higher rate of refusals than on the first (or any previous) wave.

Expect as well that interviewer morale may be a greater problem if field work becomes less rewarding and rejections more painful.

• Train interviewers to expect more frequent, persistent, third-party interruptions. In interim conversations, both respondents and family members have had some kind of reaction to the first interview, which colors their reactions to the second.

• Unless a considerable time has elapsed between interviews, respondents will mentally connect their interview experiences. Rewrite the introduction to tell respondents that we are ''just checking again to see how things stand today,'' or ''to learn what has happened since we talked to you before.'' Trying to pretend there is no connection between the two interviews will create embarrassment and refusals for the interviewer.

Intercept Surveys

Success of the election-day intercept survey depends on interviewers' competence in maintaining the proper sampling rate (see Chapter 2), in following the correct calling-in procedure (see Chapter 6), and on interviewing skill. Interviewing is especially difficult under harried circumstances, and interviewers, more than in other survey situations, hold the key to success for a study that must be done in one day. Since we use anonymous ''voting ballots'' for questionnaires in election-day polls, the interviewer's job does not ordinarily require reading questions but involves selecting and motivating respondents. The interviewer has only seconds to get the respondent's interest and cooperation, and the respondent has only seconds to react. The interviewer must be convincing, the respondent must be convinced, and there is no way to check the ballots or to verify responses. There is no tomorrow on this job.

As opposed to the commercial mall-intercept survey, in which interviewers often work alone and use judgmental sampling methods, the election-day survey requires team efforts and probability sampling. In addition to maintaining proper sampling rates, probability sampling requires interviewers on-the-spot to resolve (and code) problems of refusals, nonresponse, and sampling errors. Smooth teamwork is required to achieve the sample. Teams of three interviewers are ideal, with one person designated as team leader.

Team Leader. The team leader is responsible in advance of election day for locating the polling place, evaluating it for interviewing problems, securing the cooperation of officials, and, on election day, for backing up the other interviewers and for calling in the poll results to Election Central. Some suggestions for the team leader's job are itemized in the following:

• About a week before the election, locate the polling place—checking address and facilities, and correcting any discrepancies in information. Polling places frequently shift between elections.

- Locate the nearest telephone. It should be no farther than five minutes away by car. If no phone is available, arrange to use the telephone at a private residence or business. Payment is a field expense. Report the phone number to the central office. Guarantee that you have exclusive use of the phone at the times required.
- Locate other facilities—parking, eating, rest rooms. Work out full-day team schedules of time on and off the job.
- Make a drawing and record pertinent information about the polling place. Taking into account exits, expected number of voters, sampling rates, and likely directions of voter movement, make a plan showing where interviewers will stand at each exit and at what times during the day.
- Report and discuss the plan with central office staff. If agreed, make up the final work assignment sheet, including interviewing rates.
- On election day, arrive early and park legally. Set up operations using the car or some other convenient place for storing ballots and materials. Go over the work assignment with the other interviewers. Be sure they understand their jobs and have all field equipment and supplies—ballots, counters, badges, pens. Position them at the closest possible points to the exit(s). Walk around the polling station. Be sure all exits are known and planned for coverage.
- Introduce yourself to election officials, as well as the police if necessary. Even with identification and letters of authorization, it is often difficult to convince officials that the work is not electioneering but is nonpartisan research. Try to get cooperation without waving impressive documents around.
- Work inside the legal distance boundary for electioneering, if possible. Unless local officials misinterpret the nature of the work and the meaning of the local law, we try to work as close as possible to voter exits. Success depends on being able to count and encounter all voters exiting the polls before they disperse.
- If voting is done in one room in a building (the school gym), try to work inside the building. There are likely to be too many exits to cover.
- During the day, make the acquaintance of polling officials, so that you know whom to get voting counts from at the end of the day.
- Back up the other interviewers during the day. Work as hard as they do. Plan for their breaks. Morale is important for maintaining sampling rates.

Interviewers. The interviewers are responsible for counting all voters at the exit(s), recording demographic observation codes, introducing and handing out the ballots, maintaining the sampling rates, and recording refusals and other sampling or questionnaire problems.

In a three-person team, each interviewer has a different assignment. It's best to work 50 minutes, take a 10-minute break, and exchange jobs. Rotating assignments relieves boredom, gives a sense of equal participation, and reduces the influence of an individual interviewer on the results.

Voting patterns vary during the day. During the hectic periods all three interviewers will work. During the normal periods, two interviewers work together at the exit assigned to be covered during that hour (remember, different exits may be covered during different hours (see Chapter 2). The *first interviewer* (the "intercepter") counts the voters as they exit in order to determine which voters to interview according to a specific sampling rate—say, every fourth voter. Responsible for determining eligible respondents, introducing the study, and handing out the ballots, the *first interviewer* is fully occupied and should not get involved in lengthy explanations.

The *second interviewer* (the "retriever") is responsible for retrieving all ballots. She steps in to answer questions and explain the study, thereby freeing the first for the cumulative count of all voters and for intercepting respondents. She also assists the first interviewer when voters start exiting in large numbers. In this case, both are responsible for sampling rates, observation codes, and giving and retrieving ballots.

The *third interviewer* counts the ballots from the previous hour of interviewing, records results on the tally form, which are called in later to Election Central, and rests during the hour. If required, she assists the other two interviewers during busy periods.

Below are some interviewing guidelines for election day surveys:

- Determine the correct voter according to the assigned interviewing rate and counting procedure (Chapter 2).
- Record silently the appropriate observation codes for the person's gender, race, age, or whichever demographic characteristics are being observed.
- Position yourself in front of the voter. Present him with a ballot and pen.
- Introduce the study saying: "This is an Election News Poll (HAND BALLOT TO RESPONDENT). Would you mark this secret ballot the same way as you voted inside and put it into our ballot box."
- If necessary, the second interviewer assures the respondent of the following: that the ballot is secret; that it takes only a second to complete; that it is a professional, nonpartisan poll; that the results will be on the news; that the survey has official sanction and everything is legal.
- Without obtrusively showing interest, observe that the voter marks the ballot.
- When he has marked the front of the ballot, ask him to turn the ballot over to mark the items on the back. This is a critical point of possible failure in the survey. As he gives the ballot to the second interviewer, she must remind him: "Did you mark the back of the ballot too?"
- If the voter refuses the ballot, make a large X across the entire front of the ballot and put it into the ballot box. The number and type of refusals are

important to know. For this reason, the ballot's observation codes may be analyzed for possible patterns of refusal.

- If the voter walks away with the ballot or if a would-be respondent is missed, record the proper observation codes on another ballot, mark a big X across the front like a refusal, and put it in the ballot box.

- If anyone asks about the observation codes, the second interviewer should say: "The numbers just show whether you are a man or woman and your approximate age. They're just used to show who is in our study." But don't mention race or ethnic codes.

- If anyone objects to or doesn't understand the ballot, say one of the following: "It will only take a few seconds to fill out." "It's secret." "We don't ask your name, we're just reporting the voting trends from this area." "Which candidate did you vote for . . .?" (Read from the ballot and fill it in as a personal interview questionnaire.)

- If other people wonder about the interviewing or want to be interviewed, say "I'm interviewing a sample of voters according to a mathematical formula. I don't decide who to choose, I only follow the instructions my office gives me."

- If a nonrespondent insists on being interviewed, let him fill in a ballot and put it into the box. But do not fill out the observation codes; later, the ballot can be identified and discarded. Remember, do not deviate from the assigned sampling rate for any reason. We would rather have a smaller, correct number of voters than a larger number whose inclusion incorrectly alters the sampling rate

Telephone Surveys

The major differences between telephone interviewing and in-person interviewing is that the interviewer's voice is the principal source of interviewing bias. Not seeing the interviewer, respondents are free from the biases of appearance, mannerisms, gestures, and expressions. On the other hand, the interviewer's voice must project an image of a warm, pleasant person who is stimulating to talk to and who is interested in the respondent's views. The telephonic voice carries an enormous burden.

The features of telephone interviewing of interest to us here are: interviewer selection, interviewer training, and interviewer supervision.

Interviewer Selection. In hiring, select interviewers by telephone behavior alone. The interviewer's telephone image is the only personal characteristic respondents can judge. Below is a guideline for hiring telephone interviewers:

- In recruiting interviewers (by referral, advertising, or other method), do not make personal contact.

- Mail prospective interviewers a package of materials—including a page of reading material, a mock questionnaire, and interviewing instructions.
- Require each applicant to call in at an appointed time. The Project Director and trained staff should receive the calls.
- To start the telephone conversation and to put the applicant at ease, conduct a brief interview. This information is not wasted, it is part of the hiring criteria. For example, inquire about demographic and social characteristics such as residence, education, work experience, interest in public affairs, and media exposure.
- Ask the applicant to read the page of written material. As she reads, we use a specially designed questionnaire to judge various aspects of her voice quality (e.g., tone, volume, speed, enunciation, pronunciation, accent) as well as her projected personality (e.g., the degree to which she seems aggressive, friendly, warm, active, etc.).
- Then ask her to conduct an interview with us, using the short questionnaire and instructions sent to her. As she interviews we follow a script, deliberately creating small diversions and problems for her. On the scripted form, we score her ability to follow instructions to solve the problems we create and to perform credibly under stress.
- The scores for these various criteria are combined into a composite profile. Those with favorable profiles are invited in for training.

Interviewer Training. Training interviewers for telephone surveys is no easier than for face-to-face surveys. There is a tendency to believe that if we give an interviewer a WATS line and a list of phone numbers, she is automatically competent. Interviewer training has the same objectives regardless of survey mode. While training in interviewing principles can be conducted face-to-face, practice interviewing must be done by telephone. This is important because some persons who seem engaging in personal conversations become tongue-tied on the phone or stilted in reading from questionnaires. We hope our hiring procedure screened most of these people out.

Part of training should include ''crisis'' problem-solving exercises. In these, we simulate a variety of interviewing situations that require quick imagination to solve. The exercises require cassette tape recorders and patched-in telephone connections. The interviewers are divided into teams of two. Each team is given scripts, a tape recorder, and two attached headsets or telephones. The two take turns dealing with problem situations on the tapes. The sessions go something like this:

- A beginning signal is sounded (a bell or a beep).
- At the signal, the next 20 seconds on the tape are blank. The *second interviewer* presses the ''record'' button. The *first interviewer* reads the script's first questionnaire item—e.g., the survey introduction, a question in the respondent-selection procedure, or a demographic question.

- The question is read within 20 seconds. The second interviewer then presses the "play" button.
- A recorded "respondent" then replies to the interviewer's question. The reply invariably is unexpected, creating a problem for the interviewer to resolve quickly. A signal ends the reply.
- At the signal, the tape is blank again. The second interviewer presses the "record" button again. The first interviewer has another 20 seconds to deal with the respondent's reply, using the methods learned in training.
- The 20-second period is arbitrary. This is usually the time needed to permit interviewers to react to the problem without running over into and erasing the next prerecorded section of the tape.
- The second interviewer rewinds and replays the tape. The two critique the problem and the first interviewer's reactions to it, giving advice and support to each other.
- Then they let the tape play on, following the problem, and (again cued by a signal) the next section of the tape contains an "official solution" to the problem. The interviewers again review their performance looking for errors and improvements in the light of the official solution.
- The remaining segments of the tape develop in the same fashion with additional problem situations.
- Interviewers take turns at the different roles.
- This is both an effective and engrossing training device, and one that interviewers enjoy.
- Of course, tape segments are frequently erased by mistake, but several copies, re-recorded from a master, are always available.

Interviewer Supervision. Telephone interviewing should be done from a central facility. This increases control over interviewers' behavior and enables supervisors to resolve problems on the spot. As compared with interviewers working from their homes or in separate offices, central interviewing produces higher completion rates and lower costs per interview.

- Although controversial, telephone interviewing can be randomly monitored by supervisors. It is, of course, illegal to record a telephone conversation without the party's knowledge. It is not illegal, however, for a third party to listen to (*not* record) a telephone conversation, although it may seem a bit unethical to do so. The improved performance benefits from monitoring interviewers' behavior are so great that we recommend it. But we also favor having interviewers tell respondents shortly *after* the introduction–respondent-selection–warm-up sequence: "Don't be surprised if someone comes on the line. It's just my supervisor checking my work. Now, in your opinion (continue immediately with the next question). . . ."
  If the interviewer doesn't make an issue out of monitoring, the respon-

dent usually won't either. If the respondent objects, the interviewer can alert the supervisor to stay off the line. If an interviewer experiences an unusually high number of objections, the problem is probably with the interviewer, not with the respondents.

- Like in-person interviewing, about 95 percent of all telephone interviews are successfully completed within three calls. However, we have rules for the number of callbacks to make after the first call results in a busy signal or a no answer. We generally permit only three calls—one original and two callbacks—but if any of these calls produce busy signals or appointments, we allow up to five calls total.

- Disposition codes for telephone interviewing are different from the door-to-door survey:
  Code:
    1—completed interview
    2—busy signal
    3—no answer
    4—refused
    5—appointment (show date/time)
    6—nonworking number (out of order, discontinued, nonexistent)
    7—nonresidential number (commercial, office, group quarters)
    8—reached, but respondent unavailable (hospital, out of town beyond interviewing period)
    9—reached, but not interviewed (ineligible household, speech or physical problem, and the like)

- Telephone interviewing is most efficient in the evening hours and on weekends. For a national study the effective hours are from 6 P.M. to 12 midnight, if calling is done from the Eastern time zone. We would start the evening at 6 P.M. calling Eastern zone people in New York City, Pittsburgh, and Miami. Progressively moving west, we begin the Chicago calls at 7 P.M. Eastern time, the Denver calls at 8 P.M. Eastern time, and the San Francisco calls at 9 P.M. Eastern time, (at which hour we cease making Eastern zone calls. We end the interviewing evening at midnight Eastern time, 9 P.M. Pacific time. Only if we had made appointments for a later time would we call in any time zone after 9 P.M. Sample numbers are assigned by time zones to maintain this control.

- In our public affairs studies, we want both men and women interviewing at night. Only a few interviewers are needed for daytime interviewing, to keep appointments made from the previous evening. In studies that aim mostly at women who are at home during the day, interviewers obviously do their interviewing in the daytime.

- Depending on the area and time of calling, anywhere from one-fourth to

one-half of the first-attempted calls may not be successful due to no answers, busy signals, and other problems.

- When the first call produces a busy signal, the rule is to wait a half hour
  before calling again. If the second call also is a busy signal, wait a full hour
  before calling again. Repeated busy signals require a call to the local
  operator to check whether the number is no longer working.
- If the first call produces no answer, wait 2 to 3 hours before calling
  again—assuming it will still be a reasonable hour to call. If evening-time
  calls produce no answer, call during the following day.
- Dates and times of all calls, regardless of their disposition, are recorded and
  used for ongoing analysis of calling efficiency.
- It is a major management challenge to collect questionnaires marked for
  callback or appointment, maintain them in an orderly suspense file, and
  redistribute them to available interviewers at the proper times.

Mail Surveys

Previous chapters have covered most aspects of mail surveys that are important in
terms of interviewing problems. As explained, the covering letter, question wording
and page format have to do it all. There is no opportunity for interviewer skills, nor
for interviewer biases to intervene.

Sometimes mail surveys are preceded by personal or telephone interview contacts, and sometimes they are followed up in person or by phone to increase the
number of respondents or to verify responses. Television rating services and marketing studies often initiate mail surveys with personal or phone contact. The phone
contact is useful for alerting people to the coming mailing, getting their interest, and
offering incentives for their cooperation.

The self-administered questionnaire does not have to be done by mail. Instead,
the researcher can make a personal contact and then leave the questionnaire with the
respondent to be mailed back to the researcher. Such contacts are needed in studies
in which the interviewer has to explain to the respondent how to fill out the
questionnaire—such as a weekly television-viewing diary. Upon completion of the
survey period, the respondents return the form, usually in exchange for some small
reward.

Personal contacts are also important for getting permission for later surveys of
classrooms or other institutional populations. This is a type of survey that is popular
among graduate students doing theses, since large numbers of respondents can be
inexpensively obtained in groups. The self-administered questionnaire is explained,
completed by the group at that time—or over some longer period—and handed or
mailed back to the researcher.

Here the interviewing consideration is the researcher's skill in explaining carefully and simply the respondents' task, as well as ability to kindle respondent motivation to participate sincerely.

FURTHER READING

Bradburn, Norman M., and Seymour Sudman, *Improving Interviewer Method and Questionnaire Design: Response Effect to Threatening Questions in Survey Research* (San Francisco: Jossey-Bass, 1979). Recommendations based upon a careful study of interviewer effects.

Cannell, Charles F., Sally A. Lawson, and Doris L. Hausser, *A Technique for Evaluating Interviewer Performance: A Manual for Coding and Analyzing Interviewer Behavior from Tape Recordings of Household Interviews* (Ann Arbor: Institute for Social Research, University of Michigan, 1975). Useful for training and evaluation.

Converse, Jean, *Conversations at Random* (New York: Wiley, 1974). The human aspects of good interviewing.

Dexter, Lewis Anthony, *Elite and Specialized Interviewing* (Evanston: Northwestern University Press, 1970). Aspects of interviewing selected groups.

Hursh-César, Gerald, and Prodipto Roy, *Third World Surveys: Survey Research in Developing Nations* (New Delhi: Macmillan of India, 1975). Many examples of problems of interviewing in unfamiliar cultures.

Kahn, Robert L., and Charles F. Cannell, *The Dynamics of Interviewing* (New York: Wiley, 1967). Proper handling of a communications process.

Survey Research Center, *Interviewer's Manual*, revised edition (Ann Arbor: Institute for Social Research, University of Michigan, 1976). Step-by-step techniques, including telephone surveys.

CHAPTER 6

Processing Data

This chapter has three main sections. First, it tells how to prepare survey data for analysis. Second, it describes how to analyze that data for meaning. And finally, it suggests how to present the results of that analysis to users.

PLANNING FOR DATA PROCESSING

Survey results in tabular form, especially when printed out by computer, have an impressive appearance, but orderly appearance can be deceptive. Many types of human error can occur in data processing—errors in coding, sorting, punching, tabulating, scoring, analyzing. We must be as careful in these final stages as we are in all earlier stages to safeguard the survey from pitfalls.

Processing data requires accuracy, purposeful organization, appropriate techniques of analysis and evaluation, and creative thinking. Checklist 31 outlines the steps in data processing.

CHECKLIST 31

Steps in Data Processing

1. *Resource Planning*—Data-processing requirements are specified in the earliest phases of survey design, including time, cost, staff, materials, facilities, and services.

2. *Analysis Outline*—Based on the study hypotheses, a formal outline is drawn up including dummy tables for the display of independent and dependent variables, the kinds of statistics to be used, and the intended uses of the findings.

3. *Precoding*—In advance of field work, data fields (card columns) are assigned on the questionnaire to all questions, and response codes (punch positions) are designated for expected responses.

4. *Pretesting*—A dry run of procedures of data processing and analysis are as important as testing question wording and interviewing.

5. *Editing*—As questionnaires come in from the field, they are logged in and checked briefly for completeness of key identification of respondents (name, address, demographic data) and other missing data that may still be retrieved from the field.

6. *Coding*—Answers to open-end questions are classified into numbered categories based on an analysis of the most frequent and meaningful responses. Responses to closed-end questions are checked for missing, incorrect, implausible, or inconsistent codes. All codes are transferred to a separate coding form.

7. *Keypunching*—Code numbers are transformed into computer-readable form, usually by punching all codes from each questionnaire onto one or more data cards.

8. *Machine Verification*—Data cards are rechecked to make sure they faithfully reflect the questionnaire.

9. *Visual Verification*—The codes in all cards are printed (listed) for a quick visual check that all cards are present, complete, and in the proper order.

10. *Electronic Verification*—Data is checked by computer for all types of possible errors of omitted or inconsistent coding.

11. *Programming*—Instructions are written to have the computer manipulate and display the data.

12. *Recoding*—Certain data may be combined or regrouped to create new variables.

13. *Weighting*—Imbalances among demographic groups in the sample can be mathematically corrected.

14. *Compiling*—Data is transferred to electronic form by the computer for storage on tape or disk, and it is summarized into tables showing totals and percentages of responses, by single questions and by combinations of questions.

15. *Analysis*—Tables are examined for answers to questions posed by the study, and the data is submitted to statistical tests of risk in drawing conclusions.

16. *Reporting*—Results and conclusions are written out for those who intend to use them.

17. *Publication*—Where possible, conclusions are reported to professional and public audiences, and data is placed in an archive for wider use.

The first five steps, planning through editing, were described in earlier chapters. They are mentioned here to indicate that data processing is not merely tacked onto the end of a survey. Instead we plan all data processing requirements from the beginning as an integral part of the survey. It is vital that planning ensure enough resources, primarily money and time, for detailed computer analysis. After spending so much effort to procure the data, we want to exploit it fully. We aim to extract from the data every conclusion and insight that can be brought to bear on the study problem.

DATA PREPARATION

Survey data just in from the field is not ready for machine processing. The data must be checked in various ways and transformed into machine-usable form before it can be turned out as tables.

Coding

All responses must be converted to numbers for tabulating. This is called *coding*.

During questionnaire design, each question is assigned a data field—one or more columns in a machine data card—which becomes the record of each respondent's answers. Further, each anticipated answer is assigned a code number—a punch position in the column (see Chapter 4). In recording answers, interviewers circle the precode that matches the response given. But there are many possible errors in this simple process.

Closed-end Questions. Precoding never delivers completely usable data. Even for simple fixed-response questions, both interviewer and respondents can make a variety of errors. Questions may be missed altogether, and answers may be falsified. But even if the question is asked and a response given, codes may be incomplete, incorrect, implausible, inconsistent, or illegal. Examples follow:

- *Incorrect code*—The respondent says *no* (Code 2), but the interviewer circles Code 1 (for *yes*). Obviously this type of error is unlikely to be detected later unless a follow-up question reveals an inconsistency. Likewise, circling two or more codes for a question where only one is permitted is incorrect coding. Since only one punch is allowed, a decision rule should be in the coding manual: the interviewer should be consulted or the "don't know/no response" code assigned.
- *Incomplete code*—The interviewer fails to record all codes. For any question without a code, the respondent's answers are lost to analysis. If multiple responses are permitted but not all recorded, we lose detail without being aware of it.
- *Illegal code*— A code that is outside the accepted range of codes for a set of responses is illegal. If we find a question coded 5 for a set of responses for which 1 to 3 are the only accepted codes, we have an error. If such errors

are not discovered in error-checking (Steps 8–10 in Checklist 31), they will confound the tables when printed. If inspection of the questionnaire cannot clear up the problem, we recode as though there was no response.

- *Implausible code*—The respondent is coded for having been "unemployed" but also for having an income of "$35,000." His or her income may come from royalties or stocks, but we think it is implausible and suspect that one code or the other is incorrect. If the questionnaire contains this implausibility, we may want to go back to the respondent for verification.

- *Inconsistent code*—Less obviously wrong than implausible codes, the inconsistent code is one that does not fit some pattern. For example, we would expect the person with a high score on exposure to the mass media also to have high scores of knowledge of public affairs. Or, respondents may say they favor gun control, yet later say they think anyone should be able to purchase a gun. We re-examine the data records but do not automatically assume inconsistent codes are interviewer error. The respondent either may have been inattentive, may have a hidden logic resulting in two answers both seeming to express his or her views, or simply may be inconsistent. Discovering human inconsistency is one of the reasons we do research.

We cannot make over respondents according to our own logic. Coders should question all suspicious codes and try to correct them from the questionnaire if possible. Any change should be marked on the questionnaire in blue ink (to contrast with the red marks of the interviewer), should not obliterate the original marked entry (in case we change our mind), and should be initialed by the coder.

Open-end Questions. By definition, open-end questions are coded after the answers are in. To do this, we review a large sample (say, 10 to 25 percent) of all questionnaires, taking each open-end question one at a time. We read all responses to one question in the sample of questionnaires, writing down key phrases and looking for patterns of similar responses. Once we have established the pattern the responses are taking, we form categories to reflect the most frequent and relevant answers, assigning a code (punch position number) to each.

The object is to devise mutually exclusive and exhaustive categories that capture all significant data yet distinguish between truly different thoughts.

There is no fixed number of categories to establish for coding. But six or seven categories usually capture the meaningful responses to most questions. An "other" category is a catchall for the scattered, one-of-a-kind responses. If we have too many categories the first time around, or too many respondents in "other" (more than 10 percent), we go back to see if the answers are truly distinct and, if not, recategorize.

Having too few categories may hide important differences in people's feelings, yet having too many categories means too few people will appear in each group to do meaningful analysis against other questions in the survey. Also, it is intellectually difficult to hold more than a half-dozen concepts in mind during analysis.

Coincidentally, if the major open-end responses can be coded in less than eight punch positions, leaving two positions to accommodate missing data, the question will fit in one card column. The Model Survey makes the final decision on how many categories to allow for open-end questions at the coding stage, but provision should have been made for questions possibly requiring more than one card column at the questionnaire design stage.

For more complicated issues, it is difficult to code all meaningful responses into fewer than eight categories. In such instances the Model does "telescopic" coding, that is, using two (or more) columns to code each separate response to the question.

For example, suppose we ask: "What are the most important problems facing Model City today?" The answers will range across all sorts of issues—crime, health, economics, education, transportation, government ethics, welfare, sanitation, the environment, public safety, consumer protection, taxes, and more. Here we give 2-digit codes to each response, meaning that each response is coded into two columns in the data card. The first digit of the code indicates major categories, the second digit indicates specific issues within each major category. For example, suppose "economics" is the third major category and has six individual subcategories. The first digit (3) tells us the major category is economics; the second digit (1 to 6) tells the specific economic issue.

> Code 30—*Economic Issues*
> 31 — inflation; high retail prices
> 32 — recession; tight money
> 33 — high taxes
> 34 — jobs; increasing unemployment
> 35 — housing; high prices, interest rates
> 36 — credit; high interest rates
> 37 — . . . .
> 38 — . . . .
> 39 — . . . .
> Code 40—*Energy Issues*
> 41 — gasoline shortage
> 42 — nuclear dangers
> 43 — . . . .
> etc.

If people give two or more answers to the same open-end question (see the example in Chapter 3), we use the same codes, but in additional fields of two columns each. This is because we do not punch two codes in the same column.

During analysis, we can collapse these codes like a telescope to analyze the number of respondents mentioning each of the major categories by using only the first digit, or we can expand the telescope to look closely at the number mentioning any of the many subcategories by using both digits.

Coding open-end questions requires time, this being the major cause of delay between completion of interviewing and availability of results. The pretest results are valuable for devising a preliminary coding scheme for the main study, providing the question is asked the same way both times. Also, the coders can begin to work with the first questionnaires returned from the main study. We do not, however, rely only on the pretest or early returns for the final categories. Rather, we wait until all questionnaires are completed and then take a random sample of the total. This is necessary because, if a survey is in the field any length of time, intervening events can cause responses of the later days to be different from those of the earlier days.

We cannot stress too much the rigor needed in coding of open-ended questions, as the validity of all subsequent analyses rests on how soundly we have represented what respondents really had in mind.

Although much coding is clerical, it is not easy. Coding is tedious and fatiguing, requiring high tolerance for repetitive tasks and an aptitude for order. Some people are easily bored by it; others are inattentive to detail.

Before employing coders, we check their handwriting of figures. Some people have a tendency to write 1s like 7s, 2s like 3s, 4s like 9s. Still others have a natural tendency to transpose figures. We can't use such people as coders.

Coding open-end responses is also a challenging intellectual task demanding a feel for language subtleties, subject matter nuances, and local community characteristics. Model Survey coders work in a group in the same room. Discussion among coders increases insight into different response meanings and also promotes coding uniformity. The Project Director, of course, makes final decisions on how responses are to be classified. If an answer is reassigned to a different category, the coders must go back and change the already-coded questionnaires. Such changes are recorded and dated in all copies of the coding manual for future reference.

Before settling on the final scheme, however, we test the coders' ability to code the same responses in the same way on different days. We also check how well coders' classifications agree with each other by having each independently recode a sample of another's questionnaires to determine the consistency of coding agreements. If they do not reach substantial consistency we revise the categories until coding is reliable enough to proceed.

Transcribing Codes. Once codes have been assigned to all questions, they are usually copied to another sheet for keypunching. Several options for transcribing codes exist. Because most responses are precoded and the column numbers are in the margin of the questionnaire, keypunching can be done directly from the body of the questionnaire pages. Unless the questionnaire is very brief and simple, this is not a very good plan, because it requires keypunchers to glance around to locate codes, risking omissions and reducing speed. Professional keypunchers will punch from questionnaire pages only at a higher (hourly instead of piecework) charge. A somewhat better way of coding is to copy the codes next to the column number in the margin (see Figure 6.1). This saves keypunchers' time and reduces error, because their eyes can follow easily down one side of the page.

Even this, however, will not be acceptable to most data-processing centers. For them, separate coding sheets are required.

A tablet of computer programming forms with 80 numbered columns across is often used for keypunching. This is not always wise because the columns and lines are close together. Handwritten figures must be unusually small and neat. Skipping every other line helps the reading somewhat. If all responses for one respondent can be contained on a single card, this is an acceptable form for data to go to the keypunch.

When more than one card per respondent is needed, a specially designed coding sheet, one per respondent, with spaces for the codes numbered by column, improves keypunch performance (see Figure 6.2, page 316).

Having the coders rewrite the codes vastly reduces keypunch time and error but increases the potential for coder mistakes. Tests of transcription accuracy are necessary to prevent and catch errors.

A coding realiability check should be run on the completed work. This involves comparing the consistency of coding of different coders for the same questions as well as checking the consistency of each coder's own work. Depending on the number, we may check anywhere from 10 to 50 percent of each coder's work.

Q.24. In an election in Model City . . do you think a
        candidate for mayor is likely to be helped . .
        or hurt by his religion . . when it comes to
        getting votes? For example, what if he happens
        to be Protestant?   C37: _1_

                (1)--helped

                2--no difference

                3--hurt

                4--DK/NR

Q.25. What if he happens to be Catholic . . would
        he be helped . . or hurt?

                1--helped

                (2)--no difference   C38: _2_

                3--hurt

                4--DK/NR

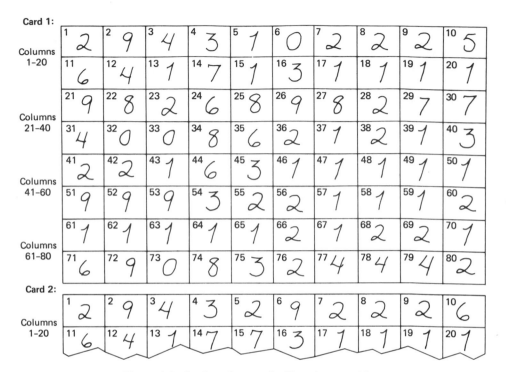

Card 1:

Columns 1-20

Columns 21-40

Columns 41-60

Columns 61-80

Card 2:

Columns 1-20

Figure 6.2. Coding sheet to facilitate keypunching.

Although zero errors is the goal, it is unlikely. For closed-end questions we can't accept less than 95 percent agreement. For open-end questions, 80 percent agreement between coders is considered very acceptable; 90 percent agreement is unusual. We include the intercoder reliability in the final report of the study.

Breaks and snacks combat coder fatigue, but if coding is interrupted by a long interval, we must go back over a few completed questionnaires to refresh everyone on how to classify certain troublesome responses. This promotes equivalence with previous coding.

Coders are reminded of the confidentiality of responses and respondent identification. They are the last staff members to see identifying information; other project workers deal only with numbers.

To fulfill our obligation of confidentiality, questionnaires are stored under lock and key. They are saved until the study is over for correcting errors that become apparent during analysis. We also read through them for verbatim comments that illustrate answers and lend color to the report. Although the questionnaires themselves are finally destroyed, we may need to preserve a master list of respondents' identification and case numbers if there is any possibility of a follow-up study.

Coding Manual

The meaning of every code and coding decision is recorded in a coding manual. This is the permanent guide to what we did. Without this Rosetta stone, the little holes in the cards will be more mysterious than hieroglyphics.

It is useful to mark up a blank questionnare with the newly established codes for open-end questions and additions or changes in precoded items. The final version of the coding manual, often itself punched on cards for computer transcription, should include all code definitions and the total count for each response from tabulation of the survey to accompany the data. Don't risk misinterpretation; the authors did this with an inherited poll, almost reporting 25 percent of a large city's respondents as farmers. Before we published this remarkable demographic item, a long-distance call to the fieldwork company extracted the admission that their coders had changed the punch position previously labeled "farmer" to mean "retired person" without bothering to update the codebook they sent with the data.

An example portion of a page from a coding manual is shown in Figure 6.3. Questions are listed column by column. All instructions are shown, for example,

Figure 6.3. Page from the Model Coding Manual [a]

Master Code Sheet—Spring 1981, Survey Number 07, page 3

C35—Respondent knows what sample ballot is (Precoded yes/no)
  —add "9" for interviewer omission
C36—Sample ballot was delivered to home (precoded for yes/no/DK)
  —add "0" for legitimate skip (C35 answered "no")
  —add "9" for interviewer omission
C37—First party's sample ballot (precoded parties)
  —add "7" for Socialist Workers party
  —add "0" for legitimate skip (C36 answered "no" or coded "0")
  —add "9" for interviewer omission
C38—Second party's sample ballot delivered (precoded parties)
  —if any party coded here, and none in C37, edit to move it to C37
  —add "7" for Socialist Workers party
  —add "0" for legitimate skip (C37 coded "0," or only 1 party mentioned)
  —add "9" for interviewer omission
C39—Respondent read sample ballot (precoded family members)
  —add "6" for lodger
  —add "8" for don't know/not sure
  —add "0" for legitimate skip (C36 coded "0")
  —add "9" for interviewer omission

---

[a]To save space, this is only illustrative. In an actual code book, we would print all question wording and all codes, even those precoded, in order to have a full record of the meaning and frequencies for all codes.

when more than one column is used for a single question, or when questions have more than one answer.

To avoid confusion in keypunching that could arise from skipping blank columns, and because many computers read a blank as zero, we use special codes to give meaning to all blank spaces on the questionnaire. We do not use a blank as a code for some response. We instead assign a 9 for interviewer omission (information that should have been obtained but isn't there) and a 0 for a legitimate skip (a question that should not have been asked if the interviewer followed directions correctly). In Figure 6.3, Column 37, 0 would be coded in the case of a respondent who did not receive a sample voting ballot from any political party; it makes no sense to ask which party's sample ballot was received, since none was delivered. Checklist 32 summarizes hints for code schemes.

CHECKLIST 32

Coding

1. Use only one code per field (one punch per column).
2. Assign only numeric (0–9) codes to responses.
3. Don't use the *11* or *12* punch positions.
4. Have some code for every column. Don't use blanks for missing data (nonentries).
5. Use *0* to mean zero or to show "not applicable." Use *8* as the highest or the "other" category in a one column field. Use *9* code for missing data, or "don't-know/no response," except where DK/NR is to be considered a midpoint as in: (1) agree (2) DK/NR (3) disagree.
6. Code real number data, such as age and income, in full.
7. Try to code simple open-end responses in fewer than eight categories.
8. If more than eight categories are needed, use 2-digit (telescopic) coding, with the first digit indicating the major categories and the combined first and second digit specifying the subcategory.
9. Code consistently in the direction of the hypothesized relationship. That is, all the "positive" responses with higher values and the "negative" responses with lower values (see Chapter 4).

These rules may seem arbitrary, but they exist to avoid difficulty at a later phase.

Some computers cannot, without special programming, handle multiple punches (more than one code per field or column), so we avoid using them. Also, most tabulation routines and statistical procedures accept only numeric data from 0 to 9, so we don't use the top two punch positions, 11 and 12, on the data card.

We usually enter raw quantitative data (e.g., age and income) because the computer can later be told to group raw data, but it can't restore greater detail to a variable that it receives already grouped.

Conventions differ on coding in the direction of the hypotheses. We feel this helps the researcher focus on the problem and get results rapidly in usable form, but some researchers prefer a standard code across all questions in all studies to avoid confusion where data is shared.[1] This requires every data user to recode the variables to test their specific hypotheses.

DATA COMPILATION

Once the translation of questionnaire data to numbers is complete, we assemble it into a format that makes possible analysis of all responses. The process is called compiling. Data compilation may be done by manual or by machine methods. The basic compilation operations involve counting, sorting, and comparing.

- *Counting* (tabulating) is important because we are interested in how many times each response is given in the survey—for example, the number of people who favor the proposal for drug education.
- *Sorting* is important because the survey sample is made up of various subgroups of the overall population—for example, men and women.
- *Comparing* is important because we are interested in knowing whether one subgroup is more likely than another to choose a particular response—for example, that women are more likely than men to say they favor drug education.

Methods of Compilation

Data compilation may be carried on by any of four basic means: (1) hand, (2) edge-punched cards, (3) machine sorting of punched data cards, or (4) electronic manipulation.

Because of its size and types of analyses to be done, the Model Survey is tabulated by computer. But a computer is not necessary for simple tabulation of small surveys. For these, programming a computer and punching the data may well take much longer and entail needless expense. A brief sketch of some alternate techniques follows.

Hand Compilation. Looking at one question at a time, we can sort, count, and compare manually. First, the questionnaires are sorted into two piles—men and

---

[1]For example, the Michigan Survey Research Center always codes a "yes," "good," or most positive response as 1; a "no," "bad," or least positive response is always coded 5. Doris Muehl, ed., *A Manual for Coders* (Ann Arbor, Survey Research Center, 1961), p. 13.

women. Then, taking each pile separately, we sort the pile of male questionnaires into piles that favor, oppose, or have no opinion on the issue. Then we count the number in each pile and prepare to see which gender has the greater likelihood of supporting the program.

Obviously, the problem with manual compilation is that we can't obtain much more intricate analysis than the present example.

Edge-punched Cards. The edge-punched card is one technological step above counting and sorting by hand. These cards are made of stiff paper, measuring usually 6 inches by 8½ inches. Each card is numbered completely around its four sides, and a hole is prepunched for each number. The center of the card is empty and can be printed with blanks for the responses from the questionnaire. Figure 6.4 shows how each response is associated with a punched hole. Here, positions 10 and 11 indicate "male" and "female" respectively. Positions 13 to 15 stand for political party affiliation, and positions 16 to 18 indicate the respondent's opinion on the issue under study.

To prepare a card for an individual respondent, the position of each response he or she gave is marked on the card and is *notched* (cut away to the edge of the card). The card in Figure 6.4 indicates a female Democrat, age 38, who favors the issue.

To do the sorting and counting for the whole survey takes several steps. First, we put the cards for all respondents together in a deck with the edges flush. Second, we insert a stylus (like a knitting needle) into the number 10 position and through all

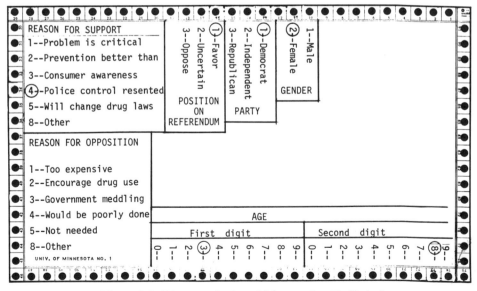

Figure 6.4. Edge-punched card (shown about half-size)

the cards. When we lift the needle, those cards impaled on the stylus are women (no notch in 10). Those that fall out are men (notched in 10). Now, taking the group of male cards, we insert the stylus into position number 13. Those that fall out this time are male Democrats. Now passing the stylus through hole 16 of that stack will drop out those male Democrats who favor the proposition. We count the cards and record the number. Similarly, we sort and count the male Republicans and Independents pro and con. We then sort the first group set aside into the various female partisans who support and oppose. To tabulate other questions, the complete deck is reassembled and other sorting done.

Punched Machine Data Cards. In any survey with large numbers of respondents or questions, hand tabulation is error prone. Edge-punched cards can only be sorted; no transformations of data and no statistical analysis can be done automatically with them. Thus we turn to machines and computers.

The traditional means of putting survey data into computer-readable form is the type of machine data card shown in Figure 6.5. The card is punched to show how figures, letters, arithmetic operators, and special characters are represented. The same kind of cards used for the computer are also used for older mechanical devices such as the counter-sorter (which is still available). One description will serve for both methods of tabulation.

Since cards are used for the Model Survey we key the questionnaire for convenient transfer to cards (see Chapter 4). The cards have 80 vertical columns, one or more of which is used as the field for recording the responses to each question. Each column has 12 punch positions, although we use only positions 0 to 9. The punch positions in a single field (usually one column) correspond to the response codes for one question. The card column will be punched out at the position corresponding to the code for the respondent's answer to that question.

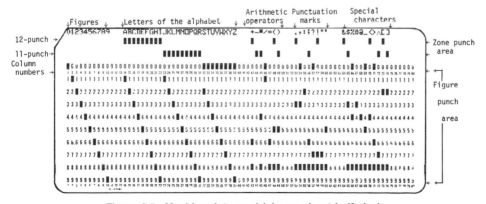

Figure 6.5. Machine data card (shown about half-size)

Keypunching. Punch cards are usually prepared with a keypunch machine. The machine has a typewriterlike keyboard. Blank cards are placed in a hopper at the top of the machine and fed automatically one at a time to the punch station in front of the operator. A pointer or digital readout indicates which column of the blank card is ready to be punched. Depressing the key punches an oblong hole through the card. The column and row location of the hole is later read by the computer (or other machine) and interpreted as the appropriate number (0–9) corresponding to the code. Letters A through Z and special characters are produced by the appropriate key making more than one punch per column. Letters and symbols are necessary for writing program instructions to the computer on separate cards, but they cannot be used as response codes without special handling by the computer.

Perforated Cards. Some cards come with the punch positions perforated. Any code can be punched out by hand with a sharp instrument, preferably on a specially designed backboard that gives support and thus avoids card mutilation. This is the kind of card punched by voters in cities using an electronic voting system. These perforated cards can be adapted for survey use, but we don't recommend them. It is too easy for respondents to punch the wrong hole or damage the card. It would be time-wasting and inaccurate to punch them by hand at the survey office. Other problems: Sometimes the chads (the small perforated oblongs) do not fall out, sticking to the back instead and fouling the machines. Unpunched chads sometimes fall out, showing up as unintended responses.

Optical Scanning. Special equipment can communicate information to the computer without using punched cards. Regular-size computer cards or letter-size pages with printed blocks that respondents can blacken in by pencil can be optically scanned to transmit the response numbers to the computer. The U.S. Census obtains its population information from such sheets mailed to every household. Although this method eliminates manual coding and punching—and the human errors associated with those steps—allowing respondents, or even interviewers, to mark their sheets for direct entry into the computer cannot be relied upon, for inevitable errors will distort results.

Direct Data Entry. Punch cards can be bypassed, if the data from a questionnaire is keyed in by the operator of a teletype or cathode-ray tube (CRT) display device linked to the computer. It is a slow process for a single operator to enter data from many respondents, and this ties up a computer portal while being done. Because many problems have plagued us in using these devices, we think that researchers are well advised to begin their survey analysis careers with punch cards; these constitute a useful physical record of the data as it is sent to the computer and can remain under the control of the researcher.

Data Storage

Ideally, the survey analysis plan anticipates all analysis needed that can be performed over a short time period. This hope is rarely met. Invariably, new data relationships unfold as the analysis proceeds. Later, other scholars might make further inquiries of the study's data. This means we need the capability to store and access data again and again over long periods.

Computers can hold large amounts of data in memory, but it is wasteful to store data in them for more than the few seconds it takes to make needed calculations. For this reason, data is kept on peripheral storage devices such as electronic disks or magnetic tapes that are either automatically available or can be hand-mounted in a few minutes and copied into the computer.

Because electronic records can be mistakenly erased (by the computer programmer or the computer service personnel) or lost by accident, we keep back-up tapes, along with coding manuals and other written records that detail how the data is stored on the tape and how it can be accessed. The original input cards themselves should be saved as further back-up until all current analysis is done. Cards have a further use in that they can be sorted mechanically on a counter-sorter machine for special analyses when the computer is not available.

Cards are not indestructible. They burn or get warped from improper storage. They are heavy to tote around or to mail to a data archive, and they take up much space.

If a survey is sensitive, security should be provided during the data analysis. Built-in passwords and account numbers on the computer are supposed to provide access to authorized users only, but the input–output desk may be a weak link, and electronic snooping is advancing as fast as the technology and procedures to prevent it.

Error Checking

Once the data is on cards we subject it to a number of accuracy checks. The aim is to make sure that all data is present, usable, and plausibly correct. We never trust ourselves or others without both visual and machine checks.

Keypunch Verification. Keypunch verification calls for "repunching" the same data cards, this time by another operator on a special keypunch. If the attempted new punch is not the same as that already in the card, the operator is warned and a nick is cut into the top of the card to flag it for correction. The assumption of repunching for verification is that two operators are unlikely to make the same keying error, although it could happen if the figure codes on the matrix sheet are sloppily written. When an error is discovered, a new card is punched. It is important when correcting a card to check all codes again to be sure new errors are not introduced.

Visual Verification. There are several ways to check cards just by looking at them. For example, we can check to make sure there is only one case number per respondent. A "case" is all the data on a single respondent, and each questionnaire is assigned a case number before the interviewer takes it into the field. In a small survey, there may be only one cardful of data per case, but a longer survey may require several cards per case. That means that for a three-card respondent study, the cards must be arranged as follows:

> Respondent 0001, Card 01
> Respondent 0001, Card 02
> Respondent 0001, Card 03
> Respondent 0002, Card 01
> Respondent 0002, Card 02
> Respondent 0002, Card 03
> Respondent 0003, Card 01
> Etc.

We can order the cards sequentially by using a counter-sorter machine (described below). Regardless of the manner in which the cards were arranged, it's essential that a check of sequence be made. If even a single card in the series is missing, the computer, expecting three cards per respondent, will read on into the first card of the next respondent, and all the rest of the responses will be misread. Likewise, if a stray extra card is mixed into the deck, all subsequent cards will be misread. If two cards from one respondent are transposed, this case will have mislabeled entries. These extra and missing card errors occur frequently in the punching process. We must prove to ourselves that the card order is correct.

A first visual check can be made by listing all cards onto paper with a special accounting machine, or by making a simple computer run that just copies the cards to output paper (an 80 × 80—read "eighty eighty"—listing). We examine the listing to see if there are indeed three cards with an identical case number in the correct order for each respondent. Scanning the listing pattern will also reveal short or long lines of print or irregular columns, indicating too few or too many punches per card. We can also detect alphabetic characters where only numbers are expected. Correction of these obvious errors before moving on will save an expensive computer run or two.

Computer Verification. All of the foregoing error checks can be done in an early, data-cleaning computer run. Any computer program will usually reveal some errors without being requested—illegal alphabetic punches, too few cards, or too many cards in total. The computer is most valuable, however, for checking the data's logical consistency. This involves setting up certain tests and instructing the computer to report if any case fails the test. For example, to check the order of cards for each case number, a test is mounted to determine: whether the first card encountered in a case bears a number other than the *1* it should contain; whether the next card bears a number other than *2* and the third card other than *3*. To check if all three of these cards are from the same case, the case number is read from each card and compared for nonequivalence.

Likewise, tests of illegal codes elsewhere in the study can be set up for the computer. If, for example, the highest code allowed for a question is 5, the computer can be instructed to report any cases in which codes are greater than 5.

Inconsistent or implausible responses can be flagged in the same manner. For example, if a respondent was too young to vote last year, the next question about whom she or he voted for should be coded 0 for "inapplicable."

The basic checks of logical consistency usually involve comparisons of two or more responses. We instruct the computer to flag any violations of certain data rules. The rules can be written very simply: In the presence of one response, another response: (1) must or must not be present; (2) must be lower, must be higher, or must be equal in value; and (3) must be of the same type, or must be of a different type. Other rules may involve sums and sizes, for example: (1) the total must be equal to the sum of its parts, (2) rows and columns of data should add to the same overall total, or (3) figures cannot be higher or lower than certain boundary values.

It is worth noting that these same checks are capable of detecting interviewer cheating under certain circumstances. An interviewer who enters responses for a nonexistent respondent is not likely to take the time to be internally consistent.

The goal of verification is to assure the physical and logical soundness of the data. When all corrections have been made, we print another copy or make another run to see that the corrections were actually entered and that no new mix-ups have been introduced. If it passes this inspection, the data is now considered "clean."

Without this step, tables will have meaningless numbers, or cases will be lost from analysis—when some code is declared missing because it is outside the expected boundary. We want to end up with every bit of data we worked so hard to get.

Tabulation

We are now ready for a preliminary look at the total survey findings. Individual cases have little significance themselves, as we are not looking for unique statements but for generalizations—what we can say about the whole sample and, therefore, hopefully about the whole population. The first step is to tabulate the data.

Counter-sorter. Between hand and computer tabulation in degree of automation is the counter-sorter. In a single pass, it sorts the cards among all punch positions found in one column, and counts the number of cards containing each punch. To tabulate a second question, the column selector is changed, and the cards are reassembled into a deck and run through the machine again. Previously the mainstay of survey tabulation, the counter-sorter these days is used mainly as an adjunct to computer analysis. It can merge decks so that all cards for one respondent are together, and in the right order. And it is useful to perform a few hurry-up sorts when the computer is not available at nights or on holidays, or when additional funds to pay for more runs are lacking.

One educational advantage of the counter-sorter is that we can see before us the same logical process that takes place inside the computer. We can work step-by-step trying further sorting on another column as soon as a new idea is triggered from looking at a previous breakdown. But sorting one column at a time becomes tedious. Also, it is possible to analyze only one card per respondent at a time, requiring that all data that is to be compared be on a single card. Worse, the counter-sorter has no memory and no capacity to do computations or comparisons of relationships. We turn to the computer to do the whole job.

Computer Compilation. The Model Survey uses a computer because it has incredible accuracy, handles hundreds of variables from thousands of cases in seconds, holds all data on each respondent at one time, and can perform the most complex and varied tests of relationships with ease.

But the computer can't work without being told what do to, and this takes time and familiarity with the process.

Instructing the computer is called *programming*. Computers are very loyal—they do exactly what they are told. But they lack intuition. They cannot figure out what we want them to do until we tell them. For a human to control a computer there must be a common language. Great developments in simplifying these languages have been made, so that people with no understanding of the computer's internal operations and no training in its use can readily utilize its great capacity. Nevertheless, it takes time to write an analysis program. The time lag can be shortened considerably by using pretest results for writing and debugging programs well ahead of actual analysis.

The Model Survey uses SPSS (Statistical Package for the Social Sciences) to produce its tables and analyses.[2] SPSS programs are written in simple English (with a few mathematical symbols for the arithmetic), and since they have predigested most data processing and statistical operations, we can trigger complex operations with a few simple statements. The logic of SPSS computer analysis described here is essentially the same for other data handling and statistical packages, so the following discussion applies to whatever system particular users may have available.[3]

[2]Norman H. Nie, *et al.. Statistical Package for the Social Sciences,* 2d ed. (New York: McGraw-Hill, 1975).

[3]For example, OSIRIS, BMDP, OMNITAB. See glossary in Ronald E. Anderson and Francis M. Sim, "Data Management and Statistical Analysis in Social Science Computing, *American Behavioral Scientist, 20* (January/February 1977), pages 406–409.

Checklist 33 lists the seven basic things we tell the computer for any program These will be explained here briefly (but see Figure 6.6 for an illustration of how the SPSS cards instruct the computer). As an example, a simple program has been worked out for some questions from the Model questionnaire.

CHECKLIST 33

What To Tell the Computer

1. *What the items are*—the names of all variables in the questionnaire.
2. *Where the items are*—the location of each of those variables, in order, on the data card for one respondent: the data format.
3. *How many respondents there are*—the number of cases (not cards, since there may be more than one card per respondent) to be analyzed.
4. *What changes are desired in the data*—variables to be recoded, or new variables to be calculated.
5. *What we want to see*—tables to be printed.
6. *When to start*—data cards to be read.
7. *When to stop*—the last task to be performed.

Two sets of cards are needed for computer analysis: (1) the data cards, which have already been described; and (2) the program cards, which tell the computer what to do with the data cards. It is the latter that will be discussed here. Program cards contain information or instructions that tell the computer the following:

What the Items Are. Although survey variables—the individual items of information gathered from each respondent—may easily be assigned a sequential number by SPSS, we prefer to use a short name with a built-in memory jog (a *mnemonic*) to identify each of the variables in the data card. One variable is named AGE, another GENDER, another RACE, another PARTYID (for party identification), another FAVDRUGP (for "favor drug education program"), and so forth. Each variable must have a distinct name, start with a letter, and be no longer than eight letters. (In a major survey, of course, we might have 100 or more variables.)

Where the Items Are. The location of each variable on the card is the same for each respondent. We have merely to tell the computer where to find an item on one respondent's card, and it will look in the same place for that item on all respondents' cards. The data locations are called the *format* of the data card. The individual items and the positions on the format card must bear a one-to-one relationship. That is, the first variable named must be in the first position, the second variable named in the second, and so on. The format specifies how many columns each field contains (e.g., "F1," "F2," or more). All information on a data card does not have to be used in a single run—columns can be skipped ("3X" means skip three columns

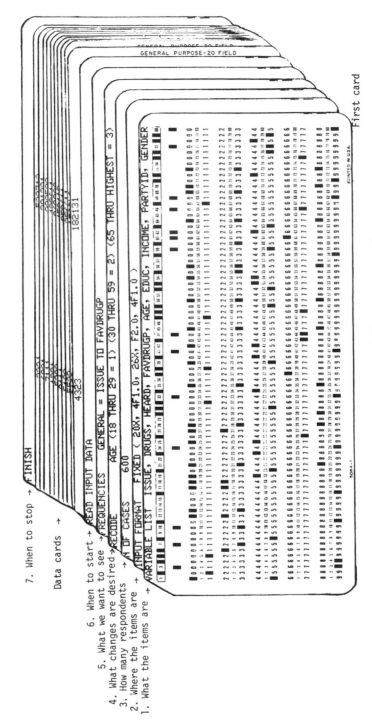

Figure 6.6 SPSS program cards for survey analysis.

7. When to stop → FINISH

Data cards →

6. When to start → READ INPUT DATA

5. What we want to see → FREQUENCIES   GENERAL = ISSUE TO FAVDRUGP

4. What changes are desired → RECODE   AGE (18 THRU 29 = 1) (30 THRU 59 = 2) (65 THRU HIGHEST = 3)

3. How many respondents → N OF CASES   600

2. Where the items are → INPUT FORMAT   FIXED (20X, 4F1.0, 26X, F2.0, 4F1.0)

1. What the items are → VARIABLE LIST   ISSUE, DRUGS, HEARD, FAVDRUGP, AGE, EDUC, INCOME, PARTYID, GENDER

before picking up the next variable). But it is usually wise to read in all the data at once to avoid getting caught without something that later turns out to be important for analysis. Variables can be added later, but the new cards must perfectly match the existing data in number of cases and order; if not, data from one respondent will be mixed up with that from another respondent.

How Many Respondents There Are. The computer has to know how many respondents are in the survey so it knows when to stop one operation and go on to another. Also, different kinds of analyses are performed with different-size groups. (Actually, SPSS has a feature that will count the cases for us, but we don't use it in the Model.)

What Changes Are Desired in the Data.   At the coding stage we tried to save all possible detail. For example, we recorded the exact age of each respondent. Now, however, we are trying to draw generalizations. We don't want responses to each question tabulated by perhaps 70 different age categories, some with only one person of that age. In order to make sense of the data, we need to establish just a few age categories.

For the Model Survey we will establish a new grouping of ages: Younger (18–29) Middle-aged (30–59) and Older (60 +). This process is called *recoding*. Instead of recoding AGE and thus losing the original detailed data, we could manufacture a new variable called NEWAGE to hold the compressed age data.

We might use recoding to create a whole series of new variables made up of other information we obtained in the interviews.

What We Want to See. We have to tell the computer what results to print. In surveys, we first want to know totals—how many people gave each response (the "frequency" of each response). Tabulating the number and percentage of the sample that mentioned each response is called "printing frequencies." Usually we ask for the frequencies of all variables to be printed in tables, one per variable, as the last step in data checking and the first step in analysis.

When to Start. We next tell the computer to read the data cards, and we insert all respondents' data cards so the computer can proceed to tabulate and print the response frequencies we ask for. If there is only one card per respondent, they do not have to be in order. But if there are several cards per respondent, all cards for each respondent must be together, in perfect sequence.

When to Stop. If a print of frequencies is all we want from our data at this time, we indicate that the job is done. Actually we could continue on with one procedure after another. One of the features of SPSS is that it allows us to save an electronic copy of the whole data and program file as it exists at the end of this computer run; later, we can start right at that point for further analysis without the time and expense of creating the file again.

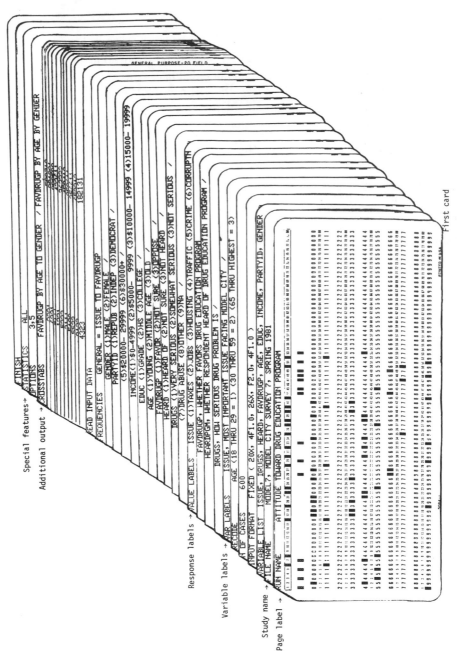

Figure 6.7. SPSS program cards for labeled survey data.

Special features→
Additional output →
Response labels →
Variable labels →
Study name →
Page label →

First card

330

Job Cards. The foregoing seven steps constitute the minimum computer instructions necessary to tabulate survey data. Of course, each computer installation requires that we add certain "job cards" to the front of our deck. These cards identify our output, give us permission to use the computer, tell where to send the bill, and ask the computer to use the SPSS Package (or some other system) to handle our cards.

Labeling. The tables the computer would produce in response to the program cards just described would identify variables only by short names, and responses only by code numbers. A worthy investment of time (that will save time and eliminate confusion later) is to attach more complete labels to the short variable names and identify the meaning of the response codes. These additions to the program deck are shown in Figure 6.7.

Output

The first output desired from survey data is a complete set of frequency tables—a simple count of the number of respondents per answer per question. A frequency table produced by the SPSS program (see version in Figure 6.7) is shown as Figure 6.8.

We usually print frequencies and percentages for all variables in the final code book, which we produce on the computer. It's also handy during analysis to write frequencies and percentages of all responses in a copy of the questionnaire (see Figure 6.9).

Despite the editing and coding checks made during data preparation, some errors will show up at this point. Errors may cause extra rows to be printed in tables

ATTITUDE TOWARD DRUG EDUCATION PROGRAM

FILE   MODEL7   (CREATION DATE =   80/08/20.)   MODEL CITY SURVEY 7, SPRING 1981

FAVDRUGP   WHETHER FAVORS DRUG EDUCATION PROGRAM

CATEGORY LABEL	CODE	ABSOLUTE FREQ	RELATIVE FREQ (PCT)	ADJUSTED FREQ (PCT)	CUM FREQ (PCT)
FAVOR	1.	325	54.2	54.2	54.2
NOT SURE	2.	93	15.5	15.5	69.7
OPPOSE	3.	182	30.3	30.3	100.0
	TOTAL	600	100.0	100.0	

VALID CASES   600   MISSING CASES   0

Figure 6.8. Computer-produced frequency table (SPSS).

Q.24: **As of right now . . do you favor the drug-education**
       program,... or not?

   325 1--Favor   *54.2%*

    93 2--Not sure   *15.5*

   182 3--Oppose   *30.3*

Figure 6.9. Entering frequencies onto questionnaire.

or cases to be lost in cross-tabulations. Each error is traced back to the case it comes from, to the coding sheet to see if it was a punching error, or to the questionnaire if necessary. Frequencies for any incorrect table will have to be rerun to get a clean, correct table.

The cross-tabulation of two variables produced by the SPSS program in Figure 6.8 is shown as Figure 6.10. The first variable mentioned in the command to the computer is the dependent variable. Its responses will be listed down the left side of the table.

The next variable is the independent variable, which will be listed across the top of the table.

A third variable (if any) will be the control variable, with one separate table—the first two variables cross-tabulated—produced for each of its response categories. Because the use of a control variable can result in hundreds of tables, it should be called for judiciously, as needed, and only after examining the frequencies for that variable to suppress printing of tables for less important or too small categories.

A later section tells how to analyze data in frequency and cross-tabular form.

```
* * * * * * * * * * * * * * * *  C R O S S T A B U L A T I O N   O F  * *
    FAVDRUGP  WHETHER FAVORS DRUG EDUCATION PROGRAM       BY  GENDER
* * * * * * * * * * * * * * * * * * * * * * * * * * * * * * * * * * * * *

                         GENDER
                 COUNT  I
                 COL PCT IMALE        FEMALE       ROW
                        I                          TOTAL
                        I      1.I       2.I
FAVDRUGP        --------I---------I---------I
                  1.   I    147  I    178  I    325
     FAVOR            I   51.9  I   56.2  I   54.2
                    -I---------I---------I
                  2.   I     63  I     30  I     93
    NOT SURE          I   22.3  I    9.5  I   15.5
                    -I---------I---------I
                  3.   I     73  I    109  I    182
    OPPOSE            I   25.8  I   34.4  I   30.3
                    -I---------I---------I
                 COLUMN      283       317       600
                 TOTAL      47.2      52.8     100.0
```

Figure 6.10. Cross-tabulation of two variables (SPSS).

Composite Variables

For ease of analysis we sometimes create a single new variable based on respondents' answers to several questions. This summarizes a large amount of information as a measure of one concept.

In effect, we find that several characteristics are related to each other in such a way that an index manufactured from a person's combined answers to all items is a better measure than his/her separate answers to individual items. The new composite variables now can be used in cross-tabulations just like variables already in the study.

In Chapter 4 there is an example of a voting screen that is a composite variable. From the screen, we conclude that respondents are *likely voters* if they are registered, know where to vote, are interested in the election, are planning to vote, and had voted in the previous election.

During data processing we construct a new variable—"LIKEVOTE"—to contain all this information. We do a series of "if" tests: *if* respondents answer *3*, meaning "registered to vote"; and *if* they answer *2*, meaning "knows where to vote"; and *if* they answer *5*, meaning "very interested" in the election; and so on—then score them *2* on the new variable "LIKEVOTE." All other respondents who don't meet the test are scored *1* on "LIKEVOTE." For analysis, other variables will be compared between these two groups to see if there is a difference.

Obviously the validity of a composite variable depends upon the soundness of our reasoning about the meaning and relationships of its components.

Another example of a composite variable would be to score people on a continuum of their media use based on answers to several questions: whether they read a daily paper, a weekly paper, a newsmagazine; whether they listen to news on radio and on television. We might construct a simple *summed index*, counting each of these activities as equal indicators of media use. Anyone who claims to do all is assigned *5* on a new variable "MEDIAUSE," while anyone who does none gets *0*, and others get scored in between. The new variable "MEDIAUSE" can now be cross-tabbed against questions on amount of information on a study topic, likelihood of voting in the referendum, or whatever.

If scores are to be calculated by coders, detailed instructions on the question numbers and eligibility codes must be provided. Usually we program the instructions to have the computer count the separate items into a summary score.

Sum scoring, as in the foregoing example, rests on assumptions that the items are of equal importance and are so closely related that they can be added together. Usually we need prior analysis to meet such assumptions. We may know from other research that TV is "twice" as highly trusted and relied on by people for public affairs information. Thus it may have to be counted twice to give it proper weight in the composite variable.

A more complicated method of creating a new variable is based on the *relative* position of respondents on each of several items combined into one index. For example, a widely used concept in survey analysis is socioeconomic status. To create this index we might add together the relative position of each respondent on, say, an eight-code income question, a seven-code occupation question, and a four-code education question. The sum of these relative standings is each respondent's status. For example, one respondent might be $5/8 + 4/7 + 2/4 = 1.69$ on a scale that ranges from 0.0 to 3.0.[4]

Again, such scaling rests on theory and evidence that both indicate the items can be added together.

Later in this chapter we describe such techniques as *factor analysis* and *multiple regression,* which are statistical methods for helping us to determine whether and with what value items can be combined into summary scores.

Weighting

At several points we have noted that we sometimes give more or less "weight" to different groups in the sample. Suppose we oversample Hispanic-speaking blacks in Model City—that is, draw a larger proportion of them from the total population than would be expected by chance. We do this to be assured of having enough of them to analyze. But in order to draw proper conclusions about the whole sample, this larger-than-normal proportion of Hispanics would have to be weighted down again (decreased by some factor) or the rest of the sample weighted up (increased) to restore the proper proportions of all groups.

Weighting is also done to make the sample more representative of the population on known traits. Suppose we know from Census data that Model City has about 24 percent adults under 30, but only 12 percent of our sample is of this age. We have underrepresented young adults by half. One way of making the sample more representative of age groups is to weight each young adult in the sample by some factor that in effect doubles their number in the sample. Several subgroups of the sample can be weighted in different ways simultaneously.

Weighting is done at the data-processing stage usually by multiplying the answers of the group underrepresented by a factor we figure will bring them into proper balance.[5] Alternatively, a group that is overrepresented in the sample can be

---

[4]Norman H. Nie, *op. cit.,* p. 100.

[5]We can figure the weight for the underrepresented group as follows:

$$W = \frac{P_u\, n_r}{n_u\, (1 - P_u)}$$

W = weight
P_u = correct proportion of the underrepresented group in the population
n_u = number of the underrepresented group in the sample
n_r = number of the rest of the sample, the correspondingly overweighted group

adjusted to its proper proportion by randomly deleting respondents of that group. The method SPSS uses for weighting has the computer duplicate the response cards of the underweighted groups until they are a proportion of the sample equal to their proportion of the total population. Since this raises the sample size, it may change the assumptions of statistical tests of sample results.

One danger of weighting is that we tend to forget how small are the numbers of real people in the underrepresented categories. We have read survey reports in which the analysts, having achieved on paper the proper proportions of each sub-group in the population, make grand generalizations on the basis of, say, six Chinese-Americans actually interviewed. We must keep in mind during analysis the actual number of respondents in the underrepresented categories.

Adjusting a sample by weighting assumes that the respondents of the underrep-resented group who are in the sample are like the ones the interviewers failed to find. If in fact they are different in characteristics related to the study topics—less mobile, higher income, more family oriented, etc.—weighting them up will tend to bias the sample in those directions. This is another danger of weighting.

Number of Tables

Producing tables is easy. The simplest SPSS command is one that produces a cross-tabulation of every variable against every other variable. If we had only 12 variables, a complete cross-tabulation would produce 144 tables, 78 of them worth-less because each variable would be cross-tabbed against itself or against a variable already cross-tabbed. Some of the other tables wouldn't make theoretical sense. And there would be too much output to digest.

It is far better to hypothesize about which cross-tabulations will yield relevant information, run them, study them, and then ask if something else is worth looking at. If the available computer facilities have an interactive keyboard, we can produce tables one at a time as needed.

While we recommend this "tiny steps for tiny feet" procedure, it is not always

---

Substituting from the example above, where the sample of 600 contains 12 percent, or 72 young adults, instead of 24 percent as it should:

$$W = \frac{.24 \ (528)}{72 \ (1 - .24)} \quad \text{or} \quad 2.3$$

Then, the effective sample size becomes:

$$N = n_r + W \ (n_u)$$

Substituting:

$$N = 528 + 2.3 \ (72), \text{ or } 694$$

To check this work, note that 2.3 times 72 is 166, which is 24 percent of 694, the correct proportion for the formerly underrepresented group.

9. DO YOU THINK IT IS A GOOD IDEA FOR THE GOVERNMENT TO BAN ABORTIONS

	STATE TOTAL	AREA IN OUTSTATE CITIES		SEX MEN	WOMEN	AGE 18-24	25-34	35 + OVER	INCOME UNDER $10000	$10000 19999	$20000 + OVER	EDUCATION NOT HS GRAD	HS GRAD	POST HS	UNION YES	FAMILY NO
A GOOD IDEA	47%	41%	53%	40%	53%	36%	42%	52%	47%	47%	44%	56%	53%	37%	47%	47%
A POOR IDEA	38%	46%	32%	43%	34%	54%	48%	30%	40%	36%	45%	26%	31%	52%	39%	38%
NOT SURE/NO ANSWER	15%	14%	15%	17%	13%	10%	9%	18%	14%	17%	11%	18%	16%	12%	14%	15%
TOTAL	100%	100%	100%	100%	100%	100%	100%	100%	100%	100%	100%	100%	100%	100%	100%	100%

Figure 6.11. Multiple table under a banner heading.

practical. If our data is compiled by a commercial company, we are usually required in advance to tell all data runs wanted, so the firm can deliver the whole package, get paid, and turn to the next customer. It is important to specify in the contract how much cross-tabbing is included in the flat price, and how much will be charged for additional runs we may need.

Typically, commercial companies will cross-tab data by "banners"—that is, a string of column headings running across the top of the printout page that they use for presentation of results for every question in the survey. A standard banner will include the results for the total sample and for major demographic groups—categorized by gender, age, education, income, residence, union membership, etc.

In one such system there are 16 columns on a page (see Figure 6.11) consisting of six different demographic variables. This single page is the equivalent of six separate tables for each question. Questions are presented one to a page. A survey with 30 questions would produce 30 pages of six variables each, the equivalent of 180 tables produced one per page by SPSS.

If we have more than six independent variables by which we want the rest of the variables cross-tabulated, or want more detailed response codes for some variables, it will require a second banner, thus doubling the cost. Once an additional banner is ordered, however, it costs no more to use all 16 available columns on a page, so we must carefully plan the desired display.

DATA ANALYSIS

Printing data in neat tables is a mechanical job, although guided by theory. Once the tables are printed, our tasks become intellectual.

Analysis is an *interactive* process by which we examine the answers to the survey's questions, seeing whether those results support the hypotheses underlying each question. Analysis is a challenging task, like the sleuthing of a detective combing over the evidence, evaluating clues in the light of experience, and testing the reliability of the conclusion. The process raises new (sometimes unexpected) questions about possible relationships that may explain the mystery.

We are aided in our search for meaning of survey data by well-developed procedures of thinking and measurement called *statistical analysis*.

Statistical Analysis

The word "statistics" often provokes an anxious response among non-researchers. The descriptions here are not technical, but are written for beginners. Our purpose is simply to introduce some of the basic notions and tools of survey analysis—to get across the logic of what we're doing when we use a sample value (statistic) to estimate a population value (parameter).

Our concern in survey analysis is to see whether and how people are alike or different. We look for *response patterns* for different groups in the sample— Protestants, Catholics, and Jews; Democrats, Republicans, and Independents. In judging the similarities and differences among these groups, we are interested in how frequently they occur, which are most typical, what are the extreme values, which are significantly different, and which are related to each other. Then, we try to relate our findings for the sample to the larger population.

Certain statistics, called "measures of central tendency," describe *typical* responses; another kind, "measures of dispersion," describe *differences*. Together, these measures show the *variation* in responses. To know whether the variations (similarities and differences) are real—not due only to errors of sampling—we have various statistical tools for testing the significance of relationships and differences. Which tools are appropriate depends on the kind of data we have.

In this section we will look at common statistics that summarize sample data. In the next, we will link the sample *by inference* to the population it estimates. Finally, we will describe basic statistical tools used to test the significance of our findings.

Frequency Distribution. Our first task in analysis is to count responses to see how frequently each is given. Let's take as an example the responses to a question about a new Model City tax to support public day-care centers for the infants of working mothers. Tabulating the responses (Figure 6.12), we can tell that most people favor the new day-care tax plan:

TABLE A : SUPPORT FOR DAY-CARE TAX

Response:	Number of People
Favor day-care tax	336
Oppose day-care tax	168
Don't know/No response	96

N = 600 (total sample)

Figure 6.12. Frequency distribution.

This is a frequency distribution, where "distribution" means the array or pattern of responses. The notion of distribution is important because our link from sample statistics to unknown population parameters is through a theoretical distribution of all possible samples, which lets us mathematically approximate the population—as will be seen shortly.

The frequency distribution is our first measure of sample variability—the pattern of similarities and differences in people's responses about themselves, their views, and their behavior. A simple frequency count is only suggestive. It is easier to compare data by changing the numbers to percentages.

Percentage and Proportion. The percent figure is very useful for comparing people. All *percentages* are calculated on the same base of 100. So even though we turn up six times as many brunettes as redheads in the sample, we can still make valid comparisons: "About one-half (54%) of the brunettes compared with only one-third (33%) of the redheads favored the new day-care tax."

When we express percentages as a part of 1.00, they become *proportions:* .54 and .33 in the present example. Converting percentages to proportions enables us to use them in statistical calculations.

The proportion is a key concept in sampling. First, we use the relative occurrence of the most important variable under study (the dependent variable) as one basis for deciding sample size (see Chapter 2). Suppose we estimate that opinions about the day-care tax will be split 50 percent for and 50 percent against. The estimate is expressed as a proportion (.50 and .50) and is part of the fomula for computing sample size.

Second, we speak of proportional representativeness of the sample. This means that we compare, say, the proportion of men and women in the sample against the Census figures to see if we have underrepresented or overrepresented either group. If so, we could weight the sample data to adjust its proportions, bringing it in line with Census proportions.

Adding percentages to the population numbers in Table A yields Table B (Figure 6.13). This makes it easier to understand how opinions divide in Model City about the day-care tax plan:

TABLE B : SUPPORT FOR DAY-CARE TAX

Response:	Number of People	Percent of People
Favor day-care tax	336	56%
Oppose day-care tax	168	28
Don't know/No response	96	16
N = 600	100%

Figure 6.13. Frequency and percentage distribution.

The figures showing the responses of the total sample are called "marginals." They are the end figures for any table that add down the columns or across the rows to 100 percent of the sample. The marginals in Table B (Figure 6.13) tell us that twice as many people favor the tax (56%) as oppose it (28%), and that about one out of every six persons (16%) cannot or will not give an opinion.

The tables in Figures 6.12 and 6.13 are one-way classifications of data. This is called *univariate* (one-variable) analysis.

Cross-tabulation. We can learn more about opinions by doing a two-way classification of the data—that is, by dividing the sample among responses on two variables simultaneously. Therefore, we divide each response on the day-care tax by men and women as in Table C (Figure 6.14). This is *cross-tabulation*. *Note:* in all example tables, we will now use the symbols "f" (frequency), "%" (percent), "n" (subtotal), and "N" (total sample).

TABLE C   :   SUPPORT FOR DAY-CARE TAX, BY GENDER

Response:	MEN		WOMEN		TOTAL	
	f	%	f	%	N	%
Favor	90	31	246	79	336	56
Oppose	132	46	36	11	168	28
DK/NR	66	23	30	10	96	16
n=	228	100%	312	100%	600	100%

Figure 6.14. Two-way cross-tabulation.

This two-variable (*bivariate*) analysis shows that most of the opposition to the day-care tax, as well as uncertainty about it, is among the men. That is, almost one-half (46%) of the men are against it, and about a fourth (23%) don't give an opinion. Most of the support is among women—about four out of every five (79%) of the women support the tax.

Suppose we suspect that marital status has something to do with the feelings of men and women about the new tax. If we further divide the data into a three-way cross-tabulation, we get Table D (Figure 6.15).

TABLE D :   SUPPORT FOR DAY-CARE TAX BY GENDER AND MARITAL STATUS

Response:	MEN				WOMEN				TOTAL			
	Married		Unmarried		Married		Unmarried		Married		Unmarried	
	f	%	f	%	f	%	f	%	f	%	f	%
Favor	78	39	12	14	184	93	62	62	262	63	74	40
Oppose	73	36	59	69	19	3	17	17	92	22	76	41
DK/NR	51	25	15	17	9	4	21	21	60	15	36	19
n =	202	100%	86	100%	212	100%	100	100%	414	100%	186	100%
N =										600		

Figure 6.15. Three-way cross-tabulation.

This three-way classification of data is a form of *multivariate* analysis. The advantage of multivariate analysis is that by analyzing several things at one time, we can learn more about their interrelationships. But a cross-tabulation such as the one here (Figure 6.15) may not be a persuasive example of the advantage, because a table with so many numbers may be confusing. We can interpret the percentages: for example, unmarried men (69%) seem much more likely than unmarried women (17%) to oppose the tax, but the numbers of such men (59 = 10% of the sample) and women (17 = 3%) are so small that we are really not sure that the differences are real—within the limits of error due to sampling. Statistical tools, to be explained later, help sort out significant from insignificant findings.

Column and Row Data. Let's go back to Table C (Figure 6.14) to look at the interpretation of columns and of rows of data.

Table C shows column totals by men and women. The percentages add to 100 percent each for both groups, which lets us compare the two groups and the total sample. For example, women (79% of them) are much more likely than men (46% of them) to support the tax. Contrast this with Table E (Figure 6.16) where the figures are totaled across the table, that is, by rows. The comparisons now are between *responses*. And the interpretations are very different and very revealing. For example, of those *favoring* the tax, nearly three out of every four (73%) are women; of those *against,* more than three out of four (79%) are men. And, of those *uncertain,* more than two out of three (69%) are men.

Regardless whether by rows or columns, we usually report findings as some comparison of likelihood, difference in size, or ratio. For example, if we were reporting the findings in Table E by rows, we could say:

- Those favoring the tax are much much more likely to be women (73%) than men (27%)
- Four out of every five persons opposing the tax are men; or, those opposing the tax are four times more likely to be men (79%) than women (21%)
- Among those uncertain about the tax, men lead women by a ratio of more than two to one (69% to 31%)

TABLE E :   SUPPORT FOR DAY-CARE TAX, BY GENDER

Response:	MEN f	MEN %	WOMEN f	WOMEN %	TOTAL N	TOTAL %
Favor	90	27%	246	73	336	100%
Oppose	132	79%	36	21	168	100%
DK/NR	66	69%	30	31	96	100%
n =	228	48%	312	52%	600	100%

Figure 6.16. Cross-tabulation, percentaged by row.

TABLE F :   SUPPORT FOR DAY−CARE TAX; BY GENDER

Response:	MEN				WOMEN					TOTAL			
	f	Col %	Row %	Men Mar-ginals	f	Col %	Row %	Women Mar-ginals	!	N	Col %	Row %	Total Mar-ginals
Favor	90	↓	→	(15%)	246	↓	→	(41%)	!	336	↓	100%	(56%)
Oppose	132	↓	→	(22%)	36	↓	→	(6%)	!	160	↓	100%	(28%)
DK/NR	66	↓	→	(11%)	30	↓	→	(5%)	!	96	↓	100%	(16%)
		100%				100%			!		100%		
Total Marginals: n =	288			(48%)	312			(52%)	!	600			(100%)

Figure 6.17. Total sample marginals.

Total Sample Marginals. Earlier, we mentioned the "marginals," the totals found by adding across the rows or down the columns of the table to produce total sample results. Table F (Figure 6.17) shows the total sample marginals of the same data given previously. We've omitted the internal column and row percentages to show the total sample marginals more clearly. The arrows show the direction of column and row totals.

Total sample marginals are important for the context they give to data. Recall from Table E (Figure 6.16) that we found that by a two to one margin those who are uncertain about the day-care tax are more often men (69%) than women (31%). But we have to be mindful that this group of men is only one-tenth (11%) of the total sample (Table F).

Suppose we were advising a group trying to get support for the tax. We see from Table F that while most women support the tax, their number is only two out of every five persons studied (41%). Yet, there aren't many women left to attract in support of the tax—only a tenth of all people (11%) are in this group, which is composed of those who oppose the tax (36 women—6% of the total sample), or who are uncertain about it (30 women—5% of the total sample). So, the tax-support group will probably have to get the support of some men. Although enough men (15% of the whole sample) support the tax to help pass it with a majority vote, nearly the same proportion of the whole sample are opposed (22%), and uncertain (11%). Because there is no clear pattern of support for the tax among men, if the "wrong" men come out in large numbers on election day, the opponents of the day-care tax may have the majority.

Measures of Central Tendency. One of our interests is to know how similar or typical responses are. There are three main measures of central tendency: the mean (average), the median, and the mode.

Mean. The mean is the arithmetical average of a set of responses, or the total value of all people's scores divided by the number of people. If one person scores 4 and another scores 6 on some variable, their mean score is 5 (6+4 = 10/2 = 5). Of the measures of central tendency, the mean is most important. It takes into account all of the scores in a distribution. Other measures do not.

Next to the percentage, the mean is the most commonly used statistic: average temperature, average size, average height, average score are all familiar terms. In surveys, we talk about "the typical score," "the average respondent," "the most likely response," and so on.

The mean is basic to measuring variation. The notion of scores varying around the mean of a distribution is a core concept for all statistical inference. The scores are called *deviations from the mean*.

Median. Once responses are ordered by size (low to high), the median score is the midpoint of the distribution. Exactly one-half the scores are above the median and one-half are below. We often use the median for rough descriptions. For example, median family income may be an important statistic. Knowing that more than one-half of the families in a neighborhood are below the poverty income line may be important information for the Department of Social Services. Or, knowing in one precinct that more than half the registered voters are Republicans may be important for campaign decisions.

Mode. The mode is the most frequent, most popular response given. Once responses are tabulated, it's easy to find the modal response. We don't make much use of the mode, because it's only a crude measure of the centrality of a distribution. But it can be important. Which candidate wins the nomination in a crowded primary election depends upon the voters' modal response. The average voter may have voted for a liberal candidate, but if there were several liberals, a single conservative could win.

Measures of Dispersion. We are interested in the differences among people and among their responses. There are three measures we use: range, variance, and standard deviation.

Range. The range shows the extremes of a distribution—the lowest to the highest score. Using the same example that illustrated the mean, subtracting the lowest (4) from the highest (6) score gives the range value (2). Like the median and mode, the range is a crude measure that only uses a little information about the distribution. It is important, however. We often use the range as context for interpreting responses.

For example, suppose we find that the average incomes for two neighborhoods are identical—$8000. Knowing that the neighborhoods are from different areas of the city, we are concerned that our measurement may be invalid. So we check the income range for each neighborhood. Suppose we find that the range of incomes in the first, inner-city neighborhood is from $4000 to $12,000. The range in the second, transitional neighborhood is from $4000 to $30,000. A few old Victorian homes have been rehabilitated in the second neighborhood, and the area is gradually giving way to new settlement. The core population still is low income, but the character of the neighborhood is changing. The range, not the average, suggests the difference.

Variance. The concepts of variance and standard deviation are central to statistical analysis. It is important to understand their meanings.

The notion of variance was introduced in Chapter 2. Variance is a measure of the differences among all responses as calculated from the mean of those responses. Variance is itself a mean. It is the average (mean) of the differences (deviations) of all scores in a distribution from the average score of that distribution.

Suppose that we know the neighborhood distribution of all responses to the income question. We compute the mean ($8000). If, one at a time, we subtract the mean income from all other incomes in the neighborhood, we get the difference— the deviations—of each income from the mean. Because individual incomes are higher and lower than the mean income, some of the deviations are positive and some are negative. If we simply add them up, the sum will be zero. Therefore, to use them for further calculation, we *square* the (plus or minus) value of each deviation in order to get all positive values. Adding up all of these values gives a measure called the "sum of squares." This sum of the squared deviations from the mean is a measure of the general variability of all scores. It is much larger when individual scores deviate wildly from the mean than when they cluster closely around the mean.

If we then calculate the average of the squared deviations, we get the variance. *Variance: the mean of all squared deviations from the mean of all scores of a distribution.*

Knowing the variance of a set of scores tells us something about their similarities and differences. Whether this is significant information can be known through further statistical analysis.

Standard Deviation. In figuring the variance, we squared the deviations from the mean to get all positive values, summed them, then averaged the result. Once we have obtained the positive values, we can determine the "actual" (not squared) deviations simply by calculating the square root of the value of the variance. Arithmetically, the opposite of squaring numbers is to find their square root. The *square root* of the variance is called the *standard deviation* (SD). Thus, the standard deviation is an average value representing actual (no longer squared) differences of scores as calculated from the mean of all scores. *Standard deviation: the square root of the mean of all squared deviations from the mean of all scores of a distribution.*

The purpose of calculating standard deviation is to get a uniform measurement that permits us to compare, with the same yardstick each time, the differences in people who are from different types of random samples and populations. The *standard* deviation is, therefore, a standardized way of handling different types of statistical data. The measure is theoretical. It is based on a proven mathematical logic that enables us to infer where people are in relation to the mean on any continuum of scores.

Statistical Inference[6]

Descriptive statistics such as the mean, percentage, range, and standard deviation describe important characteristics of any set of data. But in surveys, our problem is whether the data collected from a sample looks anything like the real world population from which it was drawn.

Recall these definitions:

- *Statistic*—a characteristic of a sample.
- *Parameter*—a characteristic of a population.
- *Statistical inference*—estimating parameters from statistics.

Statistical inference is concerned with drawing conclusions about large groups of people by studying only a few of them. Through sampling, we try to infer population characteristics—that is, we try to estimate the value of certain parameters. And/or we try to determine whether differences among subgroups in our sample suggest that these groups are drawn from the same population or from different populations.

In estimating parameters from a sample, we are usually trying to establish a range of values around our sample statistic so that we have a high likelihood of claiming that the "true" population value falls within that range. In comparing subgroups, we are usually trying to test hypotheses about differences that we expect to find in the overall population. Thus, our problem is whether the differences we find are due only to chance (sampling error) or whether they are real. The tools of statistical inference enable us to test whether the differences we find in our samples are likely to be due to chance or whether they are so great that they are not likely to have resulted from chance alone.

Suppose we want to estimate the average number of books that teenagers read during one year. If we draw two random samples of Model City teenagers, each sample is likely to produce a different value for book reading. This is simply due to chance. By chance we draw a sample of teens A, B, and C one time, who read some number of books, and of teens X, Y, and Z the next time, who read a slightly different number of books. But, both samples are taken from the same general population.

We are interested in various types of differences. Maybe the two separate samples of teens are from different populations; maybe one sample was taken on the north side of town and the other on the south side. Moreover, if within one sample we find that boys read more books than girls, we want to know if the difference between them is so great that we're really talking about two separate populations in terms of book reading. Also, we want to know whether our estimate of book reading for either sample is close enough to the "true" population value to be trustworthy.

---

[6]A number of the ideas in this and later sections are adapted from Frederick Williams, *Reasoning with Statistics,* 2d. ed. (New York: Holt, Rinehart, & Winston, 1979). This is an excellent text for beginners.

The Random Sampling Distribution. The validity of statistical inference rests both on mathematical theory and on practical demonstration that show that random sampling of populations works. Given a large enough random sample of population units, we can show a mathematical relationship between the sample and the population if each member of the population has a known and equal (nonzero) chance of being selected into the sample. We can demonstrate the relationship by repeatedly sampling the same population over and over again.

Each equal-sized random sample of the same population will produce a different value for each estimate of any proportion, mean, or variance. If we were able to draw all (infinite) random samples of equal size, we would create a *sampling distribution* for each statistic.

- Sampling distribution—a theoretical (mathematical) distribution of all possible values of any statistic from all possible random samples of the same size from the same population.

For many statistics, most of the sample estimates would be close to the "true" population values, and therefore the distribution of all sample estimates of that statistic would be domed in the middle like a bell. This is the type of sampling distribution we call "normal."

Normal Distribution. A normal distribution—called the *normal curve*—often has a bell-like shape. In other words, when a sample statistic is normally distributed, the values closest to the "true" (usually unknown) population value are likely to occur most often. The values furthest (higher or lower) from the true value are likely to occur least often.

The normal curve is theoretical. We don't really find sampling distributions that have its exact shape, but we assume that the population is normally distributed so that (1) a random sample of it will likewise be normally distributed, and (2) the sampling distribution, which links the sample estimate by inference to the population parameter, is normally distributed.

If we knew all possible sample values of a statistic, the normal sampling distribution would look like Figure 6.18 (page 346). As shown by Figure 6.18, the normal curve can be described in full by two features: its mean (M) and its standard deviation (SD). The area under the curve is measured along the baseline in units of standard deviation—the deviations from the mean are expressed in SD units. As such, the normal curve expresses the probability of any value occurring as a deviation from the true value (M).

On the baseline, the curve is divided by SD units into sections above (plus values) and below (minus values) the mean. This indicates that the chances of any value being above the mean are no better than the chances of being below it.

Each section represents some *proportion* of the total area under the curve. The total area is 1.00. Therefore, any section can be expressed numerically as a proportion—a probability—of 1.00. For example, the probability of a value occur-

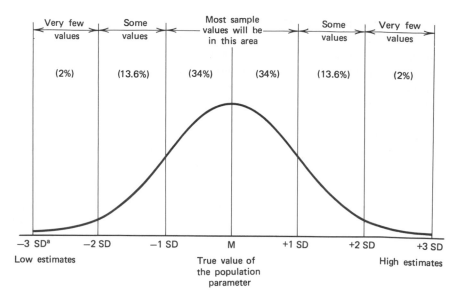

Figure 6.18. A normal sampling distribution
(SD means "standard deviation").

ring between the mean (M) and +1 SD is about .34 (or 34% of all values are likely
to be between the mean and one positive standard deviation). The probability of a
value occurring between the mean and −1 SD also is .34. Thus, about 68% of all
values will fall within ±1 SD from the Mean.

As shown above in Figure 6.18, about 47.6 percent of all values fall within the
mean and +2 SD (add 13.6% to 34%). The same falls between the mean and −2
SDs. Thus over 95 percent of all values will fall within ±2 SDs. Over 99 percent of
all values will fall within ±3 SDs. The reverse way of saying this is that: the
probability is .01 of getting a value so extreme that it would fall ±3 SDs from the
true mean. We could get more values at 4 SDs, 5 SDs, and so on. In theory, the tails
of the curve extend to infinity, but with only the tiniest proportions of all values being
so far from the mean.

The SD values given above are approximate. Actually, we know the specific
values for different areas under the curve. For example, 95 percent of all of the
area—thus of all values—under the curve will fall between ±1.96 SDs. (Later we'll
change the notation to 1.96z, but the meaning will be the same.) Similarly, 99
percent of all values will fall between ±2.58 SDs. We'll use these more precise
values in all of the following comments about the normal curve: 95 percent of all
values fall within ± 1.96 SDs, and 99 percent of all values fall within ± 2.58 SDs.

It is a convention among researchers to express their confidence in their sample
statistics in terms of being sure that "95 times out of 100" or "in 99 out of 100

identical random samples'' the same result, within a known margin of error, would have been obtained. These are called the .05 and .01 *levels of probability;* meaning that only 5 percent of the time or 1 percent of the time would a result such as the one we found be due to the chance error of sampling. The SD values associated with the .05 and .01 levels or probability are ± 1.96 SDs and ± 2.58 SDs.

Let's illustrate what we know thus far about the likely spread of sample values obtained when we sample from a population that is normally distributed. Suppose we are measuring Model City residents' knowledge about a new drug treatment program. Each respondent is given a knowledge score, and the average and standard deviation of all scores are computed. Then we assign those sample values (assumed to represent the population) to the parameters of the normal curve. On a knowledge test scoring from 0 to 100, let's say that the average score is 60 and the standard deviation is 12. Figure 6.19 shows the likely distribution of sample values if our sample comes from a population that is normally distributed. if our sample is from a large, normally distributed population, we can interpret any sample value in terms of the probability of its occurrence:

- *For ±1 SD:* the probability is about .68 that any score will be between 48 and 72; or, 68 percent of all respondents will have scores in this range. So, the probability is about .32 (1.00 − .68) that any score will be lower than 48 or higher than 72.
- *For +1.96 SD:* the probability is about .95 that any score will be between

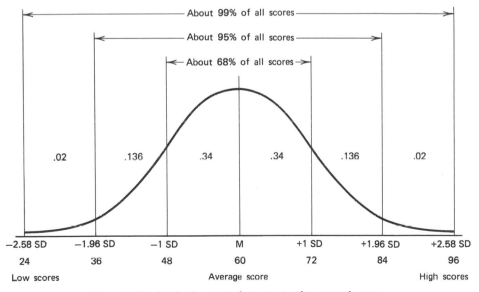

Figure 6.19. Assigning actual scores to the normal curve.

36 and 84; or, 95 percent of all respondents will have scores in this range. So, the probability is about .05 (1.00 − .95) that any score will be lower than 36 or higher than 84.

- *For ±2.58 SD:* the probability is about .99 that any score will be between 24 and 96; or 99 percent of all respondents will have scores in this range. So, the probability is about .01 (1.00 − .99) that any score will be lower than 24 or higher than 96.

In summary, the normal curve for any statistic is what we would get if we took all possible random samples of equal size from the same large, normally distributed population. The normal curve shows the probabilities of getting various values of our statistic. We think in terms of the *associated probability* of occurrence: the probability of getting any statistic is the chance of getting that value and any more extreme value in terms of distance from the true (population) value. The distance of the sample estimate is measured in units of standard deviation in either direction (positive or negative) from the true value. We judge the estimate in terms of the likelihood of its occurrence as a percentage (proportion) of all possible occurrences.

Figure 6.20 summarizes our interpretation of probability values under the normal curve.

Standard Scores. To this point we have only assumed that our sample comes from a population that is normally distributed and thus will produce statistics (e.g., means, percentages) that will have values arrayed in the bell-like form of the normal curve. But our sample values are unique to this sample. Therefore, to link our observed sample statistics to the poupulation we're trying to estimate, we have to convert the unique sample values into some universal (standard) units under the normal curve. In

Figure 6.20. Interpreting the meaning of probability levels.

Area under the Curve	Standard Deviations	Expected Level of Different Values		Meaning: a Value as Extreme or More Extreme Than the One Found Could Occur by Chance (Due to Errors of Sampling)
		Percent	Proportion	
68%	±1.00	32% =	.32	32 times out of 100 Symbol: $p < .32$
95%	±1.96	5% =	.05	5 times out of 100 Symbol: $p < .05$
99%	±2.58	1% =	.01	1 time out of 100 Symbol: $p < .01$
99.9%	±3.40	0.1% =	.001	1 time out of 1000 Symbol: $p < .001$

this way, the normal curve becomes our bridge for making inferences about the study population or any other population that we sample and that we can assume is normally distributed.

To build our inferential bridge, we have to standardize (normalize) our sample statistics. For this we use *standard scores*.

Standard scores are a way of converting any sample value into units of standard deviation under the normal curve. Standard scores (called "z scores") indicate how many standard deviations any score is from the mean of its normal distribution. Thus, z scores are analogous to the SDs of our sample, but they are standard deviations of the normal curve. Or, given the normal curve distribution for any sample, we can change any value (X) of that sample into a standard score (z) simply by finding the difference of X from the mean (M) and dividing that difference by its standard deviation (SD):

$$z = \frac{X - M}{SD}$$ (or) Standard Score = The difference between any score (X) and the mean (M) of its distribution divided by the standard deviation (SD) of the distribution (normal);

(*or*)

Standard Score = Differences from the mean in standard units of the normal curve.

Standard scores are used with "large" samples. Large samples are those with enough people that statistics based on them are likely to be normally distributed. Most statisticians say 30 people are enough.

Standard scores are interpreted for meaning in a special table, shown as Table 6.1. This *z-score table* is a table of values for areas under the normal curve. Let's illustrate the use of the z table with these figures: suppose we have a sample value of 130, the mean of its distribution is 32, and its standard deviation is 50. Using the formula above

$$\frac{X - M}{SD} = \frac{130 - 32}{50} = \frac{98}{50} = 1.96z$$

we get a z score of 1.96. Going to the normal curve table in any statistics book, we look down the left column ("z") until we find the 1.9 row. Then we look across the row to the column headed by the figure .06. Where the row (1.9) and column (.06) intersect (1.9 + .06 = 1.96), we have the area under the normal curve that lies between the mean and a point 1.96 standard units above the mean. Here the area is .4750, or 47.5 percent, of the area under the curve. If we double the value (2 × .475 = .95) we find that 95 percent of the area under the curve lies between the mean and 1.96 standard units from the mean in either direction. Or, under the normal curve, only about 5 percent of the values we would obtain would be as extreme or more

Table 6.1.   Normal-Curve Areas

z	.00	.01	.02	.03	.04	.05	.06	.07	.08	.09
0.0	.0000	.0040	.0080	.0120	.0160	.0199	.0239	.0279	.0319	.0359
0.1	.0398	.0438	.0478	.0517	.0557	.0596	.0636	.0675	.0714	.0753
0.2	.0793	.0832	.0871	.0910	.0948	.0987	.1026	.1064	.1103	.1141
0.3	.1179	.1217	.1255	.1293	.1331	.1368	.1406	.1443	.1480	.1517
0.4	.1554	.1591	.1628	.1664	.1700	.1736	.1772	.1808	.1844	.1879
0.5	.1915	.1950	.1985	.2019	.2054	.2088	.2123	.2157	.2190	.2224
0.6	.2257	.2291	.2324	.2357	.2389	.2422	.2454	.2486	.2517	.2549
0.7	.2580	.2611	.2642	.2673	.2704	.2734	.2764	.2794	.2823	.2852
0.8	.2881	.2910	.2939	.2967	.2995	.3023	.3051	.3078	.3106	.3133
0.9	.3159	.3186	.3212	.3238	.3264	.3289	.3315	.3340	.3365	.3389
1.0	.3413	.3438	.3461	.3485	.3508	.3531	.3554	.3577	.3599	.3621
1.1	.3643	.3665	.3686	.3708	.3729	.3749	.3770	.3790	.3810	.3830
1.2	.3849	.3869	.3888	.3907	.3925	.3944	.3962	.3980	.3997	.4015
1.3	.4032	.4049	.4066	.4082	.4099	.4115	.4131	.4147	.4162	.4177
1.4	.4192	.4207	.4222	.4236	.4251	.4265	.4279	.4292	.4306	.4319
1.5	.4332	.4345	.4357	.4370	.4382	.4394	.4406	.4418	.4429	.4441
1.6	.4452	.4463	.4474	.4484	.4495	.4505	.4515	.4525	.4535	.4545
1.7	.4554	.4564	.4573	.4582	.4591	.4599	.4608	.4616	.4625	.4633
1.8	.4641	.4649	.4656	.4664	.4671	.4678	.4686	.4693	.4699	.4706
1.9	.4713	.4719	.4726	.4732	.4738	.4744	.4750	.4756	.4761	.4767
2.0	.4772	.4778	.4783	.4788	.4793	.4798	.4803	.4808	.4812	.4817
2.1	.4821	.4826	.4830	.4834	.4838	.4842	.4846	.4850	.4854	.4857
2.2	.4861	.4864	.4868	.4871	.4875	.4878	.4881	.4884	.4887	.4890
2.3	.4893	.4896	.4898	.4901	.4904	.4906	.4909	.4911	.4913	.4916
2.4	.4918	.4920	.4922	.4925	.4927	.4929	.4931	.4932	.4934	.4936
2.5	.4938	.4940	.4941	.4943	.4945	.4946	.4948	.4949	.4951	.4952
2.6	.4953	.4955	.4956	.4957	.4959	.4960	.4961	.4962	.4963	.4964
2.7	.4965	.4966	.4967	.4968	.4969	.4970	.4971	.4972	.4973	.4974
2.8	.4974	.4975	.4976	.4977	.4977	.4978	.4979	.4979	.4980	.4981
2.9	.4981	.4982	.4982	.4983	.4984	.4984	.4985	.4985	.4986	.4986
3.0	.4987	.4987	.4987	.4988	.4988	.4989	.4989	.4989	.4990	.4990

This table is abridged from Table I of *Statistical Tables and Formulas,* by A. Hald (New York: John Wiley & Sons, Inc., 1952). Reproduced by permission of A. Hald and the publishers, John Wiley & Sons, Inc.

extreme (in either direction from the mean) than the one we got. Or, only five times out of 100 would we expect to get a value as extreme as we did. In summary, to know the probability associated with any sample statistic for which we can assume a normal distribution, we convert the value into a standard score (z) which we can locate on the baseline (in SD units) under the normal curve.

Standard Error. To this point we've described standard deviation and standard scores. The first is a yardstick for measuring the variation in any set of scores in a uniform way that permits us to compare other scores from other random samples. The second is a way of converting sample values to units of standard deviations under the normal curve. This shows us the location of any value under the curve, and the probability associated with its occurrence.

We turn now to the notion of *standard error*, which we need to know to test whether the sample statistic we obtain is significantly different from what we might have expected in advance of doing the survey. We compute standard error, therefore, to test our hypotheses (expectations) about the population under study. Standard error is a mathematical way of expressing sampling error. We'll ignore the mathematics.

Here, we'll talk about the *standard error of the mean*. We can compute standard error for any statistic, but we'll use the mean because it is the most frequently used statistic in estimating parameters. A single score is a less reliable (more risky) estimate of a population parameter than is the mean of several scores obtained in the same way. The mean is more conservative. Similarly, a single sample mean is a less reliable estimate of a parameter than is a mean of many means. This mean of means is a most conservative measure. The *standard error of a mean* is the *standard deviation of a random sampling distribution of sample means;* or, the likely deviation of sample means around a population mean. In effect, instead of just calculating one mean, we calculate all possible means (a random sampling distribution of means). Given a mathematically plotted sampling distribution of means, we calculate its mean—thus the grand mean—and its standard deviation. This standard measure of means deviating from the grand mean is called the standard error. Any statistic has a sampling distribution—which is, remember, the inferential link between our sample and the population. If we wanted to estimate the population standard deviation, we would calculate a sampling distribution of standard deviation values. This sampling distribution would have as its standard deviation the *standard error of the standard deviation*.

The standard error of the mean (or any statistic) is a measure of its reliability. If the standard error is small, the measure is good—the risk of using it is made acceptable by our knowledge of the probabilities associated with the normal curve. As we use the normal curve for estimating the probabilities of obtaining any single score, so do we use it for estimating the probabilities associated with any mean. That is, we calculate the random sampling distribution of mean scores in order to locate the place of our sample mean under the normal curve and the likely error that goes with it.

Although the standard error of the mean indicates the amount of variation among means taken from many samples, in real life we cannot afford to sample the population repeatedly. In practice we take one sample, add up the scores, find their mean and standard deviation, and—if we meet the assumption of the normal curve—estimate the population value from that single mean. We express standard error in units of standard deviation (converted to z-score values) under the normal curve.

In summary, the standard error of a statistic is a theoretical measure based on many identical samples of the same population. Each identically-drawn sample will have a different value for the statistic. The greater the variation in values from sample to sample, the larger the standard error and the less reliable the statistic for estimating parameters.

In practice, we usually draw only one sample and estimate the standard error of our statistic (mean, proportion, standard deviation) just from that sample itself—using the assumptions of the normal curve. Usually, the larger the size of the sample and the smaller the standard deviation, the smaller the standard error.

The standard error of a statistic has to be computed in order to "test" the statistic. We do tests to learn whether the value obtained is significantly different from the value we expected. When the formula (noted above) for the z score is appropriately modified to incorporate the sample mean, the assumed population mean, and the standard deviation of the sampling distribution, then we have a way of assessing the probability of the value of the sample mean's occurring. In other words, we can test the likelihood of getting such a value by chance. We also use the standard error to set boundaries (confidence limits) within which we are likely to find the "true" population value.

Testing Hypotheses. As noted in Chapter 1, analysis of survey data aims at testing our expectations for what we will find in the population. We express each expectation as a *research hypothesis:* a *statement of an assumed relationship.* The relationships we "expect" are between independent and dependent variables. These were defined in Chapter 1 but bear repeating here.

- *Independent variables*—things that we predict from; things that come "before" in time; things that cause other things to happen; the predictors.
- *Dependent variables*—things that we predict to; things that come "after" in time; things that are caused by other things to happen; the predicted.

Our testing usually amounts to comparing our sample statistics to see how great are the differences among them and whether the differences are greater than could have been resulted by chance—due to the errors incurred through sampling. If we find that a difference is larger than what might have occurred by chance, we say that the difference is *statistically significant*.

Our most common testing situation in survey analysis is to test the significance of the difference between two values from two groups within the same sample. For example, suppose we hypothesize zero difference in the attitude of parents and nonparents about the universal legalization of abortion. When the results of the survey come in, we compare the sources for the two groups to see if they are substantially different.

In testing sample results, we start from the point of view that, other than a tolerable amount of random error due to sampling, there is no difference between our sample statistics and the parameters they are intended to estimate.

The hypothesis of no difference is called the *null hypothesis*—where "null" means no effect, no consequence, zero, none, nonexistent. The null hypothesis states that the difference between two values is zero. If our tests show that the differences from zero are no greater than what we might expect simply as a result of sampling error, we *accept* the null: the difference we found is not significant, it is no greater than what might have occurred by chance. But if the difference is greater than the expected amount of sampling error, we *reject* the null: the difference we found is significant (real), it is not merely a chance occurrence.

The alternative to the null hypothesis is our *research hypothesis*. The research hypothesis states our expectations: the differences (thus, relationships) we expect to find.

Research hypotheses are important in planning our Model Survey. As illustrated in Chapter 1, our research hypotheses show the similarities and differences we expect to find among people in Model City in supporting or opposing the drug-abuse treatment program. These expectations are our real-world logic for doing the study. While we use the null hypothesis for purposes of statistical testing, we state the research hypotheses to show the clarity of our thinking and to enable our colleagues to critique our planning.

Testing Sample Differences. In surveys, most of our testing involves testing the difference between statistics from two (or more) groups within our sample. Suppose we are testing the significance of the difference between the percentage of men and women who do support gun control legislation. The standard error between the two percentages has to be computed before we can test the significance of the difference between them. The standard error of a difference between two statistics is computed from the standard error of each. The *standard error of the difference* between two means (or any statistic) is a key concept in statistical testing. Just as a single sample mean is a statistic, so is the difference between two means a statistic. And just as the standard error of a mean is based on a sampling distribution of all means, so is the standard error of the differences among means based on a sampling distribution of all differences. Thus, as we can compute the probabilities associated with a mean, so can we compute the probabilities associated with the difference between two means. In this connection, we have the notion of the *critical ratio*.

Critical Ratio. A ratio compares two values, showing the number of times the first contains the second: 75 percent versus 25 percent is a ratio of three-to-one ($75/25 = 3:1$).

The critical ratio is the ratio between the difference between two statistics and the standard error of their difference. Suppose men have a ''high'' mean score and women have a ''low'' mean score on favorable attitudes toward gun control. The critical ratio has to be calculated in order to test if the ''high'' versus ''low'' difference is significant. The critical ratio is computed like this:

$$\text{Critical ratio} = \frac{\text{Mean Score Men} - \text{Mean Score Women}}{\substack{\text{Standard error of} \\ \text{mean score men} - \text{mean score women}}} \text{ (or) } \frac{\text{Differences of Two Scores}}{\substack{\text{Standard error of} \\ \text{difference of the scores}}}$$

The critical ratio is ''critical'' because it tells us whether statistical differences are significant or not. It is our standard for testing differences by relating the ratio to standard scores under the normal curve. On attitudes about gun control, suppose we get a big difference between men's and women's mean scores, and find in the normal curve table an associated z score of 1.96. Recalling the characteristics of the normal curve as shown in Figure 6.21, let us see what 1.96 means to us. Notice that

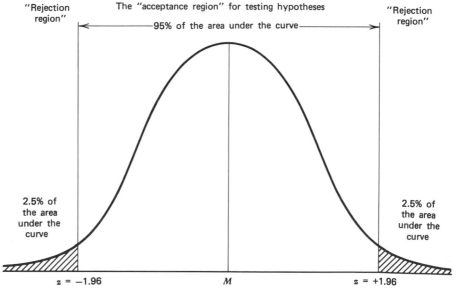

Figure 6.21. Using the normal curve to test hypotheses.

at $\pm 1.96z$ about .025 of the area under the normal curve remains at either tail of the curve. When both areas are combined they make up about 5 percent of the total area. This 5 percent corresponds to the probability statement: $P < .05$, meaning that chances are only 5 times in 100 of getting a value as extreme or more extreme than we did. The 2.5 percent of the area at either tail together constitute the *region of rejection* for testing the null hypothesis. That is, if we get a difference so large that the probability associated with it has a z score of 1.96 (or larger), we reject the hypothesis of no difference; concluding that we found a real difference not just a chance difference due to the errors of sampling.

If we don't know in which direction our difference should occur, we use both tails of the curve (called a two-tailed test) because any sample value is thought to have as much chance to occur above the mean as below the mean of the distribution. If our hypothesis is that the sample statistic should have a value greater (or less) than the mean, we would use a one-tailed test, meaning that we would calculate our 5-percent rejection region at only one side of the curve, requiring that we would use a z score of 1.65 instead of 1.96. This makes it easier to reject the null if the value is greater (positive values) than the mean. We use the one-tailed test, therefore, when our hypotheses are strong that the result will occur only in one direction. We'll talk more about the critical ratio in the next section on statistical tests of significance.

Tests of Significance

The next section briefly explains the most useful statistical tools to test significance. The availability of these tests in computer statistical packages (such as SPSS) is both a boon and a curse. It is a boon because a single command will produce any or all of the statistics on any kind of data, without our needing to do a single calculation. The curse is that the computer cannot know which tests are appropriate for which kinds of data nor what the results mean. Therefore, we are vulnerable to serious mistakes in what we ask and report about our data.

We introduce the tools here to guide their use, but are freed from the necessity of showing the calculations. Further instruction is provided in the documentation accompanying the computer statistical packages as well as in the readings listed at the end of this chapter.

The specific statistical tool we use to conclude whether a survey finding is statistically significant depends on what we are testing for and the nature of the data being tested. Figure 6.22 (page 356) shows a decision matrix and the most common statistics to test significance under different conditions.

Our goal in analysis is either to test differences or to test relationships. Depending on the nature of the data, we will use parametric or nonparametric tests.

Parametric and Nonparametric Tests. Survey research gives us estimates of population parameters. The statistical tests we use for these estimates are called

	Nature of Data		
Task	Interval or ratio	Ordinal	Nominal
	Parametric tests	Nonparametric tests	
Test differences	T test t test F test (One factor ANOVA, Multi-factor ANOVA)	Mann-Whitney U	χ^2 (chi-square)
Test relationships	r (product-moment correlation coefficient) Simple regression $r_{xy \cdot z}$ partial correlation R (Multiple correlation) Multiple regression	γ (gamma)	Q ϕ (phi) τ (tau)

Figure 6.22. Selecting appropriate statistical tests.

parametric tests. Those tests, also used with survey data, that do not try to estimate parameters are *nonparametric* tests. Which parametric or nonparametric tests we use depends on the assumptions we can make for the population and the kind of data we have. All tests are based on certain assumptions. We don't always check the assumptions each time we use a test, but the power of any test rests on the correctness of our assumptions. It's essential, therefore, to know the assumptions underlying the use of any test.

Each test is based on a *statistical model* made up of assumptions about the population studied (e.g., normal) and about the sampling done (e.g., random). Of course, we can make valid statistical inferences only from randomly drawn samples. The more we know about a population and the more specific are our assumptions for it, the more powerful are our statistical tests.

If we are testing differences, the common parametric tests are the T test, t test, and F test. The tests are based on strong assumptions. If the assumptions are met, these tests are the most powerful—that is, most likely to detect significant differences in the population—and, therefore, most likely to lead us to correct decisions about accepting or rejecting the hypotheses being tested. Parametric tests are based on these assumptions:[7]

- *Independent*—the observations are independent; the selection of one respondent or the assignment of one score does not affect the selection of any

[7]Adapted from a classic statistics text, Sidney Siegel, *Nonparametric Statistics* (New York: McGraw-Hill, 1956), p. 19.

other respondent or the assignment of any other score. This is random sampling.

- *Normal*—the population is normally distributed; any statistic calculated from the sample can be assessed in units of standard deviation under the normal curve.
- *Equal*—the variances of the population are the same; no group within the population should have values that are different in any nonrandom way from any other group, or the differences must be known as some ratio.
- *Interval*—data must be measured at least by interval scales, in order to perform the basic arithmetic calculations of adding, subtracting, multiplying, dividing.
- *Additive*—this is an assumption required only for the F test: the parts that contribute to the variance must add up to the total variance.

Nonparametric tests should usually be used when these conditions are not met—e.g., when the population is not normally distributed, when measures are nominal or ordinal, not interval scales, when variances are not equal. However, it should be noted that some parametric tests are so robust, that violating certain assumptions does not make a practical difference in outcomes related to inferences.

T Test and t Test. The T test and the t test are the most commonly used parametric tools for testing hypotheses about differences in the population. The T test is used with the z-score table shown as Table 6.1.

Suppose we want to know if there is a significant difference between liberals' and conservatives' beliefs in the sincerity of the Model City mayor's promise to reduce property taxes next year.

If the number of people sampled is at least 30 (some statisticians argue for at least 50 to 100), we would use the T test to learn if there is a significant difference between liberals and conservatives. The T test uses the *critical ratio* (z score) formula to test for significant differences. The z values in Table 6.1 are the same as T-test values or critical ratio values. Despite all of the different symbols, they mean the same thing: units of standard deviation under the normal curve.

To test the difference, we first calculate the average of each group's "belief in mayor" score. Next, we have to find the critical ratio. Recall that this is the ratio of the difference of two values and the standard error of their difference:

$$\text{Critical ratio} = T = \frac{\text{Difference of two scores}}{\text{Standard error of the difference of the scores}}$$

The formula converts differences between liberals and conservatives into standard scores (z scores) under the normal curve. The higher the value of T, the more likely is the difference to be significant.

Suppose we decide that we are willing to take only a 5 percent risk of being wrong about this difference. That means that if we get a T equal to or greater than

1.96z, we will know that this much difference between liberals and conservatives could have occurred by chance only 5 percent of the time—only 5 times out of 100 identical random samples; or $P < .05$.

If we feel that a .05 chance of being wrong is too risky, we can toughen our standards. If we require T scores to be as large as 2.58z, the differences would have to be so large that they would occur by chance only 1 percent of the time. Said another way, if we find a T value equal to or greater than 2.58z, our chance of being wrong about finding a real difference is only 1 in 100. (Recall the meanings of the .05, .01, and .001 probability levels summarized previously in Figure 6.20.)

If the sample has less than 30 people (or less than 50 or 100, depending on the preferences of the analyst), we would use the t test. The t test requires some adjustments in the calculation formula of the T test and is interpreted according to a different table (see Table 6.2).

As Table 6.2 shows, the small-sample t test involves the concept of "degrees of freedom." When we test the difference of two means from independent samples

Table 6.2. Distribution of t (two-tailed test)[a]

Degrees of Freedom (d.f.)	5% Probability of Exceeding These Values by Chance (p = .05)	Degrees of Freedom (d.f.)	5% Probability of Exceeding These Values by Chance (p = .05)
1	12.71	16	2.12
2	4.30	17	2.11
3	3.18	18	2.10
4	2.78	19	2.09
5	2.57	20	2.09
6	2.45	21	2.08
7	2.36	22	2.07
8	2.31	23	2.07
9	2.26	24	2.06
10	2.23	25	2.06
11	2.20	26	2.06
12	2.18	27	2.05
13	2.16	28	2.05
14	2.14	29	2.05
15	2.13	inf.	1.96

[a] From Fisher and Yates, *Statistical Tables for Biological, Agricultural, & Medical Research*, 4th ed. (Edinburgh: Oliver and Boyd, Limited, 1953), Table III.

(say, men's and women's attitudes toward gun control), the degrees of freedom
are $n_1 + n_2 - 2$; or the number of men (n_1) *plus* the number of women (n_2) *minus*
the number of values that are known (2) and are thus not free to vary. In this case,
the value of each mean is known, which has the effect of reducing by one the number
of values that are free to vary in *each* of the male and female subsamples. Degrees
of freedom are an important concept for many statistical tests.

One-factor ANOVA. As just seen, the t test is used to test whether the difference
between two scores is real—not caused merely by the errors of random sampling.
But when *two or more scores are compared for significance,* a different kind of test
is used. Most commonly, we use a parametric statistical test called *analysis of
variance* (ANOVA). It's simplest form is called one-factor (one-way) ANOVA. A
factor is an independent variable. So, one-factor ANOVA means that we are testing
differences related to a single independent variable.

ANOVA is also popularly known as the F test, because F is the name of the
statistic by which we interpret the significance of an ANOVA test. The F table will
be described below. The F test requires that measures be at least from interval data.
Interval measures are *continuous*—that is, they lie along a continuum. As such, they
have different (unequal) values that can be compared on the same dimension—
high/low, strong/weak, favorable/unfavorable, etc.

Continuing a previous example, let us suppose that we are measuring the
strength of people's support for a day-care tax plan, measured by a scale of several
items. The measure is continuous if its values range along a continuum from one
extreme (support) to the opposite extreme (oppose). This type of graduated measurement is different from the yes/no type of nominal measurement that has been
described. A nominal measure is called *discrete*—answers fall into categories of
equal value: yes/no, right/wrong, black/white, which cannot be compared for their
differences or relative placement. Such categories are absolute, they are not relative
to each other.

Table C (Figure 6.14) shows an example of one independent variable: how
men and women (independent) differ in their support of the day-care tax (dependent). Suppose, however, we are interested in knowing how people of different
income levels feel about the tax. In this case, we could divide the sample into three
(or more) groups: low-income, middle, high-income. Further, instead of just knowing whether the different income groups are for or against the tax plan, we will
measure the strength of support—a continuous measure.

In analysis we find the different scores for each of the three groups and
compare them. The null hypothesis is that the scores (averages) are equal, that there
are no differences between the low-income, middle, and high-income groups in
terms of their support for the tax. The analysis would look like Figure 6.23 (page 360).

ANOVA tests the significance of the *overall* distribution of the three mean
scores. Thus, ANOVA tells whether there are significant differences among the

Feeling about Day-Care Tax	Low Income	Middle Income	High Income
Average strength of support	Mean Score $_1$	Mean Score $_2$	Mean Score $_3$

Figure 6.23. One-factor analysis of variance.

three means without specifying which differences are significant. ANOVA answers the question of whether the three means are from the same population, that is, whether the three income groups differ by more than could be expected to happen by chance. To compare any two means for significance requires other tests and strong hypotheses.

As already stated, ANOVA produces a statistic called F. ANOVA does not test the differences between individual means; the value of F indicates only whether there is significant variation among all means. In our example, ANOVA looks at the pattern of differences for the three income groups (low-middle-high) and asks whether their average scores are similar enough to have come from the same population. Each group has its own mean, and each group's scores vary around the group mean. This is called *variance within groups*. All groups together have a grand mean (the average of all scores), and each group's scores vary around the grand mean. This is called *variance between groups*.

If the groups are from the same population, there should be no significant difference in the values of the variances *within* groups or *between* groups. Thus, the value of the within-group variance and the value of the between-group variance should be about equal. F is the ratio of these two variance values:

$$F = \frac{\text{Between-group variance}}{\text{Within-group variance}} \quad \text{or} \quad \frac{\text{(Group differences)}}{\text{(Individual differences)}}$$

As indicated here, the between-group variance shows the differences in groups and the within-group variance shows the differences in people. Therefore, the F ratio tells how many times the group difference is greater than our estimate of the difference in people in the population.

If there is no difference between the two variance values, their ratio would be 1.0. The further the ratio value is from 1.0, the more likely the difference within and between groups is to be significant—that is, the more likely the three groups are to be from different populations. If the difference is significant, we reject the null hypothesis that the three groups are equal.

The probabilities of F values are found in a special table (not reproduced here) that reflect normal-curve outcomes. The table has different F values at different "degrees of freedom" based on the number of groups and number of scores in the calculation.

Multi-Factor ANOVA. We often use more than one independent variable (factor) in a single analysis. Thus, we use multi-factor (N-way, multiple factor) ANOVA.

In the next example, we'll use two independent variables, though there could be more. Each independent variable must divide into two or more levels (classes, groups, categories). For making these groups, both factors do not have to be continuous measures. Here, we'll divide the three income groups by median age, so that each group has people classified as ''older'' or as ''younger.'' The analysis will now look like Figure 6.24*a*.

a. Tabular form	Low income		Middle income		High income	
Feeling about Day-Care Tax	Younger	Older	Younger	Older	Younger	Older
Average strength of support	Mean $_1$	Mean $_2$	Mean $_3$	Mean $_4$	Mean $_5$	Mean $_6$

b. Factorial design

	Age	
Income	Younger	Older
High	Mean $_5$	Mean $_6$
Middle	Mean $_3$	Mean $_4$
Low	Mean $_1$	Mean $_2$

Figure 6.24. Multi-factor analysis of variance.

In Figure 6.24*b*, the same items are rearranged into a *factorial design*. This is a ''3 × 2'' factorial design, meaning that there are two factors (income and age), the first which has three (3) levels and the second which has two (2) levels. The distinction of the factorial design is important, because each cell (Mean $_1$ to Mean $_6$) in the table represents a different group in the population and a potentially different hypothesis for our analysis.

Multi-factor ANOVA tests different hypotheses. Testing hypothses about the relationship of each independent variable (income and age) to the dependent variable (support) is called *testing the main effects* of the relationship: that is, do high-, mid-, and low-income people represent the same population in terms of support for the tax? Do younger and older people represent the same population in terms of their feeling? We test each main effect as though the other did not exist. When we test for age effects, we ignore income; and vice versa. Of course, the two independent variables may have important relationships, too. However, if the two independent variables are correlated, discovering their individual effect on the dependent variable is not a straightforward matter.

Testing the effect of the two independent variables in combination is called *testing the interaction effect*. The two age and income variables may interact—

that is, older people with higher incomes may come from a different population than younger people with lower incomes, at least in terms of each group's support for the tax. The interaction effect is not just the sum of the main effects; it results from a special combination of factors. It's possible to have main effects but no significant interaction effects, or to have interaction effects and not significant main effects. In such cases, the F-ratio would show a significant difference for one kind of test but not for the other.

The interpretation of multi-factor ANOVA follows two rules: (1) if there is an interaction effect, each main effect must be interpreted as related, not as separate; and (2) if the interaction effect is not significant, the main effects may be treated separately, since they are independent of each other. If one test shows significance, the other is likely to show significance, too, but not always. The combination may be more (or less) than the sum of its parts.

In summary, older people may differ from younger people. And people with more money may differ from those with less. Each of these differences or nondifferences is a main effect of an independent variable. Each can be tested by multi-factor ANOVA. In combination, the two independent variables may so relate as to produce interaction effects on the dependent variable. Interaction effects are additional—not simply the sum of the main effects. Interaction effects are the results of the special combination of factors. It's possible, but not typical, for interaction effects to be significant when main effects are not, and vice versa.

Nonparametric Tests of Difference. If instead of interval data we have ordinal (ranked) or nominal (categorical, yes/no) data, we must use a *nonparametric* test—one that does not try to estimate population parameters. Two will be described here.

Mann-Whitney U Test. Where we have crude measurement that tells us only that some respondents stand higher than others on some criterion (e.g., prestige) but not by how much, we use the Mann-Whitney U test to decide whether two subgroups differ significantly. The two groups are jointly ranked and a count is made of how much more often the members of the first subgroup rank ahead of members of the second. We then compute a z score and interpret it in the normal-curve table at the chosen level of significance.

Chi-Square Test. This test is the most commonly used nonparametric statistical test of differences. We use chi-square when our data cannot meet various assumptions for parametric testing. Chi-square does not assume the conditions of the normal curve.

The first use of chi-square is when we group data in nominal or ordinal categories to test differences among them. The test deals with frequencies—raw scores —not percentages or other comparative statistics. We test frequencies because the categories are discrete, not continuous, and therefore assumed to be "equal" in value

Main Transport	Observed Frequencies	Expected Frequencies
Big U.S. cars	150	150
Small U.S. cars	125	150
Small imported cars	225	150
Mass transit	100	150
N = 600		600
$\chi^2 = 58.33$		

Figure 6.25. Chi-square test of observed and expected frequencies.

but not comparable. For example, classifying people as men/women, Republican/ Democrat, Protestant/Catholic/Jew produces discrete categories. Our test is not of the "quality" of the categories, but of the differences of the "quantities" (frequencies) within categories.

In statistical analysis, chi-square tests different hypotheses for one or more variables. With one variable, we compare the difference between the frequencies "observed" in our sample against hypothetical frequencies that we would have "expected" to find if there were no differences in the population—the null hypothesis. The chi-square value obtained from calculating the differences between the observed and expected frequencies indicates whether the difference is greater than what could happen by chance.

The values of the expected frequencies are calculated on the basis that they sum up to the same total as the sum of the observed frequencies. Suppose we find that our sample of 600 Model City residents divides unevenly into four nominal groups for their main transportation, as shown in Figure 6.25. If there were no differences among the groups in the population, we would expect one fourth in each group (600/4 = 150). The chi-square value is based on calculating for each category the difference between the two columns, squaring that value, and dividing by the expected frequency.[8] The test indicates whether the observed distribution for the four groups is significantly different from that expected with 150 people in each group.

Another use of chi-square is with cross-tabulated data to see whether the variables

[8]For this example

$$\chi^2 = \frac{(150-150)^2}{150} + \frac{(125-150)^2}{150} + \frac{(225-150)^2}{150} + \frac{(100-150)^2}{150}$$

or $0 + 4.17 + 37.5 + 16.7 = 58.33$

which exceeds the value in Table 6.3 for 3 degrees of freedom (7.81). Therefore, the difference between subgroups is significant, not due to chance alone.

Table 6.3.   Distribution of Chi-Square[a]

Degrees of Freedom (d.f.)	5% Probability of Exceeding This Value by Chance (p = .05)
1	3.84
2	5.99
3	7.81
4	9.49
5	11.07
6	12.59
7	14.07
8	15.51
9	16.92
10	18.31

[a]Adapted from Catherine M. Thompson, "Tables of the Percentage Points of the χ^2 Distribution," *Biometrika,* Vol. 32 (1941), pp. 188–189.

being cross-tabulated have any relationship. The test indicates whether they are independent or not. Under the null hypothesis, we expect zero relationship between variables; they are hypothesized to be independent of each other.

Generally, the higher the value of chi-square, the greater the likelihood that the difference is statistically significant between the observed and expected frequencies: the probability is small that the difference is simply a chance occurrence.

We use a special table (Table 6.3) to interpret the statistical significance of chi-square. The logic is the same as for *t*-test and others. The table involves calculating the *degrees of freedom*. Here, degrees of freedom means literally the number of frequencies that are "free" to vary—the number that could be assigned arbitrarily after the number of categories used to group the frequencies is known. Yuker simplifies the rules as follows:[9]

- *One variable:* when chi-square is computed for one set of observations with *n* categories, the degrees of freedom is one less than the number of categories:

$$\text{d.f.} = n - 1$$

- *Cross-tabulated variables:* when chi-square is computed for cross-tabulations involving *r* rows and *c* columns, the degrees of freedom is the product of one less than *r* times one less than *c*:

$$\text{d.f.} = (r - 1)(c - 1)$$

[9]Harold E. Yuker, *A Guide to Statistical Calculation* (New York: Putnam, 1958) page 70.

We interpret the chi-square value in the same manner we would a *t* or *F* value; it indicates the probability that the value obtained is likely to reflect a real difference or is likely to have occurred simply by chance.

Testing Significance with a Nomograph. For researchers without access (late at night) to a computer, a *nomograph* of chi-square values is handy for testing whether a percentage difference between two groups is statistically significant. The nomograph in Figure 6.26 is used in two steps: (1) finding the critical value given the sample size of the two groups, and (2) finding whether the two percentages differ enough to exceed that critical value.

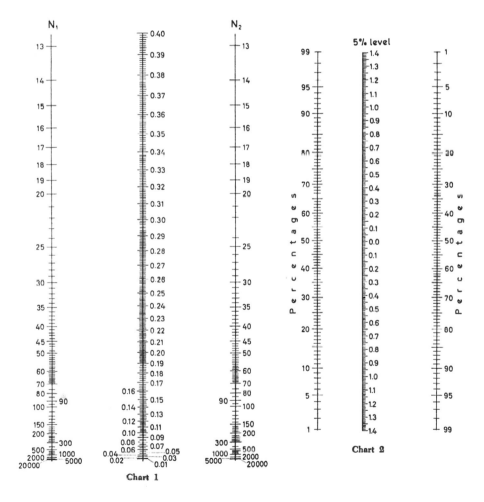

Figure 6.26. Testing percentage differences with a nomograph. [Adapted from A. N. Oppenheim, *Questionnaire Design and Attitude Measurement* (New York: Basic Books, 1966), pp. 290–291. Based on Joseph Zubin, Journal of Amer. Stic. Assn, 34 (1939), pp. 539–544.]

We illustrate the use of the nomograph with a sample of 125 men (n_1), of whom 81 percent drink beer, and 164 women (n_2), of whom 70 percent drink beer. First lay a ruler (preferably transparent) on Chart 1, between 125 on column n_1 and 164 on column n_2. Now read the critical value from where the ruler crosses the middle column (here it is 0.119). Next, move the ruler to Chart 2, laying it between the percentage for group₁ (men, 81%) and group₂ (women, 70%). Now look where the ruler crosses the middle column, labeled ''5% level.'' If this figure (here 0.14) exceeds the critical value from Chart 1 (it does), the percentage difference is significant at the .05 level.

Testing Relationships

Now we turn to the second kind of data testing—determining whether significant relationships exist.

Simple Correlation. We are often interested in how things ''go together,'' or are associated, in a population. Things are said to *correlate* (co-relate) when increases (or decreases) in one are accompanied by increases (or decreases) in the other. For example, a *positive* correlation may exist between education and income: people with more education tend to have more income; or, as education increases, income increases. A *negative* correlation may exist between education and number of children. As parents' education is higher, the number of children in the family is lower; or, people with more education tend to have fewer children. In this latter example, increases in one characteristic are associated with decreases in the other—a negative relationship.

To say things correlate does *not* mean that one causes the other to happen, only that the two tend to occur together. We know that when one characteristic is present the other tends also to be present; and as one varies upward (downward), the other varies upward (downward) as well.

Correlation is measured on an index ranging from $+1.0$ (perfect positive correlation) to -1.0 (perfect negative correlation). A perfect noncorrelation (zero correlation) is expressed as 0.0—the midpoint of the index. The index value is called the *correlation coefficient,* and its symbol is r. The correlation coefficient shows the extent to which two measures vary together—positively or negatively. The coefficient shows the size (between 0.0 and 1.0) and direction ($+$ and $-$) of a relationship. The coefficient does not tell what causes the relationship. This requires special research approaches. Nor does the coefficient tell the significance of the relationship between the two variables, nor how much change in one variable is associated with how much change in the other. Special tests must be made to show this latter feature.

We use statistical tests to assess the significance of correlation coefficients, r. Although correlation shows relationships and not differences, we use the same probability-of-occurrence logic in testing hypotheses of the significance of the correlation. The value of r can be adapted by a special formula to the t table and interpreted for significance in the same way as for t values for tests of differences.[10]

In interpreting the importance of a correlation, it's helpful to know the relationship between r and r^2—between the correlation coefficient and its squared value, called the *coefficient of determination*. The r^2 value indicates the amount of variation between two sets of scores that is common to, or shared by, the two sets. That is, r^2 is the percentage of the variance that the two scores have in common.

Suppose we have an r value of .50 between income and age, and it is statistically significant. We know that there is a definite relationship between the two variables, but how useful is this knowledge? The r^2 value (.50 × .50) is only .25; or, only 25 percent of the variation between the two sets of age and income scores is accounted for (explained by) their relationship. Frankly, being able to explain only 25 percent of the differences in a set of scores is not a very solid basis for making a policy decision that relies on that relationship holding true. However, knowing one variable that explains 25 percent of the differences in another variable is quite useful in the context of theory-building.

Although r is commonly cited, and has the important characteristic of retaining its plus or minus sign (lost when r is squared), the importance of any correlation can be judged more sensibly in terms of the r^2 value. Guidelines for interpreting the importance of r values are shown in Figure 6.27.[11] We have added the r^2 values to aid the interpretation:

Relationship is:	(r) Correlation Coefficient	(r^2) Variance Explained	Remarks about Variance
Negligible	<.20	Up to .04 =	Up to 4% of the variation in one measure is explained by its relationship with another measure.
Low-to-definite	.20–.40	Up to .16 =	Up to 16% of the variation explained.
Moderate-to-substantial	.40–.70	Up to .49 =	Up to 49% of the variation explained.
High	.70–.90	Up to .81 =	Up to 81% of the variation explained.
Very high	>.90	Over .81 =	Over 81% of the variation in one measure is explained by its relationship with another measure.

Figure 6.27. Interpreting the importance of correlations.

[10]This so-called "product-moment correlation coefficient" is interpreted in the t table with $N - 2$ degrees of freedom; where N is the number of pairs of scores. Since each respondent in this case has two scores being paired (correlated), N = the number of persons in the sample.

[11]Adapted from J. P. Guilford, *Fundamental Statistics in Psychology and Education* (New York: McGraw-Hill, 1965), p. 145.

We'll expand further on the idea of common variance in the sections below on multiple correlation and factor analysis.

Simple Regression. Whether involving only one variable or several as the basis for making predictions, regression equations tell us the extent to which we can predict one variable by knowing another. For the moment we'll deal only with trying to predict a single variable from another single variable, which is called *simple regression*. Later we'll illustrate using two or more variables in combination to predict another. This is called *multiple regression*.

The notion of prediction involves wanting to know the extent to which the differences (variance) in some dependent variable, such as income, can be explained by its relationship to some independent variable(s), such as education. The logic of prediction involves *knowing the extent to which:*

- one variable predicts another;
- the differences in one variable explain the differences in another;
- one accounts for variations in another;
- one shares common variance with another.

All of these say the same thing: the differences in one characteristic, such as education, can be used with some known degree of reliability to explain the differences in another characteristic, such as income.

Let's continue with the correlation of education and income. In a cross-tabulation, the relationship would look like Table G (Figure 6.28a).

TABLE G: RELATIONSHIP BETWEEN EDUCATION
AND INCOME

		Education	
		Low	*High*
	High		+
Income			
	Low	+	

Figure 6.28a. Relationship between two variables.

The plus signs in the table indicate that "high" education is associated with "high" income and "low" education is associated with "low" income. This relationship is graphed in Figure 6.28b.

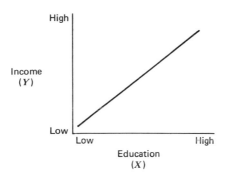

Figure 6.28b. Relationship between education and income. (Graphic)

Let's call education X and income Y. They form the X-axis and Y-axis of the graph. The diagonal line, called a "line of regression," indicates that increases and decreases in X are associated with increases and decreases in Y. The line indicates that we might be able to predict someone's income if we know his or her education. That is, if we know a person's education (the value of X) and know the exact slope (sharpness of the slant) of the diagonal line, we would theoretically be able to draw a line from the point of that person's education level on the X-axis up to the diagonal line and then across to the Y-axis, which would tell us the income level we could expect would be associated with that level of education.

The graph (Figure 6.28b) indicates one of the principal reasons why we do surveys—to find relationships between people's characteristics and to use our knowledge of one characteristic to predict another. Once we have established such relationships, we can make very practical use of our knowledge. Of course, our knowledge is never exact, but many of our day-to-day actions are taken on the basis of the risk we feel we can safely run in predicting one variable that we haven't measured from another that we have. For example, on the basis of knowing the relationship between "pocketbook" issues and how the general public intends to vote, the mayor will be wise to talk price controls to factory workers and to talk wage controls to businessmen.

As we've said, the correlation coefficient tells the extent to which two variables tend to go together. The line of regression indicates the extent to which two variables are *linearly* related—that is, whether there is a "straight-line" relationship between them. If there is a straight-line relationship between two variables, then we can determine the amount of change in one that is related to the amount of change in the other. For example, knowing the type of regression line between two variables might allow us to claim something like: if X has a value of .80, then Y is likely to have a value of .60; or if $X = .90$, then $Y = .75$—plus or minus some margin of error.

Drawing Regression Lines. Our very simple example suggests an unrealistic relationship between education and income; it suggests that a perfect straight-line relationship exists between them—as though they were perfectly correlated at +1.0.
Such perfection is an ideal. But continuing for a moment more with such simplified
examples, let us suppose we know both the income *and* education for three persons,
Sam, Sue, and Ed. We are trying to predict income (score *Y*) from education (score
X). If we plot the three person's *pairs* of scores (*XY*) on a graph, we see a perfect relationship as is shown in Figure 6.29*a*. The upwardly diagonal line connects the points (*) at which Sam, Sue, and Ed's *X* and *Y* scores are paired (*XY*).
In this example, the pairs of scores just happen to fall on a perfectly straight line.
Thus, knowing how the line connects each pair of scores from the sample tells us
what kind of a basis we have for predicting other pairs of *XY* scores for any other
person or group of persons in the same population.

The diagonal *regression line* is a hypothetical straight line that "best fits" a set
of paired scores. This best-fit line can be approximated by eye, or can be calculated
by a regression equation, which will be explained shortly. Actual pairs of scores
will not fall nicely into a straight line, but the regression equation tells us how close
to such a best-fit line our pairs are and, thus, how well we can predict the income of
any person in the population by knowing his or her education.

Although plotting all points on a graph is the best way to visualize the relationship between the two variables, in actual surveys we have so many pairs of scores
that we can't spend all of our time plotting graphs. The regression equation is
important because we must learn to visualize the plot by the size of the correlation
coefficient *r* and the values associated with it.

Let us turn now to the regression formula. Throughout this book we have

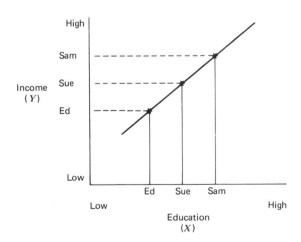

Figure 6.29*a*. A perfect regression line to predict values.

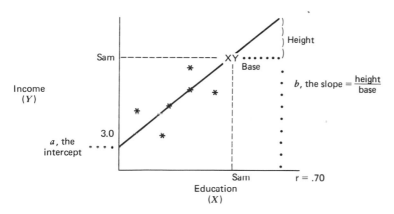

Figure 6.29b. A regression line to predict income from education.

avoided formulas wherever possible. In this case, the underlying logic of regression is important to understanding the goal of survey research: prediction. Using only Sam for the example, Checklist 34 shows the steps involved in understanding regression. The formula for the regression line is the high school algebraic formula for a straight line:

$$Y = a + bX$$

In Figure 6.29b the formula appears in graph form. Two things should be immediately apparent: first, the point, a, at which the line *intercepts* the Y-axis tells something about the *relative value* of Y and X. Second, the sharpness of the angle of the line's slope, b, tells something about the *rate of change* in Y as X changes. The symbols, a and b, are called regression coefficients (or constants). Knowing a and b in the formula enables us to estimate the value of Y for each value of X.

The coefficient, r, tells how closely the individual pairs of observations fit the regression line. Here, $r = .70$, with $r^2 = .49$, meaning that about one-half (49%) of the variation in income is explained by the variation in education. The other half of the variation is unexplained by education, and must therefore be accounted for by the nonlinear aspects of the relationship, by other variables that we may or may not have in the survey, and by errors of measurement.

CHECKLIST 34

Understanding Regression

Symbol

X	Sam's score on education, shown as the *horizontal* axis of Figure 6.29b
Y	Sam's score on income, shown as the *vertical* axis of Figure 6.29b

XY	Sam's *paired* scores for education and income. (For each other person's *X* value we would plot the corresponding value for *Y* in Figure 6.29*b*)
*	The points at which the paired *X* and *Y* values intersect when plotted.
Regression line	A hypothetical straight line that "best fits" the pairs of *XY* scores, when drawn to connect the intersection points of *X* and *Y*. Values are calculated from the regression equation (below).
$Y = a + bX$	The regression equation. It is the formula for a straight line that we learn in high school algebra. To plot the line, choose any level of education, *X*; multiply it by the slope, *b*, and add the *y*-intercept, *a*. The result is a value of income, *Y*. Plot that point. Choose another value of *X*; figure the associated value of *Y*; plot the point; draw the regression line through the two points. (Plot a third point also, to check the line.)
a	The *y-intercept*, the point at which the diagonal regression line intersects the *Y*-axis. *NOTE: a* tells the *value* of *Y* relative to *X*. In Figure 6.29*b*, suppose that the line hits the *Y*-axis at the place where the value of *Y* is 3.0. This means that at the point of interception, where *X* = 0, the value of *Y* is 3.0 units greater than *X*.
b	The *slope*, the angle of the regression line. *NOTE: b* tells the *rate of increase* in *Y* for each unit of increase in *X*. Or, *b* tells how many units that *Y* increases with each unit that *X* increases. It is shown in Figure 6.29*b* as the height divided by the base of any section of the regression line. Here it rises about .8 units for every 1 unit it moves to the right.
a and *b*	Called "regression coefficients," these are important to all formulas that predict: (1) one score from another (regression), (2) one score from another with a third held constant (partial regression), and (3) one score from a group of other scores (multiple regression). They are calculated by hand or by a computer regression program to give the best-fitting regression line for the data.
Prediction	The goal of trying to explain the difference in a dependent variable by knowing the differences in the independent variable. Once the regression line is drawn, we can pick any level of education, follow up to the line, and read across to the level of income likely to be associated with that level of education.
r	The correlation coefficient; it tells how closely we can estimate the value of one variable from the other.
r^2	The coefficient of determination; it tells what percent of the variance of one variable is "explained" by the other.

Partial Correlation. The relationship between two variables may be due to the presence of one or more other variables. Let's continue the Model City example of education and income but divide income groups into ''younger'' and ''older'' members. In a cross-tabulation with a control variable, the relationship (suggested by plus signs) would look like Table H in Figure 6.30.

Suppose our original finding showed a positive correlation between age and income as well as between education and income. Now we wonder which is the better predictor of income. First, we define income more clearly by eliminating from the analysis those people who do not earn income and who are not included in the labor force (students, retirees). Now, with a better definition of our problem, we are ready to look at the relationships.

The double plus sign (++) in Figure 6.30 indicates two very strong relationships among those studied:

- Older people with high education have higher incomes.
- Younger people with low education have lower incomes.

But two other relationships are also seen. As is indicated by the single plus sign (+):

- Younger people with high education have higher incomes.
- Older people with lower education have lower income.

Thus, regardless of age, people with higher education tend to have higher income. This is an overly simplified example, of course.

Now we have a clue that a person's education in Model City is a better predictor of income than is age. Showing this relationship statistically is called *partial correlation*—we hold constant one variable (age) to see if another (education) is the more likely explanation of the relationship with a third variable (in-

TABLE H: INCOME BY AGE BY EDUCATION

Income Level	Younger		Older	
	Low Education	High Education	Low Education	High Education
High Income		+		++
Low Income	++			+

Figure 6.30. Multiple relationships.

come). We are, in effect, "partialling" out the relationships by looking at various combinations of variables to see which are the most highly related.

The symbol for partial correlation is, for example, $r_{xz\cdot y}$, which represents the correlation of x and z while controlling for the effects of y. Partial correlation is a correlational tool; we use cross-tabulation here merely to make the education-income relationship visual.

One of the goals of predicting one variable from another is *parsimony*— reducing the numer of variables we study to the smallest possible number of key variables that are best predictors of other variables. In other words, we are trying to report accurately about the world, using as little information as is reasonable. It makes sense that if we know as much from studying 15 variables as from 30; it is more economical to study only the 15. In our example, we see that education is probably a better predictor of income than is age. If, in the interest of parsimony, we had to choose to study only one variable, we would choose to study education instead of age, since we are interested in predicting income with the best possible explanatory variable.

Knowing one variable usually is not enough information on which to base predictions of another. Rather, since variables have important relationships with other variables, we usually have more solid bases for predicting one variable, such as income, when we know several others, such as age, gender, education, occupation, marital status, ethnic group membership. This is the concept of *multiple correlation and regression*.

Multiple Correlation. Recall the following distinction: knowing that two things tend to "go together" (correlate) is a useful piece of information; but knowing the extent to which one predicts another (regression) is a higher level of knowledge.

Prediction is a goal of science. In statistical analysis, prediction is based on the notion of shared variance. That is, our ability to predict one variable from another rests on our knowledge of the variance they have in common and, thus, on the extent to which one variable can be used to explain differences (variance) in another.

To this point, we've dealt mostly with the correlation of two variables. Usually we're concerned with the correlations of more than two variables—or, the *intercorrelations* of several variables. Continuing the previous example, suppose we find the three intercorrelations shown in Figure 6.31. We can show the intercorrelations as a table, as a matrix, or graphically.

In graphical form (Figure 6.31c) the shaded areas of the circles indicate that each variable shares some of its area with another, and all three share some area in common. This is the simplest notion of multiple correlation.

In this example, the strongest relationship is between education and income. They overlap about half ($r^2 = .75^2$ or .56). Age overlaps about one-fourth with

a. Tabular form

	r
Income and age correlate	.50
Income and education correlate	.75
Age and education correlate	.40

b. Matrix form

	Age	Education
Income	.50	.75
Age	—	.40

c. Graphic form [a]

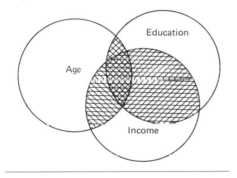

Figure 6.31. Intercorrelation of three variables.

income ($.50^2 = .25$), but age shares only about one-sixth with education ($.40^2 = .16$).

   . Printing an intercorrelation matrix is one of the early tasks of data analysis. With many variables, the intercorrelation matrix gets very large, and it is often as wasteful as the all-variables-against-all-variables cross-tabulation run. It may not cost much money to request these everything-by-everything analyses, but it's a "sorting through the garbage" approach to analysis. The analyst who does this typically lacks specific hypotheses about important relationships and simply hunts through the table for any large values of r. Later comes the problem of trying to make some sense of these values. This is not rigorous research thinking and should be discouraged.

     Rather than dealing only with pairs of correlations, we can, with the tool of *multiple correlation*, find the degree to which two or more variables relate to the dependent variable. The multiple correlation coefficient, R, is much like the simple correlation coefficient, r, in its meaning. The R value, by convention always positive, tells the size (from 0.0 to 1.0) of the multiple relationship of several independent variables (such as age and education) and a dependent variable (such as income), when all interrelations are considered at the same time.

In our continuing example, the R coefficient expresses the multiple relationships of (1) age *and* (2) education with (3) income. To indicate which multiple variables are being related to which single variable, the R is written with subscripts as: $R_{3.12} = .80$. This translates as "the coefficient of multiple correlation (R) of income (subscript 3) *with* age (subscript 1) *and* education (subscript 2) is .80." Squared, this yields the *coefficient of multiple determination* (R^2), which is the percentage of variation in the dependent variable "explained by" or associated with the other variables acting together. An R of .80 yields an R^2 of .64, indicating that about two-thirds (64%) of the variation in income is explained by variation in age and education together.

In large multiple correlation problems involving many variables, the intercorrelations are so numerous and the calculations are so arduous that a computer is mandatory. Rather than improving our explanation, however, adding more and more variables is not necessarily going to increase the multiple correlation coefficient dramatically. If we include a dozen sensible variables, one or two may be highly related to the dependent variable, and a couple of others may contribute somewhat more to the explanation. But, then, because of the interrelations of all of them, only trivial increases in the correlation coefficient will occur with other variables added to the combination.

The value of R can be tested by special formula in the F table (not shown) to see whether the multiple relationships are statistically significant. This is shown routinely in the printed output of the multiple regression procedure of SPSS.

Multiple Regression. Like simple regression, multiple regression involves prediction, but from the basis of two or more variables. Like multiple correlation, multiple regression involves knowing the relationship of two or more variables at the same time. In this case, however, the multiple variables are combined into a single set of predictors, each of which can be known for its individual contribution to the prediction statement.

Multiple regression is calculated like partial correlation coefficients. That is, all other independent variables are held constant while each individual variable is calculated for its straight-line relationship to the dependent variable.

Calculating multiple regression is complicated, but with a computer statistical package at our command, we need only summon it to do the work. We will continue our previous example to describe how multiple regression uses the separate and combined relationships of independent variables (age and education) to predict the dependent variable (income).

Multiple regression is based on knowing both how well *each* independent variable predicts the dependent variable and how well *all* in combination predict the dependent variable. The *multiple regression equation* has as its basis the same straight-line formula used in figuring the best-fit line in simple regression. But because of the presence of multiple variables, the regression equation has several different slopes (*b*'s,)—one for each independent variable in the equation.[12] These *b* slopes are *partial regression coefficients*. The coefficients are different for each predictor variable. For example, $b_{xy \cdot z}$ is a ratio of how much *y* increases for every unit of increase in *x*, with the effects of *z* held constant; while $b_{zy \cdot x}$ is a ratio of how much *y* increases for every unit of increase in *z*, with *x* held constant.

The multiple regression equation tells us the relative contribution of each predictor variable in estimating values of the predicted variable. But the mathematics are fairly complicated—involving the standardization of the *b* coefficients by first calculating so-called Beta (β) coefficients. Skipping the mathematics, once the values for *a* (the *y*-intercept) and the *b* associated with each independent variable are calculated, we can substitute actual figures of the age (X_1) and the education (X_2) of any respondent into the formula, multiply each by the appropriate *b*, and figure the likely income of that respondent. How accurate this prediction will be is shown by the value of R^2. If it is 1.00 we will be perfectly accurate in our estimate each time, but it will, of course, always be somewhat less.

In summary, calculating the separate relationship of each independent variable with income tells us how much of the difference in income can be partially explained by its common-variance relationship with each, when all other variables are controlled simultaneously. Additionally, by knowing the interrelationships of all independent variables—R^2, the coefficient of multiple determination—we can know how much income variation can be explained by its common-variance relationship with all independent variables at the same time.

Factor Analysis. Many variables in a survey are correlated. Factor analysis is a tool for simplifying and clarifying those relationships.

Recall that correlation is the notion that variables tend to "go together"—to have something in common, to share variance, to overlap each other, to vary together. Correlation is the basis for prediction.

As previously shown in Figure 6.31*a*, we make an *intercorrelation matrix* to show how variables tend to associate with each other. However, this matrix may hide a significant piece of information: that two variables may be highly interrelated but not measure the same thing. For example, "fear of strangers" and "fear of persecution" may be highly related, but they both may not be measures of paranoia.

Factor analysis is a mathematical technique that recalculates intercorrelations in terms of a few basic commonalities that may underlie them. In analysis of

---

[12]The formula is: $Y = a + b_1X_1 + b_2X_2 \ldots$, etc. (If all of the slopes are standardized so as to be in comparable units, they are called "beta weights," and the *a* drops out of the equation.)

variance (ANOVA) a "factor" is an independent variable. In factor analysis, a "factor" is a premise. It is a hypothetical concept that presumes that a few fundamental, common properties are shared by many variables, and that these common properties are more efficient explanations of human behavior than are the many variables considered individually.

So, factor analysis is a procedure for reexamining a large number of correlations, seeking to uncover certain basic properties they may have in common. If such properties exist, the variables that relate to each will tend to fall naturally into "clusters." Each cluster is composed of those variables that share common variance. Each cluster would include those variables that are highly interrelated and exclude those that have low or negative correlations. Of course, the theory is more pure than the practice.

Suppose we were studying six variables from the Model Survey: (1) knowledge of the day-care tax plan, (2) number of children, (3) newspaper readership, (4) trust in politicians, (5) past voting behavior, and (6) independence from political party affiliation. If we expressed their intercorrelations in the kind of matrix shown in Figure 6.31, they might look like Table I in Figure 6.32. (The numbers at the top refer to the same variables as along the side.)

The table shows that three variables (1, 2, and 3) are highly interrelated but have little relationship with the other three. These other three (4, 5, and 6) are themselves highly interrelated but have low or negative correlation with any of the other three. We recognize from the matrix that there seem to be two, not six, concepts being measured here. (Of course, the example is unrealistically simple.) Graphically, the six variables form two clusters as in Figure 6.32b. The circles in Figure 6.32b illustrate how the variables might look if we overlap them by the variance they have in common. Three variables cluster in one group, and the others cluster in a different group. The first cluster seems to have a dimension of *self-interest* binding the three variables together. This is only our judgment, of course, but it appears that having children is linked with a tendency to seek information about the day-care plan. *Political disinterest* seems to be common to the second cluster, in which political distrust and inactivity go together with self-styled independence from political labels. We must name the clusters according to our understanding of the common relationship; there is nothing automatic about the mathematics of factor analysis to tell us what we have found conceptually.

If converted by the mathematics of factor analysis, the clusters become factors. The analysis turns the intercorrelation matrix into a *factor matrix*. The factor matrix shows, by determining the amounts of variance held in common by all variables, the correlations of each variable with a common property—the factor. The correlations of variables with each factor are called *factor loadings*. If a variable correlates highly with a factor, it is said to have a high loading. If it correlates poorly, it has a low loading. Still using fictitious data, converting the intercorrelation matrix into a factor matrix could produce a table like Table J in Figure 6.33. (Asterisks by numbers indicate the high-loading variables in each column.) As we see. the first three

a. Intercorrelation Matrix

TABLE 1: RELATION OF AWARENESS AND FAMILY
STATUS TO POLITICAL ATTITUDES

	(1)	(2)	(3)	(4)	(5)	(6)
(1) Knowledge	1.00	.90	.95	.03	.14	.13
(2) Children		1.00	.85	.15	.10	-.07
(3) Readership			1.00	.08	-.12	-.13
(4) Distrust				1.00	.93	.74
(5) Nonvoting					1.00	.69
(6) Independent						1.00

b. Intercorrelation graphic

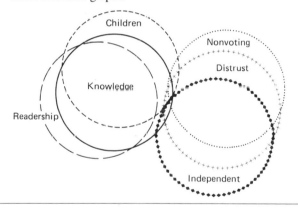

Figure 6.32. Intercorrelation of variables in two factors.

TABLE J: FACTOR LOADING OF AWARENESS, FAMILY
STATUS, AND POLITICAL ATTITUDES

Variable	Factor I Self-Interest	Factor II Political Disinterest
(1) Knowledge	.72*	.04
(2) Children	.88*	.23
(3) Readership	.79*	-.22
(4) Distrust	.21	67*
(5) Nonvoting	-.15	.83*
(6) Independence	-.01	.57*

Figure 6.33. Example of a matrix with two factors.

variables load highly on Factor I (self-interest) and load weakly or negatively on Factor II (political disinterest). The last three variables load highly on political disinterest and weakly or negatively on self-interest.

In summary, the principle of factor analysis is that it redefines the intercorrelations of each variable with each other to show how each correlates with a common property. We must name the factors according to our understanding of the common relationship.

Nonparametric Measures of Relationship. When our data does not meet the assumptions for parametric statistics, we should use nonparametric tests of relationships. Many tests have been developed for this kind of measurement. We will mention only a few. Each has certain advantages and disadvantages. The calculations are simple enough to do by hand,[13] but computer statistical packages also produce them.

Yule's Q Test. The Q test is used with nominal or ordinal variables in a 2×2 table, whether in the form of frequencies, proportions, or percentages. Like r (the correlation coefficient), Q values can range from $+1.00$ through 0 (for no relationship) to -1.00. But unlike r, values can reach 1.00 when the relationship is not perfect.

Phi (ϕ) Test. Sometimes called the index of mean square contingency, ϕ is used for 2×2 tables of nominal variables only. It can have values from $+1.00$ through 0 to -1.00 and, unlike Q, will reach 1.00 only when the relationship is perfect. It therefore has lower values than Q for the same data.

The symbol ϕ^2 represents the proportion of variation in the dependent variable that is explained by the independent variable. As an example, if we cross-tabulate attitude toward the drug treatment referendum with political party identification, and we find $\phi = .60$, then $\phi^2 = (.60)^2$ or $.36$, which means that 36 percent of the respondents' attitudes toward the proposition is associated with their party identification. This is a powerful test, and makes ϕ one of the most useful nonparametric statistics for survey data.

Goodman and Kruskal's Gamma (γ) Test. To test relationships when our data is ordinal—variables with least/greater/most response categories—we use the γ test, which accepts only frequency data. It is figured on the same principle as the Q test and, in fact, $\gamma = Q$ in a 2×2 table, but ordinal data would typically have more categories.

If we cross-tabulated low, medium, and high sense of social involvement by low, medium, and high media use, and calculated γ to be .37, we would conclude there was only a moderate relationship.

---

[13]See William Mendenhall, Lyman Ott, and Richard Larson, *Statistics: A Tool for the Social Sciences* (North Scituate, Mass.: Duxbury, 1974); H. T. Reynolds, *Analysis of Nominal Data* (Beverly Hills, Ca.: Sage, 1977); and other "Further Readings" at the end of this chapter.

Goodman and Kruskal's Tau (τ) Test. The tau test is used to measure relationships with nominal variables, as we used regression to measure relationships with interval data. It shows the proportionate reduction in prediction error on the dependent variable based on knowing the independent variable.

Other Nonparametric Measures. There are a large number of association tests for various combinations of different data types. To determine which will be effective for a particular situation, we refer to "decision-tree" tables that allow us to answer questions about our data and arrive at the appropriate statistical test.[14]

REPORT WRITING

The survey is not complete until a full written report has been given to those who need the results. We tailor-make each report for the specific data user, who may be a single commercial client, a group of government decision makers, the scholarly community, or the wider public. To each of these we offer interpretation at an appropriate level. We strive to communicate, not to impress.

In this section we offer a few general remarks about report writing, point out pitfalls in data reporting, give tips on writing style for reports and tables, and comment briefly on use of survey data.

What To Report

The report addresses the problem studied. We present first a summary of the major findings. We then take up the research hypotheses one by one, stating each specific finding and documenting it with one or more tables detailing the evidence. We then proceed to explain the differences and similarities between groups by cross tabulating with other variables.

We routinely present tables of the principal study variables, broken down by all demographic characteristics, but we don't stop here.

Journalistic polls often report nothing beyond two-way cross-tabulations, which usually consist only of demographic characteristics. How frustrating it is to read a report about the public's evaluation of the local school system that says, "People of moderate incomes, those living in the northern part of the city, Republicans, older people, and women are least likely to think Model City's schools are doing a good job." We don't know whether it's their Republicanism, age, gender, income, or location that best explains their views about the schools.

Being "older," "Republican," and "female" may merely be three characteristics belonging to the same individuals, who are thus counted three times in the

---

[14]Frank M. Andrews et al., *A Guide for Selecting Techniques for Analyzing Social Science Data* (Ann Arbor: University of Michigan, Survey Research Center, undated).

reported statement. These relationships need to be analyzed with characteristics studied individually and in clusters in order to learn what would be most explanatory to report. But without an adequate-sized sample, extensive breakdowns cannot safely be done.

The more we subdivide the data, the fewer the number of respondents per group. The fewer the number of respondents per group, the greater must be differences among groups to be significant. If we want to find out how many women (one-half the sample) over 65 (one-tenth of these) with incomes below $5000 (one-tenth of these) are Democrats (one-third of these) who live in a union family (one-eighth of these) and who will admit that union endorsement of candidates influences their vote (one-half of these), there will be precious little of a sample on which to base conclusions. The example just cited, if the proportions were actual, would yield 1/9600 of the sample in one subgroup. With a sample of 600, we probably wouldn't have even one such person.

Despite the risk, we may desire to *explore relationships* down to even a dozen individuals, which will provide speculation, though not statistical proof, about what different types of people are thinking. If some results look intriguing, further investigation may be warranted through another survey or by depth interviews restricted to people with these characteristics.

If we have a series of random sample surveys of the same population that have identical questions on some behavior that is fairly stable across time, we could *pool* them to get enough respondents (a large N) for making detailed demographic breakdowns. This would allow us to draw conclusions about specific subgroups— say, young, married, well-educated, suburban liberals. If, however, the behavior studied fluctuates over time—for example, attitudes toward candidates during a campaign—pooling samples taken over several months could be highly misleading.

Sensible Use of Statistics

Just because a survey finding is not statistically significant does *not* mean we ignore it. We report what we found on all relationships that theoretically seemed important to investigate when we undertook the survey.

Scholarly articles tend to emphasize *confirming* data only. This is a mistake, because our failure to find a significant relationship triggers a search for alternative explanations. We emulate the detective who, having proved that the butler couldn't have done it, looks more closely at the governess. But merely because we couldn't establish a relationship between two variables doesn't mean there is none. Other researchers might improve upon our methods, mount a different attack for testing the same relationship, and find something we missed.

We use statistics to help distinguish findings that are significant—not likely due to chance and, hence, safe to report—but we don't get infatuated with statistics.

Not every statistically significant difference is an important theoretical difference. With very large samples, small differences are often statistically significant, but not necessarily useful in practice. Likewise, if we cross-tabulated every variable against every other variable, significant differences may show up between groups that would make no theoretical sense to report.

Common sense is a useful guide to crediting a statistic with importance. We don't want to make too much of small differences. In the Model Survey we seldom call readers' special attention to differences between groups unless they are at least 8 percentage points apart, and even those differences are not all going to be significant.

Likewise in reports we do not necessarily confine ourselves to the bare bones of the data. We do express our personal judgments of the meaning of the data. However, we clearly label findings and the observations we offer about implications for action, so that they are distinguished for the reader. Some researchers fear that speculation is not scientific. But the scientific approach demands only clear hypotheses, sound methods, and honest reporting. Speculation, so long as it is not disguised as proof, can aid others' understanding. And the speculations of one study become the hypotheses of the next.

Pitfalls in Data Interpretation

Imaginative analysis will squeeze every insight and proof possible out of a set of survey data. But good data can be misinterpreted. An ever-present danger is that we will draw spurious conclusions based on incomplete information or bad judgment. A spurious conclusion is one drawn falsely. Some false conclusions drawn from survey (and other research) findings are those that: (1) see cause-and-effect relationships where none exist, (2) explain relationships with the wrong variables, (3) overlook the presence of important intervening variables, and (4) give undue importance to meaningless relationships. These and other problems are described below.

Assuming Cause-and-Effect Relationships. Because two conditions exist together does not mean that one causes the other. When we speak about one variable "explaining" the other, we usually mean "is associated with" rather than "makes the other happen." Example: Our preelection survey for an upcoming primary battle shows that people who read the *Model City Bugle*'s editorial endorsement of the conservative GOP candidate are more likely to vote for him. But if we rested with this knowledge, we might not have a factual explanation of that candidate's eventual victory. Instead, by doing an election-day intercept survey of voters at the polling place, we find a decisive number of Democrats are crossing over party lines to defeat the liberal GOP candidate for the purpose of helping the conservative to win whom the Democrats consider easier to beat.

In surveys we often think of demographic characteristics as "causing" attitude variations, as well as events occurring earlier in time as "causing" those that take place later. But we must be careful of our judgments. Social research seeks causal relationships, but the survey by itself is not a sufficient tool to prove them. As noted in Chapter 1, the model of the field experiment is our most appropriate approach to the study of causes and effects.

Explaining Relationships with the Wrong Variables. This is mostly a problem of weak theory or incomplete information. Consider the following example of a survey finding: Heavy smokers know less about the cancer dangers of cigarette smoking than do nonsmokers. Conclusion in the report: a public information campaign to increase smokers' knowledge of cancer dangers will cause smokers to quit. Evaluation of the report: *wrong*. In reality, what heavy smokers don't know about the dangers of cancer, they don't want to know. This facet of human behavior is called selective inattention to information that is disagreeable to the reader.

Overlooking Intervening Variables. A relationship might not be as direct as it appears. Example: the Model Survey found that age is negatively correlated with use of marijuana and with approval of its use. We might conclude that something about youth leads to approval of marijuana use. But when the question on marijuana use is made into a control for the question on approval, young people who don't use marijuana are just as likely to be opposed to its use as older people who don't use it. However, fewer youth disapprove of marijuana use.

Misinterpreting Unimportant Relationships. A relationship that coexists in space but not in individuals has been called the "ecological fallacy." Example: most minority groups are in the center city. Reported alcoholism rates in the center city are higher than elsewhere. From this data alone, it's a fallacy to conclude that minority group members are more prone to alcoholism. Surveys can try to avoid the ecological fallacy by finding characteristics that coexist in the same individual—although not all traits found in the same individuals are necessarily related in any meaningful way.

Confusing Reporting with Prediction. Example: if most respondents in the sample support the mayor, he will win the election. Not necessarily. A preelection poll typically asks, "If the election were being held today, who would you vote for . . . ?" But today is not election day. An intention to vote is not the act of voting. Events will intervene, many self-styled voters won't in fact vote on election day, and those who do vote may vote differently than they claimed they would in the comparative calm of their living room during the heat of the campaign period. Any reports of trial heats between candidates should point out the gaps that may lie between reports and later actual behavior.

Assuming a Static World. People do change opinions—in response to new situations, to new perceptions of situations, to new utterances of public officials. A view once thought intolerable (e.g., going to war) might reverse in a relatively short time with a series of national setbacks. Unwillingness to support new funds for a municipal water filtration plant may change rapidly after the media report that contamination has occurred in Model City's water supply.

Reporting the Same Relationship in Several Guises. Called *covariance,* several items might be so closely related that looking at them separately adds no new information. Normally, high income is correlated with high education. Thus, if the survey shows higher-income respondents approving a new domed stadium and higher-educated respondents also approving, it is probably reporting many of the same people twice. Instead, suppose we control for income and cross-tabulate education with stadium approval. If we then find that the few higher-educated poor in the sample are against the stadium, this would suggest that we report income as an important variable and sort out the effects of education separately.

Generalizing from Small Samples. Currently fewer young people identify themselves as Republicans than Democrats. Example: but suppose, in the Model Survey, of the very youngest people (18–21) who voted, a higher percentage (66%) voted for Ronald Reagan, the GOP winner in 1980 than did other age groups. Does this mean that the Republican party is being revived by an influx of new young voters? Not necessarily. There were only 21 such young people in the sample. Clearly, a few swallows don't make a summer.

Extrapolating to Different Populations. Extrapolation is the attempt to project findings to conditions and people different from those studied. Example: the Model Survey found the Democratic nominee for governor to be way ahead of the Republican opponent. This could discourage the Republicans unduly if they generalize from the sentiments of these center-city people to predict the behavior of the entire state's voters. We do sometimes extrapolate, because we cannot study every population, but we use care and notify the readers of the leap we are making.

Concluding No Relationship. We shouldn't be too hasty in concluding there is no relationship just because our statistics aren't significant. Before giving up, we should reexamine our methods for flaws—poor question wording, too small a sample, interviewer errors, wrong population sampled, incorrect tests, lack of understanding of subject matter subtleties. We sometimes find that out of a large number of items none seems to be related. Perhaps each truly represents distinct parts of people's lives. Perhaps we have not asked the right question to tap the various parts. Or, perhaps there is a deeper logic that allows opposite views to be expressed by the same person. For example, early surveys on the women's movement showed middle aged and older women opposed to the movement yet, at the same time, hoping it would succeed. The explanation for the contradiction seemed to be that although mature women did not want to unsettle their own accommodation with their female status, they also hoped for a new world for their daughters.

Stating the Obvious. A highly expensive survey was reported with the earth-shaking conclusion that many of the problems of the poor were associated with their poverty. The researcher went on to recommend that one solution to the problem was to raise the standard of living of the poor.

Reporting Data

It's dismaying that we so often seem willing to put great effort and care into designing and conducting high-quality surveys, only to sacrifice our potential impact with reports heavily encumbered with jargon, statistical notation, and textbook rhetoric. Research, to be used must be seen as useful. This means, first, that it must be understood and, second, that it must be relevant to the user's situation. Research reports should present the statistical data, a narrative of findings, and our interpretations of what the findings mean and what decisions may be taken based on them.

Tables are needed in reports to present details more efficiently than can be done in text discussion. But tables alone are insufficient. Most readers, including researchers, are intimidated by large masses of closely spaced, unexplained numbers. A rule of thumb is that text should be able to stand without tables. That is, if the table were omitted, the text would still convey the highlights of the findings. Similarly, tables should be so graphically clear that they can be understood without supporting text. However, we prefer that tables do not stand alone. The text must support them.

Report Style and Format. Recommendations for writing clear reports are offered in Checklist 35.

CHECKLIST 35

Tips for Writing Reports

1. *Use fractions.* Percentages can be intimidating, particularly if strung out in a long series. If close to a simple fraction, use it. Instead of saying: "65 percent of the women and 32 percent of the men . . ." say: "About two-thirds of the women and one-third of the men. . . ." Of course, stringing together several fractions can be confusing too.
2. *Put percentages in parentheses.* Using the above example, say: "About two-thirds of the women (65%) and one-third of the men (32%) said . . ."
3. *Use simple ratios.* Where possible, use ratios for comparisons: "Women by a 2-to-1 margin over men (65% to 32%) were more likely to . . ." or, "Women were twice as likely as men . . ."
4. *Think in whole numbers.* Same example: "Two out of three women (65%) as compared with only one out of every three men (32%) said . . ."
5. *Use simple fractions.* It's safe to use *one-half, one-third, one-fourth,* and *one-fifth* (one out of five) to express data. Beyond these, understanding becomes

difficult. People don't think in terms of *one-seventh* (14%). As noted in Item 7, the tenths can be used effectively to compare fractions.

6. *Use sensible fractions.* It's a bit silly to report on "... a sixteenth of the Catholics (6%) and a twenty-fourth of the Jews (4%)..." Keep it simple and sensible: "Only a handful of Catholics (6%) and Jews (4%) said ..."

7. *Use comparable fractions.* It's confusing to mix fractions. We go as far as mixing "... one-fourth of the boys and one-half of the girls ...." But otherwise we try to keep consistency in fractions: "... one-tenth of the married people as compared with three-tenths of the singles and seven-tenths of those divorced..."

8. *Use common referents.* It's also confusing to mix referents, as in, "... five-eighths of the Republicans, seven-tenths of the Democrats, and three-fourths of the Independents..." In this instance, where the numbers are close, it might be more helpful to use a common point, as: "... just about three-fourths of the Independents (76%) and slightly smaller groups of Republicans (72%) and Democrats (70%) said ..."

9. *Don't trivialize statistics.* In the text, we shouldn't report every single statistic we get. In particular, stringing together a series of percentages can impede understanding: "The answers were definitely yes (17%), probably yes (25%), probably no (27%), definitely no (14%), no opinion/not sure (8%), indeterminate/miscellaneous response (5%), refused to answer (3%), not asked the question (1%)."

10. *Don't trivialize responses.* Item 9 also is an example of overreporting of categories. We get the important information we need from knowing: "... definitely yes (17%), probably yes (25%), probably no (27%), and definitely no (14%)." We might simply report that people divided about evenly between yes (42%) and no (41%).

11. *Be sensible about small values.* Of course it is as important to report negligible numbers as it is to cite big numbers: "Only 4 percent felt...". But further analysis may be silly: "This 4 percent divided into people who were favorable (3%) or who had no opinion (1%)."

12. *Report whole percentages.* Surveys suffer from errors due to sampling. Saying "... Democrats (45.3%) and Republicans (22.6%)..." is false precision. Instead, we report whole figures, rounding off the decimal places to the nearest whole number. If the decimal is .5, a rule of thumb can be to round off even numbers *up* (44.5% = 45%) and odd numbers *down* (43.5% = 43%).

13. *Include an appendix.* Except for academic journal articles, it is very helpful to include a technical appendix in all reports. The appendix should carry all tables (with all response categories), a description of the sample, notes on the statistical tests used and how interpreted, and a copy of the questionnaire.

14. *Verbalize table highlights.* Tables should not stand alone. Many readers cannot or will not read tables. The text should highlight important findings and provide the supporting table nearby.

15. *Explain statistical significance.* In the introduction to the report, we explain what

"significance" means for this study ("Only 5 times in 100 could such a difference occur by chance—errors due to sampling.") In the text, we say: "This relationship is well above that which could be explained by chance alone." We do *not* use symbols in the text, such as $p < .05$, to make this point.

16. *Provide a guide to significance.* In the introduction, we give readers a rule of thumb for interpreting statistical significance: probability more than .05 = not significant; probability less than .05 = significant; probability less than .01 = highly significant; and probability less than .001 = very highly significant.

17. *Report no more than three significance levels.* As a convention, we report only significance at .05, .01, and .001; *not* .03, .00002, or .10. In a nontechnical report we might choose one level of significance (usually .05) and apply it throughout.

18. *Use the term "significant" exclusively.* We don't use the word "significant" to mean important, since it has a narrow technical meaning in statistical studies.

19. *Report nonsignificant findings.* It's important to report findings that fail to confirm our research hypotheses. Say, "No significant differences were found between men and women, young and old, city and farm residents."

20. *Put symbols in footnotes.* We don't like to clutter the text with all kinds of statistical symbols (χ^2, D.F. = 6, $p < .01$, ϕ, τ, $\Sigma x - y$/SD, etc.). If we have to use a formula, we usually put it into the appendix.

21. *Describe the sample.* In the introduction, we indicate the total sample size and the population from which it is drawn. Refer readers to the detailed sample description in the appendix.

22. *Admit to small numbers.* We warn readers when numbers get small: "Blue collar workers under age 20 (although there were only eight in the sample) were all opposed to the gasoline tax."

23. *Write simply.* For the lay reader, a lengthy blurb on, say, multiple regression is statistical gobbledygook. This virtually assures that busy decision makers will ignore our findings. But we run the regressions and report our findings. We could say: "We tried to predict people's reactions to the event based on our knowledge of a combination of their characteristics."

24. *Be descriptive.* Describe relationships, don't just symbolize them: "About half of the differences in scores is accounted for by respondents' age, older people being better informed than younger people." *Not:* "We found $r = .72$, which means that age explains about one-half of the variance ($r^2 = .49$) in scores."

25. *Don't hide uncertainty.* There's nothing wrong with not being able to explain some finding. Either our theory is weak or we haven't studied all relevant variables. Admit it. Simply say: "We are unable to explain the difference." It may be seriously misleading (and unethical) if we pretend to have explanations. It may be helpful to future research to point out the gaps in theory.

26. *Be consistent in tense.* A rule of thumb is to write using the tense formula: "respondents were/data are." This means that we use *past* tense when describing what people said in response to our questions (findings), but use *present* tense when

stating the meaning of the findings (conclusions). Example: "Four-fifths of the respondents (81%) *approved* of the referendum. It *appears* that the measure will pass handily."

27. *Avoid overly artistic language.* A vocabulary of perhaps 2500 words is enough to write simple, declarative sentences for most clients' research needs. Straining for artistic, colorful language can be an obstacle to readers' understanding. The worst case could be phraseology that suggests "vive la difference" when the real finding is consistency and similarity.

28. *Avoid absolutes.*[15] It's misleading to say "The public feels . . ." when, in fact, we mean only that a large proportion of our respondents expressed a certain feeling. Surveys look for similarities and differences among people. We don't expect to find too many absolutes in human behavior.

29. *Distinguish intensity and extensity.* A common mistake is to report that " . . . there is strong support among Model City residents (85%) for this issue . . ." when we mean ". . . there is widespread support." How strongly (intensity) each individual supports the issue is different from the number (extensity) of people who support it.

30. *Report sampling error.* We periodically remind the reader that any finding is likely to be in a range of plus-or-minus some margin of error. In the introduction, we say: "Findings are not likely to be off by more than 4 percentage points in either direction, although conclusions for smaller parts of the sample, for example the 303 Democrats, will be less precise." At the relevant sections in the text, we note the amount of sample error associated with different types of findings.

31. *Be careful with sampling error.* Our survey may have four to five percentage points of sampling error in either direction from our estimate. As such, we should not report: ". . . A majority (51%) said 'yes and a minority (49%) said no . . .". The actual proportion of those saying yes may be anywhere between 46 and 56 percent. Similarly, 45 percent of the respondents is not a plurality when 42 percent of the respondents give a different answer. The difference is "too close to call," and should not be labeled as majorities or pluralities. People reading our report in haste may be unaware of the range of sampling error bracketing our estimates.

32. *Be approximate.* No figure is exact in a survey. Rather than pretending great precision, we report data as being "about," "around," "close to." It's one reason we use fractions, to convey a proper humility about social data— ". . . roughly half of the people . . ." or ". . . about two out of three . . .".

33. *Don't be surprised.* One person's surprise is another's naiveté. The kinds of judgments we avoid are those that suggest we have some stake in the outcome, such as: "It was surprising to find . . ." or "Remarkably few people said . . .".

---

[15]Some of the following points are adapted from Leo P. Crespi, *Some Technical Guidelines to Better Survey Reporting* (Washington, D.C.: International Communication Agency, 1971 [mimeo]).

We are not supposed to be surprised, only to find evidence that helps us accept or reject our hypotheses.

34. *Report the population.* If the sample is representative of the population, we should report the population ("Model City voters") and avoid such sample-oriented words as "respondents," "interviewees," "those surveyed," and the like. We use such terms only when we are skeptical of whether those studied do represent the population they're supposed to.

35. *Report timely events.* Because contemporary events influence answers and because intervening events may cause answers to change, it's important to tell readers what was happening at the time of the survey: ". . . the Mayor was indicted for tax fraud," "the Gay Rights rally turned into a riot," "the police went on strike . . ." and other ordinary events in Model City.

36. *Reprint the question.* Although a questionnaire is included in the appendix, we often reprint the entire question with the appropriate table in the text in order that readers know exactly what was asked. This enables them to check our interpretation.

37. *Don't use excessive footnotes.* Unless we're writing for an academic journal or a graduate thesis, footnotes should be used sparingly. Like formulas and tables, footnotes can be intimidating—especially to the busy, practical-minded executive. Don't for the sake of show (the so-called practice of building one's "scholarship index") pile up a long list of references in the text. The appendix can cite by major themes the literature that was reviewed.

38. *Write an executive summary.* Each report should have a brief overview of key findings and implications organized thematically. This is for many reports the make-or-break opportunity to catch the readers' interest. It must be brisk, straightforward, and action-oriented (whether "action" means a campaign decision or a call for further research). There is no room here for complicated analyses, statistical formulas, tables, or much else other than simple, lively, readable prose.

39. *Write to communicate.* Many writers write for themselves rather than for their clients. Much of this writing is self-conscious—overly artistic, complex, lofty. We follow an old advertising dictum in our reports: "If the Smiths can get it, the Smythes will get it too."

40. *Remember the code of ethics.* In Chapter 1, we described the minimum information about survey methods that ethically must be reported to clients and the public. The information includes survey dates, population, sample size, sample type (random or not), sampling error, question wording, and sponsorship. Additionally, we report nonresponse rates and any known biases that seem to have crept in and affected our findings.

Of course, we could have found more items for Checklist 36. Tips to good writing are endless. Perhaps the most important tip is to *want* to let readers understand our findings—both "what" was found and "how." This attitude rests on the belief that the reader has a right to comprehend us, and that our responsibility is to keep out of our writing anything of style or substance that obstructs the reader's ability to understand.

How Large Is Vast? For years researchers have argued over the adjectives used to describe findings. Some research has been attempted to quantify such terms as "vast majority," "sizable minority," "huge percentage," "great difference," "substantial proportion," "large plurality," "very few," and other terms that convey findings in *qualitative terms* that connote differences in sizes varying from minute to magnificent.[16]

There are no easy rules of thumb, but we offer a general guide for reporting sizes and differences. The aim is to make it easy for the report writer to be consistent by setting out only a few adjectives to connote consistently how much larger is one value than another or how much greater is one difference than another. Figure 6.34 presents a range of percentages and shows the simple fractions we associate with each as well as the phrases we use to convey size. Of course, the aptness of the phrase depends on whether we're at the lower or upper end of each range shown in Figure 6.34 (page 392). The following examples may help in reading Figure 6.34.

- We would interpret 9 to 11 percent as a "tenth" of the respondents; a "handful" as a group.
- We would interpret 31 to 35 percent as "a third" of the respondents; a "large minority" as a group.
- We would interpret a 44 percent versus 40 percent division of respondents not as a plurality for the first, but as "about two-fifths" in both cases.
- We would interpret 48 to 52 percent as "about half" of the respondents.

Next, Figure 6.35 (page 393) distinguishes several varying uses of the terms *significant* and *difference*.

Tables. Tables, as mentioned, are essential in the report as supplement and documentation to the text.

SPSS and other data handling packages can produce print-ready material—labeled tables one to a page that can be torn apart from the continuous computer printout. If desired, these can be reduced by a copying machine to 8½ × 11 inch sheets that can be neatly inserted in reports. Or, electrostatic printers can vary the size of the pages initially, and use a wide variety of book typefaces. But often we

---

[16]Leo P. Crespi, *How Many Is a Vast Majority?* (Washington, D.C.: International Communication Agency, 1971 [mimeo]). This test booklet illustrates some of the research efforts to quantify the meanings of phrases (*vast, overwhelming, substantial,* etc.) used with survey data. The subject is not yet closed.

Figure 6.34. Percentages, fractions, and meanings.

Percentage Range	Simple Fraction	Size as a Group
01–10	One-tenth	Negligible Very few A handful
11–20	One-fifth	Small Few
21–30	One-fourth A quarter Three-tenths	Minority
31–40	One-third Two-fifths	Large minority Plurality (if true)
41–49	Nearly half	Very large minority Large plurality (if true)
50	Half One out of two	Evenly divided (if close to 50–50)
51–60	More than half Three-fifths	Majority Most people
61–70	Two-thirds Seven-tenths	Large majority Substantial Considerable
71–80	Three-fourths Four-fifths	Very large majority Great
81–90	Nine-tenths	Overwhelming Very great
91–99	More than nine out of ten	Nearly everyone Almost all

will want to retype computer results into simpler tables that speak directly to the point and appear right where reference is made in the text.

Tables also can be made more understandable by observing a few basic principles. (These are outlined in Checklist 36, which is followed by example tables in Figures 6.36 to 6.39.)

Figure 6.35. Terms describing differences and significance.[a]

Significance Levels	Interpretation
$p > .05$ not significant	No significant difference Slight difference (if close to sampling error)
$p < .05$ significant	A difference Real difference
$p < .01$ highly significant	Great difference
$p < .001$ very highly significant	Great difference

Difference between Values	Interpretation
Within range of sampling error	No difference
Close to the limits of sampling error but not significant	Slight difference
Beyond sampling error: 　　　　　　$\pm 10\%$	 Different Somewhat more likely
$\pm 20\%$	Great difference More likely
more than $\pm 30\%$	Very great difference Much more likely

[a]Remember, with very large samples, small percentage differences may be statistically significant. Common sense must guide our interpretation.

CHECKLIST 36
Hints for Tables

1. *Report response rates in percentages.* Frequencies often confuse.
2. *Report the number of respondents on which the percentages are based.* Report the numerical base at the bottom of the table columns. Use $(n = \quad)$ for subgroup totals and $(N = \quad)$ for total sample (see Figure 6.36c).
3. *Account for all respondents.* The basic tables should include even those who do not answer a question; show the "no response" to the question percentage. Where needed for interpretation, the analysis is based on a subgroup, but then the table heading is labeled by that subgroup, such as "supporters only" (to show support for a referendum) or "Republicans only" (for candidate preference in a primary election). (Compare Tables K and L, Figure 6.36.)
4. *Round off to whole percentages.* Surveys of human populations produce "soft" data, and sampling error is almost always larger than 1 percent.

5. *Force tables to total 100 percent.* For the same reason as Item 4, do not say
    pretentiously, "Tables may not add to 100 percent due to rounding." Raise or
    lower the largest figure being added, since a percentage point affects it less.

6. *Place the percent symbol (%) at the top and bottom.* Use the percent symbol at the
    beginning of a column of figures, and use "100%" at the bottom of the column to
    indicate how the figures were added (see Table M, Figure 6.36).

7. *If figures are percentaged by rows:* Place the percent symbol (%) after the leftmost
    figures and show "100%" at the right end of each row (see Table N, Figure
    6.36).

8. *Use a uniform format for tables.* In cross-tabulations of two variables, place the
    dependent variable—the "row" variable we are predicting—at the left of the
    table. Place the independent variable—the "column" variable that we are predict-
    ing from—across the top of the table, with percentages calculated vertically (see
    Table M, Figure 6.36).

9. *As necessary, use "control" variables.* If a control variable appears to explain
    difference in the relationship of two other variables, or if differences are masked
    without holding the third variable constant, include it in the table (see Table O,
    Figure 6.36).

10. *Do not add when totals are more than 100%.* Instead of adding percentages for
    questions to which each respondent was permitted more than one response, indi-
    cate that multiple responses were permitted. Or, show percentages as "percent of
    all mentions" (see Figure 6.37).

11. *Avoid cross-tabulating more than three variables.* This is too complicated. If
    three or more variables need breaking down, use a "tree format (see Figure 6.39).
    Report frequencies (in parentheses) rather than percentages, because the subgroup
    sizes (n's) become so small in a typical community survey.

12. *Run several cross-tabulations against a single variable.* Doing this in one table
    saves space and improves comparison, for example, of demographics (see Figure
    6.38). In this instance, put the dependent variable at the top of the table, since it is
    the common thread. List independent variables down the side, skipping a line
    between the groups of response categories for each independent variable. Percent-
    ages must be figured across the rows of the table. Sometimes in newspaper
    column tables there will not be room for "no response," "100%," and "n
    = ..." Not every category of each independent variable need be listed (e.g.,
    people of other religions are left off Figure 6.38).

13. *Beware of too much data breakdown.* Don't break down tables by such detailed
    cross-tabulations that fewer than five respondents are left in one cell.

14. *Indicate significant findings with asterisks.* In the introduction and the appendix,
    provide a legend to denote levels of significance. Where significant findings appear
    in tables in the text, simple notation like an asterisk can denote statistical signifi-
    cance, instead of using symbols like $p < .05$.

15. *Make the table heading fully descriptive of the contents.* Tables should be capable
    of standing alone from the text, although they should be supported by text.

a.   Percentages based on total sample   b   Percentages based on those responding
                                                      to this question

TABLE K :   TABLE L :
ATTITUDE TOWARD SUBWAY SYSTEM   ATTITUDE TOWARD SUBWAY SYSTEM

	%
Favor	49
Undecided	21
Oppose	25
No response	5
	100% (N=600)

	%
Favor	51
Undecided	22
Oppose	27
	100% (N=570)

c.   Two-way cross-tabulation, percentaged down

TABLE M : PARTY IDENTIFICATION OF RACIAL GROUPS

		RACE		
		Black	White	Total
PARTY		%	%	%
	Republican	10	48	40
	Democratic	90	52	60
		100%	100%	100%
		(n=120)	(n=480)	(N=600)

d.   Two-way cross tabulation, percentaged across

TABLE N : RACIAL COMPOSITION OF PARTIES

		RACE		
PARTY	Black	White	Total	
Republican	5%	95	100%	(n=240)
Democratic	30%	70	100%	(n=360)
	20%	80%	100%	(N=600)

e.   Three-way cross-tabulation (cross-tabulation with a control variable)

TABLE O: PARTY IDENTIFICATION OF RACIAL GROUPS, CONTROLLED FOR AGE

	AGE								
	YOUNG			OLD			TOTAL		
	Black	White	Total	Black	White	Total	Black	White	Total
PARTY	%	%	%	%	%	%	%	%	%
Republican	10	10	10	10	85	70	10	48	40
Democratic	90	90	90	90	15	30	90	52	60
	100%	100%	100%	100%	100%	100%	100%	100%	100%
n=	(60)	(240)	(300)	(60)	(240)	(300)	(120)	(480)	(600)

Figure 6.36. Examples of tables for reports.

Q.1.   "What are the most important problems you see facing Model City Today? "

	% (of respondents)	% (of all mentions)
Taxes	65	49
Crime	45	33
Air pollution	15	11
Poor bus service	10	7
	*	100%

(* totals more than 100%
because some respondents
mentioned more than one
problem.)

Figure 6.37. Table with more than one response permitted.

TABLE P: ATTITUDE TOWARD DRUG-EDUCATION REFERENDUM

Total sample responding	51%	22	27	100%	(571)
Men	49%	26	25	100%	(280)
Women	53%	18	29	100%	(291)
Young (18 - 29)	60%	20	20	100%	(180)
Middle-aged (30-59)	52%	18	30	100%	(200)
Old (60 plus)	41%	28	31	100%	(191)
Grade school	30%	10	60	100%	(60)
High school	50%	20	30	100%	(340)
College	60%	30	10	100%	(171)
Republicans	75%	20	5	100%	(110)
Independents	50%	19	31	100%	(228)
Democrats	41%	25	34	100%	(228)
Protestants	67%	22	11	100%	(252)
Catholics	29%	20	51	100%	(142)

Figure 6.38. Several variables cross-tabulated against a single variable.

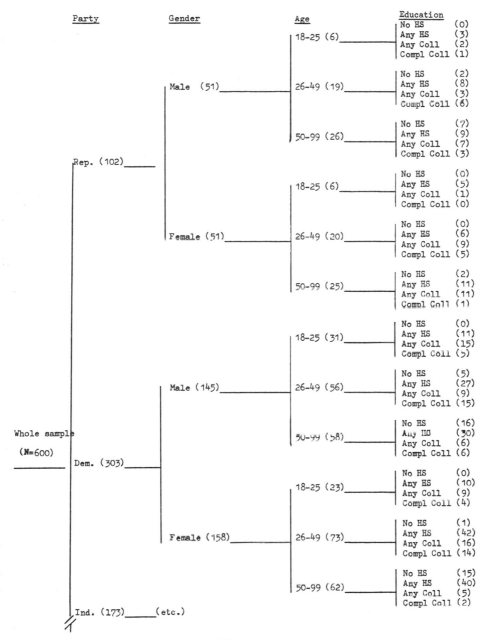

Figure 6.39. Breakdown tree.

Additional Reports

It may be necessary to go beyond straightforward reporting to make the survey useful. Certain ancillary materials are also helpful. Several ideas are introduced below.

Figure 6.40. Distinguishing findings and action statements [a]

Findings	*Descriptive statements: Data* Tells what is there: —what conditions exist —and how they compare with other conditions: e.g., how large, how many, who, where, how intense, how frequent, when . . . etc. —report in the past tense
Conclusions	*Interpretive statements: Meaning* Tells why it is there, and so what: —explains causes and relationships —tells why important in time and context —gives reasons and logic —suggests what the condition indicates —relates to previous/future conditions —relates to present policy —report in the present tense
Implications	*Predictive statements: Guidance* Tells what to do, and what will happen if you don't —actions to take (options) —consequences to expect from inaction —reactions to expect to action (impact) Advocates what it takes to change conditions —suggests courses of action —compares alternative outcomes
Recommendations	*Prescriptive statements: Allocation* Tells how to do it; what it takes to act: —allocates resources required for each action: e.g., quantity, type, time and cost of human and material resources —schedules convergence in time and space —dictates tone, quality, direction of position —sets specific achievement indicators.

[a] Adapted from Gerald Hursh-César, *Analysts' Guide* (Washington, D.C.: International Communication Agency, 1980 mimeo).

Action Reports. For some users, a report that includes only findings will not be sufficient. If the survey was done to suggest a course of action, such as for a candidate planning an election campaign, a lobbying effort, or an evaluation of a government program, the report should include the implications of the findings.

Figure 6.40 distinguishes the various types of statements we might make in reporting our findings and their implications. At what level we can comment depends upon the kinds of other information available to us. Obviously, we have to be pretty knowledgeable to state an implication leading to a change in policy; or to make a recommendation for the investment of time, money, and other resources. An example of implications drawn for the mayoral reelection campaign in Model City is presented in Figure 6.41. Note that directly following a table and its narrative interpretation, we can place a pertinent comment. We label and indent it to indicate that it is not data from the survey but the application of the background knowledge of the researcher to suggest implications for action.

Additional Reports. A series of initial reports should answer all of the questions the client has asked or the researcher has hypothesized. But the utility of a survey can be magnified with special reports based on a thorough analysis of a single question, or an attitude profile of a single demographic group.

There is no end to the analysis that can flow from a set of survey data. Reading the initial reports will generate questions from the data users about seeming inconsistencies, surprises, and anomalies. We do not close shop until all explanations have been given. The survey budget should anticipate additional computer data analysis beyond initial printouts.

> **Nearly three-quarters of the people in his own party believe that the mayor is not a strong leader or a hard worker, while three-fifths think he is not firm enough in his stands. But he is overwhelmingly seen as loyal to the party and as being honest.**
>
> *COMMENT:* **Model City is essentially a one-party town. It is the mayor's party, and his perceived loyalty gives him a great advantage to exploit in the campaign. The party is stronger than the candidate, and must therefore become the predominant campaign theme. It can carry him to victory.**
>
> **Much can be made of the mayor's perceived honesty—particularly since the voters say "honesty" is an important reason for voting for a mayoral candidate. Use his honesty to counteract the negatives about his industry and leadership. For example, develop the theme:** *"He's working hard to give you an honest chance."*
>
> **We must combat the "wishy-washy" and leadership image head-on. Take the two controversial issues (liquor control and industrial pollution) on which our opponent's stand is unclear to the voters, and have the mayor take firm positions, never wavering once from them. Project his firmness, and make an issue of the opposition's uncertainty.**

Figure 6.41. Labeling researchers' comments.

Follow-up

Even though the complete report has been delivered, our work on the survey may not yet be over. We need to follow up to make sure it is fully used.

Ensuring Use. Often "truth" will not win without an advocate. In campaign research, we often have to stack the survey data up against the folk wisdom of the wise old "pols" who surround the candidate and try to preserve their influence by defaming the survey and the "pollster." In evaluation of government programs, we may have to defend the research against attacks by program managers whose careers are threatened by critical findings. In academic research, our results may contradict establishment "laws" that have been ensconced in textbooks and often die hard. Or, in corporate research, our findings may conflict with a top executive's pet idea that has already been sold to the board of directors.

Researchers seldom are the final decision makers. Our skill is limited in satisfying the policy maker's need to take into account other concerns—financial, ethical, social, political. But we should make certain that the survey findings are given a hearing and are correctly perceived. If decisions are made contrary to the survey findings, it should not be because we failed to argue our case.

The problem may be more serious than nonuse of findings. If a user deliberately and publicly misrepresents the data, we may have to protect our reputation as researchers by disavowing misstatements.

We should also try to protect the user from overreacting to the findings. Candidates are notorious for reacting with work-slackening euphoria when shown to be ahead in a survey and with debilitating depression when behind. Some political managers refuse to share much of their self-commissioned research with their candidates for this reason. The survey questionnaires are not the decisive election-day ballots.

Sharing Data. Full utilization of survey data by the immediate client is rare. Media researchers skim off the cream for a series of topical reports. They will contend that the public's attention span will not extend to deeper analysis. Campaigners seldom have the time to absorb more than basic tabulations during the campaign, and they almost never have the money, energy, or incentive to follow up their polls after the election. Commercial researchers are usually rewarded for their decision-making advice, not for theoretical implications of their work.

All this means is that the wider society loses out. Here academics can make a major contribution. With access to surveys produced by others, scholars can more patiently reexamine the data for important relationships. This is called secondary analysis.

In order to encourage wider research use, archives are needed. Preeminent in the social sciences is the Inter-University Consortium based at the University of

Michigan's Survey Research Center (SRC). The consortium compiles its own studies for its members and promotes sharing of individual scholars' data as well. The Roper archive at the University of Connecticut receives syndicated poll materials, copies of which can be purchased.

Much remains to be done to capture for scholarly use the fugitive results of candidate surveys. Understandably there is sensitivity about releasing this information during or soon after a campaign. But respected neutral agencies such as state historical societies and universities can cultivate potential donors by timely approaches and by assuring limited access to sensitive data until a suitable time. Media organizations are often amenable to others using their polls but cannot take time to service requests for additional interpretation or duplication. Scholars will have to arrange to get copies of data and codebooks.

Commercial polling firms usually do not reveal their clients, but they might be induced to ask clients routinely if, after a period of time, someone with academic goals could use the data.

As archiving of survey data becomes more common, comparability can be facilitated by developing standardized codes and data storage techniques. Ideally, the data would be stored in a form accessible by remote computer terminals. Researchers could then tap into the data stored across many studies, many years, and in many places.

Publication. The widest possible use of survey data is ensured by publication. The substantive results may themselves be interesting to people beyond the immediate users. But the data will quite often reveal more fundamental aspects of human behavior that if properly circulated, may trigger other researchers to new discoveries of their own. That is why we seek to publish in news releases, popular and specialized magazines, and in scholarly journals. No one gains if we squirrel away our data for exclusive use on some far-off day that may never come.

PROCESSING DATA FOR OTHER KINDS OF SURVEYS

All other kinds of surveys—phone, mail, panel, and intercepts—converge at the point of data compilation, so few adjustments in data processing and analysis need be made. Major adjustments, however, in the speed of processing are required for election day intercept surveys.

Panel Studies

Since we reinterview the same individuals at least once in a panel survey, we must make sure that any new data is correctly associated with the old data of the same respondent. This is done by matching case numbers. There will always be shrinkage in the size of the sample, because we will fail to find some of the original respondents, or because they refuse to be interviewed again. We will have to have the computer designate those cases as "missing data" from the second wave.

Data Cards. It is unwise to add data to already-punched cards. There is danger of overpunching, resulting in the destruction of first-wave data. Therefore, a new set of cards is used. Additional cards from the reinterview must contain the basic study and case number, a new card number, plus the addition of a prefix digit to indicate the wave number. If a rotational sample design is used as described in Chapter 2, the different rotating groups have to be designated.

At some computer installations, the new data cards will have to be physically integrated with the old. This requires checking to make sure no case is lost or interchanged. A card will have to be prepared for each member of the first wave, with an indication of whether data was obtained in the second wave on that case.

For those using SPSS, it is possible to merely add a new deck, with an ADD VARIABLES instruction, but the cards must be in the exact order of the original deck. This means that there must be a card for every original respondent, although all but the study and case number will have to be shown as missing data for the uncontacted respondents. A computer check of the match of case numbers is mandatory to avoid mixups.

Analysis. The purpose of doing a panel study is to measure changes in single individuals. Because the successive surveys are of the same sample, statistics appropriate for independent samples cannot be used to analyze panel change. Instead, we use *contingency analysis,* with statistical tests such as chi-square. The basic purpose of panel analysis is to identify those who change between time 1 and time 2. Suppose we were interested in knowing how much new support or opposition has developed for the Model City drug-abuse treatment program that we described previously. This can be easily shown with a simple 2×2 table that compares respondents' answers (for or against) to the second interview with their answers to the first (see Figure 6.42).

Note the four groups shown in Figure 6.42.

- Group A—"positive changers": those who were against the program previously but are for it now.
- Group B—"negative standpatters": those against the program both previously and now.
- Group C—"positive standpatters": those for the program both previously and now.

		Second interview	
		For	*Against*
First interview	*Against*	A	B
	For	C	D

Figure 6.42. Panel analysis of changes in people's responses.

- Group D—"negative changers": those for the program previously but against it now.

Suppose we were campaigning for the drug program. Each group is interesting in its own right. For example, we would want to know for groups A and D what changed their minds, when, why, and how strongly do they feel now. We might write off group B as the diehards against the program whom we should not waste further campaign resources to convert to the cause. We might examine group C in depth to try to understand the core reasons that hold their support. This panel analysis can be most useful for practical decisions—especially when we link people's support or opposition to specific sources of information, to themes that appeal to them, to trends in other aspects of their lives, and to intervening events occurring between the surveys.

Intercept Surveys

For an election day intercept survey, data processing above all must be speedy. Its usefulness lasts only a single night, as far as the sponsoring media are concerned.

Advance Preparation. First, the survey should be completely precoded. No time can be taken for establishing codes on open-end questions. All programming to report data must be done in advance and proved by rehearsal to work as expected. All possible relevant display tables must be ordered and tried out with the use of dummy (but plausible) data cards. Many tables will turn out to be wasted when the hypotheses they tested get no support, but they have to be available. (Destroy the dummy cards before election night!)

Data Transmission. Likewise we must arrange for almost simultaneous transfer of the interview data from the field to the survey headquarters. At a fixed time early in the day, interviewers are scheduled to call in the responses they have received to give us a head start in entering the data into the computer file. Then interviewers make second calls with the remaining responses after the polls have closed. Survey headquarters predetermines the exact time for call-ins—based on number and length of calls expected at each time period—to avoid jam-ups. The number of operators and phones required is worked out, and all participants are given a live rehearsal.

Headquarters operators use a script to elicit the information needed from the interviewers (who get the same script in their training kits). This process economizes on time and eliminates misunderstandings. (Figure 6.43 presents an example of a ballot with reading instructions superimposed.) The operators enter the precoded responses onto coding sheets or, alternatively, use a computer input device while on the phone, sending the data directly to the computer without keypunching by another operator. This latter procedure is dangerous because it skips verification.

Weighting. A brief review of the way the intercept sample was drawn (see Chapter 2) will identify the occasion in which weighting of incoming data is required. Recall the basic design:

- All precincts in the city are separated into three sample strata desired for analysis (we use three distances from the center of the city).
- Within each stratum, precincts are rank-ordered (alternating high to low with low to high) by partisan vote (percent Republican) in a typical past election. This is our base year for projecting voting turnout and interviewing rates.
- The number of precincts in which interviewing is to be done is decided. We use 25 precincts because our purpose here is only to provide color commentary to the election night analysis, not to predict the results—for which we would need a larger sample.
- The skip interval for selecting precincts is calculated by dividing total voter turnout in the city in the base year by the number of precincts (25) for interviewing.
- Within each stratum, we cumulate precinct voting figures, just as we do with block populations in the Model in-the-home Survey. That is, we treat all precincts as one list—a string of voting figures—and we move through the list cumulating vote totals and marking off as sampling points those 25 precincts indicated by the skip interval.
- Each of the 25 sampling-point precincts represents $\frac{1}{25}$ of the total city vote, so each has equal weight in the sample, although each is not equal in size. Remember, the size of the precinct for interviewing purposes is no more relevant than the size of the block in the Model Survey. In each case, we are going to try to obtain the same number of interviews per sampling point (5 per block in the Model, and 100 per precinct here).
- Because each precinct equally represents $\frac{1}{25}$ of the city's vote, we will try to interview the same number of people in each. We decide on 100 interviews per precinct, based on considerations of precinct sizes, statistical reliability, and interviewing work loads.

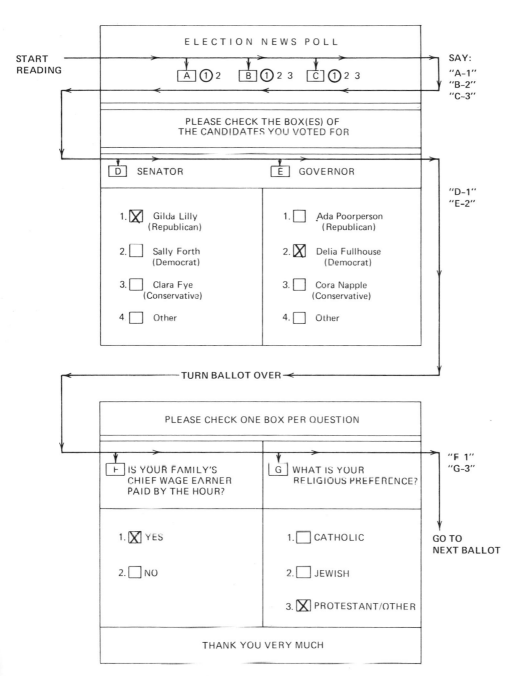

Figure 6.43. Example of the sequence in which answers are called in for each election day ballot.

- For its (first-stage) selection into the sample, the precinct is only a device for locating respondents around the city. However, the size of the precinct is important for determining the rate (second-stage sampling fraction) at which we try to interview people there. Since precincts do vary greatly in numbers of voters, we figure a different sampling fraction for each by dividing the precinct's total vote in the base year by 100.
- Thus, in a sample precinct with 1500 votes in the base year, we instruct interviewers to intercept every 15th voter; in a precinct with 200 votes, we intercept every second voter.

    If everything goes as planned on election day, meaning that we actually get 100 interviews per precinct, no weighting is required. And we proceed with the analysis counting every respondent equally.

But not all intercepted voters will agree to be interviewed. Suppose that no one refuses in one precinct, giving us 100 interviews, but that one-fifth of those stopped refuse in another precinct, giving us only 80 interviews. Since all sample precincts represent an equal $\frac{1}{25}$ of the city's voters in the base year, we must weight the 80 respondents in the second precinct so that they will count as heavily in the final results as do the 100 in the first precinct. This is done by weighting each respondent in the second precinct by a factor of 1.25 (100/80). This is done by the computer (e.g., by a standard procedure in SPSS).

There is another instance in which a precinct may require weighting. Suppose that we have a very small precinct of only 50 voters. We would assign a 100-percent sampling rate to this precinct, but—even if no one refuses—we would get only 50 interviews. Because this precinct like all others represents $\frac{1}{25}$ of the city's voters, its respondents have to be weighted by a factor of 2 (100/50) in order for it to have equal influence on the overall result. Weighting by a factor of 2 means, in effect, counting every voter twice.

We don't always weight when the numbers are different from expected. If, in some precincts, the sampling rate turns up many fewer contacts because voting turnout is so much lower than expected, we do not weight the completed interviews up to 100. Rather, we must let the actual number of contacts reflect the actual turnout.

Conversely, if many more people than expected come out to vote this year, and therefore we get more than 100 interviews by application of our sampling rate, we do not weight that number down. Instead, we must let the actual number of interviews reflect the larger-than-expected turnout.

The two situations of refusals and higher (or lower) turnout rates often occur together. For example, if we find that by use of our sampling rate, the interviewers attempt 200 contacts instead of the expected 100, but that only 160 interviews are successful, then we must weight the figures to take both refusals and turnout into account. That is, we must weight the number of interviews (160) up by a factor of 1.25 in order to equal the number of contacts made (200).

The reverse would be true if the contacts were much fewer than 100. Suppose that, instead of the expected 100, our interviewers can attempt only 75 intercepts and can obtain only 50 completions. Then, rather than weighting up to 100, we weight up only to 75 to reflect actual turnout.

Reporting. The computer program needs built-in monitoring to flag questionable data. If the sample is used to project the election winners, the computer also needs statistical tests to note the threshold that indicates it is safe to report a finding. The computer prepares the summary data tables and transmits them to display screens for research analysts and correspondents who will write or broadcast the conclusions (and who also need to be rehearsed to gain confidence in the system).

As should be apparent, the intercept survey for election reporting is a one-time, all-or-nothing effort that taxes human, technical, and financial resources to the limit.

Application to Other Surveys. The techniques developed to automate and speed up data processing for election day intercept surveys can be adapted to any other survey to reduce the time between completion of interviewing and distribution of print-ready data for analysis.

Telephone Surveys

When telephone surveying is done from a central headquarters, no time is lost transmitting questionnaires back to the office. Coders are on hand as the interviewing period starts. Quality checks can be done on the sample as the interviewing moves along, and management decisions can be made to correct weaknesses on the spot.

All other processing and reporting will be identical to face-to-face surveys.

Mail Surveys

Without trained interviewers to mark the questionnaires, coding may present more of a challenge. Some mail surveys may not be precoded, even for standard items respondents are asked to check. This is to avoid cueing respondents, who might think a 5 is a more desirable answer than a 1, though we have used them solely as labels.

Coding of an unprecoded survey can be facilitated if a plastic overlay is made, with column numbers and response codes indicated in the proper positions either with a grease pencil or "burned" into the plastic by running a sheet containing them through an office duplicating machine onto a special glassine sheet (see Figure 6.44a). Coders can then simply lay these coding masks over each mail questionnaire in turn, observing the respondent's answers and noting the code numbers on a coding sheet (see Figure 6.44b).

Other data-processing steps are the same as for other surveys.

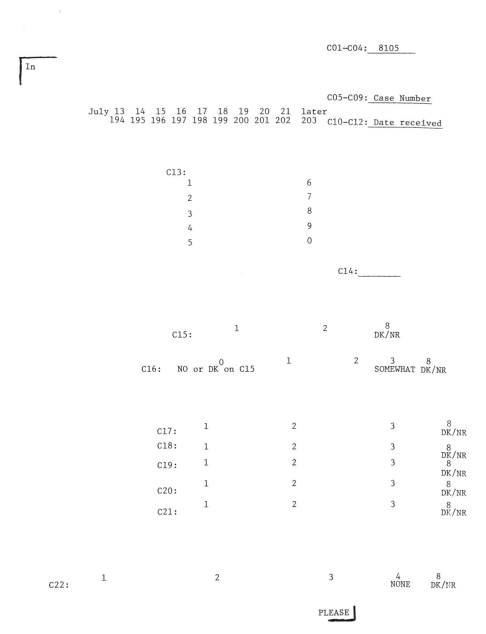

C01–C04: 8105

In

C05–C09: Case Number

July 13 14   15   16   17   18   19   20   21 later
     194 195 196 197 198 199 200 201 202   203 C10–C12: Date received

C13:
        1   6
        2   7
        3   8
        4   9
        5   0

C14:_____

C15:   1   2   8
                                             DK/NR

                        0   1   2   3   8
C16:   NO or DK on C15   SOMEWHAT DK/NR

C17:   1   2   3   8
                                                 DK/NR
C18:   1   2   3   8
                                                 DK/NR
C19:   1   2   3   8
                                                 DK/NR
C20:   1   2   3   8
                                                 DK/NR
C21:   1   2   3   8
                                                 DK/NR

C22:   1   2   3   4   8
                                              NONE   DK/NR

PLEASE

Figure 6.44a. Coding overlay.

RECEIVED

C01-C04: 8105

In order for us to get the views of more people, please complete this questionnaire at this time -- it takes only about 3 minutes. Then mail it today in the postage-paid envelope to the address on the back.
(All answers are confidential.   Your name is not required.) C05-C09: Case Number

July 13	14	15	16	17	18	19	20	21	later
194	195	196	197	198	199	200	201	202	203

C10-C12: Date received

PUBLIC AFFAIRS SURVEY OF CITY ACTIVITIES

- Which of the following activities of city government especially interest or concern you?

C13:

PUT AN X BY AS MANY AS YOU ARE CONCERNED ABOUT

____ 1 Parks, recreation   X 6 Property tax rates
____ 2 Library service   ____ 7 Dutch Elm disease control
____ 3 Street repair   ____ 8 Police protection
  X 4 Help for the needy   ____ 9 Job opportunities
____ 5 Trash removal   ____ 0 Other: _____
                                         (write in)

- Now go back and CIRCLE the ONE SINGLE item in the list that concerns you most.

C14: _____

- Have you ever written, or telephoned, the Mayor or your Alderman about any problem you had with the city?

C15:   X 1   ____ 2   8
          YES   NO   DK/NR

- Did you get a reasonable, satisfactory response?

C16:   NO or DK on C15   ____ 1   X 2   3   8
          0   YES   NO   SOMEWHAT DK/NR

- If city services must be CUT, how much of each of the following would you prefer to see cut?

PUT AN X IN EACH LINE SHOWING HOW MUCH TO CUT

		1 CUT MUCH	2 CUT A LITTLE	3 DON'T CUT	8 DK. NR
Police patrols	C17:	____	____	X	
Neighborhood fire stations	C18:	____	____	X	
Number of school buildings	C19:	____	X	____	
Trash collection	C20:	____	____	____	
Street repair	C21:	X	____	____	

- NO ONE LIKES TAXES, But . . .

If more money had to be raised to keep the city services you want most, mark here how you think the city should raise that money:

C22:   ____ 1   ____ 2   X 3   4   8
          Property tax   Sales tax   Income tax NONE   DK. NR

OVER, PLEASE

Figure 6.44b. Coding overlay laid over mail questionnaire.

FURTHER READINGS

Andrews, Frank M., Laura Klem, Terrence N. Davidson, Patrick M. O'Malley, and Willard
     L. Rodgers, *A Guide for Selecting Techniques for Analyzing Social Science Data* (Ann
     Arbor: University of Michigan, Survey Research Center, no date). A decision tree.
Blalock, H. M., Jr., *Causal Models in the Social Sciences* (Chicago: Aldine, 1971). Rela-
     tionship of variables.
———, ed., *Measurement in the Social Sciences: Theories and Strategies* (Chicago: Aldine,
     1974). Path analysis and multiple indicators related to factor analysis.
Crespi, Leo P., "Some Technical Guidelines to Better Survey Reporting," unpublished
     paper, International Communication Agency, Washington, 1971. How to be straight-
     forward and clear.
———, "The Communicative Precision of Terms of Indefinite Number," unpublished
     paper, International Communication Administration, Washington, 1970. Beginning
     empirical research on what people mean by numbers.
Davis, James A., *Elementary Survey Analysis* (Englewood Cliffs, N.J.: Prentice-Hall, 1971).
     Follows a survey through with one statistical tool—Yule's Q.
Frankel, M. R., *Inference from Survey Samples* (Ann Arbor: Institute for Social Research,
     University of Michigan, 1971). Empirical investigation of statistics used from nonran-
     dom samples.
Henkel, Ramon E., *Tests of Significance,* Sage University Paper series on Quantitative
     Applications in the Social Sciences, series no. 07–001 (Beverly Hills, Sage, 1976).
     How, when, and why to use them.
Hildebrand, David K., James D. Laing, and Howard Rosenthal, *Analysis of Ordinal Data,*
     Sage University Paper series on Quantitative Applications in the Social Sciences, series
     no. 07–001 (Beverly Hills, Sage, 1977). Prediction analysis and traditional methods for
     handling comparative concepts.
Hyman, Herbert H., *Secondary Analysis of Sample Surveys: Principles, Procedures, and
     Potentialities* (New York: Wiley, 1972). Sources of survey material, opportunities, and
     cautions for use.
Iverson, Gudmund R., and Helmut Norpoth, *Analysis of Variance,* Sage University Paper
     series on Quantitative Applications in the Social Sciences, series no. 07–001 (Beverly
     Hills, Sage, 1976). Technique explained by working with actual data.
Johnson, Allan G., *Social Statistics Without Tears,* (New York: McGraw-Hill, 1977). Clear
     explanations of tables, distributions, relationships, testing.
Kim, Jae-On and Charles W. Mueller, *Introduction to Factor Analysis: What It Is and How
     To Do It,* Sage University Paper series on Quantitative Applications in the Social
     Sciences, series no. 07–001 (Beverly Hills, Sage, 1978). Exploratory and confirmatory
     data reduction using SPSS examples.
Mendenhall, William O., Lyman Ott, Richard F. Larson, *Statistics: A Tool for the Social
     Sciences* (North Scituate, Massachusetts: Duxbury, 1974). Statistical tests of all kinds.
Muehl, Doris, ed., *A Manual for Coders: Content Analysis at the Survey Research Center*
     (Ann Arbor, Survey Research Center, Institute for Social Research, 1961). Kinds of
     codes, conventions, problems.
Nie, Norman H., C. Hadlai Hull, Jean G. Jenkins, Karin Steinbrenner, and Dale H. Bent,

SPSS: Statistical Package for the Social Sciences, 2d ed. (New York: McGraw-Hill, 1975). Lucid manual, and discussion of individual statistics.

O'Muirchearlaigh, Colm A., and Clive Payne, *The Analysis of Survey Data,* 2 vols. (New York: Wiley, 1977). Data structures and model fitting.

Reynolds, H. T., *Analysis of Nominal Data,* Sage University Paper series on Quantitative Applications in the Social Sciences, series no. 07–001 (Beverly Hills, Sage, 1977). Compares measures of association, including those for multi-variate categories.

Rosenberg, Morris, *The Logic of Survey Analysis* (New York: Basic Books, 1968). Basic introduction.

Siegel, Sidney, *Nonparametric Statistics for the Behavioral Sciences* (New York: McGraw-Hill, 1956). Basic.

Sonquist, John A., and William C. Dunkelberg, *Survey and Opinion Research: Procedures for Processing and Analysis* (Englewood Cliffs, N.J.: Prentice-Hall, 1977). Professional-level editing, coding, analysis, and administration.

Weisberg, Herbert F., and Bruce Barnes, *Introduction to Survey Research and Data Analysis* (San Francisco: W. H. Freeman, 1977).

Williams, Frederick, *Reasoning with Statistics,* 2d ed. (New York: Holt, Rinehart, & Winston, 1979). Graphic explanations. A lively, understandable, helpful introduction.

Yuker, Harold E., *A Guide to Statistical Calculation* (New York: Putnam, 1958). Simple explanations.

Zeisel, Hans, *Say it With Figures,* 5th ed. (New York: Harper & Row, 1968). Percentages, tables, indices, interpretation.

Epilogue

Conscientiously following all of the steps outlined in the foregoing pages will virtually guarantee a first-rate survey. But some of us may feel like the person who, when told by his physician that the "best" thing for him would be to give up liquor, cigarettes, steaks, and socializing, cried out, "But I don't *deserve* the best—what would be second best?"

The Model Survey presented here is a goal—the ideal we work toward but never fully reach. As we have said, in the survey process we are humans using other humans to help us gather information about still other humans. To be human does *not* mean to be second best (since there are *no* superhumans). It does mean having limits and slipping now and then, yet still having the capacity to envision a goal and to strive to change our behavior and move toward it. Available material resources are—and should be—always a constraint on the kind of survey possible.

We suggest a simple optimizing strategy—doing the best survey we can under the circumstances, but making the inevitable compromises and trade-offs with our eyes open to the consequences. We also attempt at every stage to be aware of the methodological weaknesses of the survey tool and to research our own methods each time we exercise them. We want every survey we do to be a little better than the last. This not only results in self-improvement, but it also will advance the respectability of survey research in general.

INDEX

Page numbers in *italics* indicate figures or checklists. Plurals are implied.